Terrorism Unjustified

Terrorism Unjustified

The Use and Misuse
of Political Power

Vicente Medina

ROWMAN & LITTLEFIELD
Lanham • Boulder • New York • London

Published by Rowman & Littlefield
A wholly owned subsidary of The Rowman & Littlefield Publishing Group, Inc.
4501 Forbes Boulevard, Suite 200, Lanham, Maryland 20706
www.rowman.com

Unit A, Whitacre Mews, 26-34 Stannary Street, London SE11 4AB, United Kingdom

British Library Cataloguing in Publication Information Available

Library of Congress Cataloging-in-Publication Data
Medina, Vicente.
Terrorism unjustified : the use and misuse of political violence / Vicente Medina.
    pages cm
Includes bibliographical references and index.
ISBN 978-1-4422-5351-3 (cloth : alk. paper) — ISBN 978-1-4422-5352-0 (electronic)
1. Terrorism. 2. Terrorism—Political aspects. 3. Terrorism—Social aspects. I. Title.
HV6431.M43367 2015
363.325—dc23   2015024384

♾™ The paper used in this publication meets the minimum requirements of American
National Standard for Information Sciences—Permanence of Paper for Printed Library
Materials, ANSI/NISO Z39.48-1992.

Printed in the United States of America

To Mimi
From whom I learned the power of love and the courage to be.

Contents

Contents

Acknowledgments

Many people have contributed to this project in more than one way. Regrettably, I am unable to acknowledge all of them. The following persons, however, have contributed more than their fair share in helping me to bring this project to fruition. I would like to express my gratitude to my colleague and friend David O'Connor. David not only encouraged me in this arduous venture, but he also volunteered to reread several chapters of this book. His suggestions and criticisms were most helpful to me. Next, Chris Herrera has been an enthusiastic supporter of this project. Chris read the whole manuscript more than once. His unwavering support and generosity were instrumental in my finishing this project. Alan Goldman went out of his way to read the whole manuscript, and he provided me with invaluable suggestions for improving it. I am convinced that without David's, Chris's, and Alan's support, this work would have never been published. I am indebted to them.

Other colleagues and friends have helped me to avoid careless mistakes. For quite some time, David Benfield and I have engaged in serious philosophical conversations about terrorism. Perhaps my views will never pass David's rigorous scrutiny; however, I have always learned from him. I am also grateful to my colleague and friend Yvonne Unna for patiently rereading some sections of the manuscript and for her incisive suggestions. My colleague and friend Mark Couch has generously read the whole manuscript, providing me with valuable suggestions for improving it too. I am grateful to them all.

Other colleagues and friends in the Department of Philosophy, including Bill Smith and Abe Zakhem, have contributed to my clear understanding of my views on terrorism. I would like to thank Abe, chair of the department, for his support. I would also like to express my gratitude to all members of the department, to the dean of arts and sciences Michael Zavada, and to the provost Larry A. Robinson for having approved a sabbatical that allowed me to finish the first draft of my manuscript. In addition, I must acknowledge the contribution of Mia Anderson, who graciously proofread the whole manuscript. Mia saved me from one too many embarrassing mistakes.

I developed and taught for about ten years the course Ethics and International Affairs for the School of Diplomacy and International Relations at Seton Hall University. I tested many of the ideas and arguments found in this work on my students. I have also shared these ideas with the students who have enrolled in my seminar on Terrorism. My views on terrorism have to a large extent been conditioned by their insightful questions and comments.

I have also explored my views on terrorism with members of my family. My sister Mary and I have engaged in fruitful conversations about many of the issues that I address here. Her enthusiasm and support have inspired me to finish this project. I also appreciate the contributions of my brother-in-law, Tony Concepción, who went out of his way to help me in my research. My son Vicente-Alexander, who is a constant inspiration in my life, has raised numerous questions about my research on terrorism. His perceptive questions and comments have on more than one occasion helped me to revise my views. My wife, Celia, has been and continues to be a source of strength and optimism. Without her unconditional love and encouragement, this work would have never seen the light. I am most grateful to her. Lastly, I am grateful to Jon Sick, Natalie Mandziuk, and Karen Ackermann of Rowman & Littlefield for their support. Needless to say, I exonerate the above-mentioned individuals of any responsibility for the views expressed in this book. For those I am solely responsible.

Introduction

From the numerous books and articles published on terrorism, it is evident that there are reasonable people who still continue to disagree vehemently about its nature, justification, or excuse. Despite their disagreements, I argue that terrorism is a grave crime.

I offer a hopefully compelling defense of the view of those whom I refer to as hard-core opponents of terrorism. For hard-core opponents like me, terrorism is categorically wrong and, therefore, morally and legally unjustified. I view terrorism as either equivalent to murder or manslaughter in domestic law, or equivalent to crimes against humanity or war crimes in international law. I offer and defend the following definition of terrorism: terrorism is the use of political violence by individuals or groups who, with the aim of influencing a domestic or an international audience, deliberately or recklessly inflict substantive undeserved harm or threaten to do so on those who can beyond reasonable doubt be conceived of as innocent noncombatants.

I categorically object to terrorism based on a deontological or nonconsequentialist view of morality, which I view as depending primarily on people's intentions and only subsidiarily on the consequences of their actions. By contrast, those who view morality as depending primarily on the consequences of people's actions, namely consequentialists, are likely to disagree with a categorical objection to terrorism.

I distinguish between opponents of terrorism and apologists of terrorism. Opponents of terrorism, be they hard core or soft core, typically, though not necessarily, espouse a deontological view of morality. For them, terrorism is in principle categorically wrong. By contrast, apologists of terrorism, be they hard core or soft core, typically, though not necessarily, espouse a consequentialist or teleological view of morality. For them, terrorism is equivalent to homicide that can, at times, be justified. I argue, however, that apologists' arguments and reasons are insufficient to justify terrorism.

If my argument is compelling, at least two important results follow from it. First, that under no circumstances is terrorism justified. A terrorist is someone who knowingly engages in morally and legally wrong acts, such as murder, kidnapping, or piracy. As a result, there is no such thing as "good" and "bad" terrorism. And second, that even if my argument were to be compelling, it will not necessarily end debates about the nature, justification, or excuse of terrorism.

If we, hard-core opponents of terrorism, want our view of terrorism to be practical rather than only ideal, we will need to allow for the possibility that while terrorism is never justified, it might sometimes but rarely be excused during anomalous catastrophic situations. Apologists of terrorism, of course, will likely agree that terrorism can be justified or excused. Still, given the different moral intuitions that opponents and apologists of terrorism hold, they are likely to disagree on the conditions for justifying or excusing terrorism.

Despite our rich but diverse cultural, religious, political, and moral values, people's undeserved suffering matters to most of us because we have a natural repugnance against other sentient beings' needless suffering. Regardless of whether we have moral knowledge, we seem to share, as Rousseau has argued, two fundamental principles: self-love or *amour de soi* and commiseration or fellow-feeling for other people's suffering. The first principle is essentially self-regarding, while the second principle is essentially other-regarding.

As individuals capable of rational and reasonable judgments and having a natural aversion to undeserved needless suffering, we recognize a compelling natural duty of nonmaleficence to avoid deliberately or recklessly harming the impeccably innocent by commission or omission. Those who engage in terrorism violate their compelling natural duty of nonmaleficence. This duty entails two fundamental moral principles: (1) the presumption of innocence and (2) the principle of noncombatant immunity (a.k.a. PNCI), that is the deliberate avoidance or the reckless harming of innocent civilians who are impeccably innocent. Because terrorists violate these two fundamental moral principles, I argue that—whether they act on behalf of a state or as nonstate agents—they engage in categorically wrong and hence unjustified acts.

Civilians are presumed innocent unless they present an evident threat to someone that justifiably overrides their presumed innocence or unless they are known to be guilty of serious wrongdoing. For example, by deliberately and recklessly targeting innocent civilians, those responsible for the September 11, 2001, attacks on the World Trade Center and the Pentagon (a.k.a. 9/11); the March 11, 2004, attacks in Madrid (a.k.a. 11-M); the July 7,

2005, attacks in London (a.k.a. 7/7); and similar attacks elsewhere violated both the presumption of innocence and the PNCI. Hence, both their intentions and the consequences of their acts are a testimony to their inexcusable behavior.

I have divided the book into five sections. In the first section, I briefly explore the modern origin of terrorism and David Rapoport's four waves typology for understanding different types of terrorism, including religiously inspired terrorism. I then go on to address the challenge that Robert Pape's argument raises against Rapoport's fourth wave, understood as religiously inspired terrorist violence.

In the second section, I address disputes about the term "terrorism," explore the nuances of my proposed definition of "terrorism," and assess the strengths and weaknesses of some typical definitions of "terrorism." I underscore that these typical definitions are either too broad or too narrow. Hence, they are inadequate definitions.

In the third section, I divide opponents of terrorism into hard core and soft core. Hard-core opponents of terrorism, such as Michael Walzer, Tamar Meisels, and C. A. J. Coady, condemn terrorism absolutely. For them, terrorism is equivalent to murder, and since murder can never be justified, it follows that they never justify terrorism. Soft-core opponents of terrorism, such as Igor Primoratz and F. M. Kamm, prima facie but seriously condemn terrorism too. While Primoratz justifies terrorism only if it can prevent or stop an unfolding catastrophic situation, such as a genocide, Kamm justifies terrorism only if it brings about a greater good.

In the fourth section, I divide apologists of terrorism into hard-core and soft-core. Hard-core apologists of terrorism, such as Ted Honderich, refuse to condemn terrorism absolutely. Honderich and like-minded people defend the thesis that terrorism is justified if and only if it improves humanity overall. Soft-core apologists of terrorism, such as Virginia Held, James Sterba, and Andrew Valls, however, justify terrorism by appealing, at times, to just war considerations. They typically argue that if terrorism resembles war, and wars when just can be justified, terrorism when just can also be justified. Nonetheless, I will show how their view of terrorism differs from soft-core opponents' view of terrorism.

In the fifth section, I explore the ambiguity of the commonly used expression "whatever it takes" and its relevance for debates about terrorism. I argue that the use of this ambiguous expression, as well as some of its cognates, such as "extreme crisis," "extreme necessity," or "supreme emergency," is worrisome. Oftentimes, those who invoke any of these expressions try to justify or excuse morally questionable actions.

Finally, in the postscript, I sum up my views on terrorism and reaffirm my commitment to the hard-core opponents' view of it. I underscore that terrorist groups will not be defeated once and for all anytime soon. While the threat of terrorism is real, we need to learn how to live with this menace without succumbing to an unreasonable fear of it that could permanently undermine our civil and political rights. The probability of being a victim of a terrorist attack outside interstate or intrastate armed conflict zones is rather low or virtually negligible. This leads me to conclude that as citizens of liberal constitutional democracies we need to be vigilant to avoid compromising some of our hard-won civil and political rights because of an unreasonable fear of terrorism. That would be too high a price to pay in the so-called "war on terrorism."

Chapter 1

Brief History of Terrorism

A. MODERN ORIGIN OF TERRORISM

The term "terrorism" has a long and controversial provenance. Its modern origin dates back to the French Revolution. The Jacobins and sansculottes used it in a positive sense to describe their rampant politically inspired violence against their opponents.[1] This period of the French Revolution lasted from March 1793 to July 1794, and it is known as the Reign of Terror or the Red Terror. During this period, people lived in constant fear of being arbitrarily executed or imprisoned for their alleged counterrevolutionary beliefs or activities.[2]

The use of violence to instill fear or terror among one's alleged enemies, however, has a long-standing pedigree in human history. For example, the Thugs, the Zealots, and the Assassins were ancient sects that aimed at killing and thereby intimidating their opponents. The Thugs were influenced by Hinduism, while the Zealots, especially the Sicarii, were influenced by Judaism, and the Assassins by Islam.[3]

One can understand terrorism in a generic sense as a form of deliberate and, at times, reckless violence directed against one's alleged enemies but also against bystanders. By using reckless violence, contemporary terrorists might try not only to frighten but also to coerce a domestic or an international audience. In doing so, they forcefully try to change a nation's domestic or foreign policies including, when possible, promoting regime change. They use violence as a means of trying to exert power on their alleged enemies to try to obtain their political goals. As a result of using deliberate and reckless violence against their alleged enemies, they oftentimes end up seriously harming innocent noncombatants whose innocence is beyond reasonable doubt, since they do not harm or threaten to harm anyone by commission

1

or omission. They are harmless or guiltless, such as ordinary citizens who go about their quotidian lives without seriously harming others who do not deserve to be so harmed.

Terrorists often believe, whether rightly or wrongly, that their use of violence can beget favorable outcomes that otherwise they would be unable to obtain through peaceful and popular supported means. This is why people oftentimes conceive of terrorists as being antiestablishmentarians. However, they need not be so conceived. They might use terrorism to preserve, change, or undermine an established political order or to try to create a new one. Their terrorist violence is ideologically multifarious depending on the goals that they are trying to bring about, such as promoting nationalism, authoritarianism, white supremacism, religious fundamentalism, or any combination of "isms" that sanction the use of violence for political goals.

The present practice of suicide bombings or "martyrdom operations" by militant Islamists or jihadists is a paradigmatic example of contemporary terrorism. Unfortunately, jihadists' use of deliberate or reckless violence against those whom they identify as infidels or enemies of Islam shows the extent to which some can portray Islam as promoting a religious duty to kill for political reasons.[4] Nevertheless, we need not rush to judgment against Islam. There is sufficient historical evidence to demonstrate that almost any theological and eschatological conception of the world has the potential for sanctioning violence against alleged infidels or enemies of the faith.

Islam and Christianity have their own idiosyncratic way of trying to justify political violence. Islamist scholars offer elaborate interpretations of jihad based on the Quran as the revealed Word of Allah to the prophet Muhammad, and on the Hadiths or collection of the prophet's words and deeds as reported by others. Christian theologians and canonists have developed what has come to be known as the just war tradition based on the revealed word of God in the Bible and the views of the Patristic fathers. A controversial perennial issue, however, has been and continues to be whether religiously or secularly inspired violence can be morally justified.

One can trace back to antiquity attempts to justify acts of political violence, such as the political assassination of tyrants or tyrannicide.[5] So no single culture, religion, or political ideology has a monopoly on political violence. Even though the term "terrorism" and the expression "the reign of terror" became popular during the eighteenth century in Europe, the use of violence to try to instill fear and, hence, terrorize one's adversaries to promote or achieve political goals has been a constant in human history. The practice of warfare, whether justified or not, by rulers and governments of different ideological persuasions is a good example of using political violence to try terrorizing and thereby vanquishing one's enemies.

Despite frequently using political violence to inflict terror on their enemies, defenders of a just war approach from antiquity to the present attempt to justify the practice of warfare not only on legal but, more importantly, on moral grounds. Nonetheless, people's conception of the practice of warfare as being just could be mistaken. I am assuming, however, that one can justify political violence in principle and in practice, provided some conditions are met, among which the following three are necessary: defending one's community from an aggressor—assuming the community is a morally worthy or a minimally decent community; preventing or stopping abominable acts, such as substantive violations of human rights; and avoiding deliberately targeting innocent noncombatants. That is, respecting what is known in contemporary parlance as the PNCI.

When social policy experts and scholars discuss issues related to terrorism, they usually refer to the violence perpetrated by nonstate agents or groups rather than to state-sanctioned violence. Their unstated assumption is that states, especially democratic ones, do not normally engage in terrorism, while nonstate agents regularly do so. However, that is a gratuitous assumption that flies in the face of compelling historical evidence.

By their nature, states have a monopoly on the use of physical force or violence. For example, Weber aptly defines a state as "a human community that (successfully) claims the *monopoly of the legitimate use of physical force* [his emphasis] within a given territory."[6] The justification of such physical force, however, might depend on its use. If a state uses physical force to seek morally worthy goals, such as protecting fundamental human rights, its use of force might be morally justified. By contrast, if a state uses physical force to violate fundamental human rights, its use of force is rather a misuse of it and therefore morally questionable. Since it is reasonable to believe that all states at one point or another have violated and are likely to violate some of the fundamental human rights of people—either domestically or abroad—their justification for using physical force needs to be evaluated on a case-by-case basis.

Unfortunately, states, including democratic ones, have frequently used excessive or unjustified physical force to deliberately intimidate their alleged internal or external enemies in order to accomplish political goals. Sometimes their alleged internal enemies are simply nonviolent opponents who oppose questionable domestic or foreign policies. When government officials who act on behalf of a state inflict excessive or unjustified force against their alleged enemies, their actions are oftentimes labeled as "state terrorism." While labeling a given state practice as terrorism carries a moral condemnation, such label has no legal force because the term "state terrorism" has no legal standing in international law. Still, those acts that are frequently labeled as state terrorism can instead be denounced as war crimes or crimes against humanity, both of which are proscribed by international law.

Unlike nonstate agents, however, states are bound by domestic and international norms. So regardless of how powerful states are, they can be held accountable more often than nonstate agents can because nonstate agents, such as terrorist groups, operate on the fringe of society, frequently ignoring domestic and international norms. As a result, many social policy experts and scholars have chosen to identify as terrorist those nonstate agents or groups who use deliberate or reckless violence without compunction against culpable and inculpable individuals alike.

Despite being on the fringe of society in an age of increasing globalization, modern terrorist groups have been rather successful in achieving some of their immediate political goals, including attracting the attention of the international community to their alleged grievances. Oftentimes whether their grievances are legitimate remains an open question. Still, if we want to develop successful strategies for dealing effectively with modern terrorist groups, it is only reasonable that we try to understand where they are coming from, the goals that they are trying to achieve, and their grievances.

It is important to dispel the false belief that terrorists are common criminals motivated by self-serving reasons alone. They are rather trying to promote political goals. By using deliberate or reckless violence against their alleged enemies, they are sending not only a message of violence and destruction against their alleged enemies, but they are also sending a message of hope to their acolytes. Whether their message of hope represents a morally questionable or a morally worthy ideal might be a contentious issue that cannot be settled by ad hominem attacks against those who defend such an ideal. We instead need to appeal to sound reasoning and arguments to determine whether their ideals pass moral scrutiny.

In seeking a holistic understanding of modern terrorist groups, it is important to avoid conflating understanding with support for these groups. As Louise Richardson pointedly explains, "the best way to contain terrorism is to understand its appeal and to use this understanding to forge effective counterterrorist policies."[7]

For counterterrorist policies to succeed, they must be based not only on an accurate understanding of terrorist groups' capacities to launch attacks against their targets on the ground, but also on an accurate understanding of the reasons why these groups resort to violence to try to accomplish their goals in the first place. If we misunderstand their ideological convictions, whether political, religious, or otherwise, our counterterrorist policies will be based on false assumptions. Basing counterterrorist policies on false assumptions is likely to bring about three probable but unwelcome outcomes: (1) they could simply achieve mixed results in curbing and preventing terrorist acts, (2) they could promote rather than curb and prevent terrorist acts, or (3) they could end up harming the wrong people, namely, the impeccably innocent.

B. FOUR WAVES OF TERRORISM

David C. Rapoport offers a historically based working typology for elucidating the modern and contemporary use of politically inspired violence by non-state agents. While some might disagree with Rapoport's typology, he offers pithy but informative guidelines to try to understand modern and contemporary usages of terrorist violence. We can debate ad nauseam whether there are other reasonable ways to classify modern and contemporary practices of terrorism, including the use of state terrorism, which Rapoport neglects. Nevertheless, I think that his typology can help us understand the variegated nature of terrorism and how modern and contemporary nonstate agents use terrorism to try to achieve their political goals.

Rapoport's typology is illuminating for a historical understanding of modern and contemporary practices of terrorist violence. Following his typology, one can divide the practice of modern terrorism into roughly four waves: the "anarchist wave" of the 1880s, the "anticolonial wave" from the 1920s to 1960s, the "new left wave" from the 1960s to 1990s, and the "religious wave," which began in 1979 and continues to the present.[8]

During the first wave, anarchists were mostly involved in high-profile political assassinations, such as the killing of Czar Alexander II in Russia by members of the anarchist group *Narodnaya Volya* ("People's Will") in 1881. Anarchists wore the label of terrorist with pride because, at the time, those who engaged in political assassinations wanted to distinguish themselves from common criminals.

During the second wave, those involved in anticolonial struggles and, hence, wars of national liberation called themselves freedom fighters or guerrilla fighters.[9] Since these groups confronted powerful enemies with vast resources, namely nation-states, they avoided engaging them in conventional wars. So they chose to employ hit-and-run tactics that violated the laws of war or the law of armed conflict (LOAC), namely, the collection of conventional agreements among nation-states for regulating interstate armed conflicts.[10]

As a result, colonial powers viewed urban and rural guerrilla groups as terrorists. Frequently, these groups did use indiscriminate violence whereby innocent civilians were seriously harmed or simply killed. Among these groups, for example, were the *Irgun Zvai Leumi* (National Military Organization in the Land of Israel) (1931–1948) and the EOKA (National Organization of Cypriot Fighters) (1955–1959). The first fought to expel the British from Palestine and to establish the state of Israel, while the second fought the

British to try to establish the republic of Cyprus. Similarly, the FLN (National Liberation Front) (1954–1962) fought French colonial rule in Algeria until they succeeded in achieving their independence.

Needless to say, colonial powers, especially French paratrooper forces in Algeria, also engaged in terrorist practices. In their counterterrorist practices, they used indiscriminate violence and rampant torture against guerrilla fighters and innocent civilians too.[11] Thus, we can describe their counterterrorist practices as a form of state terrorism, namely, using deliberate indiscriminate or reckless political violence against innocent and noninnocent people alike.

Terrorist groups from the third wave espoused a mélange of Marxist radicalism and nationalism, such as *Euzkadi Ta Askatasuna* (Basque Nation and Liberty), better known for its acronym ETA in Spain, and the IRA (Irish Republican Army) in Northern Ireland. In addition, a number of small radical leftist groups tried to undermine democratic regimes worldwide to show their solidarity with allegedly oppressed groups in Third World countries or at home. Among these groups are, for example, the American Weather Underground in the United States, the Red Army Faction in former West Germany, the Red Brigades in Italy, and the Red Army in Japan.

One can also identify large and well-organized guerrilla groups in Latin America, such as the FARC (Revolutionary Armed Forces of Colombia). In Asia one finds, for example, the Liberation Tigers of Tamil Eelam (LTTE), who fought a protracted guerrilla war for independence against the Sri Lanka government but were defeated at a great cost to the civilian population. They have been credited with masterminding the use of suicide bombings.[12]

Cases of contemporary suicide bombings or what critics call "suicide terrorism" and sympathizers call "martyrdom operations" can be traced back to the attacks carried out by Hezbollah in Lebanon during the 1980s. The most prominent of these attacks was the one against the US Marine barracks and the headquarters of French paratroopers in Lebanon on October 23, 1983, where 241 US soldiers were killed along with 58 French paratroopers.[13] Whether one could describe this attack as an act of war against foreign soldiers, which might be justified or excused, or as suicide terrorism remains questionable. During the third wave, the Palestine Liberation Organization (PLO), an umbrella organization fighting the state of Israel to try to establish an independent Palestinian state, emerged as the epitome of terrorist violence.

The fourth or religious wave is a rather peculiar wave. In the former three waves, secular ideologies such as anarchism, nationalism, and Marxism were instrumental in motivating those who use terrorist violence. In the fourth wave, however, religion, and especially Islamic fundamentalism, seems to play a significant role as a legitimizing ideology. The systematic use of suicide bombings or "martyrdom operations" has become an international trademark of Islamist terrorist groups belonging to the fourth wave, such as Al-Qaeda and its international affiliates.

During the fourth wave, some non-Islamic terrorist groups inspired by religious convictions have also emerged, such as *Aum Shinrikyo* in Japan, which has been influenced by unorthodox views of Buddhism, Christianity, and Hinduism. On March 20, 1995, members of the *Aum Shinrikyo* released a deadly sarin gas in Tokyo subway trains, killing twelve and injuring more than five thousand people. The mixed motives of those who belong to the fourth wave demonstrate that the old ideological labels of "rightist" or "leftist" terrorism seem inadequate to distinguish among groups motivated by a mixed and, hence, amorphous quasi-religiously inspired terrorism.[14]

1. Does Religion Matter?

Some scholars object to the prominent role assigned to religious beliefs in motivating people to perpetrate terrorist attacks. They challenge the idea of a fourth wave. According to Robert Pape, "there is little connection between suicide terrorism and Islamic fundamentalism, or any one of the world's religions."[15] Instead, he argues that in general those who carry out suicide attacks are motivated by secular goals, such as "to compel modern democracies to withdraw military forces from territory that terrorists consider to be their homeland."[16] For example, Pape has collected empirical data that conclusively demonstrates that the Tamil Tigers in Sri Lanka, a purely secular guerrilla group that fought for independence, committed more suicide attacks than any Muslim terrorist group has committed thus far.[17] According to Pape, 143 members of the LTTE carried out 76 suicide terrorist attacks, killing 901 people.[18] Hence, there is compelling evidence that no necessary causal link exists between the practice of suicide terrorism and Islam.

Despite the absence of a necessary causal link already mentioned, many suicide terrorists are evidently influenced by a militant interpretation of Islam, or so they publicly advocate. If we want to avoid distorting what they advocate, we are to take them at their word. If so, what lesson can we learn from Pape's empirical data? Apparently, those who voluntarily engage in suicide terrorism need a legitimizing ideology, either secular or religious; they need a community to support them; and they need to feel a deep-seated grievance shared by members of their supportive community.

For example, according to Louise Richardson, suicide terrorists are motivated by long-term and short-term political objectives, among which are revenge, renown, and reaction. She refers to these motives as the three R's. Moreover, she argues that those who engage in suicide operations are disaffected individuals supported by a community with a legitimizing ideology.[19] Their deep-seated grievance can easily turn into deep-seated resentment against powerful nations, which they blame for a medley of unjust states of affairs. For example, they might blame the US government for continuing to maintain a presence in Islamic countries, including supporting despotic and nepotic regimes, such as the present Kingdom of Saudi Arabia.

A militant interpretation of Islam provides the legitimizing ideology necessary for militant Islamists to sanction their suicide attacks or "martyrdom operations" against the alleged infidels. Since in Islam there is no supreme authority that one could appeal to in trying to settle disputes regarding theological dogmas, one could argue that whether or not their militant interpretation is the correct interpretation of Islam remains contestable. Even if such an authority were to exist within the international Islamic community or *umma*, there would be no way to guarantee general compliance with the dictates of this supreme authority. For example, consider the recently issued fatwa signed by all twenty-one members of Saudi Arabia's top cleric council declaring that terrorism is a heinous crime under sharia law and that those who engage in terrorism must be punished severely.[20] While this fatwa might dissuade some members of the fundamentalist Sunni majority from supporting or even engaging in terrorism, it is unlikely to prevent militant Islamists across the globe from continuing their violent campaign against those whom they identify as infidels, especially against the United States and its allies.

By focusing on the grievances of terrorists, one could help the international community to develop sound political and legal strategies to address effectively such grievances. Moreover, by focusing on their beliefs, whether religious or otherwise, one could also help in trying to dissuade or deter some potential terrorists from acting on some of their spurious beliefs. Perhaps moderate Islamic leaders might be able to persuade potential terrorists that their beliefs sanctioning violence against the alleged infidels are unfounded. Even though potential terrorists could sincerely believe that their motives are compatible with the letter and spirit of Islam, they might be only rationalizing their criminal behavior as martyrdom operations.

Members of the international community, especially moderate religious leaders and scholars, could play a positive role in persuading pious believers that terrorism is incongruous with the letter and spirit of major religious doctrines, such as those propounded by Islam, Christianity, and Judaism. In this way, those who hold moderate religious views could be instrumental in promoting peaceful goals. They could help to undermine the militant religious views of those who resort first to violence and self-immolation rather than to peaceful means in trying to obtain their goals. So religion and religious leaders could play a prominent role in preventing, solving, or at least taming international conflicts exacerbated, in part, by communities holding different religious beliefs.[21]

In any major religion, martyrdom is the exception rather than the norm. Otherwise, an act of martyrdom would be equivalent to an act of suicide, which is forbidden by most major religions, including Islam. An act of martyrdom should be looked upon as a pis aller rather than as a first course of action. If so, the international community could play an important role in supporting and bringing together moderate religious leaders and scholars who could play a crucial role in disarming the arguments and ideas of militant extremists. So those soi-disant martyrs who use indiscriminate or reckless violence against combatants and innocent noncombatants alike would cease being perceived as martyrs in the eyes of the majority of their respective communities.[22] Such a majority might condemn rather than praise their self-immolation and disregard for innocent human lives.

Policy makers, political pundits, and journalists frequently complain about the lack of criticism by moderate Islamist religious leaders and scholars against militant Islamist groups and their indiscriminate use of violence. But they sometimes criticize these extremist groups, especially their so-called "martyrdom operations." Unfortunately, the news media oftentimes ignore their criticisms of these groups.

Militant Islamist groups are the most conspicuous members of the religious wave, such as Hamas in the Gaza Strip, Hezbollah in Southern Lebanon, Palestinian Islamic Jihad, Jemaah Islamiyah in Southeast Asia, Jamaat al-Islamiyya in Egypt, and the global terrorist organization of Al-Qaeda with its various international affiliates. The following are good examples of Al-Qaeda's international affiliates: Al-Qaeda in the Arabian Peninsula (AQAP), which has been active primarily in Saudi Arabia and Yemen; Al-Qaeda in the Islamic Maghreb (AQIM), which has been active in Northern Africa, especially in Algeria; and Al-Shabaab, which has been operating in Somalia and neighboring countries, especially in Kenya.

The civil war in Syria to try to overthrow the despotic regime of Bashar al-Assad and the power vacuum left in Iraq after the departure of US troops on December 18, 2011 has allowed for the emergence of a different militant Islamist group in the region. The newly created Islamic State of Iraq and the Levant (a.k.a. ISIL), also known as the Islamic State of Iraq and Syria (a.k.a. ISIS) or Islamic State (a.k.a. IS), which has been fueled by the ongoing civil war in Syria and by the Sunni discontent in parts of Iraq, is competing with Al-Qaeda's global leadership in trying to win the hearts and minds of militant Islamists worldwide.

Al-Qaeda's leaders have launched an international campaign of terror whose main objective is to try to establish a Pan-Islamic state based on Islamic law or sharia.[23] Unlike Al-Qaeda's global aspirations, ISIL's leaders aspire to establish an Islamic state in their already conquered territories in parts of Syria and Iraq. While they have been recruiting jihadists from all over the world, including Western nations, their aspiration in trying to carve and create an Islamic caliphate at this time appears to be mostly local rather than global. Hence, the level of threat that presently ISIL poses to the United States seems to have been exaggerated.[24] Nevertheless, it seems that as a response to President Obama's initiative to form an international coalition to attack and presumably destroy ISIL, ISIL's leadership has urged its followers to attack indiscriminately citizens of the United States and citizens of those nations that have joined the coalition.[25]

Unlike some of the other militant Islamist groups that are inspired by local conflicts, such as the Israeli-Palestinian one and the Syrian civil war, the global scope of Al-Qaeda's campaign of terror is evident by the number of successful transnational attacks against Western democracies and their allies that Al-Qaeda and its acolytes have perpetrated. Consider, for example, the car bombing of the World Trade Center on February 26, 1993; the bombing of US embassies in Kenya and Nairobi on August 7, 1998; the attack on October 12, 2000, on the American naval ship *USS Cole* docked on the port of Aden in Yemen; the September 11, 2001, airplane collisions into the World Trade Center in New York City and the Pentagon in Washington, DC, including the crash of United Flight 93 in Pennsylvania; the car bombing of a nightclub in Bali, Indonesia, on October 12, 2002; the March 11, 2004, bombings of the subway trains in Madrid and a similar attack of the London subway trains and bus on July 7, 2005; and the multiple suicide bombings in Bali, Indonesia, on October 1, 2005. As a result of these well-coordinated and indiscriminate attacks, thousands of innocent people have lost their lives, and many more have been seriously harmed, including families and friends who have lost their loved ones in these attacks.

Al-Qaeda's cadres worldwide, but not them exclusively, have shown no compunction about launching reckless lethal attacks against innocent civilians. Such a level of coordination, cruelty, financial resources, and especially self-immolation seems unprecedented. However, Sunni rebels who are members of the newly created ISIL are committing similar atrocities if not worse than Al-Qaeda's cadres continue to commit worldwide.[26]

The religious wave, however, is not completely new. During different historical epochs, religion has played and continues to play a significant role in attempting to justify violence and terrorism against alleged infidels. So to identify the religious wave with the so-called "new terrorism" is somewhat misleading because the new terrorism shares similar characteristics with previous terrorist practices. While the expression "new terrorism" might not be fully accurate, it seems that the magnitude of the threat posed by present-day religiously inspired terrorism, especially militant Islamists, is far greater than in the past.[27] That is, terrorists try to influence a domestic or an international conflict by using indiscriminate or reckless violence against their alleged enemies, including innocent bystanders, as their preferred weapon to try to achieve their political goals.

There seems to be a widespread misunderstanding that terrorists rarely achieve their goals.[28] Despite some evidence to the contrary, terrorists sometimes succeed in accomplishing their goals. The truth of this conclusion depends on how one defines "terrorists' goals." On the one hand, if one defines their goal as totally defeating their enemies, such an outcome rarely happens, especially if they engage in a civil war against a more powerful enemy. On the other hand, if one defines terrorists' goals, for example, as gaining recognition from the international community, forcing their enemies to sit at the negotiating table, or gaining concessions for their multifarious grievances, it is evident that terrorists oftentimes accomplish some of these goals.[29] In addition, even though some terrorist groups, such as Al-Qaeda, have tried but failed to acquire weapons of mass destruction (WMD) to use them against their enemies, there is always a real possibility that they might succeed in acquiring them in the future. If that were to happen, it would truly be a game changer for how the international community addresses the challenge posed by those who engage in the practice of international terrorism.

During the so-called Cold War, the development of nuclear weapons altered our conception of war by recognizing the possibility of mutual assured destruction (MAD). Similarly, the existence of WMD nowadays, including chemical, biological, radiological, and nuclear weapons, and the possibility that terrorists can get hold of them, has altered our view of contemporary international terrorism.[30] Yet the expression "weapons of mass destruction" is ambiguous not only regarding what specific weapons it refers to but also regarding the meaning of the term "mass destruction." Nevertheless, the expression has been used and continues to be used in international treaties and domestic law to refer at least to nuclear, chemical, and biological weapons.

The possibility that terrorists can acquire WMD seems more likely during the fourth wave than during the past three waves. A similar possibility exists that they might blackmail the international community, or that they could even bring about catastrophic results. However, unlike low-level chemical, biological, or radiological attacks by terrorist groups that seem highly probable in the near future, the possibility of catastrophic nuclear attacks by terrorist groups resulting in tens or perhaps even hundreds of thousands of victims does not seem feasible at the present time.[31]

Even though some scholars might argue that the possibility of terrorist groups, such as Al-Qaeda, getting hold of or developing WMD has been exaggerated, the possibility remains real.[32] As long as this possibility remains real, international terrorist groups, such as Al-Qaeda and its international affiliates, present a formidable threat to the stability of the international community.

The development of an increasingly multipolar international community has provided fertile ground for terrorist groups to recruit, finance, incite, and coordinate successful terrorist attacks around the globe. Their threats have become more lethal and frequent. In addition, the globalization of conflicts has added new concerns about how to deal effectively with the significant threat that international terrorism presents to the international community. Consider, for example, the war in Afghanistan; the presence of virtually failed states, such as Somalia and Sudan; the development of WMD by rogue states, such as North Korea; and the precarious nature of weak democracies such as Pakistan whose WMD could fall into the hands of zealots or black marketers. Moreover, the extensive use of the Internet, including innovative communication technologies, is allowing international terrorist groups to create criminal global networks to support their attacks—networks that even with a high level of international cooperation are rather challenging to identify.

Ironically, the increased cooperation in the international community in facing terrorist threats has been mimicked by what appears to be an increased cooperation and coordination of terrorist groups with international organized crime. Such cooperation and coordination increase the likelihood that terrorists could develop WMD or obtain them so they can use these weapons against their alleged enemies.[33] It seems, however, that the process of convergence between terrorist groups and organized crimes has been going on for quite some time despite controversies about the nature and possible continuity of such interaction.[34]

Still, one must not be distracted by the claims of some scholars, policy experts, policy makers, and government officials who try to hide or ignore an incontrovertible truth—that the number of innocent victims killed as a result of terrorism by nonstate agents pales in comparison with the millions of innocent victims that have been killed, maimed, and tortured by state-sponsored political violence or state terrorism.[35] For example, Bern Kiernan calculates that in the twentieth century alone "at least 30 million people perished in genocide across the globe," and R. J. Rummel calculates that from 1900 to 1987 alone approximately 169,202,000 people were killed by governments worldwide.[36]

Also, heads of states and government officials worldwide typically exaggerate the threat of terrorism to try to justify investing billions of dollars in counterterrorism efforts, which oftentimes provide a temporary false sense of security. Nevertheless, the risk of any person dying as a result of a terrorist attack outside interstate or intrastate armed conflicts is rather low.[37] The previous claim, however, need not be construed as a way to minimize the real threat that terrorists, mainly militant Islamists, pose nowadays to nations and people around the globe, specifically but not exclusively to liberal constitutional democracies and their allies.[38]

C. STATE TERRORISM AND POLITICAL VIOLENCE

One can conceive of state terrorism as the deliberate misuse of political violence by states' agents who inflict significant undeserved harm on people, either domestically or internationally.[39] However, the fact that so-called state terrorism has harmed more innocent people than nonstate agents' terrorism has harmed provides no justification or excuse for the latter to do the same, since *injuria non excusat injuriam* (i.e., one or more wrongs do not justify another). Whether a wrong is permissible or not depends on contextual circumstances and extenuating considerations, including the number of impeccably innocent people that other people's actions might positively or detrimentally affect.

Given the suspect history of political violence by state and nonstate agents alike, we need to be circumspect rather than rash about trying to justify or excuse the use of political violence, regardless of the legitimacy of people's grievances. One can only hope that political violence, understood as interstate or intrastate armed conflicts, is to be used as a last resort to settle disputes, especially in an age where there is an abundance of WMD. If one or more of these weapons were to be used, it could bring about unprecedented suffering to a vast number of people. It is precisely the suspect history of political violence that has provided and still provides pacifists and those who are sympathetic to some kind of pacifism with evidence to argue that nothing can justify people's killing one another on such a grand scale as during war.[40] However, even if pacifism were widely accepted, so long as we keep having standing armies, the possibility of ending the practice of warfare to settle disputes seems improbable.

It was Marcus Tullius Cicero (103–43 BC), a Roman political philosopher, constitutional scholar, and statesman, who acknowledged in antiquity that one may use political violence as a last resort. At the time, the practice of warfare was far less lethal than it is nowadays. According to Cicero, there are two types of conflict: one people can settle by argument or reason, and the other one people can settle by force. He writes, "Since the former is the proper concern of man, but the latter of beasts, one should only resort to the latter if one may not employ the former."[41] It took the international community over two thousand years to achieve a consensus for codifying such an insightful thought into the UN Charter, which is the foundation of contemporary international law.[42]

States have been slowly but progressively moving toward the recognition of what is known as international humanitarian law (IHL), the laws of war, or the law of armed conflict (LOAC) as a way of regulating the use of political violence in interstate and, to some extent, intrastate armed conflicts to prevent the harming and needless suffering of civilians or noncombatants.[43] But while states have been progressively moving toward the regulation of armed conflicts, terrorist organizations, such as Al-Qaeda and its international affiliates, continue to deliberately use indiscriminate violence as their preferred means to try to achieve political goals.

Some argue that terrorism is the preferred tool of weak nonstate agents against powerful states.[44] If weak nonstate agents were to challenge powerful states by using political violence according to LOAC, they would likely be defeated regardless of the legitimacy of their grievances. Moreover, if they were to use nonviolent methods against powerful states, they would almost certainly be defeated. In an asymmetrical armed conflict, so the argument goes, the only way that weak nonstate agents can level the play field is by resorting to unconventional tactics, such as terrorism, to make the citizens of a powerful state feel vulnerable.[45] The assumption is that in asymmetrical conflicts the weak might be justified in or at least excused for using terrorism to try to achieve their legitimate goals. According to Michael Ignatieff, this is an appeal to a lesser evil argument. Assuming that weak nonstate agents have right on their side, if they choose to fight a powerful unjust state according to LOAC norms, they will be crushed. Hence, their grievances will never be redeemed.[46]

The above-mentioned assumption, however, seems specious. One could in principle agree that, under extraordinary circumstances, such as facing the threat of genocide, one might find terrorism to be an excusable or permissible option. Still, the threat of genocide by itself is insufficient to excuse using terrorism. One would also need to demonstrate that the following conditions exist: that those who engage in terrorist violence have legitimate grievances for doing so (obviously a real threat of genocide would constitute a legitimate grievance), that they have explored and reasonably exhausted peaceful means to try to settle their grievances (assuming that they were able to have done so), and that a reasonable possibility exists that by engaging in terrorism they would succeed in achieving their presumably commendable goal. For example, they might succeed in preventing or stopping an unfolding genocide.

One could grant that members of Al-Qaeda might have legitimate grievances against Western presence in Islamic countries, Western support for despotic and nepotic Islamic regimes, and the United States' lopsided support for the State of Israel in the Israeli-Palestinian conflict. But members of Al-Qaeda and the communities they claim to represent face no threat of genocide. Moreover, by making unreasonable demands on the United States and its allies, namely, demanding total abdication of the alleged infidels, Al-Qaeda's leadership shows evident disregard for trying to settle their grievances peacefully.

Despite the low probability that Al-Qaeda and its affiliates could achieve any of their substantive goals, such as regime change in any of their designated apostate states, they have chosen terrorism as the first rather than as the last reasonable course of action. Al-Qaeda's cadres continue to use indiscriminate violence against innocent and noninnocent alike. So they present a significant threat to the international community, especially if we keep in mind the real possibility that they could sooner or later acquire WMD. They might have no scruples in using such weapons against their alleged enemies, disregarding any distinction between culpable and inculpable individuals.

There is something idiosyncratic about the use of violence by groups belonging to the fourth or religious wave, such as Al-Qaeda and its international affiliates, and ISIL. They deliberately use indiscriminate violence on a grand scale against those whom they identify as their enemies, disregarding the presumption of innocence of their victims.[47] In their minds, their goals justify the means used to try to obtain them, including their deliberate killing of innocent noncombatants. They might reason as follows: since they do not enjoy widespread support in Islamic nations, they are unlikely to obtain their goals through peaceful means. Therefore, they must try to obtain their goals through widespread use of reckless violence and terror.

After the catastrophic 9/11 attacks on the World Trade Center and the Pentagon, the international community realized the vulnerability of any nation in the face of the new terrorist threat. Hence, in solidarity with the United States and in trying to provide an international legal framework for the international community to defend itself from such a threat, the UN Security Council adopted Resolution 1373 on September 28, 2001. This resolution together with Resolution 1535 adopted on March 26, 2004, unequivocally condemns terrorism and urges all member states to "become party, as a matter of urgency, to all relevant international conventions and protocols relating to terrorism."[48]

Regrettably, while there are international conventions and protocols condemning the practice of international terrorism, there is no universally binding definition of international terrorism. Having such a definition could facilitate bringing terrorists to justice and thereby avoid arbitrariness in designating and prosecuting them according to the rule of law.

D. TERRORISM AND WAR

Emotionally charged terms, such as "terrorism" and "war," have negative connotations. These terms evoke unsettled feelings about undeserved suffering and destruction. Still, something stirs up our emotions when we hear the term "terrorism" that is generally different from when we hear the term "war." Despite our unsettled feelings about war, in our ordinary parlance we oftentimes debate about just or unjust wars. Those who debate so assume that wars could be just or unjust. Apparently, the same cannot be said about terrorism. To argue about whether terrorism is just or unjust seems somewhat paradoxical.

For many ordinary citizens, terrorism is equivalent to murder. So how can terrorism be just if it is conceived of as murder? Also, for many other citizens such a conception of terrorism is simply a controversial assumption. For them, terrorism could be equivalent to war. So if there is nothing paradoxical debating about the justice of war, then likewise there is nothing paradoxical debating about the justice of terrorism.

Some might argue that our ordinary parlance is purely partisan and subjective because singling out terrorism depends on our biased political ideas and preferences rather than on any objective criterion. They might propose that if by terrorism one understands the use of violence to achieve a given political objective, then terrorism, like war, can be described as just or unjust.[49] They could argue that the justification of terrorism would depend on the nature of the goals the terrorists are trying to accomplish and their means of achieving them.[50] People who so argue oftentimes refer to groups engaged in political violence as revolutionaries, insurgents, partisans, guerrillas, or freedom fighters rather than as terrorists. Others distinguish between ill-advised terrorism and "good terrorism." For example, the late Osama bin Laden stated, "America and Israel practice ill-advised terrorism, and we practice good terrorism."[51] Still others maintain that "terrorism could be justified as a response to structural violence."[52]

In my view, nonstate agents and states, including government officials, can engage in terrorism when they deliberately or recklessly inflict or threaten to inflict substantive harm, whether physical or psychological, on those who are guiltless or harmless. Those who are guiltless or harmless are truly innocent because they threaten no one by commission or omission. By virtue of their guiltlessness or harmlessness, they can be aptly conceived of as impeccably innocent. To deliberately kill or substantively harm them would be a serious crime.

One can reasonably distinguish between political violence that targets combatants, such as the attack perpetrated by members of an Al-Qaeda cell against the US Navy guided missile destroyer *USS Cole* while harbored in Yemen on October 12, 2000, that killed seventeen sailors and wounded a number of others, and the 9/11 attack on the World Trade Center where thousands of innocent victims, including innocent bystanders, were indiscriminately targeted by members of Al-Qaeda.[53] The first might be described as an attack against declared enemies and combatants, while the latter can be described as a terrorist attack against innocent civilians and bystanders. One could even try to make a legitimate distinction between the 9/11 attack on the Pentagon building in Washington, DC, as a possible military target and the attack on the World Trade Center. Domestic and international law, however, prohibit the act of hijacking commercial airplanes. Also, by deliberately killing the innocent passengers in the plane, they committed an act of murder.

Since Al-Qaeda had declared war on the United States and its allies, the Pentagon was a legitimate military target. International law experts who are purists, however, could argue that a nonstate agent, such as Al-Qaeda, has no standing in international law to declare war on a state because by war they understand an armed conflict between political units or states. If that were to be so, then, strictly speaking, a state could not declare war on a nonstate agent. One can then argue that the so-called "war on terrorism" can be seen as a malapropism, as a euphemism, or as a pretext to try to justify unilateral action by strong states against weak or failed states that sponsor or harbor terrorist groups.

The definition or criterion of war operating in international law seems too narrow, and, more importantly, it also begs the question. For example, if one were to adopt Clausewitz's definition or criterion of war "as an act of violence intended to compel our opponent to fulfill our will,"[54] then Al-Qaeda's targeting of the Pentagon could be interpreted as an act of war. To say so is not to justify or excuse the attack on the Pentagon but to establish a plausible distinction between military and civilian targets.

According to international law, military objectives are "limited to those objects which by their nature, location, purpose or use make an effective contribution to military action."[55] If that is so, then the Pentagon, being the headquarters of the US Department of Defense, is a clear military objective for those who might declare war on the United States, which Al-Qaeda had already done. If one interprets the 9/11 attacks as acts of war, then it follows that those involved in planning and carrying out the attacks ought to be treated according to the LOAC.[56]

By contrast, civilian objects are those that are not military objectives. The attacks on the World Trade Center and similar civilian targets elsewhere can be described as terrorist attacks that are also acts of war. One can also describe an attack on a military target, such as the Pentagon, as an act of war rather than as a terrorist attack. One can similarly describe, for example, the December 7, 1941, surprise military attack by the Japanese on Pearl Harbor. Even though some civilians were killed as a result of the attack, that was an act of war but not necessarily a terrorist attack.

Ordinary reasonable people find the practice of terrorism morally reprehensible for at least two reasons. First, more often than not, terrorists deliberately or recklessly inflict substantive harm on civilian bystanders who are impeccably innocent. As a result, they end up violating the presumption of innocence of some of their victims. And second, they deliberately or recklessly end up using their impeccably innocent victims only as a means in trying to achieve their political ends or goals, thereby violating the physical, psychological, and moral integrity of their innocent victims. So their terrorist acts are seriously wrong and hence morally unjustifiable.

The deliberate or reckless use of violence against those who are impeccably innocent creates a feeling of frustration, animadversion, and horror among those who are unwilling to sacrifice people's bodily, psychological, and moral integrity to promote a given political agenda, regardless of how morally appealing this agenda might be. Yet some could reply that the history of human conflicts from antiquity to the present is a vivid reminder of how the innocent have been used and continue to be used to promote and achieve other goals, especially political ones.

The above reply, although accurate, is unconvincing. That which has been or is the case carries no moral weight. A historical event is just a description, but it is not necessarily an evaluation of that which ought to be. Furthermore, we can always try to educate future generations about our past moral failures to prevent similar failures from reoccurring. Nothing could guarantee our success in the prevention of heinous crimes. But, if having the opportunity to try to prevent them, we simply choose to ignore them, it will be difficult for future generations to disregard our complicity in such crimes.

Being aware of the carnage and abuses perpetrated on the innocent throughout the ages should not exempt us from being overwhelmed when confronted with specific cases of horror. Take for example the March 20, 1995, attack in Tokyo; the April 19, 1995, attack in Oklahoma City; the September 11, 2001, attacks on the World Trade Center and the Pentagon; the August 19, 2003, attack on the UN in Baghdad; the March 11, 2004, attacks in Madrid; the September 1, 2004, Beslan School massacre in the North Ossetia region of the Russian Federation; the July 7, 2005, attacks in London; the October 1, 2005, bombings in Bali, Indonesia; the November 26, 2008, coordinated attack in Mumbai, India; the July 22, 2011, attacks in Norway; and similar attacks elsewhere. As a result of these attacks, thousands of innocent civilian bystanders were deliberately killed or seriously harmed.

Despite our horror and justified rage about these events, it is in our best interest to try to understand the terrorists' motives behind their heinous crimes. Such an understanding need not impede us from judging their acts as morally abhorrent and from trying to develop effective domestic and international policies to bring to justice those responsible for having committed the above-mentioned abominable acts. However, we need to be aware that terrorists sometimes might have legitimate grievances motivating them to commit their crimes. By having a good understanding of their grievances, we might be able to address them effectively. In so doing, for example, we might succeed in undermining their propaganda campaign for recruiting new foot soldiers. If we choose to overlook or undermine the seriousness of their sometimes legitimate grievances, we do so at our own peril.

It is important to highlight that explaining the plausible motives and reasons of those who planned and carried out the above-mentioned terrorist attacks is not a way of justifying or excusing their actions. For example, the United States' unilateral foreign policy decisions supporting despotic and nepotic Islamic regimes are no excuse for targeting innocent US citizens who might have been opposed to such unilateral foreign policy decisions to begin with. Likewise, Great Britain's and Spain's support for the wars in Afghanistan and Iraq provide no excuse for targeting their innocent citizens. Those who argue for a moral equivalence between a nation's foreign policy, such as the one supported by the United States, Great Britain, or Spain, and the already mentioned terrorist attacks perpetrated in these countries have a substantial burden of proof. They must demonstrate in what sense those who perished in the attacks were threatening anyone or whether they were morally and legally culpable in any significant way to deserve such fate.

One is always free to adopt a skeptical, cynical, or aesthetic view of terrorism. Some skeptics might adhere to moral relativism. They might argue that it is doubtful that there are objective moral facts to distinguish between right and wrong conduct across cultures or communities. If so, what might be conceived of as terrorism in a given culture or community might not be so conceived of in a different culture or community. Even within the same culture or community, however, we encounter serious disagreements about fundamental moral and political issues, such as terrorism. For example, those who defend the adage "one man's terrorist is another man's freedom fighter" oftentimes try to illustrate how different people's perspectives and conflicting moral values can condition their view on terrorism and whom they identify as a terrorist or as a freedom fighter.

Some cynics might argue that if terrorism helps a person or group to achieve their objectives, terrorism is right for that person or group. And some who defend an aesthetic view of violence might simply argue that the justification of violence is purely subjective, so its approval or disapproval is in the eyes of the beholder. I will explore in a later chapter the pros and cons of these views. For now, it seems that people who adopt any of the already mentioned views have a rather blasé attitude toward human suffering.

For those who take human suffering seriously, such a blasé attitude in the face of what one might aptly describe as human evil provides a feeling of discomfiture. Adopting such an attitude could simply lead to human indifference to other people's undeserved suffering. That is a rather frivolous attitude, especially when one is in a position to prevent undeserved human suffering without substantive risk to oneself or others and simply chooses to ignore it.

Still, reasonable people disagree about the justifiability of political violence whether in the form of terrorism or in any other form. Thus, since the term "terrorism" is a loaded term with motley meanings for different people, those who adopt any of the already mentioned relativist views could in principle maintain that there is no independent objective way to assess the justifiability of terrorism. One could similarly so argue about political violence, since it is also a loaded concept. However, with the exception of radical pacifists, there exists a consensus that one can justify political violence based on its aims or goals and on the way people go about pursuing these aims or goals. The use of political violence for self-defense, to help those who have been unjustly attacked, to prevent great undeserved suffering, or to punish great evil has a long and well-established legacy, namely, the just war tradition that goes back to antiquity.

Those opposed to the just war tradition could argue that historical arguments do not justify what ought to be as a matter of right. While theirs is a pertinent objection, one can always reply that historical arguments provide us with a broad contextual understanding of the issues in question. For example, by reverting in time to try to explore the arguments and reasons offered in favor of the practice of slavery, one can have a better understanding of such an appalling practice. By the way, I am referring to the practice of slavery in general and not only to the practice of African slavery. Those who defended slavery back then can be viewed nowadays as having been cruel and morally blind to the suffering of others. Nevertheless, all of them were certainly neither sadists nor insane individuals. Many were reasonable individuals whose reasons and arguments do not seem compelling to us nowadays because in hindsight their beliefs appear suspect to an overwhelming majority of people for whom human decency should not allow for such an abominable practice.

Some might have appealed to brute force and ancient practices to justify slavery since, for them, the victor ought to have despotic or absolute power over the vanquished. Others might have justified the practice of slavery based on a given natural order. Still others might have tried to justify it based on the assumed superiority of a given race or culture, such as racial or cultural imperialism. Yet others might have tried to justify such an execrable practice based on economic considerations, such as the provision of inexpensive labor. Presently, there seems to be an international overlapping consensus that these arguments are specious because our contemporary conception of human dignity or at least human decency has no room for the subordination of some individuals to the despotic will of others.

Similarly, we can go back in time to try to understand the nuances of the just war tradition and the arguments and reasons offered in defending its use of political violence. Those who defend the use of political violence by appealing to such a tradition are typically reasonable individuals whose reasons and arguments must be understood and gauged contextually. Also, one needs to ascertain whether their arguments are compelling. Apologists of terrorism and those who practice it can argue likewise. They could go back in history to try to contextualize the nuances of terrorist violence against despotic political power. Still, a fundamental moral issue is whether the arguments defended by those who espouse a just war approach and those who espouse terrorism are equally morally compelling.

Some might try to justify terrorism as a last resort of the weak against a powerful opponent. Although in principle that could be seen as a plausible justification, more often than not in practice those who engage in terrorism are usually not interested in pursuing peaceful ways to try to settle a given conflict. They are rather intransigent in their demands because they view themselves as upholding the high moral ground. So they are unwilling to compromise. In their worldview, compromise amounts to moral weakness and abdication. Others could try different routes to excuse or explain the use of terrorism.

For example, they can understand terrorism as the practice of war by other than legally established means. They might adopt General William Tecumseh Sherman's view that "war is hell." General Sherman never recalled having said that, although he did say something akin to it. In an impromptu speech delivered on August 11, 1880, he addressed a group of veterans as follows: "there is many a boy here today who looks on war as all glory, but, boys, it is all hell."[57]

Even if one were to accept General Sherman's characterization of war as hell, the expression itself is ambiguous. It could mean that if war is hell, then everything is permissible in trying to win a war. One can absolutely do whatever it takes, including the deliberate killing and harming of the innocent, to win a war regardless of whether one is in the right or not. Thus, the victor imposes what they view as right on the vanquished—the so-called "victor's justice." As a result, those who support this view would argue that "might makes right." This line of argument has a well-established pedigree going back to Thucydides's *Peloponnesian Wars* and Thrasymachus's views in Plato's *Republic*.[58]

One can conceive of at least two more different views contrary to the one already mentioned. The first view is the antithesis of right viewed as power, namely, right viewed as a matter of reason. This line of argument goes back to Socrates and the Stoics. For them, power alone cannot establish that which is right or just. Hence, right or justice must be established by reason alone in conformity with fundamental moral principles. For defenders of this view, war is a regrettable state of affairs, but it is not necessarily beyond moral evaluation.

The second view is another plausible interpretation developed by moral and legal scholars going back to the Roman and Christian natural law tradition. Because they conceive of war as being indeed rather cruel and inhumane, they argue that people have the power of reasoning to try to regulate it. In doing so, they can try to minimize innocent casualties and unnecessary destruction of property as long as those involved in the conflict are willing to be bound by mutually agreed principles of conduct. Presumably, hell is for unredeemable sinners. In war, however, many of the victims are innocent noncombatants. This conventional juristic tradition has contributed to the development of international law as a way of regulating armed conflicts among states to try to minimize human suffering. Whether such a juristic tradition has accomplished the goal of minimizing human suffering remains controversial.

E. SUMMARY

In this section, I have briefly explored the modern origin of the term "terrorism." Despite its origin during the French Revolution, I underscored that the practice of political violence to instill terror among one's alleged enemies has a long ancestry. I offered a provisional definition of terrorism in a generic sense as a form of deliberate or reckless violence directed against one's alleged enemies and bystanders regardless of their innocence. I used David C. Rapoport's four waves typology for understanding modern terrorism: the anarchic wave of the 1880s, the anticolonial wave from the 1920s to the 1960s, the new left wave from the 1960s to the 1990s and the religious wave from 1979 to the present. Subsequently, I explored Robert Pape's objection against the prominent role assigned to religion during the current fourth wave, especially Islam, in motivating suicide terrorism. Next, I explored the relationship between state terrorism and political violence. The fact that political violence sponsored by states has harmed more innocent people than nonstate agents have harmed is no excuse for the latter to engage in terrorism. In antiquity, Cicero argued that political violence should be used as a last resort. But Al-Qaeda's acolytes seem to use political violence as their first way of attempting to accomplish their goals, namely, to expel Western presence and influence from Islamic nations, especially from the Holy Land of Islam, and to establish a worldwide modern-day caliphate ruled by sharia law. Lastly, I explored the distinction between the different responses that terrorism and war elicit among ordinary reasonable people. One of the fundamental reasons why level-headed people find terrorism appalling is because terrorists deliberately or recklessly inflict undeserved harm on the impeccably innocent.

Chapter 2

Disputing Terrorism

A. PERSPECTIVISM AND POLITICAL VIOLENCE

"Terrorism" is a polysemic, emotionally laden term. Belligerent groups could be labeled "terrorist" by some and "freedom" or "guerrilla" fighters by others. Similarly, the same organization or group could be labeled "terrorist" by some and "humanitarian organization" by others. Hence, depending on which perspective people take in a given conflict, and how the international community reacts to the conflict in question, members of different organizations or groups might end up being classified in a negative sense as terrorists or in a positive sense as freedom fighters. Such perspectivism partly explains why so much disagreement exists on the meaning, justification, or excuse of terrorism.

For example, those who support the so-called martyrdom operations, namely, suicide bombings employed by Hezbollah, Hamas, and Islamic Jihad against Israeli civilians, consider them martyrs (*shahids*), holy warriors or jihadists, or simply Islamic guerrilla fighters or mujahideen engaged in an asymmetric conflict against a more powerful enemy. By contrast, those who oppose the indiscriminate use of violence against innocent civilians consider them terrorists or murderers. Thus, the controversy on how to use the term "terrorism" appropriately, or whether it can be so used, seems endless.

Different actors in various conflicts continue to use and manipulate the meaning of the term "terror." According to Raymond Aron, for example, the term "terror" has been used in contemporary parlance in four different contexts. First, "by the Germans to designate the bombing of cities" during World War II; second, "by those seeking to conserve an established power . . . to stigmatize the action of the resistants or nationalists"; third, "by all authors to characterize one of the aspects of totalitarian regimes"; and "lastly by usage to designate the relation of dual impotence between the two great powers armed with thermonuclear bombs."[1]

Over 109 definitions of terrorism have been offered by several scholars and social policy experts. They, however, have identified two significant traits among these definitions, namely, the use of violence or force for political purposes.[2] In the light of these findings, I suggest that terrorism could arguably be understood as a species of political violence that is morally unjustifiable, since terrorists deliberately or recklessly inflict harm on combatants and innocent noncombatants alike. Such a deliberate infliction of harm or the threat of it for political purposes frequently causes widespread fear or indignation among intended audiences. Still, while terrorists have control over their actions, they have no control over how an audience might react to their terrorist acts. So their intention to intimidate an audience could be unpredictable and, at times, might simply backfire.

Again, my working definition of terrorism is this: the use of political violence by individuals or groups who deliberately or recklessly inflict substantive undeserved harm or threaten to do so on those who can be conceived of as innocent noncombatants beyond reasonable doubt, aiming at influencing a domestic or an international audience. I am assuming that the terms "innocent noncombatants," "innocent civilians," and "innocent bystanders" are interchangeable because they refer to the same class of people, namely, those who are innocent by virtue of being legally and morally inculpable of substantive wrongdoing and, hence, deserving of no violence or punishment. Since they are guiltless or harmless, they belong to the class of those whom I call impeccably innocent.

As any proposed definition or characterization of terrorism, mine is also contestable. While it would be naïve to pretend to settle definitional disputations about terrorism once and for all, I can still try to present reasonable and hopefully persuasive arguments to defend my working definition of terrorism. In doing so, I will need to explain the nature of undeserved harm, what a threat means, and who the innocent noncombatants are beyond reasonable doubt. I will explore the nuances of these concepts as my argument unfolds in later chapters.

Other proposed definitions or characterizations of terrorism face similar challenges. So to try to avoid endless debates among those who hold different definitions and characterizations of terrorism, I hope to demonstrate that my definition of terrorism coheres with our deep-seated intuitions, especially regarding the presumption of innocence of those who can be characterized as evidently guiltless or harmless noncombatants.

Definitions are important for attempting to isolate distinctive characteristics of acts of terrorism vis-à-vis other acts that might be morally and legally impermissible but need not be classified as terrorist acts, such as tyrannicides, sabotages, kidnappings, extortions, or simply incontrovertible acts of murder. One can view any of these acts as terrorism if the perpetrators of the act deliberately or recklessly harm or threaten to harm innocent civilians as a way of promoting domestic or international political goals.

For example, one might describe the assassination of Prime Minister Yitzhak Rabin of Israel in 1995 by Yigal Amir, a lone-wolf Jewish religious zealot who was vehemently opposed to Rabin's peace initiative with the Palestinians, as an act of terrorism. Also, the assassination of Egyptian President Anwar Sadat in 1981 by members of Islamic Jihad can be similarly described. In the eyes of their assassins, as heads of states, Rabin and Sadat were promoting questionable policies. Because their assassins were hoping to change those policies, they targeted them.

Still, there are relevant differences between Rabin's and Sadat's assassinations. First, Rabin was an elected official of the parliamentary democracy of Israel. A lone wolf murdered him with the intention of forestalling the rapprochement policy toward Palestinians. Militant Islamists opposed to Sadat's tyrannical rule and recognition of the State of Israel murdered him. As a result, they conspired to promote regime change in Egypt. In the eyes of those who opposed their policies, both Rabin and Sadat were conceived of as enemies and not necessarily as innocent. However, the fact that some people conceive of them as enemies is insufficient to justify killing them.

Next, consider whether one can conceive of an act of sabotage as a terrorist act depending upon the intention of those who perform the act or its consequences. For example, when groups opposed to the US presence in Iraq blew up oil pipelines presumably intending to harm innocent civilians in order to put pressure on US forces to withdraw from Iraq, their acts could be described as terrorism. Nevertheless, if one could reasonably demonstrate that they did not intend to harm innocent civilians, the above-mentioned acts might not be conceived of as terrorism but rather as sabotage. Determining that these are nonterrorist acts is insufficient to exculpate the perpetrators for having killed innocent civilians, but it could be a mitigating factor if and when they are brought to justice.

Nonterrorist acts of sabotage, for example, are those committed by disgruntled employees against their current or former employers, or spontaneous acts of violence by individuals or groups against private or public places with no real political objective in mind. Similarly, one might classify acts of kidnapping as terrorism depending on the intention of the perpetrators and the consequences of their acts. If the persons being kidnapped are innocent civilians rather than combatants, and the kidnappers intend to influence a given political outcome, such as the withdrawal of US forces from Afghanistan or the release of Al-Qaeda prisoners from Guantánamo Bay prison, then one might conceive of their act as a terrorist act.

If kidnappers, however, are members only of a mafia or a gang who are requesting a ransom for their own benefit, then their act is just a domestic criminal act. Both kidnapping acts are despicable acts of violence against innocent civilians, but one is a terrorist act that can be described also as an act of war, which is proscribed by international criminal law (ICL), while the other one is just a domestic crime. Still, a kidnapping act could also be an act of piracy such as those that are being committed by Somali pirates who seize ships in the Indian Ocean and the Gulf of Aden demanding hefty ransom for releasing those who have been kidnapped. International law, however, proscribes piracy. Since pirates do not represent anybody other than themselves, they are considered as *hostis humani generis* or enemies of humanity. They are international outlaws. Therefore, they can be apprehended and punished by any nation.

Legal definitions are important for holding individuals accountable when they violate domestic or international law. However, we can offer a connotative or a denotative definition of a term. We can define a term by focusing on its meaning or by focusing on its referent. In the first case, we can provide an account of the term "terrorism" by explaining, for example, that "terrorism is unexcused and, therefore, unjustified political violence against the innocent." In the second case, we can provide an account of the term "terrorism" by singling out particular acts that people openly or tacitly agree to label as terrorist acts. Presently, there is no non-question-begging universally accepted connotative definition of terrorism in international law. There is, nonetheless, ubiquitous agreement on a denotative aspect of terrorism. This ubiquitous agreement is shown by the multilateral conventions and protocols sponsored by the UN designating certain acts as terrorist acts. The UN has approved fourteen universal legal instruments and four amendments to prevent terrorist acts.[3]

Unfortunately, some states have not become signatories to some of these conventions, treaties, and protocols, and others, even though they are signatories, have failed to ratify some of these legal instruments. Hence, they are not necessarily bound by them. As members of the UN, however, they are bound by customary international law. That is, the unwritten body of rules that supervenes upon state practice and *opinio juris*. While state practice describes how states actually behave, *opinio juris* describes whether they act according to binding legal obligations.[4] Yet to establish whether states act from expediency or from recognizing their legal obligations can, at times, be rather challenging.

Despite some general agreement on the denotative aspect of terrorism, substantial disagreement remains regarding its connotation. Whatever meaning we agree on, the term "terrorism" will likely have an impact on its denotation or referent. Consequently, definitional disputations whether legal or not are quite vexing. They might be too broad or too narrow, or they might beg the question by assuming that which needs to be proved. For example, that terrorism is categorically impermissible while other kinds of political violence, such as a just war to repeal and punish an aggressor, might not be so.

Some definitions are more controversial than others. Still, that should not prevent us from classifying certain acts as being morally and legally inexcusable and, therefore, unjustifiable regardless of whether we single them out as terrorism. For example, war crimes and crimes against humanity are heinous acts that have been recognized as such by IHL since the establishment of the Nuremberg Charter in 1945 for prosecuting war criminals after World War II.

Ironically, had the Axis powers won the war, they presumably could have tried the Allies for war crimes and crimes against humanity too.[5] In his interview with Errol Morris for the documentary *The Fog of War*, Robert S. McNamara, who was a captain in the USAAF responsible for analyzing bombing efficiency during the latter part of World War II, candidly admits that if the United States had lost the war, he and his superiors would have been tried for crimes against humanity for their firebombing of Japanese cities that resulted in the estimated deaths of one million civilians.[6] Similarly, US General Curtis LeMay, who implemented the policy of firebombing Japanese cities, admits to McNamara that if they had lost the war, they probably would have been prosecuted as war criminals.

McNamara then asks a rather pointed question: "what makes it immoral if you lose and not immoral if you win?"[7] For some, morality is not about winning or losing. For example, one could argue that morality is about fulfilling our duties by preventing deliberately harming the innocent and by deliberately helping the needy whenever possible. And yet there is no universal consensus on any particular view of morality.

Despite different conceptions of morality, states, by virtue of their membership in the international community, are bound not only by the UN Charter but also by IHL. The terms "international humanitarian law," "international law of armed conflict," and "the laws of war" are sometimes used interchangeably to refer to the *jus in bello* or the rules governing interstate and, to some extent, intrastate armed conflicts.[8] These rules prohibit the targeting of civilians, whether innocent or not, when they are caught in the midst of armed conflicts. A civilian, according to IHL, is essentially any person who does not belong to the armed forces, militias, or volunteer corps, and who does not spontaneously take arms to resist an invading force in a nonoccupied territory.[9]

The UN has been effective in focusing on achieving a consensus on the criminality of certain acts in addition to the ones already identified by ICL, such as genocide, war crimes, and crimes against humanity.[10] Such a consensus is evidenced by the conventions, treaties, and protocols that foster cooperation among states regarding the nature and criminality of certain acts; for example, those proscribed by laws against aircraft hijackings, against targeting internationally protected persons, against the taking of hostages, against terrorist bombing of public places and people, against the financing of terrorism, and against nuclear terrorism, to mention only a few.[11]

International cooperation can also prove effective in trying those convicted of any of the already mentioned crimes under the aegis of international law. Even though not all those considered terrorists by some will be successfully tried under international law—at least some will be. While admitting that selective justice is arbitrary and hence unfair, we can always argue that, in practice, it is preferable to have imperfect justice than no justice at all.

Those who are trying to defend or excuse the use of political violence by certain groups for presumably worthy goals might argue against the idea of classifying these groups or organizations as terrorist. It is lamentable that those who hastily embrace the use of political violence for presumably worthy goals, such as wars of national liberation or against viciously oppressive regimes, tend to ignore that their goals might not justify the means used in trying to achieve them. For example, when they deliberately, indiscriminately, or recklessly target combatants and innocent noncombatants alike, their violence could be as vicious as that used by their oppressors.

By refusing to distinguish between their enemies or adversaries and the innocent, groups who engage in political violence quite often embrace a policy of collective punishment to try to spread terror among the general public. Despite the contestability of terrorism, IHL proscribes the practice of collective punishment. Protocols I and II to the Geneva Conventions state, "Acts or threats of violence the primary purpose of which is to spread terror among the civilian populations are prohibited."[12] While the first Protocol applies only to international armed conflicts, the second applies to intrastate armed conflicts as well. Therefore, the use or threat of violence against the civilian population, whether in interstate or intrastate armed conflicts, is prohibited by international law. Unfortunately, the enforcement of individual responsibility under ICL for serious violations of human rights abuses in peacetime as well as in wartime remains erratic.[13]

B. DEFINITIONS OF TERRORISM

1. Terrorism Internationally Defined

Controversies about terrorism in international law have a long ancestry. One could argue that the efforts to try to formally achieve an international consensus on a general definition of terrorism goes back to the 1937 Convention for the Prevention and Punishment of Terrorism sponsored by the League of Nations.[14] Article 1 (2) of the convention defined acts of terrorism as follows: "criminal acts directed against a State and intended or calculated to create a state of terror in the minds of particular persons, or a group of persons or the general public."[15] However, the Convention was never adopted.

Contemporary legal scholars, such as Cassese and Duffy, have argued that the international community has nonetheless reached a tacit consensus on a general definition of international terrorism as described in UN General Assembly resolution A/RES/49/60 on December 9, 1994.[16] Paragraph 3 of the Annex builds upon the 1937 definition by defining terrorism as follows: "Criminal acts intended or calculated to provoke a state of terror in the general public, a group of persons or particular persons for political purposes are in any circumstance unjustifiable, whatever the considerations of a political, philosophical, ideological, racial, ethnic, religious or any other nature that may be invoked to justify them."[17] Based on this definition, Cassese argues that international terrorism may constitute a war crime, a crime against humanity or, if neither of those two, at least a discrete crime if it fulfills the following three conditions: (1) the act must be a crime under domestic legal systems, (2) those who perpetrate it aim at spreading terror to influence government behavior, and (3) they are politically motivated.[18]

Although approved by the UN General Assembly, the above-mentioned definition is nonbinding because it is not a treaty, convention, or protocol signed and ratified by member states. Hence, its *jus cogens* status as a global international norm is controversial. Despite contemporary concerted international efforts to fight terrorism, some states still avoid their international obligations for politically expedient reasons, for example, by focusing on the ambiguity of the term "terrorist" and its congener "freedom fighter." Neither of these two terms is defined in international law. As a result, these terms are neither legally binding nor legally meaningful. Other states neglect their international obligations because they have neither the will nor the resources to discharge their obligations.

The emphasis on the criminality of certain acts might seem a welcome development in promoting a global consensus on a definition of international terrorism. And yet governments, either democratic or authoritarian, can always criminalize the behavior of some of their alleged political opponents by enacting controversial antiterrorist legislation labeling their behavior as terrorist acts. If there is a real risk that certain behavior might be unjustifiably criminalized as terrorist acts by liberal constitutional democracies that more often than not adhere to the provisions of the rule of law, it is even more likely that such a risk would increase exponentially under authoritarian governments that show virtually no respect for the provisions of the rule of law.

The newly proposed legislation on terrorism by the People's Republic of China is a good illustration of the above-mentioned risk under an authoritarian government. China has adopted new antiterrorism legislation to amend current criminal laws. By trying to align their newly proposed definition of terrorism with those adopted by other countries, the Chinese government is trying to inch closer to an international understanding of terrorism. That seems to be a positive development by Chinese officials in recognizing the value of international law for their domestic law. The new law defines "terrorist acts as those which are intended to induce public fear or to coerce state organs or international organizations by means of violence, sabotage, threats or other tactics." [19]

The new Chinese law defining terrorism uses open-ended expressions, such as acts "intended to induce public fear" or "threat or other tactics." By using these expressions, the mere reporting of a natural catastrophe that induces public fear might be conceived of as terrorism under the new Chinese legislation. Similarly, a peaceful protest by those who object, for example, to corrupt government practices or the mere threat of strike by workers demanding better working conditions might be also classified as terrorism.

In this way, the Chinese government can use their newly enacted legislation to stifle peaceful political dissent at home. For example, Chinese government officials have consistently and publicly accused and continue to accuse the Dalai Lama, the Tibetan spiritual leader in exile and a well-known pacifist advocate of Tibet's autonomy, to be responsible for promoting self-immolations or what Chinese officials call "terrorism in disguise." [20]

With their new legislation, the Chinese authorities have now the tools to legally charge the Dalai Lama with instigating terrorism. Ironically, the new legislation might also be used against workers who publicly demand fair wages and better working conditions. So what seems like a welcome development in Chinese's domestic law has actually created a legal precedent for silencing their political opponents and legitimate workers' demands.

The Chinese experience is not the exception but rather the norm of authoritarian governments for dealing with the threat of terrorism at home. On January 31, 2014, the Saudi authorities promulgated the Penal Law for Crimes of Terrorism and its Financing whereby they criminalize not only violent acts but also speech in a rather broad sense. For example, the following nonviolent acts, among many others, are criminalized: any act intended to "insult the reputation of the state," "harm public order," or "shake the security of society." According to Human Rights Watch, the Saudi law fails to "clearly define" any of the already mentioned crimes.[21]

What lessons can we learn from the newly proposed or enacted legislation against terrorism? I think that citizens in general, but especially those of us living in liberal constitutional democracies, should be vigilant about government efforts to adopt broad definitions of terrorism that might end up undermining our fundamental civil and political rights. In addition, we should voice our concerns about the potential or actual abuses that might be perpetrated by any government, whether democratic or authoritarian, against their citizens whose only crime might be to peacefully and publicly express their disagreement with controversial government policies.

2. Terrorism Scholarly Defined

I propose next to explore typical definitions of terrorism offered by some leading scholars and social policy experts, and of others found in documents sponsored by domestic institutions and regional organizations. In doing so, I wish to demonstrate how daunting it is to achieve an international consensus on the meaning of such a highly contestable term.

Fixing the meaning of the term "terrorism" is a challenging enterprise. It is rather difficult to come up with a non-question-begging definition that ordinary reasonable people could agree on. A good definition must fulfill the following conditions: it should not be so broad that it would include acts that are not ordinarily classified as terrorism, such as acts of sabotage, kidnapping, and assassinations motivated by self-regarding reasons alone; it should not be so narrow that it would exclude acts that are ordinarily classified as terrorism, such as acts of deliberately targeting or recklessly harming innocent civilians for political purposes; and it must conform with people's ordinary use of the term "terrorism."

For example, consider Bruce Hoffman's definition of terrorism:

Terrorism: "the deliberate creation and exploitation of fear through violence or the threat of violence in the pursuit of political change."[22]

An immediate difficulty with this definition is that the use of violence per se might or might not be morally justified depending on who is being targeted and the political change that one is trying to bring about. Under Hoffman's definition, individuals or groups who use discriminate violence against military targets of an oppressive regime to establish or reestablish a constitutionally democratic regime are considered terrorists and, therefore, their behavior is morally and legally disqualified. They are considered criminals rather than freedom fighters.

Those who subscribe to this definition must on pain of contradiction object to all partisan or insurgent groups, such as those who fought the Nazi occupation in Europe, those who participated in Third World liberation movements irrespective of their goals and tactics, and even those who participated in the North and South American wars of independence during the eighteenth and nineteenth centuries. Under Hoffman's definition, even George Washington could have been conceived of as a terrorist by the British. Perhaps even President Lincoln during the American Civil War would fit Hoffman's definition. He allowed the Union General William Tecumseh Sherman to carry out an indiscriminate campaign of terror against Confederacy troops and civilians in the South during the American Civil War, inflicting collective punishment on a whole population, neglecting, at times, the distinction between culpable and inculpable individuals.

One might think that an advantage of Hoffman's definition is that it appears to allow for the possibility that states, as well as nonstate agents, can be held responsible for terrorist acts. According to him, however, "terrorism is . . . perpetrated by a subnational group or non-state entity."[23] This assumption is unwarranted. Hoffman distinguishes between the term "terror" conceived of as state-sanctioned violence against a government's alleged political opponents and the term "terrorism" conceived of as violence perpetrated by nonstate agents against their alleged political opponents.[24] While this distinction might be useful at times to avoid the ambiguity of the term "terrorism," it might be viewed erroneously other times as a virtue rather than as a vice to try to justify the infliction of terror upon a government's alleged political opponents.[25]

It is evident, however, that states have used indiscriminate political violence that could be conceived of as terrorism because they, like nonstate agents, have targeted innocent civilians and peaceful opponents domestically and internationally. In addition, states oftentimes provide financial and military support to foreign governments knowing or at least suspecting that these governments have engaged in terrorist violence against their citizens. Despite public statements to the contrary, such a policy can be accurately described as a policy of abetting terrorism.[26]

One can describe the following events as typical examples of state-sponsored terrorism or simply state terrorism: the use of rampant political violence by the Jacobins against their alleged opponents during the French Revolution, especially during the Reign of Terror from 1793 to 1794; the political violence unleashed by the Bolsheviks during and after the Russian Revolution, especially during the Stalinist period of the 1930s; the one perpetrated by National Socialism in Nazi Germany and Fascist regimes elsewhere in Europe during the 1930s and 1940s; the one orchestrated by Mao against all those who were opposed to his policies of forced collectivization during the Chinese Cultural Revolution in the late 1960s; the campaign of terror and annihilation against the civilian population carried out by the Khmer Rouge in Cambodia during the 1970s; the death squads sponsored by some Latin American governments against leftist insurgents and peaceful opponents during the 1970s and 1980s; the indiscriminate use of violence by the Burmese military regime, nowadays Myanmar, against peaceful demonstrators in 1988; the Tiananmen Square massacre that resulted from the use of deliberate indiscriminate violence by the Chinese Army against peaceful demonstrators in 1989; and the genocide of the Tutsi population sponsored by Hutu extremists governing Rwanda in 1994. The list could go on ad nauseam. As a result of state-sponsored terrorism, millions of innocent civilians and peaceful opponents have lost their lives. Many have been tortured. Others have disappeared with no consolation for their loved ones. And many others have been incarcerated for prolonged periods of time under harsh conditions by despotic governments or ill-advised government officials.

By trying to be morally and legally neutral, Hoffman's definition winds up being too broad and too narrow. Any deliberate violent act with the intent of causing fear in order to bring about political change would be a terrorist act according to his definition. Consider, for example, a group of individuals who object to a government's domestic or foreign policy and decide to burn the flag and effigies of government officials as they march along while threatening to use physical violence in the future if their demands are unmet. Under Hoffman's definition, their act could be classified as terrorism. Such an act, however, is better described as an act of political protest, which is legally allowed by liberal constitutional democracies worldwide. Even though his definition per se is silent regarding the use of violence by state or nonstate agents, his decision to restrict its applicability only to nonstate agents makes it too narrow.

Consider next Virginia Held's definition of terrorism, which seems to compensate for some of Hoffman's deficiencies:

Terrorism: "political violence that usually involves sudden attacks to spread fear to a wider group than those attacked, often doing so by targeting civilians. It most resembles small wars."[27]

Held's definition of terrorism improves over Hoffman's because hers underscores the tragic component of targeting civilians. In addition, she allows for state and nonstate agents to be held responsible for terrorist practices. Held justifies the use of political violence depending on the goal that one is trying to achieve and how one goes about achieving it. Thus, according to her, "terrorism" can have a positive or negative connotation, since it resembles political violence as used in wars, especially intrastate wars.

One of the fundamental problems with Held's definition is that there are laws which regulate the practice of interstate wars, namely, the laws of war or law of armed conflict.[28] The legal regulation of small or intrastate wars is highly contestable. The common practice in international law is to understand the concept of war as "armed conflict between political units."[29]

The expression "political unit" is frequently understood as referring to states, but, as I have already argued, that need not be so. Thus, the traditional conception of war in international law, which refers to interstate armed conflicts, automatically excludes Held's conception of terrorism as resembling small wars. Belligerents in intrastate armed conflicts, such as civil wars, are mainly protected by Article 3 common to the 1949 Geneva Conventions and by the 1977 Geneva Protocol II related to noninternational armed conflicts.[30]

Nation-states, however, have been reluctant to extend the full protection of the LOAC or of IHL to intrastate armed conflicts, such as civil wars.[31] Still, some progress has been made in that direction, especially with the establishment of the International Criminal Tribunals for the former Yugoslavia and Rwanda authorized by Chapter VII of the UN Security Council, and with the establishment of the International Criminal Court (ICC).[32]

Held and like-minded scholars could always contend that their proposed definition is an invitation for a paradigm shift in our understanding of terrorism. That is, they are offering to switch from a statist and legalist model where the state has a monopoly on the legitimate use of political violence to a nuanced one where nonstate agents might enjoy some kind of legitimacy in their use of political violence. In doing so, Held and those who think like her are exploring the possibility of morally justifying political violence as in the case of urban or rural guerrilla groups in intrastate armed conflicts.

The term "terrorism," however, appears to carry greater negative connotation than the term "war." It is a trademark of terrorism that frequently those who practice it make no effort to discriminate between targeting culpable individuals and combatants and targeting innocent noncombatants. Therefore, they sometimes target those who ought not to be so targeted. One can level similar charges against the behavior of states that engage in wars. There is ample historical and empirical evidence to substantiate the claim that, in war, the majority of victims are innocent civilians rather than combatants. The harm caused to innocent civilians, however, is euphemistically described as "collateral damage." Collateral damages are nonintended consequences during an armed conflict. Whether one might justifiably describe the harm inflicted on innocent civilians during an armed conflict as nonintended consequences oftentimes remains contestable, depending on which side of the conflict one is on.

Still, one can plausibly argue that a substantive difference exists between terrorism and war, including so-called small wars. States have progressively tried to contain wars by means of international law, including the LOAC or IHL, and international human rights law. Unlike states, contemporary terrorist groups, such as those who promote suicide bombings, have no qualms about using indiscriminate violence. In their eyes, their goals justify using political violence against innocent and noninnocent alike.

Some of the terrorist groups already mentioned adopt a rather faux-Manichean view of the world—either you are a supporter of their view and hence a friend, or you are critical of their view and hence an enemy. In religiously inspired terrorism, such as the one that Al-Qaeda advocates, no room exists for the innocent in what appears to be an eschatological conflict between their belligerent view of Islam and the differing views of the rest of the world. According to Held's definition of terrorism, since most, if not all, bombing campaigns in a given war aim not only at destroying strategic objectives but also at spreading fear among the general populations, one might describe such bombing campaigns as terrorism. So the scope of Held's definition is too broad.

We can always try to shift our focus from open-ended definitions or characterizations of terrorism to internationally legally entrenched definitions of terrorism. Consider, for example, Brian M. Jenkins's tidy definition of terrorism based on international criminal law (ICL):

> Terrorism: "would comprise all acts committed in peacetime that, if committed during war, would constitute war crimes."[33]

This is a pithy definition of terrorism. Nevertheless, since this definition is based on international law, it suffers from similar shortcomings associated with the conception and implementation of international law. For example, strong nations design international law oftentimes neglecting the legitimate aspirations and needs of weak nations.

Given the predominance of state sovereignty in international affairs, powerful states comply with the principles and rules of international law when it is expedient for them to do so. By contrast, weak states are forced to comply with the dictates of international law because powerful states make sure that they do so. Otherwise, respect for international law would be precarious, leading to possible anarchy in the international community. An anarchical state of affairs would benefit no one, especially weak states. So despite the frequent double standard demonstrated by the behavior of powerful states, it is nonetheless in the best interest of weak states to abide by the principles and rules of international law.

Even if the international community were to achieve consensus regarding the above-mentioned definition of terrorism, one might still consider it too broad because almost any act of sabotage or political assassination would seem to fall under it. In addition, the definition appears too narrow because it focuses on the criminal aspect of the acts in question and neglects the political objectives of terrorism. The rationale behind Jenkins's definition is as follows: if ICL classifies the acts as crimes during wartime, namely, during a stressful situation under which one might try to justify or excuse some acts as a matter of necessity, ICL should classify the same acts as crimes during peacetime when presumably no emergencies exist to justify or excuse them.

While terrorists oftentimes intend to inflict terror on their victims, it is not necessarily only terror for the sake of terror. Terrorism is violence aimed primarily, although not exclusively, at achieving a given political outcome. Even though the probability of terrorists achieving their political goals by solely using violence, whether discriminate or not, is frequently rather slim, their infliction of violence and the threat of it perpetuate a state of war to prevent their enemies from enjoying a state of peace.

Even the term "peace" is elusive because it typically refers to the absence of formal hostilities between states. From the point of view of terrorist groups, however, once they have publicly declared war or simply engaged in political violence against an identified enemy, for example, a given government, group, or even an institution, a state of peace no longer exists between them and their alleged enemies.

The concepts of crimes against peace, war crimes, and crimes against humanity are well entrenched in customary international law. So the norms against some of these crimes have acquired the status of peremptory norms or *jus cogens*, such as those against aggression, genocide, slavery, and torture.[34] These norms aim at protecting fundamental values recognized by the international community. Moreover, another fundamental norm can only modify them. Therefore, they create universal obligations or obligations *erga omnes* that are owed by each state to the international community.[35]

However, the above-mentioned norms are highly controversial because no undisputable mechanism exists for ranking them. Consequently, if there is a clash between two fundamental norms, and there is no universal consensus as to which one should take precedence over the other, then there seems to be no certain and uncontestable way to settle a dispute. The likelihood is that powerful states will ultimately decide such a dispute. If there is a serious ideological clash among powerful states, it is likely to result in a stalemate or détente as was the case during the so-called Cold War between the former Soviet Union and the West.

Under conditions of uncertainty regarding the letter of international law, powerful states find it easier to promote and, hence, impose their self-regarding views of international law on weak states. Such an imposition has been the norm rather than the exception. A good illustration of the already mentioned biased approach is when those who are tried for war crimes are the ones who have lost a war even though the victors might have committed similar crimes. Hence, those who are vanquished are prosecuted and convicted by the rules of so-called "victor's justice." As McNamara has pointedly implied, those who are classified as war criminals would depend, in part, on who the vanquished ones are in a given armed conflict.

3. Terrorism Institutionally Defined

Consider next the definition of terrorism by a domestic institution, such as the US Department of State, in order to establish national and international policies to deal effectively with the looming threat of terrorism. The US Department of State defines terrorism as follows:

> Terrorism: "means premeditated, politically motivated violence perpetrated against noncombatant targets by subnational groups or clandestine agents."[36]

There are several problems with this definition. First, like Hoffman's definition, it is too narrow because it counts as terrorism only acts perpetrated by nonstate agents. As I have already argued, states have engaged and continue to engage in what might be aptly described as state terrorism. Thus, to always privilege the state over nonstate agents seems one-sided because both can engage in morally questionable practices that one can fittingly describe as terrorism.

Perhaps it is more feasible to hold states rather than nonstate agents accountable for their behavior, especially if these are liberal constitutional democracies where the rule of law prevails. But powerful states can oftentimes try to hide behind their notion of sovereignty by choosing to skirt or just ignore the universal jurisdiction of certain aspects of international law.[37]

Second, the idea of noncombatant immunity is controversial because it begs the question by assuming what needs to be proved, namely, that civilians and off-duty unarmed military personnel pose no threat to anyone. In addition, they are assumed to be innocent in a morally and legally relevant sense. That is, they are assumed to be guiltless or harmless. This assumption, however, is unwarranted because there are plenty of civilians who could be contributing directly to a war of aggression against another state or some of its people. For example, government officials and politicians who, despite being civilians, are instrumental in making decisions in favor of an aggressive war. Moreover, civilians working in munitions factories and scientists involved in the planning and developing of weaponry to continue with the war effort present a real threat to the enemy. Even if one were to conceive of them as innocent in a moral and legal sense because they might have been coerced to work in these projects, they still would be presenting a real threat to the enemy. Therefore, their civilian immunity is compromised.

As Michael Walzer contends, "The relevant distinction is not between those who work for the war effort and those who do not, but between those who make what soldiers need to fight and those who make what they need to live, like all the rest of us."[38] Private contractors who deliver ammunitions and armaments to one of the parties involved in a conflict, or who engage in the detention and cross-examination of the enemy, are helping in the war effort. More importantly, they are acting as soldiers usually act. Sometimes they might be acting as mercenaries. Civilians who take sides in a given armed conflict by being informants and collaborationists with government organizations might engage in serious human rights abuses of peaceful opponents or innocent civilians. If so, they could lose their civilian immunity too. Moreover, military personnel, whether voluntary or conscripted, could always, in principle, be a threat to those who are opposed to the state and policies that they are bound to defend. Consequently, they are fair game in armed conflicts.

Rather than focusing on a domestic definition of terrorism, that might or might not be accepted by other members of the international community, one could focus instead on an effort by a regional organization, such as the Organization of the Islamic Conference (OIC) (presently the Organization of Islamic Cooperation), to foster consensus among its members on a commonly accepted definition of terrorism. It is somewhat paradoxical that some regional organizations, such as the OIC, support the right of self-determination of oppressed people, but they also repudiate the practice of terrorism.[39] The OIC defines terrorism as follows:

> Terrorism: "means any act of violence or threat thereof notwithstanding its motives or intentions perpetrated to carry out an individual or collective criminal plan with the aim of terrorizing people or threatening to harm them or imperiling their lives, honour, freedoms, security or rights or exposing the environment or any facility or public or private property to hazards or occupying or seizing them, or endangering a national resource, or international facilities, or threatening the stability, territorial integrity, political unity or sovereignty of independent States."[40]

In the preamble of the same document the OIC states:

> Confirming the legitimacy of the right of peoples to struggle against foreign occupation and colonialist and racist regimes *by all means* [my italics], including armed struggle to liberate their territories and attain their rights to self-determination and independence in compliance with the purposes and principles of the Charter and resolutions of the United Nations.[41]

A clear tension exists between their commitment to fighting international terrorism and to supporting the right of self-determination of oppressed people "to struggle . . . by all means" to achieve their independence. If by "by all means" they mean absolutely "whatever it takes" to accomplish such a goal, including the targeting of noncombatants, then their position is incongruous. The LOAC, UN treaties and protocols, and international human rights law forbid the targeting of noncombatants. By contrast, if by "by all means" they mean all actions "in compliance with the purpose of the Charter and resolutions of the United Nations," then their position is coherent, provided that they impartially condemn all acts of terrorism, especially those identified as terrorist acts by the UN treaties and protocols.

Moreover, the OIC definition of terrorism is too broad because almost any act of dissent by a disaffected person or group could fall under the rubric of terrorism, including those who exercise their right of freedom of speech to protest against the leaders of a given state or their questionable policies. Apparently, the OIC has agreed on casting a wide net to describe terrorism as aiming not only at developing effective policies to deal with domestic and international acts of political violence but also at stifling peaceful political dissent at home. In addition to the draconian nature of sharia that sanctions cruel and inhumane punishments, leaders of Islamic States who embrace the supremacy of sharia have frequently manipulated and still manipulate the application of such law to perpetuate themselves in power. The plasticity of sharia, without the checks and balances of the rule of law, promotes authoritarian and, oftentimes, tyrannical regimes.[42]

The OIC definition, however, is also too narrow because by disregarding the "motives or intentions" of individuals or groups who engage in violent acts, member states neglect to address the political component of terrorism. We must remember that terrorism aims at promoting political goals domestically or internationally. Whether those goals are morally and politically desirable might be an open question. But what does not seem open to question is the categorical objection against targeting innocent noncombatants. Allowing for the targeting of innocent noncombatants would amount to sanctioning a policy of violating the physical, psychological, and moral integrity of those who are innocent beyond reasonable doubt. That is, they are impeccably innocent. Adopting such a policy would be equivalent to sanctioning murder.

C. SUMMARY

In this section, I explored the contestability and nuances of the term "terrorism." I underscored that, despite discrepancies among different definitions of terrorism, they all seem to share a significant trademark—the use of violence or force for political purposes. I distinguished between terrorism, sabotage, and kidnapping to illustrate the unique features of terrorist acts. Next, I argued that although member states of the UN have been unable to agree on a universal legally binding definition of international terrorism, their disagreements have not prevented them for achieving consensus on several legal instruments or "sectoral" conventions against specifically designated terrorist acts. I moved next to explore previous international legal efforts at trying to define terrorism within the boundaries of international law. I subsequently explored various scholars' and social experts' definitions of terrorism. I argued that either their definitions are too narrow by focusing primarily on violence perpetrated by nonstate agents, or they are too broad by including destruction of property and fear. I also argued that a definition based on ICL suffers from the weakness of international law. Lastly, I argued that institutionally based definitions of terrorism, such as some typically offered by national government organizations or by international organizations, have similar shortcomings as the ones offered by different scholars.

Chapter 3

Critics of Terrorism

A. WHY TERRORISM IS MORALLY OFFENSIVE

1. Presumption of Innocence

Having already discussed some typical definitions of terrorism, I will now explore the specific features that ordinary people find morally offensive about terrorism. The first feature that people usually find objectionable about terrorism is the violation of the presumption of innocence of their victims. Civilians are presumed innocent until proven guilty by an impartial court of law—either domestic or international. One can defend this immunity based on two fundamental intuitions.

The first intuition is that we, as moral agents, have a compelling natural duty of nonmaleficence, refraining from intentionally bringing about undeserved harm or significant risk of it against the impeccably innocent. One can argue that the natural duty of nonmaleficence derives from a fundamental moral principle, namely, that we ought not to deliberately harm the impeccably innocent. If we were to allow people to deliberately harm the impeccably innocent, then the concept of innocence would be meaningless. Similarly, the frameworks of morality and legality would be useless, since both frameworks are based on protecting the innocent. If that were to be so, then chaos rather than order would prevail around the globe.

One might conceive of a duty as natural in a secular or a religious sense. In a secular sense, the duty of nonmaleficence is natural by virtue of our inherent capacity for recognizing a reciprocal moral standing in other people. Therefore, we owe this duty to one another regardless of any social arrangements or conventions.[1] In a religious sense, however, one might view the duty of nonmaleficence as natural by virtue of being derived, for example, from a

Christian conception of natural law. St. Augustine offers a typical Christian understanding of such a duty.

According to Augustine, a harmonious concord among people in society is established by observing two fundamental moral rules: to do no harm to anyone and to help others if possible.[2] The first rule entails the duty of nonmaleficence, while the second entails the duty of beneficence. These rules with their corresponding natural duties follow from the two foundational precepts of Christianity: to love God and to love one's neighbor. For St. Thomas Aquinas, however, these natural duties follow from his conception of natural law, which he derives from his first fundamental principle of practical reason, namely "that good is to be sought and done, evil to be avoided."[3] One finds a similar view in Islam. The Quran states, "Let there arise out of you a band of people inviting to all that is good, enjoining what is right, and forbidding what is wrong: they are the ones to attain felicity."[4]

Our natural duty of nonmaleficence is compelling rather than just prima facie because, in principle, people can never justify deliberately violating it. One might excuse its violation only under exceptional circumstances. In addition, this duty presupposes that people have important but derivative natural rights, such as the right to life and liberty. They can forfeit these rights only when they become morally or legally culpable of wrongdoing.[5]

The second intuition whereby one can defend the presumption of innocence principle is precisely that the violation of this principle might lead to serious injustices. This moral and legal principle is widely recognized not only in domestic but also in international law.[6] Only if one establishes a person's guilt beyond reasonable doubt in an impartial court of law can s/he then be rightfully punished. Regardless of its legal ancestry, one could argue that the presumption of innocence in a legal system follows from the fundamental moral principle of nonmaleficence, which forbids deliberately harming the impeccably innocent by commission or omission.

While the principle of presumption of innocence is entrenched in the Anglo-American tradition of common law, it is not explicitly stated in the Magna Carta, the English Bill of Rights of 1689, the Declaration of Independence of the United States, or the Constitution of the United States.[7] One finds the spirit of the principle, for example, in the Fifth and Fourteenth Amendments' due process clause. That is, people cannot "be deprived of life, liberty or property without due process of law." Also, one finds the spirit of the principle in William Blackstone's classic work, *Commentaries of the Laws of England*. Blackstone states, "It is better that ten guilty persons escape than one innocent suffer."[8] Nevertheless, the principle was first established in US jurisprudence in the Supreme Court decision *Coffin v. United States* (1845). Justice Edward Douglas White delivered the opinion of the court by citing the long ancestry of the principle going back to Roman and canon law.[9]

When terrorists profile and target their alleged enemies, they increase the risk of seriously harming the impeccably innocent, which is the norm rather than the exception in terrorist attacks. Even in liberal constitutional democracies where the rule of law is the norm, issues of racial, ethnic, religious, or political profiling have occurred frequently. For example, in the United States, which upholds the presumption of innocence, law enforcement officers and government officials have used and still use racial, ethnic, religious, or political profiling of individuals. However, the harm that one might suffer in profiling by law enforcement officers is usually not equivalent to the harm one might suffer during a terrorist attack. But harm it is nevertheless.

Yet profiling is not always the result of a questionable practice in the fight against criminals, including fighting terrorists. Sometimes members of racial, ethnic, religious, or political groups might be involved in certain criminal activities more often than the general population at large is. In those cases, one must weigh the presumption of innocence against the immediacy and severity of the threat posed by members of the profiled group to the rest of society, such as during national emergencies. A war, whether interstate or intrastate, or an imminent terrorist threat is a good illustration of a national emergency. Still, to avoid treating individual members of the profiled group unjustly, the burden of proof, even in the case of national emergencies, is on the government to demonstrate that individual members of the profiled group are likely to commit a crime.

Weighing the right of the presumption of innocence against the safety of the general population during national emergencies is rather challenging. Some scholars defend the presumption of innocence based on a compelling right of the defendant to avoid being wrongfully punished.[10] Andrew Stumer, for example, argues against balancing the interests or rights of the community against the presumption of innocence of individuals, even during national emergencies.[11] Other scholars, such as Judge Richard Posner, would conceive of Stumer's defense of the presumption of innocence as formalistic. As a good legal pragmatist, Posner insists in a balancing approach between the interests of the state or the community and the rights of individuals, especially during hard cases, such as national emergencies.[12]

Geoffrey A. Stone alerts us to what can happen, especially in wartime, when we ignore the presumption of innocence principle and the politics of expediency trumps the rule of law.[13] Regrettably, in times of great peril, the courts, including the US Supreme Court, frequently sanction the excesses of the legislative and the executive branch. For example, during national emergencies, the US Supreme Court has kowtowed to military expediency, especially on the following infamous World War II decisions: *Hirabayashi v. United States*, 320 U.S. 81, 1943, and *Korematsu v. United States*, 323 U.S. 214, 1944.

In the above-mentioned decisions, US citizens of Japanese ancestry were forcibly removed from the US west coast and were sent to internment camps, as a result of which many of them lost their jobs, businesses, and properties. The US military worried that, after the Japanese attack on Pearl Harbor, some Japanese Americans could engage in acts of sabotage on behalf of the Japanese government. No Japanese American, however, was ever convicted of acts of sabotage or treason. In hindsight, US citizens' constitutional rights were deliberately violated based on racial prejudice and fear. Therefore, they were significantly harmed. It took nearly fifty years for Congress to apologize and President Ronald Reagan to sign the Civil Liberties Act of 1988 authorizing reparation payments of twenty thousand dollars to each surviving internee as a belated acknowledgment of the undeserved harm inflicted on Japanese Americans.[14]

The above is a cautionary tale alerting us to the risks involved in profiling, even during times of national emergencies. Those targeting members of a profiled group presume them to be guilty rather than innocent. The law penalizes other people's acts. So it is simply arbitrary and unfair to penalize people just because they belong to a given group that shares certain distinctive characteristics, such as their racial or ethnic background, or certain religious or political beliefs. In so doing, government officials and even the courts are risking committing grave injustices against individual members of the profiled group.

In the eyes of ordinary reasonable people, being insouciant about the presumption of innocence principle can have serious deleterious consequences for the innocent and the noninnocent alike, and for the legitimacy of a penal system, including the rule of law. What transpired after the 9/11 terrorist attacks in the United States is a good illustration of what can happen when law enforcement and government officials ignore the presumption of innocence during a national emergency. Hundreds or perhaps even thousands of Muslim and Arab young males were rounded up and quite a few were detained for weeks without sufficient incriminating evidence. Their only offense was being noncitizens and members of a targeted group. In addition, some of them might have committed minor noncriminal offenses, such as having expired visas.[15]

Given the gravity and uncertainty of the situation at the time, including the risk of immediate terrorist attacks against innocent civilians, one could argue that the behavior of US government officials and the courts might have been excused. The extenuating circumstances at the time were dire enough to allow for such behavior. As Judge Posner writes, "In times of danger, the weight of concerns for public safety increases relative to that of liberty concerns, and civil liberties are narrowed."[16] Perhaps that was the only reasonable option available to US government officials and the courts to attempt to secure public safety by trying to prevent subsequent terrorist attacks, or so they say.[17] Government officials faced a rather stark dilemma of balancing the rights of few individuals against securing the rights of many others or of balancing the personal liberty of the few against the public safety of the many.

Nevertheless, the rights of those who were unjustly detained were violated, which goes against the rule of law and against the values of our democratic institutions. Every time that we violate the rights of the innocent, we are undermining the values of that which we are trying to protect, namely, the moral, psychological, and physical integrity of individuals and the democratic institutions that make such protection possible. As the late Ronald Dworkin underscored in his criticism of the Bush administration's detention policies, "we damage ourselves, not just our victim, when we ignore his humanity, because in denigrating his intrinsic value we denigrate our own."[18]

If, as proposed by the late John Ashcroft after 9/11, preventing terrorist attacks becomes "the chief mission of US law enforcement," then the risk of violating innocent and noninnocent people's rights is likely to increase. By sacrificing the presumption of innocence in trying to prevent terrorist attacks, the former attorney general and other government officials have undermined innocent and noninnocent people's rights, especially the rights of those who are allegedly guilty of wrongdoing. That is so because, in order to prevent violating their rights and unjustly convicting them, those who are allegedly guilty are presumed innocent until proven otherwise in an impartial court of law.

Acting on the presumption of guilt can certainly allow law enforcement and government officials, and a complacent and sometimes complicit judicial system, to violate people's fundamental human rights. If that is true of those who are normally constrained by the rule of law, it would likely be worse of those who simply ignore and, hence, regularly violate the rule of law, such as terrorist groups and authoritarian governments.

The People's Republic of China, for example, while recognizing the principle of the presumption of innocence in theory, routinely ignores it, especially in their summary application of the death penalty.[19] Other authoritarian governments, such the Republic of Cuba, presume that citizens might be guilty before committing crimes. For example, Cuba's Penal Code Articles 72 and 73 criminalize drunkenness and so-called "dangerous behavior," even though citizens charged with these offenses have committed no actual crime. They are presumed guilty of potential crimes. The government routinely incarcerates political opponents by designating them as being engaged in "dangerous behavior."[20]

Domestically, violation of the presumption of innocence by law enforcement and government officials can have a harmful impact on the impeccably innocent for several reasons. First, sometimes it is extremely difficult to prove one's innocence if, for example, there are no witnesses, or, even though people have relevant information that could exonerate you, they are reluctant to testify on your behalf. Second, it would be exceedingly difficult, if not impossible, for some defendants, such as indigent ones and noncitizens, to prove their innocence given their lack of financial resources, their likely ignorance of legal matters, and the potential prejudices of juries and judges. And third, the presumption of guilt already stigmatizes those who are presumed to be guilty without having the possibility of defending themselves in an impartial court of law.

It is difficult enough for an innocent person to be a defendant in a court of law. However, it would be even worse if, while being innocent, one is considered guilty before even having one's day in court. Defendants would likely be viewed as pariahs by others, increasing the risk of their being ostracized and ultimately discriminated against by large numbers of people in society. For example, after the September 11, 2001, attacks in the United States, the March 11, 2004, attacks in Madrid, and the July 7, 2005, attacks in London, peaceful Muslim individuals and their Islamic communities in the United States and Europe have been victims of unfair Islamophobic antagonism and ostracism by both public officials and the general public.

Internationally, the presumption of guilt might allow powerful nations to violate the letter and spirit of international law for several reasons. First, they might use unilateral actions, such as preemptive attacks against weak nations, without sufficient evidence for their decisions. Second, such unilateral behavior can undermine the letter and spirit of the Charter of the United Nations that promotes cooperation and consensus among member states.[21] And third, the use of preemption can result not only in violating the sovereignty of other nations but, more importantly, in violating the fundamental human rights of their citizens. If we take seriously our compelling natural duty of nonmaleficence, then we ought to abide by it whether domestically or internationally. To act otherwise is likely to risk jeopardizing the physical, psychological, and moral integrity of the impeccably innocent.

2. Attacking the Innocent

Ordinary people usually find terrorism morally offensive. They object to the targeting of innocent noncombatants or innocent civilians. That is, targeting or recklessly harming those who should not be harmed because they are presumably guiltless or harmless unless proven otherwise. Those who are guiltless or harmless have neither harmed nor have they intended to harm anyone in particular. Moreover, they have not intentionally neglected their prima facie natural duty of beneficence to help those who are in serious distress. Therefore, one could not claim that they deliberately harmed them by omission. Also, their mere presence or social role in society poses no substantive threat to others. Hence, by virtue of their guiltlessness or harmlessness, they should enjoy categorical immunity. Consequently, it is always wrong to deliberately target or to recklessly harm those who are innocent beyond reasonable doubt, namely, those who are impeccably innocent.

The 9/11 attacks are an example of terrorists aiming at harming those who are presumably innocent beyond reasonable doubt—except those who worked in the Pentagon. The militant Islamists who carried out the attacks aimed at harming innocent civilians as their secondary target to punish and influence the behavior of their primary target, namely, the US government. One can plausibly argue that in the 9/11 attacks, the nineteen Al-Qaeda hijackers who carried out their so-called "martyrdom operation" used the civilian passengers in the airplanes and those inside the World Trade Center towers, including the surrounding bystanders, as their secondary targets. Whether their attack on the Pentagon aimed at a secondary or a primary target is debatable, since the Pentagon houses the US Department of Defense. Because Al-Qaeda had already declared war on the United States, the Pentagon could be conceived of as a primary and legitimate target. Whether the militant Islamists aimed at primary or secondary targets, they deliberately killed nearly three thousand people, most of whom were innocent civilians.

By targeting innocent noncombatants, the militant Islamists tried to punish and thereby influence the behavior of the US government. They wished to punish American citizens in general and US government officials in particular. In their eyes, even those opposed to US foreign policy in the Middle East and to US support for despotic and nepotic Islamic governments are in some elliptical sense guilty by directly or indirectly contributing to foment what they view as US misguided foreign policies. Therefore, they viewed all Americans as their enemies. By deliberately or recklessly inflicting terror on the populace, they hoped to achieve at least three goals: first, to successfully punish US government officials; second, to coerce them to change US foreign policies in the Middle East; and third, to force them to remove US presence from Islamic countries, especially from the Holy Land of Islam.

One can offer a similar assessment about the March 11, 2004, (a.k.a. 11-M) attacks in Madrid perpetrated by Islamist terrorists and the July 7, 2005, (a.k.a. 7/7) attacks in London perpetrated by four Islamist suicide bombers. In the Madrid attacks, militant Islamists planted about ten bombs in four trains heading into Madrid, killing 191 innocent civilians and injuring nearly 2,000 others. In the London attacks, three militant Islamist suicide bombers detonated their bombs in the underground commuter trains, and another suicide bomber set off a bomb in a double-decker bus, all together killing fifty-two innocent civilians and injuring over seven hundred others.

As in the 9/11 attacks in the United States, the militant Islamists in Madrid and London used the innocent civilian passengers and the surrounding bystanders as their secondary targets whereby they tried to influence their primary targets, that is, Spain's and Great Britain's foreign policies supporting the wars in Afghanistan and Iraq. In the case of Spain specifically, they probably also had in mind influencing the outcome of Spain's presidential election where the PSOE (*Partido Socialista Obrero Español* or Spanish Socialist Workers Party) defeated the incumbent PP (*Partido Popular* or the People's Party), which supported the invasion of Iraq. The PSOE had promised that if they were elected, they would pull out their troops from Iraq, which they ultimately did. Apparently, the terrorists were trying to punish the Spanish and British governments for supporting the US invasion of Iraq. By deliberately and indiscriminately inflicting terror on the populace, they hoped not only to successfully punish Spanish and British government officials but also to simultaneously coerce them to change course and ultimately withdraw their troops from Iraq.

By focusing on the above-mentioned typical instances of contemporary terrorism, we can understand why many people conceive of these attacks as heinous crimes—their secondary targets were innocent civilians. Ironically, some of their victims might even have been opposed to the wars in Afghanistan and the invasion of Iraq. One can understand that militant Islamists can harbor grievances, whether legitimate or not, against certain government policies and the rank-and-file officials responsible for implementing those policies. But it is beyond the pale to deliberately and indiscriminately inflict unmerited substantive harm on ordinary innocent civilians whose responsibility in designing and implementing government policies is negligible at best. Even in liberal democratic societies, such as the United States, Spain, and Great Britain, ordinary citizens have no direct control over foreign policy. Therefore, to hold them accountable for that which they have no direct control over is simply unjust.

3. Collective Punishment

By acting on the nebulous notion of collective guilt and its corresponding notion of collective punishment, terrorists target those allegedly guilty because they belong to a given group who share some common features. They tend to overlook that such common features might be irrelevant for designating someone as an enemy.

For example, in the Israeli-Palestinian conflict, Hamas's leaders frequently framed the conflict in such a way that they tried to justify the use of indiscriminate violence against all Israelis based on the assumption of collective guilt. When Jessica Stern interviewed Ismael Abu Shanab, one of Hamas's leaders, she asked him: "Who are the combatants in your dispute with Israel?" He replied, "There are no civilians in Israel because every citizen is required to serve in the army."[22] A similar view has been expressed by some Israeli military officials, such as retired Major General Giora Eiland, former head of Israel's National Security Council, who during the 2014 Gaza conflict claimed that Gaza residents in general "are to blame for the situation just like Germany's residents were to blame for electing Hitler as their leader and paid a heavy price for that, and rightly so."[23]

Regrettably, the State of Israel oftentimes collectively punishes Palestinians and deliberately inflicts disproportional harm on innocent and noninnocent alike.[24] If so, one can classify their morally questionable practices as reprisals. When states engage in these morally questionable practices, critics of acts of reprisal often view these acts as state terrorism. Regardless of whether one would prefer to view these morally suspect acts as reprisals or as state terrorism, the pernicious effect of acting on the presumption of collective guilt is evident.

Consider, for example, the human suffering brought about by the endless Israeli-Palestinian conflict. By implementing policies based on a dubious presumption of collective guilt, both camps only exacerbate the use of indiscriminate violence against innocent civilians. These policies support acts that might be fittingly described as war crimes.[25] In the latest confrontation between the state of Israel and Hamas, accounts and mutual accusations of war crimes have already started to emerge.[26]

In an armed conflict, once both camps determine that the concept of "innocent civilian" is vacuous and, therefore, they agree that the distinction between civilians and combatants is morally and legally irrelevant, the result is total war or mayhem. Under those conditions a peace agreement would be just a truce to prepare for when the next armed conflict would flare. The late Golda Meir, former Israeli prime minister, understood the horror of killing people, especially the innocent, when in a press conference in London in 1969 about two years after the 1967 war, she stated: "When peace comes we will perhaps in time be able to forgive the Arabs for killing our sons, but it will be harder for us to forgive them for having forced us to kill their sons."[27] Even granting former Prime Minister Meir some poetic license, forgiving those who kill or seriously harmed our loved ones is always a great challenge that only very few exceptional persons can transcend. Similarly, for those who possess a moral conscience, deliberately killing or seriously harming others, especially the impeccably innocent, is also difficult to transcend. In any case, her claim cuts both ways. It also applies to Arabs and Palestinians who might feel remorse for having killed innocent Israeli civilians.

The implementation of policies based on the assumption of collective guilt creates an insidious level of distrust among Israelis and Palestinians alike that makes it virtually impossible for them to negotiate a bona fide peaceful and fair settlement around their otherwise intractable differences. If we take, for example, Immanuel Kant's suggestions for bringing about perpetual peace among nations, they seem to consistently violate one or more of Kant's categorical provisions for establishing a future state of peace between current belligerent nations or states.

On the one hand, those who refuse to recognize that the Palestinians have a right to a viable state underscore that, despite Kant's idealism in politics, his views are just moot regarding the Israeli-Palestinian conflict. Since a Palestinian state does not exist yet, they describe the Israeli-Palestinian conflict as a civil war rather than as a conflict between belligerent states. Even in a civil war, however, IHL must be honored by all parties who are involved in the armed conflict. On the other hand, those who refuse to recognize the de jure existence of the state of Israel, such as Hamas, describe the conflict as a war against a foreign occupation. But even in war against a foreign occupation, the PNCI must be respected. Regrettably, by supporting and committing terrorist acts, Hamas violates frequently PNCI.

As a militant Islamic organization that sponsors terrorism, Hamas is committed to do whatever it takes to destroy the State of Israel.[28] Yet Hamas's morally questionable actions provide no justification or excuse for the State of Israel to use reprisals or excessive indiscriminate use of force against culpable and inculpable Palestinians alike.[29] The conflict between Israel and Hamas is not only an armed conflict but a political battle for winning the hearts and minds of public opinion. For this reason, not only the total number of people who have been killed in the latest Gaza conflict is relevant for ascribing responsibility and blame to those who participated in the hostilities, but the ratio of civilians to combatants who actually perished in the armed conflict, while highly contestable, is also relevant for ascribing such responsibility and blame.[30]

One can grant that Kant's idealism in politics might not fully explain the contemporary nuances involved in the Israeli-Palestinian conflict. However, one can still argue that diplomats and government officials from both camps could learn from his proposed six preliminary reasonable articles for bringing about a state of peace among nations. Of these six preliminary articles, one, five, and six are categorical. Article one maintains that peace treaties should rule out future wars, article five rules out interference in the internal affairs of another state, and article six rules out acts that would undermine mutual trust in a future state of peace.[31] In addition to violating articles one and five, some of the acts that Kant lists in article six as impeding the realization of a state of perpetual peace have been consistently and systematically committed by Israelis and Palestinians alike against one another, such as "the employment of *assassins . . .* or *poisoners . . . breach of agreements, the instigation of treason,* etc."[32]

Some might argue that since the Palestinians have no independent state, the primary burden of seeking a state of peace falls on the shoulders of the most powerful, namely, on the state of Israel. Although the Palestinians have no independent state, the international community recognizes that they have a legitimate claim to establish one. Moreover, they have succeeded in having some kind of acknowledged representation by Fatah and Hamas groups who are seeking to establish an independent and viable Palestinian state. By employing tactics that can legitimately be conceived of as terrorism, such as using indiscriminate violence against all Israelis, Palestinians undermine their cause in the eyes of the international community. Likewise, by continuing to expand its settlements in the occupied territories, its policy of targeted assassinations, and its policy of collective punishment, the state of Israel undermines its moral legitimacy in the eyes of the international community too.

All parties in the Israeli-Palestinian conflict have the responsibility of seeking a state of lasting peace. Those who frequently argue that nonstate terrorists are the only ones to be blamed for the failure of achieving a lasting peace are adopting a one-sided evaluation of the conflict. The institutionalized indiscriminate use of violence by states has been and still is a common practice in the history of human conflicts. Oftentimes the practice of terrorism by nonstate agents is a reaction to the excessive and discriminatory use of state violence against citizens who do not deserve to be so treated. Nonstate terrorists are not exclusively to be blamed for having an agonistic view of reality. Unfortunately, some world leaders have a similar agonistic mentality, since they sponsor policies that can aptly be described as state terrorism.

4. Agonistic View of Reality

Terrorists embrace not only an agonistic but also a faux-Manichean conception of politics—those who do not support their political agenda are necessarily against them. For terrorists, oftentimes the existence of neutrals is inconceivable or irrelevant to them. However, there are two types of political Manichaeism: Manichaeism on the left and Manichaeism on the right. Jean-Paul Sartre's argument against supporters of colonialism is a good example of Manichaeism on the left. Sartre writes, "If you [pacifists] are not a victim when the government you voted for . . . commits 'genocide'. . . , then you are undoubtedly a torturer."[33] By contrast, President George W. Bush's remarks after the 9/11 terrorist attacks are a good example of Manichaeism on the right. He stated, "Either you are with us, or you are with the terrorists."[34] Both Sartre and Bush might have used such an agonistic Manichaeism as a rhetorical device to attract supporters to their cause. Still, whether or not they truly meant what they said, such a belligerent sophism has cost many innocent lives.

Once people embrace such a bifurcated view of the world, they will likely have no compunction about harming others who nonetheless can be conceived of as innocent by any reasonable standard. The idea of innocence has virtually no meaning in a terrorist eschatological conception of the world. In that sense, terrorists generally assume that their use of violence has a redeeming nature, either worldly or otherworldly, in trying to bring about their political goals.

Those who engage in terrorism, especially nonstate agents, have a one-sided agonistic view of reality. Such a skewed view of reality, however, is not a necessary feature of all partisan warriors or belligerents. For instance, some leaders of revolutionary guerrilla groups have objected to the use of terrorism, even though they have done so mostly for strategic reasons. For example, Leon Trotsky, one of the leaders of the 1917 October Bolshevik Revolution, objected to the use of individual terror because it promotes false expectations in the masses: they hope for "a great avenger and liberator who some day will come and accomplish his mission."[35] Nevertheless, he defended the so-called revolutionary terrorism or the Red Terror of the proletariat against the bourgeoisie. He wrote, "The revolution does require of the revolutionary class that it should attain its end by all methods at its disposal—if necessary, by an armed rising: if required, by terrorism."[36]

The iconic Argentine Marxist guerrilla leader Ernesto (Che) Guevara distinguished between the practice of sabotage and the assassination of high-profile targets, which he favored, and the practice of terrorism as indiscriminate violence, which he objected to early on in his life.[37] Still, in his 1967 "Message to the Tricontinental," he seems to have had a change of heart, and thereafter he embraced a conception of total war that is indistinguishable from terrorism. He writes, "We [the guerrilla fighters] must carry the war into every corner the enemy happens to carry it: to his home, to his centers of entertainment: a total war."[38]

Others, however, had serious moral qualms about the use of indiscriminate violence. For example, Abraham Guillén, a Spaniard anarchist who influenced the Tupamaro movement in Uruguay during the 1960s and 1970s, favored the practice of urban rather than rural guerrilla tactics but objected to the use of indiscriminate political violence partly on moral grounds.[39] Groups belonging to the fourth wave, however, seem to be more successful in using deliberate or reckless violence on a grand scale than groups belonging to the first three waves.

Since the survival of guerrillas or partisan groups depends on achieving widespread support from the masses, it is only reasonable to expect them to minimize innocent civilian casualties to acquire or maintain a high level of general support. But no general pattern exists among those who advocate and engage in guerrilla warfare regarding the use of terrorism against civilians.

For example, at some point Che Guevara and Mao Zedong were opposed to it, while Carlos Marighella considered it a legitimate weapon in the revolutionary struggle against the bourgeoisie.[40]

Strategically, it is in the guerrillas' best interest to avoid being viewed as criminals. They would rather be envisaged as having the high moral ground vis-à-vis those whom they are fighting against, namely, their alleged enemies or oppressors. However, there is no guarantee that once they come to power, they would not abuse their newly acquired power against their alleged enemies.

Whether those identified as enemies or as oppressors are truly so might still be debatable—depending on the nature of the conflict in question. For example, is the armed conflict a war of liberation from colonial oppression? Is it about imposing an authoritarian or totalitarian ideology on the rest of society? Is it about defending, restoring, or establishing a legitimate constitutional democracy? Are there reasonable, peaceful, and viable means of expressing one's grievances to try to change what one perceives as an unjust political order? One needs to answer these questions before attempting to justify or excuse the use of political violence against an already recognized opponent.

There is enough compelling evidence to demonstrate that, once political violence occurs, innocent victims will likely be killed or seriously harmed. That is the indisputable tragic nature of violence. Once violence is unleashed, no one is saved from its ominous consequences. So those who ignore the above questions show a clear disregard for the physical, psychological, and moral integrity of innocent noncombatants.

Terrorism is political violence aimed at deliberately or recklessly killing, maiming, or coercing people regardless of their innocence. One might think of political violence as the use of physical force intending to perpetuate or to transform a domestic or international political order. The use of such violence frequently, although not always, concomitantly brings about widespread destruction of property. That explains why some scholars and policy makers associate terrorism with destruction of property.

Coady, for example, defines terrorism as follows: "the organized use of violence to attack noncombatants . . . or their property for political purposes."[41] A good example of this wide-ranging interpretation of terrorism can be found in the US federal definition of terrorism as stated in Title 18 of the US Code 2332b, which describes it as "an offense that is calculated to influence or affect the conduct of government by intimidation or coercion, or to retaliate against government conduct" and goes on to specifically name a long list of typical criminal actions such as the killing, murdering, kidnapping, or maiming of persons in addition to those affecting property relating to, for example, "arson within special maritime and territorial jurisdiction," "arson and bombing of property used in interstate commerce," "protection of computers," and "destruction of communication lines, station, or systems," among others.[42] Even under this broad definition of terrorism, for an act to be considered terrorism it must aim at "influencing or affecting" government conduct.

Terrorists might engage in political violence with different aims in mind. They might use political violence in a conservative or a transformative way. I am using the term "conservative" in its etymological sense meaning "preserve" rather than in its ideological sense referring to those who defend traditional views in areas such as politics, religion, economics, or morality. On the one hand, one can use political violence in a conservative way to try to preserve a given political order (either domestic or international). On the other hand, one can use political violence in a transformative way to try to change a given political order (either domestic or international). Regardless of how terrorist violence influences government conduct, terrorism is objectionable because it harms innocent noncombatants by deliberately or recklessly killing, maiming, or substantively harming them whether physically or psychologically.

In principle, conceiving of using political violence for its own sake seems oxymoronic. Terrorism is not nihilistic, as some might argue, but rather purposive. While Ignatieff, for example, argues that those who engage in terrorism and counterterrorism can easily be tempted by nihilism, namely, killing their opponents just for the sake of wantonly killing them, I think that history would show it to be the exception rather than the norm. Terrorists and counterterrorists generally kill for the sake of certain political goals, whether domestic or international.[43]

Terrorists calculate their acts rationally to obtain immediate or long-term political goals. They seem to operate with a sense of rationality being conditioned by what they believe is a higher good rather than with a cost-benefit analysis understanding of rationality. As a result, they are willing to make the ultimate sacrifice in order to try to bring about such higher good. They might conceive of the higher good, for example, as achieving national liberation, as an imposition of a political or religious ideology, or as a mélange of any of the above.

5. Terrorism and "Revolutionary Justice"

When people blame terrorists and their apologists for their indiscriminate and reckless use of violence, the latter frequently use a red herring to shift the attention to their so-called view of "revolutionary justice." In their eyes, their conception of revolutionary justice is necessarily related to their higher good that they are trying to bring about. Frequently, however, their acts of so-called revolutionary justice are simply acts of revenge masquerading as subliminal justice, since their victims are presumed guilty with no recourse of appeal. Whether their past or present grievances are legitimate or serious enough to justify using political violence against those whom they perceive as being responsible for their grievances is oftentimes of no concern to some terrorists. But it is of concern to reasonable and fair-minded people who care about whether any grievance is serious enough to justify using deliberate or reckless political violence against innocent and noninnocent victims alike.

Frequently, terrorists are militant intolerant people who are intransigent because they base their conception of politics on exclusion rather than on inclusion. As a result, they are likely to hold dangerous intolerant beliefs, such as xenophobic, misogynistic, racist, chauvinistic, or a combination of any of these questionable beliefs to try to justify targeting those whom they conceive of as their enemies.[44] They use their victims, namely, their enemies, only as means to promote their grand political schemes, such as trying to establish a xenophobic white supremacist political order or a new caliphate where sharia law would prevail. According to their one-sided agonistic view of reality, they view those who prefer a different political order as enemies whom they could remorselessly kill—justifiably or not. So the notion of a liberal constitutional democracy founded on respect for liberal and demo-cratic values, such as tolerance, diversity, and the rule of law, is inimical to them. Terrorists typically believe that anyone and anything that interferes with the realization of their grand political schemes is fair game. Since citizens of liberal constitutional democracies and their respective institutions are an anathema to the realization of terrorists' grand political schemes, they are fair game for them.

Let us consider, for example, the terrorist attack on the Oklahoma City federal building in 1995, where 168 people died and hundreds of others were injured. This was not a fortuitous attack or an improvised act of sabotage. It was rather a well-planned and calculated attack of revenge or what some might call an act of "revolutionary justice" against the US federal govern-ment, presumably carried out by Timothy McVeigh in cooperation with Terry Nichols and Michael Fortier. These individuals were allegedly associ-ated with white supremacist militias. Whether McVeigh was just a lone wolf sympathetic but not necessarily associated with any specific militant white supremacist militia remains debatable. Regardless of how one might think of him, McVeigh thought of himself as a patriot who was trying to vindicate white supremacist values against a presumably corrupt federal government— the same government that a year before had killed members of the Branch Davidian cult when federal agents stormed their compound in Waco, Texas. Timothy McVeigh honestly believed that he was in the right. Consequently, he felt no remorse for his terrorist act.

Anders Behring Breivik, who perpetrated the terrorist attacks in Norway, exhibited a remarkably similar way of reasoning as McVeigh did in attempting to justify the above-mentioned attack in Oklahoma City. On July 22, 2011, Breivik, a Norwegian right-wing extremist, carried out coordinated terrorist attacks against government headquarters in the capital of Oslo and against members of the youth division of the Norwegian Labor Party. In the first attack, he used a car bomb, killing eight people and injuring others. Two hours later, he dressed in police uniform to gain access to a youth camp on the island of Utøya where he systematically hunted down and killed sixty-nine people, mostly teenagers, and injured several dozen more.

Like McVeigh, Breivik conceived of himself as a patriot. He acknowledged that he needed to commit a "small barbarism" by killing sixty-nine people and injuring several dozen others to prevent a "bigger barbarism" in the future. According to Breivik, the Labor Party has betrayed the Norwegian people by accepting Muslim immigrants who in the long run will undermine Norwegian homogeneous culture. Hence, his apologists could describe his terrorist attacks as acts of "revolutionary justice."

Consider next the 9/11 suicide terrorist attacks that destroyed the World Trade Center and partially damaged the Pentagon, resulting in the deaths of almost three thousand people, including the nineteen hijackers. The hijackers conceived of themselves as jihadists who, as members of Al-Qaeda, the terrorist organization led by the late Osama bin Laden and Ayman al-Zawahiri, spent years planning the attack to avenge their Muslim brothers and to protect the *umma* from the US government's policies in the Middle East.[45] They also thought of themselves as *shahids* or martyrs who sacrificed their lives in a jihad against the United States and its allies. Thus, in their minds and in the minds of those who support their militant Islamist ideology, they engaged in a so-called martyrdom operation rather than in a suicide mission, which is allegedly forbidden in the Quran.[46] As a result, their attack, like the above-mentioned terrorist attacks by right-wing extremists, could be portrayed as an act of "revolutionary justice." Or, perhaps, since the hijackers were militant Islamists, they might have thought of their attack as divine retribution or divine justice against infidels.

Unlike McVeigh and Breivik, the 9/11 hijackers committed suicide or "martyrdom operations" in carrying out their terrorist attacks. Moreover, unlike McVeigh and Breivik, they were inspired by their militant view of Islam. But their way of reasoning in trying to justify their terrorist acts were remarkably similar to McVeigh's and Breivik's way of reasoning. They assumed the high moral ground. They also viewed themselves as warriors in a just struggle against evil as incarnated in liberal constitutional democracies. So they viewed their acts as heroic acts rather than as heinous crimes.

Moreover, since they believe themselves to be in the right, their victims were used as necessary scapegoats in their struggle to impose their grand political worldview on others.

The above-mentioned executioners of so-called "terrorist justice" embraced a redeeming view of violence. A belief in a redeeming view of violence, however, is not unique to terrorists and their apologists. Excepting radical pacifists who categorically oppose the use of lethal violence on a grand scale, representatives of nation-states and most of their citizens, even if reluctantly, occasionally believe in the redeeming nature of lethal violence at least for self-defense or to combat great evil.

One might justify political violence depending on the goals that one is trying to achieve and the way that one goes about achieving these goals. If so, terrorists and their apologists could try to justify the redeeming value of their use of political violence. Opponents of terrorism, however, presuppose that terrorism is the deliberate or reckless exercise of political violence frequently resulting in the infliction of substantive harm on the guiltless or harmless. Yet deliberately or recklessly inflicting substantive harm on guiltless or harmless people, when avoidable, is categorically wrong, because when doing so, terrorists violate two fundamental moral principles: (1) the presumption of innocence and (2) the principle of noncombatant immunity to avoid deliberately or recklessly harming innocent civilians.

B. OPPONENTS OF TERRORISM

I divide opponents of terrorism into two groups: hard core and soft core. Hard-core opponents of terrorism, such as Michael Walzer, Tamar Meisels, and C. A. J. Coady, absolutely condemn terrorism with no exception or excuse. They defend the following thesis: terrorism is never justified. They seem committed to interpreting the PNCI unconditionally. Under no circumstances would they justify deliberately using violence against innocent noncombatants who are impeccably innocent. Some of them, including myself, believe that terrorism is analogous to murder or manslaughter in domestic law, or analogous to crimes against humanity or war crimes in international law.

Soft-core opponents of terrorism, such as Igor Primoratz and F. M. Kamm, prima facie but seriously condemn terrorism too. They defend the following thesis: sometimes terrorism is permissible. Unlike hard-core opponents of terrorism, soft-core opponents of terrorism allow that under extraordinary circumstances, terrorism might be justified. For example, they are likely to consider terrorism as murder or as justifiable homicide depending on contextual considerations.

Based partly on recognizing the right to the presumption of innocence, hard-core and soft-core opponents of terrorism defend the categorical immunity of the impeccably innocent. In principle, for them, terrorism is categorically wrong.[47] In practice, however, soft-core opponents of terrorism allow for the possibility that under exceptionally extenuating circumstances, terrorism might be justified or permitted.[48] There seems to be a tension between their theory against terrorism in principle and justifying occasionally but rarely some terrorist acts. Nevertheless, I am assuming that exceptionally extenuating circumstances must exist to excuse rather than to justify the deliberate infliction of substantive harm on the impeccably innocent. Perhaps one can conceive of some of these extenuating circumstances as a kind of moral Armageddon where terrorism against the innocent might be permitted to avoid, for example, genocide and only if doing so would prevent such a heinous crime.[49]

The onus, however, is always on those who defend the exception to demonstrate that there are no other reasonable ways to accomplish the valuable goal in question without deliberately and substantively harming the impeccably innocent. In addition, one can reasonably expect that by substantively harming the impeccably innocent, the valuable goal would be realized. And yet, past events can sometimes be opaque. So we can easily be tempted to rationalize them in trying to justify or excuse our actions ex post facto. In doing so, we can end up, whether bona fide or not, deceiving ourselves and others too. Since it is only retroactively that we can in hindsight determine with some plausible degree of certainty that targeting the impeccably innocent might have been justified or perhaps excused, we ought to be rather circumspect before engaging in such a potentially morally suspect behavior.

For hard-core opponents of terrorism, terrorism is a form of political violence that is in principle and practice morally and legally impermissible, since it is equivalent to the deliberate unlawful killing of one human being by another, which amounts to murder. Since under no circumstances can murder be justified, and, according to hard-core opponents, terrorism is equivalent to murder, then it follows that, for them, under no circumstances can terrorism be justified. Like hard-core opponents, soft-core opponents of terrorism in principle conceive of terrorism as murder. But, unlike hard-core opponents, they allow that in practice terrorism might be justified or permitted under extenuating circumstances. Moreover, since hard-core and soft-core opponents of terrorism defend in principle the categorical immunity of the impeccably innocent, they are reluctant to make trade-offs by using the impeccably innocent only as a means to achieve other valuable ends or goals. To do justice to their view, I once again offer the following working definition of terrorism:

<u>Opponents' working definition of terrorism:</u>$_{df}$ The use of political violence by individuals or groups who deliberately or recklessly inflict substantive harm or threaten to do so on those who can be conceived of as innocent noncombatants beyond reasonable doubt, aiming at influencing a domestic and/or an international audience.

There are three important contestable components in the above definition of terrorism: political violence, substantive harm, and innocent noncombatants beyond reasonable doubt, which belong to the class of those whom I refer to as the impeccably innocent. For some, I am making a controversial omission in the above definition, namely, the lack of reference to inflicting widespread fear among the victims or intended audience. I will address first the notion of fear.

1. Is Fear Necessary for Terrorism?

Some might wonder whether widespread fear or terror must be necessary for terrorist violence to be classified as such. For example, Carl Wellman defines terrorism in a broad sense as "the use or attempted use of terror as a means of coercion."[50] While less broad than Wellman's definition, Virginia Held describes terrorism "as a form of violence to achieve political goals, where creating fear is usually high among the intended effects."[51] Anne Schwenkenbecher adopts a similar view.[52] Both Held's and Schwenkenbecher's views of terrorism are consistent with the one offered by the International Commission of Jurists (ICJ).

The ICJ admits the difficulty of trying to provide an internationally acceptable definition of terrorism; however, they claim that there is wide international agreement in several core elements. Terrorism, so they argue, "consists of criminal acts committed with the intent to cause death or bodily injury with the purpose of provoking terror in order to compel governments or international organizations to do or abstain from doing any act."[53] By contrast, C. A. J. Coady prefers to exclude fear from a definition of terrorism for two reasons: first, "stress upon this intended effect tends to preclude any serious concern with . . . the type of method used to generate fear"; and second, "we are prejudging an empirical investigation into the specific motives of those who choose to attack noncombatants."[54] His reasons seem compelling to me. To speculate about the specific motive of bringing about fear in a given audience by those who deliberately use violence against noncombatants or about people's emotional reactions to such violence is to distract attention from the event itself and those responsible for perpetrating it.

By including the promotion of fear or terror into a definition or characterization of terrorism, Wellman, Held, Schwenkenbecher and others who hold similar views distract people from that which is seriously objectionable about terrorism, namely, the deliberate or reckless targeting of innocent noncombatants. Moreover, by including fear into a definition of terrorism, one can end up classifying acts of benign intimidation as terrorist acts when these acts might have been motivated by diverse reasons, including bantering, amusing, or simply educating others.

Consider, for example, (Microsoft founder) Bill Gates's stunt act of releasing mosquitoes at an elite Technology, Entertainment, Design (TED) conference intending to cause fear and thereby alert the audience about the devastating consequences that malaria has on people living in underdeveloped countries. He also intended to demonstrate that "there is no reason only poor people should be infected."[55] One could plausibly assume that if people in the audience thought that they were being exposed to malaria-infected mosquitoes, most of them would have been probably terrified for being so exposed. I am sure that many were quite relieved when Gates assured them that the mosquitoes were malaria free!

Some members of the audience, however, might not have been persuaded by Gates's assurance. Suppose that Gates had ordered his bodyguards to lock all doors to prevent members of the audience from leaving the conference room before he finished his lecture. Moreover, he publicly announced that he had issued such an order and that his bodyguards would enforce it. Assuming that some people in the audience would have preferred to leave the room rather than be exposed to the mosquitoes, one could argue that those who would have preferred to leave the room but could not have done so had been coerced to stay. So their freedom of movement would have been seriously restricted. One might view such an act of coercion as a form of violence. Suppose also that Gates's aim had been primarily political to make sure that those sitting in the room would lobby their governments, especially those representing wealthy nations, to continue providing or increasing aid to poor nations, in particular those affected by malaria.

If one allows that the intention to spread fear needs to be incorporated into a definition of terrorism, then one could portray Gates's stunt as a terrorist act. Hence, he could be thought of as a terrorist. After all, in the hypothetical example, he used violence for a political goal, and he intended to spread fear among the audience, although only for a brief moment and for a good cause. But this result seems far-fetched, since the mosquitoes were malaria free, and presumably Gates never intended to harm anyone. Even if he inadvertently did harm those who would have chosen to leave if they have been allowed to do so, the harm seems negligible.

One could argue that perhaps the harm described above might seem negligible to some but not to others. Let us assume the same scenario, but after Gates released the mosquitoes, most members of the audience panicked, and while stampeding to the doors, people were seriously hurt. Some were physically harmed, while others were psychologically harmed. Could one then conclude that Gates's act resembles a terrorist act? That seems a hasty conclusion.

Perhaps Gates should have foreseen the possible deleterious consequences that his supposedly benign act could have had on the audience. So he could be held morally responsible for the consequences of his act. It would be a stretch, however, to argue that his stunt act resembles terrorism in any meaningful sense. Unlike terrorists, he never intended to inflict serious harm on anyone because the mosquitoes were malaria free, and his aim was altruistic, namely, to help those who are suffering from a devastating but preventable disease. One could argue that he simply miscalculated the reaction of the audience, and that was regrettable. If so, Gates's stunt could simply be excused.

Terrorists might intend to intimidate not only those chosen as their immediate target but also a given domestic or international audience to try to accomplish their goals. Regardless of their intentions, however, they have no control over how the intended audience will react to their violence. Whether terrorist violence can actually bring about widespread and long-lasting fear or terror on their immediate victims or on those whom they are trying to influence is highly questionable.

For example, Nazi officials miscalculated how British citizens were going to react to the indiscriminate but limited bombing attacks (namely, terror bombings) of London and Coventry at the beginning of World War II. British citizens were emboldened to stop the Nazi aggression. Moreover, British prime minister Winston Churchill used the Nazi limited terrorist attacks as foils to implement a policy of area bombing attacks aimed at Germany's civilian population. As the Germans did, the British gambled and actually miscalculated how the German population was going to react to their indiscriminate and widespread area bombing attacks (namely, terror bombings) of German cities during the early stages of World War II.

Despite being stunned by the indiscriminate killing of innocent civilians, ordinary German citizens were actually galvanized to resist the British attacks. Therefore, instead of undermining popular support for the Nazi government, as the British anticipated, their indiscriminate attacks on innocent German civilians contributed to a rally of support for the Nazi government.

One finds similar reactions on the contemporary Israeli-Palestinian conflict. The more Palestinian suicide bombers attack innocent Israeli civilians, the more steadfast ordinary Israelis become in resisting those attacks. Likewise, the more collective punishment Israeli officials inflict on innocent Palestinians, the more determined Palestinians become in their struggle for establishing a viable independent Palestinian state. Hence, the use of political violence against the impeccably innocent to try to undermine the morale

of one's alleged enemies might have the opposite unintended effect on
the populace.

2. Is Political Violence Necessary for Terrorism?

The practice of political violence is necessary for terrorism; otherwise,
there would not be much difference between terrorist violence and the
widespread use of violence in society, such as the one found in ordinary
crimes including murder, theft, arson, or destruction of property. Political
violence has distinctive features. It is purposive or goal oriented, aiming at
preserving, influencing, or radically transforming a domestic or international
political order.

Some might object that the opponents' working definition of terrorism
is too narrow because, among other factors, it leaves out of consideration
the practice of household or domestic violence and rape. Claudia Card, for
example, argues in favor of expanding the meaning of terrorism to include
the vices of domestic violence and rape among others.[56] Similarly, Alison
Jaggar offers a broadly defined concept of terrorism. She writes, "Terrorism
is the use of extreme threats of violence designed to intimidate or subjugate
governments, groups, or individuals. . . ."[57] By adopting such a broad view of
terrorism, she allows for the possibility that hate crimes, rape, and domestic
violence can be conceived of as terrorism.[58]

Even though household violence and rape can certainly terrorize those
who experience it, it seems that such abhorrent acts have narrower scopes
than the one people normally associate with terrorism. Those who engage in
individual and isolated cases of rape and household violence are not intending to influence or transform any local or international political order. They
just want to inflict pain and suffering to control their victims and sometimes
satisfy their libidinousness. Nevertheless, since household violence and rape
are crimes recognized as such by virtually all civilized nations, they can be
prosecuted under these nations' domestic law rather than under international
criminal law. Only if there is an evident failure in a nation's domestic laws to
prosecute household violence and rape, could one rightfully appeal to international law to prosecute such vicious criminal behavior.

In the case of rape, one can argue that if a nation or state deliberately and
systematically uses such an abominable practice against their opponents in
an armed conflict to terrorize them, it could then be classified as terrorism,
perhaps sexual terrorism. This should be so because the practice of rape,
a despicable criminal act, becomes a weapon of oppression for political
purposes against a specific group of people.[59] While the deliberate and
systematic practice of rape and sexual abuse of all kinds has been a common feature of international and domestic armed conflicts, it is lamentable

that rape per se has only recently been included among the grave breaches of IHL.[60]

Still, since nowadays IHL recognizes rape as a grave breach, describing rape as terrorism would ultimately be misguided for the following reasons. First, doing so would open a highly contestable debate about whether rape should be conceived of as terrorism. This debate might be as intractable as the one trying to fix the meaning of terrorism. And two, it would make the meaning of terrorism so broad that the term "terrorism" might simply lose its moral and legal grip.

There is a general consensus among civilized nations that the practice of household or domestic violence and rape are morally odious vices that should be punished. Unfortunately, legal systems frequently fail to act quickly and effectively against such scourges of society. Sometimes the punishment might be too lenient, depending on where the offense occurs. Even worse, sometimes offenders might get away with it with shameless impunity. Hence, advocates for the abused who are trying to change the law because it is, at times, too lenient or because it is at best enforced erratically get oftentimes understandably frustrated.

Some who argue against household violence and rape, in addition to the practice of honor killing and female genital mutilation, are trying to influence or change a domestic or international approach to these and other abominable practices by campaigning against them. Certain powerful groups in rather hierarchical societies have a vested interest in perpetuating and promoting myths and false beliefs to foster such shameful practices. Unfortunately, these shameful practices are so entrenched in some cultures that, to stop them, it might be necessary to radically reform the societies where they occur. That takes time, resources, and the political will to do it. Regrettably, the political will is oftentimes lacking because those who are in a position of power might themselves be guilty of such crimes.

One is unlikely to accomplish any substantive moral or legal gain by suggesting that we should classify the practice of rape as terrorism unless, as I have already underscored, the latter becomes a deliberate and systematic weapon of oppression. If that were to be so, then the practice of rape would fall under grave breaches of IHL, and that would impose an obligation on all nations to prosecute those responsible for deliberately perpetrating or allowing such an abhorrent practice. Unfortunately, some nations and cultures not only ignore but also condone such barbaric practices.

Unlike rape, we are better off conceiving of household violence as an odious crime rather than as terrorism. To argue otherwise is to conflate undisputable domestic criminal activity having no political objective with unjustifiable domestic or international political violence. Such a conflation could be a further impediment in trying to agree on a universally acceptable definition of terrorism that could help the international community develop coherent and effective policies against the threat of terrorism. If we were to use the term "terrorism" too broadly, then its meaning would become so diluted that it would be even more difficult to achieve consensus on its connotation. In so doing, the connotation of terrorism as an abhorrent and, hence, unjustified practice could lose its moral grip on the minds of those who object to it.

Evidently, one can always venture to offer a Humpty Dumpty definition of terrorism. That is, terrorism would simply mean whatever we want it to mean. And if and when someone challenges our definition, we can always answer à la Humpty Dumpty—the question is not whether we can make words mean so many different things, as Alice objected to Humpty Dumpty's arbitrariness in assigning his own meaning to a word, but rather, who is to be the master in assigning the meaning to a word, as Humpty Dumpty replied.[61] Such an ad hoc approach to the meaning of words seems unhelpful for promoting a concerted global effort to deal effectively with the threat of terrorism.

The term "terrorism" need not be "Humpty Dumptied." It can refer to the deliberate or reckless use of political violence by a person or group aiming to substantively harm their alleged enemies without regard for the infliction of undeserved harm on the impeccably innocent. Terrorists, whether they act on behalf of a state or on behalf of nonstate actors, are those who deliberately or recklessly inflict substantive undeserved harm on others to further domestic or international political objectives.

3. Is Inflicting Undeserved Harm Necessary for Terrorism?

Like "terrorism," the term "harm" is also protean. Joel Feinberg, for example, distinguishes among three different senses of harm: (1) harm in a derivative or broad sense whereby virtually anything can be said to be harmed, such as via the destruction of property or the neglect of a crop whereby people's interests in those things are directly defeated; (2) harm as when someone maliciously defeats people's interest when they have a stake in something valuable for their well-being; and (3) harm as when a person unjustifiably or inexcusably wrongs another person by violating his or her rights. While (2) and (3) sometimes overlap, they are not necessarily the same.[62]

In addition, one might harm people directly or indirectly. They are directly harmed when terrorists deliberately target innocent noncombatants, as in the 9/11 attacks on the World Trade Center. They are indirectly harmed when they need help and those who can help them neglect to fulfill their positive duty of beneficence. Presumably, they could have fulfilled their positive duty of beneficence without unreasonably risking harming themselves or others who deserve no harm. In both instances of harm, one assumes that those who unjustifiably and inexcusably violate innocent people's rights harm them. The 1994 Rwanda genocide is a vivid reminder of an inexcusable and, hence, unjustifiable act of omission by the international community to prevent such an apocalyptic event. In 1994, in just one hundred days, extremists of the Hutu's majority massacred the Tutsi's minority, killing an estimated eight hundred thousand people while the international community stood by nonreactive.[63]

Oftentimes there are significant moral and legal differences between acts of commission and acts of omission, especially regarding mens rea or criminal intent. For example, it is evident that the perpetrators of the 9/11, 11-M, and 7/7 attacks intended to deliberately harm impeccably innocent civilians, and they succeeded in doing so. In the Rwanda genocide, however, Africans and Western nations could have acted promptly to prevent the conflict from escalating and ending in such a catastrophic way. While Western nations had the resources to prevent the genocide, they lacked the political will to act in the face of evil. Hence, they shamefully ignored the unfolding genocide.

African and Western nations, however, did not deliberately participate in or encourage the mayhem. They flagrantly failed to act in a timely fashion to fulfill their positive duty of beneficence. On March 25, 1998, President Clinton issued a belated and anemic apology for failing to act in the face of evil.[64] But his claim of ignorance was disingenuous at best. At the time, the international community did not have the political will to act. For that reason, they can be held morally accountable. Yet while their behavior was morally inexcusable and hence appalling, it remains an open question whether there is an international legal obligation to act to prevent genocide before it unfolds.[65]

One can harm people physically or psychologically. One can define physical harm as bodily incapacitation or disfigurement that reasonable people would, under normal circumstances, never consent to. One can define psychological harm as mental or emotional incapacitation that would prevent people from enjoying a good life and, hence, under normal circumstances they would also never consent to. The infliction of physical harm is generally more evident and, as a result, its detrimental effects on the victims are less controversial to ascertain than is the infliction of psychological harm. Still, psychological harm can also have devastating effects on victims and their loved ones, especially when one realizes that psychological harm ultimately manifests itself as physical harm. There is ample and well-documented evidence about the psychological terror and agony experienced by those held in solitary confinement, those kidnapped, and those hijacked, to mention only a few examples of victims of physical and psychological harm.[66]

The fact that one might harm people and therefore wrong them in various ways should not be an excuse to avoid holding individuals accountable for their actions or inactions. When one argues that someone has been undeservedly harmed, one usually means that the person has been wronged even though s/he has done nothing to merit having his or her rights violated. For example, it is difficult to fathom in what sense ordinary reasonable people could contend that most of the victims of the 9/11 attacks in the United States, the 11-M attacks in Spain, and the 7/7 attacks in England and similar attacks elsewhere deserved such a fate.

A crucial burden of proof is on individuals, groups, or states that are ready to jump the gun in using violence against others. When a state or a nonstate agent uses political violence against opponents, it is only fair to expect them to fulfill the following reasonable and necessary conditions to try to justify their use of political violence. First, they need to demonstrate that they are in the right by defending fundamental moral and political principles upheld by the international community. While there are fundamental disagreements among different cultures and states about specific contentious issues—such as the value of traditional marriage vs. gay marriage, capital punishment vs. life imprisonment, or social and economic rights vs. political rights, to mention only a few—states are nonetheless bound by international law. Therefore, they are not allowed to hide behind the façade of cultural differences to harm the impeccably innocent.

Second, they must provide compelling and convincing evidence to the international community that their opponents are indeed guilty of serious moral or legal misconduct, such as engaging in egregious and systematic violation of human rights. And lastly, they must show their goodwill by providing compelling and convincing evidence that reasonably peaceful methods have failed to bring about the commendable goals in question. If we are genuinely committed to the protection and enhancement of human dignity or at least human decency, we should demand a stringent burden of proof to justify using political violence against others, including the use of violence during humanitarian interventions against those responsible for oppressing impeccably innocent victims.[67]

a. Human Dignity

Like the terms "terrorism" and "harm," the term "dignity" is polysemic. One can interpret the term "dignity" either in a secular or a religious sense. Classic interpretations of dignity in a secular moral sense are found, for example, in Cicero's recognition of human beings as worthy of respect by virtue of their capacity for reasoning and inquiry, and in Kant's second formulation of the categorical imperative exhorting human beings to respect others, including themselves, as ends rather than as means only by virtue of their capacity for reasoning and self-determination.[68] Also, in a contemporary secular sense, the term "dignity" is widely used in international and domestic legal discourses where the term designates a recognition of fundamental claims, including a right to equal consideration and respect before the law, such as in the 1948 Universal Declaration of Human Rights, the 1966 International Covenant on Civil and Political Rights, and in the *Grundgesetz* (basic law) for the Republic of Germany.[69]

A classic interpretation of dignity in a religious sense is found in the Judeo-Christian tradition wherein people are recognized as worthy of respect because they are created in the image of God.[70] Similarly, in Islam one finds that the children of Adam are to be honored because of their privileged status in God's creation.[71]

Since the term "dignity" connotes a sense of worthiness and hence respect, the above secular and religious interpretations of dignity are, in principle, consistent with one another. Moreover, moral, legal, and religious conceptions of dignity value human beings by virtue of their belonging to a class whose individuals typically share certain properties, such as having a capacity for reasoning and self-determination.

Opponents of terrorism generally refuse trading off the life of impeccably innocent people for consequentialist benefits during normal circumstances. Similarly, those holding either a secular moral Kantian or neo-Kantian view, a Judeo-Christian religious view of human dignity, or an Islamic view of human dignity would generally refuse to engage in trading off people's dignity for consequentialist benefits during normal circumstances. Whether they or opponents of terrorism would excuse such trading off during exceptional circumstances as in war or when confronting serious moral dilemmas remains an open question. Such trading off, however, is commonly found in domestic and international law, for example, by negotiating plea-bargain agreements in domestic courts of law or in international legal tribunals. Hence, unlike those who conceive of dignity in a purely legal sense, those who uphold the above-mentioned views of moral and religious conceptions of human dignity conceive of dignity as a nonnegotiable intrinsically valuable moral property.

As a result, those who embrace any of the above-mentioned views of human dignity presuppose that the dignity of one person is as valuable as the dignity of every person. So by violating the dignity of one person, one is in principle violating the dignity of each person. That is, if we justify violating the dignity of one person in a given situation, then we are in principle justifying violating the dignity of any person who happens to be in a relevantly similar situation.

Opponents of terrorism, whether hard core or soft core, argue in favor of respecting in principle the categorical immunity of the impeccably innocent. In doing so, they are openly or tacitly acknowledging the dignity of the impeccably innocent, and thus the impeccably innocent are not to be treated as means only for bringing about a net value of good in society, such as in punishing the innocent few to save or improve the life of the innocent many. Rawls rightly objects to such a practice, since it is misconstrued as punishment. That is, those who experience the untoward consequences of punishment do not deserve to be so treated by virtue of being innocent rather than being wrongdoers. He calls this practice "telishment."[72]

The practice of telishment, as well as similar practices that trade off the rights of the innocent few to improve the life of the innocent many, violates the following three important moral principles: Socrates's principle of no harm, St. Paul's principle of avoiding evil, and Kant's categorical imperative. According to Socrates, under "no circumstances must one do wrong," not "even when one is wronged."[73] That is because "to do wrong is the greatest of evils."[74] Hence, if one has to choose between doing wrong or suffering wrong, Socrates "would choose rather to suffer than to do it."[75]

St. Paul develops his absolute principle of avoiding evil in his letter to the Romans, and it is generally referred to as the Pauline principle, namely, "evil may not be done so that good may ensue."[76] For Kant, morality requires that we act primarily motivated by our unconditional respect for the moral law. As a result, we have an absolute obligation to act compatibly with his categorical imperative so that we ought to "act in such a way that you always treat humanity, whether in your own person or in the person of any other, never simply as a means, but always at the same time as an end."[77] Allowing for the violation of any of the already mentioned principles would jeopardize people's moral integrity and hence their human dignity.[78]

b. Innocents' Immunity

Depending on how one conceives of the innocents' immunity, one might categorically oppose, justify, or allow using deliberate or reckless political violence against them. If one conceives of their immunity in principle as absolute or quasi-absolute, as opponents of terrorism do, then one would categorically argue that using deliberate or reckless political violence directly aimed at the impeccably innocent is never justified. Nevertheless, one might be justified in indirectly harming them as a result of using deliberate political violence aimed at noninnocent individuals or combatants who are unjustifiably threatening us or other impeccably innocent people. By contrast, if one conceives of the innocent's immunity in principle as contingent, as apologists of terrorism do, then one could justify using political violence aimed directly against the impeccably innocent depending on the goals or ends that one is trying to promote, how one goes about promoting these goals or ends, and the likelihood of achieving them.

While the practice of war has been, at times, variously characterized as just or unjust, the practice of terrorism has been frequently characterized as gravely wrong. For opponents of terrorism, however, this practice is in principle categorically wrong. This is so because deliberately or recklessly inflicting substantive harm on the impeccably innocent, such as killing, maiming, or coercing them, is an instance of the *summum malum* that any ordinary reasonable and fair-minded person should avoid.

One is a reasonable and fair-minded person only if one respects innocent people's physical, psychological, and moral integrity. Whoever uses the impeccably innocent only as means for other ends would likely lose credibility in the eyes of those who uphold the natural duty of nonmaleficence, which entails respect for the presumption of innocence and the PNCI. Yet some scholars argue that the PNCI is "generally expressed in the language of rights." However, one might argue instead that traditional just war theorists, be they pagan or religiously inspired, operate with a tacit or an open notion of the PNCI based on a recognition of a natural duty of nonmaleficence. The notion of rights is virtually absent from traditional just war thinking. It is only in contemporary just war thinking that the notion of rights plays an important role.[79]

Those who attempt to justify terrorism could always allege that the target audience is noninnocent in some elliptical sense, such as having benefited directly or indirectly from the oppression and suffering of others. But that is a questionable way of ascribing guilt to others. For example, it is reasonable to assume that many white Americans and likewise many Europeans have directly or indirectly benefited from the exploitation and oppression that their ancestors inflicted on Native Americans, African Americans, and native populations all over the globe. Can we then plausibly argue that those who have benefited from past injustices without having contributed to them are noninnocent and, hence, guilty of that which they had no control over? That would seem a rather paradoxical sense for ascribing guilt. For example, as if one were guilty of having been born in a developed European country, such as Germany, rather than in an undeveloped African country, such as Rwanda, or having been born into a wealthy family rather than into an impoverished one. That is a matter of luck or nature's lottery that we have no control over.

One could reasonably argue, however, that we do not deserve the privileges that we have not earned.[80] Nevertheless, we are certainly not guilty of what we have no control over, such as when and where we are born, our racial or ethnic background, our IQ, our genetic makeup, or the original wealth of our families, to mention only a few undeserved privileges that we might enjoy. We have no control over nature's lottery or kismet. So we should not feel remorse for some of the privileges bestowed upon us. Still, the enjoyment of those privileges that we do not deserve should not exempt us from having a feeling of sympathy for and even a desire to help the unlucky ones who do not deserve the misfortunes that have befallen them.

Those who justify terrorism might argue that the target audience is noninnocent, since the members of such an audience have contributed directly or indirectly to harming others by bringing about or by perpetuating an unjust state of affairs. A fundamental question, however, for ascribing responsibility is not so much whether they are noninnocent because they might be so in a rather Pickwickian sense (i.e., as innocent threats or as involuntary objective threats), but rather whether they are guilty and, hence, liable for deliberately causing or perpetuating an unjust state of affairs.

Before ascertaining a person's guilt and liability, one would need to demonstrate rather than assume the injustice of such a state of affairs. Moreover, the ascription of guilt would depend, to a large extent, upon a person's intentions or mens rea. One could argue that people are noninnocent and, hence, guilty (directly liable) if they deliberately intend to inflict undeserved harm on others by commission or omission. That is, they primarily aim at harming them. Or one could argue that they are noninnocent but indirectly liable because their role or position is such that they present a serious threat to the well-being of others despite having no intention to harm them. That is, they are indirectly harming them. Because they present a so-called innocent threat or an involuntary objective threat, they are not necessarily guilty.

The notion of indirect liability is rather murky. Perhaps one could plausibly argue that in some sense people who are relatively well-off living in developed nations are indirectly harming the less fortunate ones living in undeveloped or developing nations. The well-off, for example, could make pecuniary contributions to palliate the misery of the needy without bringing about equivalent or greater harm to themselves and others.[81] One could argue that, to the extent that the well-off can help the needy but choose not to do it, they are neglecting their obligation or positive natural duty of beneficence to help the needy. If so, then they are indirectly harming them. Therefore, they might be viewed as noninnocent by not acting as a Good Samaritan would.

Is it evident that people who are well-off are noninnocent, meaning responsible and, hence, liable for choosing not to fulfill their positive natural duty of beneficence? On the one hand, one could plausibly argue that they are noninnocent, assuming they could help the needy without bringing about equivalent or greater harm to themselves and others who do not deserve it. However, they abstain from doing so. On the other hand, they need not be directly responsible for the dire conditions the needy are in unless one could convincingly argue otherwise. Presumably, those who are well-off are entitled to their wealth because they have earned it fairly, such as by investing their money wisely, legitimately inheriting it, or winning it, as a matter of luck, in a fair lottery. If so, then they are to have discretion on how to invest their resources. Some could argue that whether those who are well-off choose to help the needy is a matter of charity rather than obligation, provided they have not brought about the needy's misery.[82]

Even if one were to assume that a moral failure had occurred on the part of people who are well-off to fulfill their natural positive duty of beneficence, it need not follow that they could be rightfully targeted for indirectly harming those who need help. To justify or excuse targeting those who are well-off, one would need to demonstrate the following conditions: that they could have helped those in need without great cost to themselves or others; that they deliberately and, hence, maliciously neglected to fulfill their positive natural duty of beneficence; that fulfilling such a positive duty did not prevent them from fulfilling a weightier duty; and that discharging their positive duty would have benefited the majority of people affected by it.

Fixing the locus of responsibility for those who neglect their natural duty of nonmaleficence by directly harming people who neither deserve nor consent to be so harmed could, in principle, be reasonably established. But trying to do the same for those who neglect their positive natural duty of beneficence by indirectly harming others who do not deserve to be so harmed could, in principle, be challenging and, hence, questionable. We indirectly, unwittingly, or involuntarily affect many people's lives. Moreover, there are too many variables that we have no control over. Those unknown variables should not be an excuse for grossly ignoring great suffering of the impeccably innocent, especially when it is reasonable to expect people to have known about it, and having the means to prevent it chose to ignore it, such as world leaders did in the case of the Rwanda genocide.

To argue that one could target those who indirectly harm others for failing to act as Good Samaritans is likely to generate chaos and anarchy domestically and internationally. We could easily revert to a Hobbesian state of nature where all people's lives would be precarious.[83] Such a precarious state would not be in the best interest of anyone, especially the most vulnerable members of society.

c. Innocent Threats

The idea that one or more persons could present a serious threat to other people's well-being without intending to harm them raises the specter of "innocent threats" or what one might call "involuntary objective threats." Although those who are causing an innocent threat are unaware of it, they are, nonetheless, the ones who are causing it. Unlike those who are causing an innocent threat, those who are involved in an involuntary objective threat, while innocent themselves, are reluctantly but unavoidably associated with instruments or objects that aggressors use to threaten innocent people's lives. Their threat is objective because it exists independently of anybody's perception of it. Regrettably, whether innocent or an involuntary objective threat, oftentimes there is no way to effectively neutralize these threats without harming the innocent people associated with such threats.

The possibility of an innocent threat or an involuntary objective threat confronts us with the following issue: whether we could justifiably target or at least be excused for attempting to neutralize a given threat to innocent people's lives. That would depend on the nature of the threat and the capacity that we might have for effectively addressing it by avoiding it or eliminating it if necessary.

Suppose, for example, that prior to the actual 9/11 attack on the World Trade Center, the US government had collected sufficient and reliable evidence that the hijackers were on a suicide mission. Let us also assume that the government agencies learned about their mission after the commercial airplanes had already been hijacked and were in the air. The tragic reality is that nothing other than shooting down the airplanes would have prevented the hijackers from carrying out their suicide mission. So, based on sufficient and reliable evidence, government officials and military leaders counterfactually decided to order the shooting down of the commercial airplanes. In doing so, they and the pilots who carried out this mission would have chosen to destroy the commercial airplanes knowing that they would have killed the hijackers and the innocent passengers too.

The onerous and dreadful decision of shooting down the airplanes, however, might be excused and, hence, permissible since the passengers' deaths were inevitable as a result of the hijackers' determination to bring their suicide mission to fruition. The passengers in the airplanes were not strictly speaking an "innocent threat" to anyone because their being there under normal conditions would have harmed no one if the hijackers had not used the airplanes as weapons. The passengers, nonetheless, posed an involuntary objective threat because they were necessarily involved with the hijackers' chosen weapons, namely, the airplanes. So there was no way to eliminate the threat posed by the hijackers without also killing the innocent passengers. Yet by merely being on board the hijacked airplanes (wrong place at the wrong time), namely, having bad luck, the passengers were reluctantly but unavoidably involved with the objects used to harm the innocent people who were inside the World Trade Center towers and the bystanders.

Should US government officials have been excused for giving the order to shoot the airplanes down and killing the hijackers and the innocent passengers? I am afraid there is no simple answer to the moral dilemma embedded in this question. On the one hand, if US government officials had given the order to shoot the airplanes down, they would have deliberately killed the innocent passengers and possibly bystanders on the ground, which is bad enough. On the other hand, if they had allowed the hijackers to carry out their suicide mission or so-called "martyrdom operation," then it is likely that more innocent people would have died, which is even worse. Hence, the death of innocent people would have been unavoidable.

The above is not a far-fetched scenario, and it could plausibly occur in the near future somewhere in the world. So a good understanding of how to deal with potentially lethal threats whether innocent or involuntary objective threats could help states and government officials react reasonably and hopefully fairly by developing contingency plans to try to deal effectively with these unpredictable terrorist threats. The German government approach is a good case in point. The German government has addressed this issue head-on by attempting to develop an adequate legal framework to deal with serious terrorist threats such as the one already described. Germany's Federal Constitutional Court has ruled that the military can take effective measures within Germany "during states of emergency of catastrophic proportions."[84]

In the face of catastrophic moral dilemmas, such as the one already described, the distinction between justifying a reprehensible act and excusing it would seem to be moot for the family and friends of the innocent victims who would be killed by shooting the airplanes down. More likely than not, there would not be any consolation in those distinctions for the family and friends of the innocent victims. Nevertheless, for government officials who would have given the order and for those who would have carried it out, the distinction could be meaningful while no less tragic. They would have deliberately killed the innocent passengers whose lives they should have protected instead. Yet the innocent passengers inevitably were going to die. In shooting down the airplanes, those responsible for executing the government's order would have saved the lives of many more innocent people on the ground. That is their consolation. Under such a stressful state of affairs, the number of people who would have been saved seems to matter.

Perhaps rather than asking the above-mentioned question, we could ask the following: should US government officials be not only excused but also forgiven by those who lost their loved ones as a result of having given the tragic order to shoot down the airplanes, killing everyone? It seems that once we reach a certain threshold of unavoidable human-made suffering, notions of moral justification and excuse exhaust their meaning.

We need to look elsewhere for meaningful notions that would allow us to make reasonable and fair judgments about intractable moral dilemmas. That is probably when notions like forgiveness and remorse might have a role to play in judging such moral dilemmas. Those who lost their loved ones might not only excuse but also forgive those who would have given the order and the ones responsible for carrying it out because it would not have been humanly possible to do better. That was the best they could have done under such precarious circumstances.

The notion of forgiveness implies exonerating or excusing those who have been involved in some kind of wrongdoing, even when such a wrongdoing could be reasonably described as a lesser evil. Had those who would have given the order to shoot down the airplanes and those who would have obeyed it done wrong? There is no easy answer to such a difficult question. By deliberately killing the innocent passengers, it is evident that they would have wronged them, even though the innocent passengers were going to die regardless. But it is also evident that they would have done right in saving the lives of many more impeccably innocent people on the ground. So one can excuse and thereby permit their tragic act as an instance of that which one may refer to as a permissible harm.[85]

Oftentimes people allow a permissible harm because the act of harming the innocent brings about a greater good. While the innocent never consented to be so harmed and their continued living was valuable to them, they were going to die nevertheless. Still, those who would have given the order and those who would have obeyed it by carrying it out would probably have been condemned to live the rest of their lives with an uneasy feeling of remorse.

Even innocent people have been, at times, conceived of as liable because they have been seen as potential foot soldiers and, therefore, as potential enemies in a given armed struggle. The well-respected Muslim medieval legal scholar and philosopher Averroes (Ibn Rushd, 1126–1198) defended this position. According to him, during war Muslims agree that "all adult able-bodied, unbelieving males may be slain." However, "it is forbidden to slay women and children, provided that they are not fighting."[86]

The late Osama bin Laden and his cohorts defend an even more radical view than did Ibn Rushd. They tried to justify the targeting of infidels based on their militant interpretation of the Quran. By doing so, they announced a jihad against Jews and Crusaders in their declaration of the newly formed World Islamic Front on February 23, 1998. In their declaration, they make no distinction between culpable and inculpable individuals or between adult able-bodied males and women and children, as Ibn Rushd did. They incite Muslims worldwide to kill not only American soldiers but also American civilians and their allies. They write, "To kill Americans and their allies—civilians and military—is an individual duty incumbent upon every Muslim in all countries."[87]

Bin Laden's extremist interpretation of Islam is inconsistent with moderate interpretations of Islam. According to Muhammad Abdel Haleem, for example, the Prophet and his successors defend the principles of discrimination and proportionality in war so that civilians are protected, including women, the elderly, and religious people.[88]According to bin Laden and his cohorts, every Muslim has not only a right to kill any American or American ally, but they also have a duty to do so.

d. Apologists of Violence

The above-mentioned mentality is not idiosyncratic to jihadists or militant Islamists alone. It is also found in Western terrorists and in their apologists. For example, consider Jean-Paul Sartre's controversial preface to Frantz Fanon's *The Wretched of the Earth*, where he openly advocates the use of indiscriminate political violence. Sartre argues that Third World natives, namely the colonized, have "a single duty, a single objective: drive out colonialism by *every* means." He seems to have meant absolutely every means, including the indiscriminate use of violence against all European colonizers regardless of their guilt or innocence. Apparently, for Sartre, being a European in a colonized Third World country was sufficient to make one suspect and, hence, presumably liable for serious moral wrongdoing. Later he claims, "For in the first phase of the revolt killing is a necessity: killing a European is killing two birds with one stone, eliminating in one go oppressor and oppressed."[89]

Similarly, Fanon also glorifies violence when he claims, "The colonized man liberates himself in and through violence." Later he argues, "At the individual level, violence is a cleansing force. It rids the colonized of their inferiority complex . . . It emboldens them, and restores their self-respect."[90] The pernicious effect of violence, however, especially widespread violence, such as in an armed conflict, is evident. Widespread use of violence tends to have a rather long-lasting detrimental effect on both perpetrators and, most importantly, on those who experience the violence on their own flesh and blood and on their loved ones. We might conceive of violence as a necessary but lesser evil than other options available to stop a greater evil. Thus, we need to be cautious in approving the use of violence. Despite its apologists, it is reasonable to believe that since there is abundant and incontrovertible evidence of its destructive effect, the use of violence should be always a last resort.[91]

Hannah Arendt argued against precisely the above-mentioned glorification of violence. Sartre and Fanon missed the point, according to Arendt. It is just unwarranted to think that people will become more humane by using violence against one another. If that were true, as she perceptively contends, "revenge would be the cure-all for most of our ills."[92] Yet historical evidence tells us otherwise. Revenge could likely perpetuate an endless circle of violence. Still, one can justify the use of political violence to try to stop great evils, such as aggression, tyranny, and crimes against humanity, but not at the expense of deliberately targeting the impeccably innocent. Nevertheless, the expiatory power of violence seems paradoxical and tragic in light of the destruction and suffering that necessarily come with it.

Also consider, for example, Carlos Marighella's views on the use of political violence to bring about a socialist revolution in Brazil. In his *Minimanual of the Urban Guerrilla,* which has become a classic for many Latin American and Third World organizations that sponsor terrorism, he contends that the cost of the socialist revolution should fall on capitalists, imperialists, latifundistas, and obviously the government too because they oppress the people. So, according to him, "men of the government, agents of the dictatorship and of North American imperialism principally, must pay with their lives for the crimes committed against the Brazilian people."[93]

An infamous disciple of Marighella's glorification of political violence, namely, Ilich Ramírez Sánchez, surpassed him in his callousness. Ramírez Sánchez, a well-known Venezuelan terrorist whose *nom de guerre* is Carlos, is known to many as "Carlos the Jackal" for his unscrupulous killing of innocent and noninnocent people alike. In an interview with a Venezuelan newspaper while serving a life sentence in a Parisian prison, he boasted that he had carried out more than one hundred attacks. As a result of these attacks, he killed over two thousand people, for which he feels no remorse. Why should he feel any remorse if his victims, according to him, were mostly imperialists? He admits that he considered those deaths inconsequential. By his calculations, about two hundred innocent civilians were killed.[94] And yet, some people, including heads of states, have praised him for being a "freedom fighter" rather than a terrorist.[95]

One finds a similar mentality among those who defend the use of political violence to fight leftist or communist regimes. For example, in an interview, the late Orlando Bosch, who was an anti-Castro and anticommunist militant, when asked about his alleged role in a terrorist act that blew up a Cuban airliner in 1976, killing seventy-three innocent people, many of them athletes, his answer was terse but revealing. He said, "We were at war with Castro, and in war, everything is valid."[96] Presumably, in his mind and in the minds of those who think like him, even the deliberate killing of people who can be reasonably identified as impeccably innocent would be valid. Those who choose terrorism as their preferred course of action typically subscribe to such an unscrupulous glorification of political violence.

For opponents of terrorism, the above-mentioned attempts to justify the indiscriminate use of political violence are instances of terrorism. In advocating indiscriminate or reckless political violence, terrorists and their cohorts share a simplistic agonistic "us vs. them" mentality based on a fallacious assumption of their opponents. Terrorists and their cohorts presume that their opponents are guilty of serious moral or legal wrongdoing just because the latter share certain characteristics. For example, they belong to a given nationality, a given ethnic group, a given economic class, a given religious group, or a given political party whose ideology the terrorists reject.

Terrorists and their cohorts might claim to have legitimate grievances against members of the above-mentioned groups. They believe that members of these groups have benefited from presumably unfair national or international arrangements, including at times using political violence themselves. That is why one should not rush to judge those who resort to terrorism as being necessarily without grounds. They frequently base their reasons on questionable beliefs, but reasons they are nonetheless. They engage in premeditated and calculated violence with specific political goals in mind. So, if we want to show that their beliefs are unwarranted, we need to assess their grievances. Still, even if their grievances were legitimate, according to opponents of terrorism, such grievances would not, in principle, justify the practice of terrorism against those who for all practical purposes could be conceived of as impeccably innocent.

e. The Wrongfulness of Terrorism

While agreeing with the last statement, a hard-core opponent of terrorism, such as Michael Walzer, defines terrorism as "the deliberate killing of innocent people, at random."[97] He contends, "Every act of terrorism is a wrongful act."[98] But as Robert Fullinwider argues in contrast to Walzer, "It is . . . too easy to foreclose questions of justification . . . by definitional sleight of hand."[99] This is so because when terrorists choose their targets, they usually think of them as being noninnocent. Thus, to avoid begging the question against terrorists and their cohorts, one needs to answer whether their intended target can be reasonably conceived of as impeccably innocent.

Yet Fullinwider misses an important presupposition of Walzer's definition of terrorism, namely, that those who engage in terrorist violence oftentimes refuse to acknowledge any legitimate distinction between innocent noncombatants and noninnocent ones. But in international law and in many nations' domestic law people are presumed innocent until proven otherwise. Hence, more often than not, terrorists deliberately violate the presumption of innocence. Therefore, those who use terrorist violence become both judges and executioners. They judge who the noninnocent are, and they choose without compunction to inflict substantive harm or significant risk of it on those whom they so identify.

From their terrorist point of view, whether those whom they identify as noninnocent could be reasonably identified as innocent is insignificant. Terrorists act as if they were exercising what Walter Benjamin poignantly refers to as "divine violence," namely, sovereign violence that is beyond our assessment of what is humanly good or humanly evil. As Benjamin underscores, "The expiatory power of violence is invisible to men."[100] One can argue that if the expiatory power of violence is indeed invisible to people and people are fallible, they ought to be cautious in trying to justify or excuse the use of violence. It seems that for Walter Benjamin divine violence is not only sovereign but also necessarily right and hence beyond justification. However, some critics have conflated Benjamin's conception of divine violence with concrete historical manifestations of violence whose justification is questionable.[101]

For terrorists, however, the expiatory power of violence is transparent. But regardless of whether one conceives of the expiatory power of violence, the burden of proof is on those who resort to violence. If that is so, then the arbitrariness of a so-called terrorist vengeance is evident. Those deemed noninnocent have no right of appeal to try to demonstrate their innocence because terrorists, by fiat, have declared them collectively guilty.[102]

Not only terrorist groups but also states that are expected to uphold the rule of law can sometimes act on questionable moral grounds when punishing certain individuals or groups. For example, despite denials of government officials, the Bush administration condoned the practice of torture.[103] In addition, they refused to grant the status of prisoners of war to several hundred inmates who have been held at Guantánamo Bay, Cuba. Ironically, President Obama, who was highly critical of former President Bush's policies while campaigning for the US presidency, once elected into office, has not done enough to deviate from his predecessor's questionable policies.[104] By still classifying the inmates as "enemy combatants," they are being kept incarcerated for an indefinite period of time. These practices are not only morally suspect but also legally questionable under domestic and international law.

In *Boumediene v. Bush*, 553 U.S. (2008), the US Supreme Court insisted that even enemy combatants have a right to a fair trial. After spending seven years without being charged with any crime, and having being classified as an enemy combatant by the US government, Boumediene was finally released from prison. Justice Kennedy, who wrote the majority's opinion, acknowledged that even enemy combatants enjoy the fundamental right of habeas corpus, which requires a writ or written order issued by a court directed to those who are detaining others to test the legality of the detention or imprisonment of a person before a court or judge.[105] He wrote, "We hold that petitioners may invoke the fundamental procedural protections of habeas corpus. The laws and Constitution are designed to survive, and remain in force, in extraordinary times. Liberty and security can be reconciled; and in our system they are reconciled within the framework of the law. The Framers decided that *habeas corpus*, a right of first importance, must be a part of that framework, a part of that law."[106] Boumediene remains adamant about his innocence.[107] Unfortunately, in perilous times, the presumption of innocence is often eclipsed by the so-called necessity of war, especially during an unconventional war, such as the one that has been waged against international terrorist groups.

Like guilt, innocence is a matter of degree. A person can be more or less guilty and, hence, more or less innocent depending on her intention, her knowledge, her ability to act, and whether her action or inaction has harmed others. She might be considered guilty and, hence, blameworthy by virtue of her intention to harm, her action to cause harm, or her inaction to allow undeserved harm to others, especially if she could have prevented their harm without great sacrifice to herself or others. But when evaluating people's behavior, the ascription of innocence takes precedence over the ascription of guilt. Whether we are in a court of law or not, we are presumed innocent until proven guilty. Being innocent is presupposed and needs no justification. It is the imputation of guilt and culpability that needs justification. Still, the term "innocent" is potentially ambiguous, since it can be used in more than one sense. Therefore, to avoid ambiguity and misunderstanding we need to explore some of the different ways in which the term "innocent" can be used or misused.

C. WHO ARE THE "INNOCENT"?

The term "innocent" is not only ambiguous but also contestable. Different scholars offer and defend various interpretations of this term. For example, Jeff McMahan states that the term "innocent" in its generic sense means "not a legitimate target of military attack."[108] In addition, he identifies two other meanings of this term, namely, the morally innocent or inculpable and the harmless. Nevertheless, for him, "the primary and substantive sense of 'innocent' in just war theory" is not to be *nocente* or harmful but rather harmless.[109] While he admits that this is the primary sense of the term in modern just war theory, it is not the primary sense that late medieval scholars, such as Vitoria and Suárez, used in debates about war during the sixteenth century.[110]

Other scholars, such as Jeffrie Murphy, argue against using the term "innocent" to refer to those individuals who are not directly engaged in fighting a war. Thus, unlike McMahan, he argues, "the classical worry about protecting the innocent is really a worry about protecting *noncombatants* [his emphasis]."[111] Yet the term "noncombatant" is too broad, especially when it encompasses civilians who engage in deliberately committing egregious acts, such as directly contributing to initiating and conducting a war of aggression. Hence, the unqualified protection of noncombatants seems morally suspect.

Despite McMahan's observations and Murphy's reservations about the term "innocent," one can conceive of people's innocence in five different ways: in a mens rea sense, in a Good Samaritan sense, in a blameless sense, in a harmless sense, and in a guiltless sense. First, in a purely mens rea sense, one can conceive of those who are not intending to harm others who deserve no harm. Second, in a Good Samaritan sense, one can conceive of those who avoid intentional failure to help others who are in grave distress, provided they could help them without unreasonably risking harming themselves or others who deserve no harm.[112] Third, in a blameless sense, one can conceive of those who pose no significant innocent threat or involuntary objective threat to others who do not deserve it.[113] Fourth, in a harmless sense, one can conceive of those who are inoffensive to others. And fifth, in a guiltless sense, one can conceive of those who have committed no fault of their own.[114]

Therefore, those who are harmless or guiltless are morally and legally blameless for their behavior. Hence, there is no reasonable description under which one could identify them as being noninnocent. They are innocent beyond reasonable doubt, namely, impeccably innocent. By virtue of their unquestionable harmlessness or guiltlessness, one can never justifiably target them. As a result, they ought to enjoy categorical immunity.

In a mens rea sense, people's intention or lack thereof is necessary and sometimes sufficient for determining if they are innocent and, hence, blameless of serious moral or legal wrongdoing. In a Good Samaritan sense, questions about people's intentions might still be necessary for determining whether they are morally blameworthy or, as in the case of Minimally Decent Samaritans, perhaps even legally culpable. But people's intentions are insufficient for making such a determination. The emphasis is on whether it is reasonable to expect people to fulfill their positive natural duty of beneficence to help those in distress, especially when doing so might involve no significant harm to themselves or others who deserve no harm. In a blameless sense, as in the case of an innocent threat or an involuntary objective threat, questions concerning people's intention to harm others are simply moot because they are noninnocent by virtue of the substantive threat that their mere role, presence in society, or location actually pose to others who deserve no harm.

The following example provides a good illustration of the mens rea sense of innocence. Let us assume that I am a pilot involved in an armed conflict, and I am assigned a mission to bombard an enemy target. My superiors have informed me that the target is a command and control center. I have reason to believe that the information provided is reliable and, hence, warranted since, in the past, my superiors have never been mistaken in selecting military targets. Unbeknownst to me and to my superiors, however, there is a bomb shelter underneath the selected target full of innocent civilians. I go ahead and complete my mission by pulverizing what I thought was a military target. In so doing, I unintentionally but voluntarily killed all the innocent civilians who were in the bomb shelter underneath the command and control center. Am I morally and/or legally blameworthy for having done so?

One might argue that I am innocent in the ordinary sense of being guiltless although not necessarily harmless. I never intended to harm innocent civilians, and to the best of my knowledge I aimed at a military target, which is legally permissible act under the LOAC. Whether it is also morally permissible remains controversial, because that would depend on whether or not one is a pacifist, or whether one is involved in a just or in an unjust war.

Putting pacifism and the justice of the war aside, however, I am not necessarily guilty and, hence, blameworthy for serious wrongdoings over which I have no control. I inflicted undeserved harm on innocent civilians, but it seems that I was not at fault. An actual similar incident occurred during the first Gulf War in 1991. American F-117 pilots were instructed to drop GBU-27 bunker-busting bombs on the Al Firdos bunker located in the Ameriyya suburb of Baghdad, killing hundreds of civilians. American intelligence thought that the bunker was an important command and control center. The bunker, however, was constructed as air-raid shelters for the general population of Baghdad. It was later upgraded to protect Iraqi government officials. American intelligence mistakenly thought that the bunker was being used by the Iraqi intelligence service. But it was actually used by the families of the intelligence officials and probably other civilians.[115] This was an unfortunate accident that might be described as an intelligence failure or as purely bad luck.[116]

Although one may describe the above-mentioned act as morally wrong since I inadvertently but voluntarily killed innocent civilians, I can be excused because of my benign ignorance. I never intended to kill civilians. I was acting on what I had reason to believe at the time was reliable information. At the time, I believed that the information about the chosen target was warranted. With hindsight, however, I later realized that I had done something wrong. Had I known that underneath the selected target there was a bomb shelter full of innocent civilians, I would probably not have aimed at it. I would have instead aborted my mission. Hence, although the act of voluntarily killing innocent civilians was morally wrong, my benign ignorance excuses it. Therefore, I seem to be neither morally responsible nor legally liable for my action.[117]

In the next example, we see the Good Samaritan sense of innocence. Suppose that while I am at the pool drinking a martini, I realize that a child is drowning and no one else seems to notice, including the lifeguard. I am not such a good swimmer; however, by extending my arm I could easily save her, and thereby I choose to do so. So I am rightly praised for my selfless act! In this scenario, to raise a question about my innocence would be inappropriate.

Suppose instead that I am aware that the child is drowning. Still, I choose to finish my martini before actually extending my arm to try to help her, or I simply ignore her distress, assuming that somebody else in the pool will come to her rescue. After all, there is a lifeguard working at the pool.

Regrettably, the child drowns. So it seems that I neglected my positive natural duty of beneficence to help someone who was in distress. Hence, in the latter scenario, I am arguably guilty and, therefore, culpable of serious moral failure and indecent indifference to undeserved human suffering. I failed to act not only as a Good Samaritan but as a Minimally Decent Samaritan should have acted because, without much effort, I could have saved the innocent child. And yet, whether I am legally blameworthy remains an open question.

Consider the following example of the blameless sense of innocence as in an "innocent threat" or an involuntary objective threat. Suppose that I am in a poorly ventilated room with someone infected with a deadly strain of the swine flu. This person, by virtue of his infection and my proximity to him, would imminently and substantively threaten my life and well-being, since the swine flu is highly contagious and possibly lethal. He presents what is commonly known as an innocent threat because he is unaware of his infection. Given his ignorance, he would be unable to prevent risking my life or that of anyone who comes near him. Therefore, he is certainly innocent in the mens rea sense and also in the Good Samaritan sense, since he does not deliberately violate his positive natural duty of beneficence. Yet he seems noninnocent in an unusual material sense because his mere presence in the room represents a substantive although involuntary objective threat to my life and well-being.

People, nevertheless, would likely be reluctant to argue that the aforementioned person is guilty and, hence, blameworthy for his swine flu infection. To argue otherwise would seem odd. It would be equivalent to arguing that he is "guilty" of having contracted the swine flu even though his way of life is similar to the way of life of any ordinary person who takes reasonable care to preserve and improve his or her well-being. Some might try to argue that since his mere presence substantively threatens the life of innocent persons, one may conceive of him as an aggressor. However, that view seems unconvincing. An aggressor is one who initiates or threatens to initiate hostile action against another person. And the person with the swine flu takes hostile action against no one. Hence, the analogy with an aggressor seems weak and, even, far-fetched.[118] We are confronted with an anomalous situation when dealing with people who pose innocent but objective threats.

While one can view a person as noninnocent in a material sense by virtue of a substantive involuntary objective threat that his mere presence poses to others, one can simultaneously describe him as not being blameworthy because he intends to harm no one. Moreover, he cannot help those whom he is unintentionally threatening. Nor can he be thought of as an aggressor in any plausible sense because he initiates or threatens to initiate hostile action against no one. As a result, the class of all those who are noninnocent is not coextensive with the class of those who are guilty. Under the law, criminal intent is necessary for being guilty. Those who are classified as innocent have no criminal intent. Hence, it follows that they are not criminally guilty. This is the spirit of the criminal law principle *actus non facit reum nisi mens sit rea.* To be guilty of a crime, a person must have criminal intent.

Apparently, one can typically use ordinary senses of innocence as being harmless or guiltless when the absence of intention to harm is necessary or sufficient to persuade an audience that people are not guilty of any serious wrongdoing or when one can reasonably establish that they did not intentionally neglect their positive natural duty of beneficence to help those in distress. One can typically use the material sense of innocence when the already mentioned ordinary senses of innocence fail to do justice to the complexity of the situation, as in the case of involuntary objective threats. Even though the issue of people's intention to harm or their intention to help might not arise, they might still present a substantive involuntary objective threat to others.

For example, one could argue that during armed conflicts, scientists might be misled to work on research projects secretly designed for developing military technology to be used in the war effort. Even though these scientists have no knowledge of the military goals of their projects and, therefore, have no control over such goals, one can still conceive of their status as analogous to the status of combatants because they represent a substantive objective threat to the opposing camp. Similarly, munitions factory workers who are coerced and threatened with serious harm if they refuse to work can be so conceived too.

The difference between deceived scientists and coerced munitions workers is that the first have no knowledge or control over the ultimate goals of their work while the latter are fully aware of what they are reluctantly doing. Their choices, however, are limited: the first by their ignorance and the latter by the so-called sword of Damocles that hangs over their heads. Hence, one may describe the deceived scientists and the coerced munitions factory workers as noninnocent because, even though their behavior might be described as involuntary, they still represent a material threat to others. Given that they sufficiently resemble innocent or involuntary objective threats, questions about their guilt are superfluous. So their adversaries can legitimately target them under LOAC because they represent a legitimate threat.

An important remaining issue is whether those representing innocent or involuntary objective threats, or those relevantly resembling such threats, as the examples already mentioned showed, should enjoy categorical immunity based on their innocence. This is a thorny issue. Whether one can view them as enjoying categorical immunity would depend, to a large extent, on contextual considerations.

If, in addition to the impeccably innocent, we were to argue that those representing innocent or involuntary objective threats ought not to be targeted by virtue of their innocence, then it would be extremely difficult to justify a war. That is so because many of the victims of the tragic consequences of war are impeccably innocent. Others are innocent threats or involuntary objective threats. Perhaps that provides a legitimate reason for pacifists and those sympathetic to some kind of pacifism to argue against the practice of war.[119] Unlike the impeccably innocent, however, those who can be conceived of as innocent or involuntary objective threats might nonetheless still be harmful rather than harmless.

Regardless of contextual considerations, I am assuming that those who are impeccably innocent because they are harmless or guiltless should enjoy categorical immunity. This is so because they intentionally neglect neither their natural duty of nonmaleficence nor their positive natural duty of beneficence. In addition, one cannot presume that they represent a serious innocent threat or an involuntary objective threat to anyone.

One can argue that some ordinary senses of innocence fail to capture the harmless or guiltless senses of innocence that seem necessary if one wants to do justice to certain groups of people, such as innocent noncombatants during armed conflicts. This would be the case whether one describes a conflict as an interstate or as an intrastate armed conflict. We can classify certain people as innocent noncombatants in a mens rea sense, in a Good Samaritan sense, or in a material sense of innocence as representing innocent or involuntary objective threats. Or we can classify them as harmless or guiltless because they resemble sufficiently the class of innocent noncombatant beyond reasonable doubt. They intend to harm no one, so they neglect neither their natural duty of nonmaleficence nor their positive natural duty of beneficence. In addition, they pose no substantive threat or involuntary objective threat to anyone in particular. They are indeed impeccably innocent. Targeting them would seem to be capricious and, therefore, categorically wrong.

D. IS ANYONE "INNOCENT"?

Some argue that including the term "innocent" in definitional disputations of terrorism is referentially opaque. For example, Frey and Morris contend that "even if we understand terrorism narrowly, as involving attacks on the innocent, it may not be clear . . . exactly who is innocent."[120] They underscore the difficulties we can face when dealing with innocent threats, such as those who inadvertently and unintentionally threaten other people's lives. Similarly, Virginia Held argues, "another difficulty with building the killing of civilians, or noncombatants, or 'the innocent,' into the definition of 'terrorism' is that . . . it is not at all clear who the 'innocent' are as distinct from the 'legitimate targets.'" She goes on to admit that "small children are innocent, but beyond this, there is little moral clarity."[121]

While one might concede that occasionally the distinction between combatants and innocent noncombatants is referentially opaque, oftentimes it is not so. As a result, the above authors seem to overstate their case against the illuminating role that the concept of innocence could play in distinguishing between combatants and impeccably innocent noncombatants in a given armed conflict.

In Held's case, her lack of attempt to distinguish between civilians, noncombatants, and the innocent is baffling. That is so because she is an avid advocate of international law.[122] While one can argue that the term "innocent" is not entrenched in international law, the terms "civilian," "combatant," and "noncombatant" are well entrenched in it. Yet the primary distinction in LOAC among people involved in interstate armed conflict is not between combatants and noncombatants but rather between combatants and civilians.[123]

Combatants are members of the armed forces of a party to a conflict other than medical personnel and chaplains who have the right under international law to participate directly in hostilities.[124] Everyone else belongs to the class of noncombatants, and, hence, they have civilian immunity under international law. But if they engage in an act of *levée en masse* or choose to use arms against an approaching enemy, even in self-defense, they lose their immunity.[125] As defined above, all of those who are noncombatants belong to the class of civilians. Moreover, when there is doubt about a person's civilian status, international law requires that such a person be treated as having civilian immunity.[126]

Held's objection regarding the referential opacity of the term "innocent," however, has some merit. International law defines the term "civilian" too broadly. So international law ascribes civilian immunity not only to ordinary citizens who, more often than not, are impeccably innocent, but also to public and government officials who seriously violate their moral duties; for example, those public and government officials who help initiate and sustain a war of aggression, genocide, or crimes against humanity. If so, the international community can rightfully blame them for their grave breaches of international law. Whether they can be brought to justice would be a different matter.

Despite international law, the use of political violence against public and government officials who directly authorize or engage in planning a war of aggression, genocide, or crimes against humanity remains an open question. No open question exists, however, regarding the moral and legal impermissibility of targeting ordinary citizens who threaten no one in particular by commission or omission, or whose threat to other people's physical integrity and well-being is just de minimis.

Even when citizens in liberal constitutional democracies publicly advocate their support in favor of a war of aggression by voting for a political party or for political candidates who support such a war and war-related efforts, they need not automatically lose their legal immunity under international law. One can offer the following reasons in support of their legal immunity. First, in a genuine democracy, a citizen's vote is secret to avoid manipulating the will of the people by coercion or nepotism. Hence, it would be extremely difficult to determine who voted for a given party or a given candidate.

Second, a citizen's vote of support for a party does not guarantee that the party will win a majority in a fair election. Moreover, even if a party were to win, it would not follow that the elected officials representing the party would act on all of their promises. Similar reasoning applies to individual candidates or specific policies adopted in a party's platform. A vote of support for a given candidate does not guarantee that she would be elected into office. In addition, even if she were elected, nothing and no one could guarantee that she would act on her promises.

Third, even if we could single out with reasonable certainty those citizens who voted for a party or elected officials supporting a war of aggression, their motives for having done so could be mixed. Their reasons for voting in a certain way could range from having some false beliefs about the war to refusing to see the injustice of a war of aggression. For instance, they might have been exposed to yellow propaganda and newspeak, which is the norm rather than the exception prior to the outbreak of hostilities. For example, the Bush administration's accusations that Saddam Hussein possessed WMD in Iraq and that he was associated with Al-Qaeda are contemporary instances of yellow propaganda and newspeak. Both accusations have proven to be unfounded. Hence, the American public was led to believe that they were supporting a war of "liberation" when they were, in fact, supporting an aggressive war based mostly on self-serving reasons.

Sometimes people could vote based simply on peer pressure or they could vote spontaneously based on their passions rather than on reasonable grounds. Fourth, their vote is so distant in the causal chain leading to the outbreak of hostilities that to argue that they should lose their civilian immunity under international law because of their vote seems extreme.

And fifth, even if we could determine with any plausible degree of certainty that ordinary citizens voted in favor of candidates who support a war of aggression, they should not automatically lose their civilian immunity. Assuming so will likely condone a policy of collective punishment against ordinary citizens (innocent and noninnocent alike), which contravenes the letter and the spirit of international human rights law and basic human decency.

Such a policy is morally and legally suspect for indiscriminately and recklessly risking violating the rights of impeccably innocent noncombatants who should enjoy categorical immunity.

Still, even if we agree that by voting for a war of aggression citizens do not necessarily lose their civilian immunity, they nonetheless engage in grave moral failure, especially if they live under liberal constitutional democracies where they can freely express their views. That is, they could choose to dissent and even to oppose publicly government policies that they find objectionable. Even those who live under authoritarian regimes are not always coerced into publicly supporting morally or legally questionable policies. Sometimes they might simply do it for self-serving reasons. If so, they might be morally blameworthy for supporting dubious policies, such as supporting a war of aggression or supporting oppressive policies against peaceful domestic opponents.

While strictly speaking those who vote for morally dubious policies might not be morally innocent, they seem to fall under the class of noncombatants because each of their votes represents a rather distant threat in the causal chain leading to those who are being unjustly harmed. To describe their behavior as a substantive threat to others who do not deserve to be so threatened would be overstated. Ultimately, elected and appointed government officials are the ones who have the authority to launch a war of aggression abroad or to implement oppressive policies at home. So when they authorize a war of aggression, promote genocide, or condone crimes against humanity against a targeted group of people, they are blameworthy and legally liable for transgressing international law. In addition, they are morally responsible for violating the fundamental human rights of their victims.

Even if elected and appointed government officials were engaged in a just war, they would still lose their innocence in the eyes of the aggressor. By being responsible for the decision to wage war against an aggressor, elected and appointed government officials, like combatants, represent a threat to the physical integrity of the aggressor. According to international law, however, they belong to a legally protected class of people.[127] Hence, they need not lose their civilian immunity. Yet, as Primoratz contends, despite not wearing uniforms and not being engaged in actual fighting, the political leaders of a country at war are legitimate targets.[128] As a result, from a moral perspective, their civilian immunity might be dubious, especially if they were to engage in an unjust war.

Current international law is too broad and also too generous in classifying civilians as noncombatants, even when some of them might engage in approving and directing a war, especially an unjust war, such as a war of aggression with imperial ambitions or a genocidal campaign against one's real or alleged political opponents. As Norman argues, since the political leaders of a nation are the ones who ultimately decide whether or not to engage in war, they are the ones who are primarily responsible and, therefore, liable for deciding to engage in an unjust war. If so, that "would imply that the most clearly legitimate targets in war be not the combatants, but the politicians."[129]

Unlike current IHL, traditional just war thinkers, whether pagans or Christians, would accord civilian immunity neither to soldiers nor to the political leaders of a nation who deliberately engage in approving or directing interstate unjust wars or an intrastate vicious campaign against real or alleged political opponents. Therefore, according to traditional just war thinkers, both political leaders and soldiers can be legitimately targeted. The literature on tyrannicide from ancient Rome to the Middle Ages provides us with reasons to think that those who on moral grounds support the killing of tyrants in domestic affairs, such as Cicero, John of Salisbury, and Thomas Aquinas, would also support the killing of tyrants and their political supporters who engage in interstate unjust armed conflicts.[130]

It seems arbitrary that political leaders who are responsible for sending soldiers, especially conscripted ones, to engage in wars of aggression or vicious campaigns against their real or alleged political opponents, enjoy civilian immunity under international law—while soldiers, whether conscripted or not, so long as they are in active duty but not necessarily representing a threat to the enemy, have no such immunity. Putting aside for the moment the legality of assassinating political leaders, one needs to address the following challenging question: Is it morally permissible to target soldiers but not to target those who are responsible for sending them to engage in, for example, an interstate unjust war or an intrastate campaign to oppress their real or alleged political opponents?

Despite the above-mentioned question, international law and in some instances the domestic law of nations, such as the United States, have moved away from the idea of allowing assassinating individuals, especially political leaders of other nations.[131] Such an understanding of international and domestic law has not precluded some nations, including for example the United States, Israel, Russia, and Pakistan, from deliberately targeting so-called enemy or unlawful combatants if and when they represent a threat to the security of the nation and presumably they cannot be apprehended to be tried and punished according to the rule of law, either domestically or internationally.[132]

If by killing political leaders of a nation, for example, one means "assassinating them," then it seems that IHL might prohibit such acts depending on how we understand the term "assassination." Article 23 (b) of the 1907 Hague Convention IV disallows "[the killing or treacherous wounding of] individuals belonging to the hostile nation or army."[133] But since the term "treachery" is not defined in international law, whether it is legally permissible to target the political leaders of an enemy nation or group with whom one is engaged in an armed conflict is controversial.

Still, if the term "treachery" falls within the meaning of the term "perfidy," then acts of perfidy are certainly prohibited in IHL as expressed in the Protocol I of 1977 Additional to the Geneva Conventions of 1949, Relating to the Protection of Victims of International Armed Conflicts.[134] But if one party to an armed conflict uses acts that can be reasonably understood as acts of perfidy, then they might lose some protection of IHL and, hence, they might be legitimately targeted.[135] Regardless of their use of acts of perfidy, all parties to an armed conflict are bound by the rules of IHL, including the principle of proportionality.

Unlike the terms "noncombatant" or "civilian," the term "combatant," as defined in LOAC, is too narrow. LOAC identifies combatants as members of the armed forces of a party to a conflict, other than medical personnel and chaplains, who have the right under international law to participate directly in hostilities.[136] But the status of those who are not so organized—such as guerrilla groups, insurgents, partisans, so-called freedom fighters, private contractors, and paramilitary groups—is not well established in international law, even though some of them might actively engage in the preparation and actual conduct of hostilities.

For example, the provisions of the Geneva Conventions and Additional Protocol I, which generate legal obligations to prosecute and punish those responsible for committing grave breaches or serious violations of international law in interstate armed conflicts, do not automatically apply to those involved in intrastate armed conflicts.[137] And yet intrastate armed conflicts, like civil wars, are oftentimes more vicious than interstate armed conflicts. Moreover, as I have previously argued, government officials are frequently instrumental in promoting, for example, a war of aggression. So to claim that they should enjoy civilian immunity and, hence, should not be targeted seems morally insidious.

Still, those who question the relevance and applicability of the distinction between combatants and noncombatants face the following dilemma: either they accept this distinction by granting that, at times, it can be conceptually opaque, or else they reject it by allowing for the possibility of justifying or at least excusing the targeting of impeccably innocent people. In the absence of truly extenuating circumstances, allowing for targeting impeccably innocent people would amount to sanctioning acts of reprisal. That is, they would end up deliberately violating the physical, psychological, and moral integrity of those who are guiltless or harmless beyond reasonable doubt.

Those who approve acts of reprisal would be approving murder, namely, the deliberate unlawful killing of impeccably innocent people, which is categorically forbidden in domestic and international law. One could, nonetheless, argue that in light of the complexity of modern warfare, the distinction between combatants and noncombatants (or civilians) needs to be revisited to make sure that it does justice to such complexity. There is no guarantee that we could achieve complete moral clarity on this highly controversial distinction, but even if we were to do so, there is no guarantee that an international consensus on this distinction would be achieved. Nevertheless, it would be worthwhile trying, since the lives of the impeccably innocent are at stake.

An important issue that supervenes upon the distinction between combatant and noncombatant is the extent to which a person or group could be considered noninnocent in a relevant sense.[138] The noninnocent poses a substantive threat to others if s/he deliberately harms or threatens to harm their physical or psychological integrity. This agonistic sense of noninnocent is instrumental for singling out those who are classified as actual or potential threats to others.

We can include among the noninnocent state and nonstate agents alike; for example, members of the armed forces and related agencies and even public and government officials responsible for enacting and implementing policies aiming at harming the innocent and nonstate actors, such as guerrilla groups, private contractors, paramilitary groups, and mercenaries who act likewise. There seems to be no convincing reason for leaving states outside the class of noninnocent, especially keeping in mind that states, including liberal constitutional democracies and their leaders, have been responsible for committing reprehensible crimes against innocent people on behalf of their sometimes hypocritical view of humanity. They try to justify their morally and, at times, legally questionable actions on behalf of saving humanity. As a matter of fact, however, they are only acting with mixed motives among which expedient considerations frequently trump humanitarian considerations.

Occasionally, one may reasonably disagree about who the innocent are. For example, the status of munitions factory workers is contentious, since in making a living they are directly contributing to the war effort. Hence, they pose an objective threat to the enemy. The scenario becomes even murkier if they are coerced to work in munitions plants, since they might be posing an involuntary but still objective threat to the enemy. Similar considerations apply to scientists working in developing or enhancing military technologies that contribute to the war effort and also to conscripted soldiers. They pose an objective threat to the enemy regardless of whether they are coerced into their roles. That is because, as Michael Walzer underscores, they are engaged in the business of war.[139] To engage in "the business of war" means to authorize, plan, contribute to, or participate in actual hostilities.

Controversial cases should not preclude us from offering plausible and convincing arguments to classify as innocent beyond reasonable doubt groups, such as the underaged, the elderly, the mentally challenged, the severely disabled, and the chronically ill. Only under exceptional circumstances may one conceive of members of these groups as noninnocent because they present an evident threat to someone, regardless of whether one could reasonably describe their threat as a culpable, an innocent, or an involuntary objective threat; for example, when they point a gun at others threatening to kill them, when they wear a belt or vest full of explosives as suicide bombers do, or when they work in the above-mentioned industries that are instrumental for conducting the war. In these examples, they cease being impeccably innocent, and they become belligerents or combatants, or just innocent or involuntary objective threats like those who are coerced to work in munitions factories.

Given the contestability of the term "innocent," opponents as well as apologists of terrorism could rather focus on the term "noncombatant." But the classes denoted by the terms "innocent" and "noncombatants" are not coextensive. In a war, noncombatants are mostly civilians who are engaged in making a living without contributing to the armed conflict, such as those working in retail, food, and manufacturing industries unrelated to the war effort. So, presumably, they pose no substantive threat to others. Nonetheless, as I have already argued, such a presumption is sometimes questionable when, for example, civilians contribute intentionally, involuntarily, or inadvertently to an armed conflict. For example, some civilians might intentionally become informers. Others might be coerced to work in munitions factories or intelligence-related projects. Still others might be working inadvertently in scientific research projects that, while not evidently related to the war effort, could contribute to it, such as those who engage in developing software programs that could be used by the military or the intelligence community for offensive or defensive purposes.

Judgments about the recognition of the noninnocent can be foggy, and sometimes can even be incompatible with the letter of international law. International law, however, is constantly evolving. Moreover, international law has been designed by those representing strong nations, oftentimes neglecting the legitimate aspirations and needs of the citizens of weak nations. Still, despite its shortcomings, international law is a reasonable instrument nation-states presently have to prevent, palliate, and arbitrate interstate conflicts. For example, the distinction between the innocent and the noninnocent or between the combatant and the noncombatant is at times conceptually opaque. If based on such conceptual opaqueness we were to ignore the already mentioned distinctions, we could inadvertently allow for total war or mayhem.

The expression "total war" is ambiguous: (1) it could be used to describe a policy of massive or universal mobilization of resources and people in a given armed conflict, or (2) it could be used to describe a policy of indiscriminate

use of violence with no regard for the innocent and aiming at unequivocally vanquishing the enemy.[140] These usages are not mutually exclusive.
Objections to the second, however, outweigh objections to the first because
the second clearly violates our compelling natural duty of nonmaleficence
whereas the first need not do so.

The implementation of a policy of total war in the second sense would necessarily lead to sanctioning a policy of collective punishment. The practice of
such a policy would show serious disregard for the life of innocent noncombatants who belong not only to a legally but also to a morally protected class.
By challenging the distinctions between the innocent and the noninnocent or
between the combatant and the noncombatant, those who argue in favor of a
total war in the second sense appear to show a callous disregard for human
life. As Coady explains, "this challenge to the distinction requires there be
no serious moral difference between shooting a soldier who is shooting at
you and gunning down a defenceless child."[141] But there is a serious moral
difference between the first and the second scenarios. The first is an act of
self-defense while the second is just a heinous crime. As Alan Ryan has aptly
underscored, "'Total war' is . . . terrorism under the aspect of war."[142]

Chapter 4

Apologists of Terrorism

Like opponents of terrorism, I divide apologists of terrorism into two groups: hard core and soft core. Hard-core apologists of terrorism, such as Ted Honderich, refuse to absolutely condemn terrorism. Honderich and like-minded people defend the following thesis—that terrorism is justified if and only if it improves humanity overall. So, unlike hard-core opponents of terrorism who conceive of the PNCI in theory and practice unconditionally, hard-core apologists of terrorism interpret the PNCI in theory and practice conditionally.

Soft-core apologists of terrorism, such as Virginia Held, James Sterba, and Andrew Valls justify terrorism by appealing to just war considerations. They reason as follows: if terrorism resembles war, and wars when just can be justified, terrorism when just can also be justified. For them, like for soft-core opponents of terrorism, sometimes terrorism is justified. Like soft-core opponents, soft-core apologists of terrorism are likely to consider terrorism as murder or as justifiable homicide depending on contextual considerations.

As a result, apologists of terrorism, be they hard- or soft-core, agree that terrorism can be justified. They might justify terrorism on one or more of the following considerations: just war analogy, consequentialism, relativism, supreme emergency, or last resort. Unlike opponents of terrorism who, in principle, assume that terrorism is narrowly conceived of as equivalent to murder, apologists of terrorism, in principle, assume that terrorism is broadly conceived of as equivalent to political violence that might be contextually justified.[1]

For apologists of terrorism, terrorism is a form of political violence that can be justified depending on the nature of the conflict in question and the goals that those who use violence are trying to achieve. In an attempt to capture the spirit of their view, I offer the following working definition of terrorism:

Apologists' working definition of terrorism:$_{df}$ The use of political violence by
individuals or groups, provided they are not engaged in an interstate armed
conflict, who deliberately inflict substantive harm or threaten to do so against
their alleged enemies, aiming at influencing a domestic or international
audience.

Some might question whether the above proviso is necessary, since many
individuals and groups are involved in intrastate armed conflicts, such as partisans or guerrilla fighters. Despite this fact, the proviso is necessary to distinguish between those who engage in terrorism and soldiers or combatants
in uniform fighting an interstate armed conflict who, according to the LOAC,
have the right to harm members of the opposing armed forces.

Still, one can ask the following pointed question: Why exclude those
partisans, guerrilla fighters, or freedom fighters engaged in intrastate armed
conflicts, especially when such conflicts are frequently more vicious than
interstate armed conflicts? The simple answer is that international law grants
the unquestionable legal status of combatants only to those who are engaged
in interstate armed conflict. So the standing of partisans and guerrilla fighters
in international law is at best controversial.

Traditional legal scholars assume that whenever there is an intrastate
armed conflict, there is a sovereign authority that the parties engaged in such
a conflict can appeal to in order to settle their differences peacefully. Yet that
is a gratuitous assumption, especially, although not exclusively, when an
intrastate armed conflict occurs in a failed state, such as Somalia. That seems
to be one of the reasons why IHL has progressively moved to recognize that
the notion of "grave breaches" of international law applies to both interstate
and intrastate armed conflicts.[2]

Whether engaged in interstate or intrastate armed conflicts, belligerents are
required to respect LOAC. If they violate *jus ad bellum* principles (namely,
the right to wage war) or *jus in bello* principles (namely, the rights and duties
of the parties involved in actual warfare), they would risk being prosecuted by
international criminal tribunals, such as the 1993 International Criminal Tribunal for the former Yugoslavia and the 1994 International Criminal Tribunal
for Rwanda. As a result, they could be charged with grave breaches or war
crimes. The notion of grave breaches, however, falls under the notion of war
crimes within the ICC, which is becoming part of customary international
law.[3] Consequently, the notion of grave breaches has been progressively subsumed under the notion of war crimes.[4]

Unlike opponents of terrorism, who focus on the impeccably innocent,
including innocent noncombatants, apologists of terrorism prefer focusing on alleged enemies to justify the use of political violence against them.

In doing so, they are assuming that their perception of enmity can oftentimes trump people's presumption of innocence. Nevertheless, perceptions can frequently be deceiving and, hence, unreliable. Therefore, a fundamental problem they face in trying to justify political violence is that people's perceptions might result in misperceptions or, at times, self-deceptions influenced by false beliefs. For example, their analogy with just war might be a rather weak analogy. Moreover, their consequentialist calculus, as well as their relativism, their call to supreme emergency, or their call to last resort might be one-sided. I will address these issues in later chapters.

Apologists' misperceptions could be based on rationalizations to try to justify or excuse using political violence against an opponent who presents no real or imminent threat to them but whose elimination could be politically expedient. Such a way of reasoning, however, is not only peculiar to non-state agents and their apologists but to decision makers in general, including government officials and statesmen.

Consider, for example, President George W. Bush's authorization to invade Iraq on March 19, 2003, to depose Saddam Hussein and thereby put an end to his truculent dictatorship. President Bush perceived Saddam as a dangerous enemy of the United States and its allies. But the decision to invade Iraq was based mainly, although not exclusively, on the belief that there were weapons of mass destruction, allegedly posing a real and imminent threat to the United States and its allies. President Bush's decision could be viewed as a typical case study of either misperception or overconfidence in foreign policy, especially in war.[5] Whether the misperception or the overconfidence was justified given the evidence available at the time remains debatable. Yet it is evident that WMD have never been found. So even with hindsight, the onus for having initiated the hostilities against Saddam was never met.[6]

Since I have already explained the contestable components of the opponents' view of terrorism, such as the notions of political violence, harm, and the innocent, I will focus now on a contestable component found in the apologists' view of terrorism, namely, the concept of enmity. The ordinary use of the term "enmity" is as deeply subjective and debatable as the ordinary use of the term "terrorist," which is found in the often-heard expression "one person's terrorist is another person's freedom fighter."

People who use the often-heard expression are oftentimes committed to cynicism and subjectivism in politics; or to some form of relativism, whether cultural or moral. According to those who hold a cynical and subjectivist view of politics, being identified as a terrorist or an enemy and being identified as a freedom fighter or a friend is just a matter of expediency. Hence, the platitudinous expression "the enemy of my enemy is my friend."

One can, nonetheless, offer a somewhat objective friend-enemy distinction that could help us understand the terrorist–freedom fighter distinction. Whoever is identified as a terrorist is necessarily someone's enemy in the political sense of this term. That is, a terrorist is an individual or group who uses violence against another individual or group aiming at influencing a domestic or an international audience. A person or group is identified as our political enemy only if we have reason to believe that they are actually threatening our lives or they will threaten our lives in the not too distant future, and we are, in principle, willing to take action against them whenever possible, even to the extent of killing them if necessary.

By contrast, whoever is identified as a freedom fighter is necessarily someone's friend in the political sense of this term. A person or group is identified as our political friend only if we have reason to believe that we share similar political interests and we are willing to take action in order to protect them. The level of risk we are willing to take to protect our political friends would depend on how high the stakes are for protecting and promoting our political interests in a given conflict either domestically or internationally.

One of the fundamental problems that we encounter when dealing with a term such as "enmity" is that its meaning is not fixed or entrenched in contemporary international law. So assuming the enmity of any person or group is not legally meaningful. As a result, the term lacks projectability. One could argue that a term would be meaningful and, hence, entrenched in international law if the following conditions are met: (1) its meaning must be understood and generally agreed upon by parties who sign and ratify different legal instruments, such as treaties and protocols; (2) it is reasonable to expect states to act compatibly with the generally agreed-upon meaning of the term; and (3) if they fail to so act, then they would be blameworthy and, hence, liable for their failure.

Terms like "combatant" and "civilian," despite their sometimes unsettled meaning in moral arguments, are meaningful and, hence, entrenched in contemporary international law. So they have projectability. Consequently, those who deliberately target civilians or treat combatants harshly are blameworthy and, hence, liable for having violated international law, such as LOAC or IHL.

Even though the terms "innocence" and "enmity" are not entrenched in international law, the latter seems to be more polemical than the first. That is so because, despite its lack of projectability, the concept of innocence plays a foundational role in both domestic and international law. There is widespread international agreement about its meaning and value. By contrast, there is no widespread agreement about the meaning and value regarding the concept of enmity. Presumably, an enemy is one who deliberately tries to harm someone, but whether s/he is justified in doing so is a different matter.

A. WHO ARE THE "ENEMIES"?

The concept of enmity has a long ancestry going back to the Greeks. According to Plato, true enmity and, hence, war was possible between the Greeks and the barbarians who were considered aliens and hence foreigners, but not among the Greeks who were considered friends.[7] So the term "enemy" is ambiguous. One can refer to a public enemy or *hostis* who declares their intention to engage us in a military confrontation. By contrast, one can refer to a private adversary who might hate us but whose intentions are not well known to us. Or one might refer to pirates who, by refusing to recognize any laws and representing no one other than themselves, are identified as universal enemies of humanity or as *hostis humani generis* to whom we owe no respect.[8]

One can identify public enemies, however, simply by their behavior toward their opponents. Cicero's definition of an enemy as "him who bears arms against you" provides a good illustration of a public enemy.[9] That is, one who is predisposed to significantly harm you and who has publicly declared his intention for doing so according to internationally recognized laws of war or rules of engagement.[10]

Cicero even recognizes the concept of a *just* enemy, namely, one who fights according to the laws of war and with whom agreements are possible.[11] By adopting the definition of enemies as "those who have officially declared war upon us, or upon whom we have officially declared war," medieval legal and political scholars continued to embrace the tradition of enmity as an act of public hostility between two or more different human collectivities.[12]

Those who try to harm others without a public declaration of war and who do not represent a given political collectivity are viewed as bandits, robbers, or pirates rather than as public enemies. They might claim that they are representing others belonging, for example, to a given social class, an ethnic group, or some disenfranchised group. But their power of representation is arguably limited unless they are successful in gaining recognition from the international community, or at least from some of its powerful players, such as all or some of the permanent members of the UN Security Council. This view of public enmity explains the reluctance of legal scholars from antiquity to the present to classify intrastate armed conflicts, such as civil wars and guerrilla or partisan warfare, as real wars between public enemies.

Despite the concerns of legal scholars, we can identify public enemies as those who have declared openly by word or deed their intention to harm an opponent, and proceed to act accordingly regardless of whether one describes the hostility as an interstate or an intrastate armed conflict. By refusing to grant the status of public enemy or combatant to those who engage in promoting intrastate armed conflicts, such as those engaged in urban or rural

guerrilla warfare, international law presupposes that they are unlawful combatants. International law presupposes that guerrilla fighters who threaten a
given constitutional order could in principle appeal to such an order if they
want to settle their grievances peacefully. As I have stated before, such a
presupposition is at times unfounded.

There are tyrannical regimes that refuse to settle grievances democratically
and peacefully. For example, the People's Republic of China has systematically violated the rights of the Tibetan people to self-determination, and
the rights of peaceful opponents who have questioned the monopoly of the
Communist Party; and the Burmese junta, until recently, has crushed and
incarcerated peaceful opponents who have demanded democratic reforms.
Also consider ruthless and long-lasting contemporary tyrants who have
oppressed their citizens by terrorizing them into submission. For example,
the late Saddam Hussein in Iraq, the late Muammar Gaddafi in Libya, and
the current president of Syria, Bashar al-Assad, have forcefully imposed their
will on their people, and have shown no compunction in killing and torturing
their opponents. The paragon of contemporary ruthless tyranny, however,
is the Democratic People's Republic of Korea (a.k.a. North Korea) that
for many years has been sending opponents to concentration camps where
they are regularly shot, tortured, or allowed to starve to death.[13] Under such
tyrannical regimes, there is not much hope for a peaceful opposition.

While applying the terms "public" or "private" to relationships of enmity
seems noncontroversial, applying the terms "just" and "unjust" to these relationships seems vexing. When one designates some people as enemies, be
they public or private, one believes them to be unjust; otherwise one would
not have identified them as enemies in the first place. If one does not conceive
of enemies as acting unjustly, at least one must believe that their character
or conduct is morally or legally suspect. If not, then one would be using the
term "enemy" equivocally or cynically to identify some people as enemies
for self-regarding reasons to promote one's selfish ends. If that were to be
the case, then the meaning of the term "enemy" would be purely subjective.

If one believes that the term "enemy" can be used objectively to designate
those who have declared openly by word or deed their intent to harm an
opponent and proceeds to act accordingly, then it is possible that one's beliefs
about specific enemies could be mistaken. So the person or group that one
identifies as an unjust enemy could be neither unjust nor an enemy. By contrast, if one were to describe some people as just, one would not conceive of
them as enemies. As Kant states, "a just enemy would be one that I would be
doing wrong by resisting; but then he would also not be my enemy."[14] Thus,
the expression "just enemy" appears to be oxymoronic. While not necessarily
oxymoronic, the expression "unjust enemy" is nevertheless ambiguous.

One could think of enemies as unjust when they engage in flagrant violations of international law. They might violate international law in different ways; for example, when those representing a nation-state engage in a war of aggression, thereby violating the *jus ad bellum* principle of self-defense, or when they deliberately attack innocent noncombatants, thereby violating the shared *jus ad bellum* and *jus in bello* principle of discrimination. They might violate the principle of discrimination in various ways by engaging, for example, in genocide, war crimes, or crimes against humanity. A war initiated on behalf of imperial ambitions is an unjust war as are wars intending to defend or to establish tyrannical regimes that violate fundamental human rights.

Still, the following is an important practical question: Who determines whether an enemy is unjust? For example, Kant proposes the following definition and test to determine the nature of an unjust enemy. For him, an unjust enemy is one "whose publicly expressed will (whether by word or deed) reveals a maxim by which, if it were made a universal rule, any condition of peace among nations would be impossible and, instead, a state of nature would be perpetuated."[15] He goes on to argue, "violation of public contracts is an expression of this sort."[16] It is reasonable to expect that consistent violations of international treaties and protocols that have already been ratified by different nations would certainly undermine the fundamental principle of *pacta sunt servanda*, which is the bedrock of international law.[17] Despite occasional violations of this principle, especially by powerful nations, there is an international consensus that without honoring this principle, the practice of international law would be virtually impossible.

A consistent disregard of *pacta sunt servanda* would likely lead into a state of nature or anarchy and, hence, a potential state of war among members of the international community of nations. Kant's proposed definition of unjust enmity, however, is more philosophical than juridical, since violations of international public contracts might be controversial, depending on the perspective one takes in a given dispute among nations and how powerful these nations might be in trying to impose their will on other nations. Moreover, there is no single international authority that could in principle determine who an unjust enemy would be in a given context. Even if such authority were to exist, holding the so-called unjust enemy accountable could be rather difficult if the international community had no political will to do so. Or if trying to do so would be too costly.[18]

So even when a clear violation of international law has been established by an independent tribunal, such as the ICC, enforcing the court's decision could be at times logistically difficult. Consider, for example, the warrant issued by the ICC for the arrest of President Omar al-Bashir of Sudan for war crimes and crimes against humanity against the civilian population of Darfur.[19]

Unfortunately, many Islamic States have refused to enforce this warrant, and he has traveled freely to and from such states.

Given the allegedly criminal behavior of President al-Bashir, he seems to flunk Kant's test of unjust enmity because he brought about a state of nature to the Darfur region. But can one conceive of him as an unjust enemy? The Bush Doctrine of preemption and prevention in Iraq would probably flunk Kant's test of unjust enmity too, because if all states were to embrace preemption and prevention to deal with perceived threats, then the international community would return to a state of nature or anarchy. So was former President Bush an unjust enemy too? Kant's universal test to establish who an unjust enemy is seems too broad. From the perspective of international law his test seems of no avail.

Was Saddam Hussein's government in Iraq an unjust enemy? Is the current Iranian government an unjust enemy? Is the North Korean government an unjust enemy too? It is difficult to fathom who would have the moral and legal authority to determine so. One could persuasively argue that since the concepts of just and unjust enemy are not entrenched in international law, they are unhelpful for addressing international conflicts. So from an international legal perspective, the above concepts seem legally hollowed, although not necessarily morally empty. Given that nation-states have engaged in serious moral failures throughout history, perhaps the most that we can reasonably expect from them is that they act decently toward their members (whether citizens or not) and to avoid engaging in wars of aggression against other nation-states.[20]

While Kant's test for determining which states could, in principle, be identified as an unjust enemy seems unhelpful, his test when applied to individuals or amorphous terrorist organizations, such as Al-Qaeda and its affiliates, could be helpful. By words and deeds, members of Al-Qaeda have shown a callous disregard for international law, domestic law, and fundamental moral and political principles. Since they have publicly declared war against the United States and its allies, they can be identified as public enemies.

The rank-and-file members of Al-Qaeda and its affiliates, as well as members of ISIL, have chosen to become not only enemies of Western nations, but also enemies of Islamic nations that do not conform to their militant view of Islam. Such disregard for normative considerations other than their own religious and geopolitical convictions put them in a class of their own. Since conviviality with them would be impossible, they seem to be more than public enemies. Perhaps they could be appropriately classified as paragons of unjust enemies. So even though strictly speaking they are not pirates, they could nonetheless be reasonably classified as *hostis humani generis* or enemies of humanity.[21]

Yet we need to be cautious not to push the analogy between piracy and terrorism too far. Pirates use violence primarily to promote their own selfish interests. Unlike pirates, however, terrorists generally use political violence for other-regarding reasons. They use deliberate or reckless political violence against their alleged enemies and the innocent alike to influence a domestic or an international audience. Hence, while pirates and terrorists might share similar practices such as kidnapping, reckless use of violence, or the infliction of terror on their actual or potential victims, their motives frequently differ. One could plausibly argue that viewing terrorism as a form of piracy might have inspired member states in the UN to sign and ratify some multilateral conventions addressing different forms of terrorism.[22] Other UN multilateral conventions on terrorism, however, have no kindred relationship with the conception of piracy.[23]

B. APOLOGISTS' ARGUMENTS

One could argue that both working definitions of terrorism, the one presupposed by opponents of terrorism and the one presupposed by apologists of terrorism, beg the question to some extent. Opponents of terrorism might assume that the concept of innocence is fully transparent and, hence, noncontroversial. But that is a questionable assumption. While the concept of innocence is well entrenched in domestic law as referring to those individuals who are harmless and, therefore, guiltless of legal wrongdoing, that is not the case in international law where the concept has been substituted for the terms "civilian" and "noncombatant." As I already argued, classifying a person or group as civilian or noncombatant might not absolve them of grave moral failure. Whether that is the case, one would need to argue so contextually. Likewise, determining who the innocent are must be done contextually rather than a priori.

Apologists of terrorism, however, might assume that the concept of enmity is fully transparent and noncontroversial. But that need not be so. Unlike the concept of innocence, the concept of enmity is neither well entrenched in domestic law nor in international law where the concept has been substituted for the term "combatant." Current international law uses the term "combatant" in a morally and legally neutral sense. Hence, the designation of someone as combatant in international law implies neither blame nor liability. Nevertheless, combatants can engage in serious moral and legal failures, such as when they engage in genocide, war crimes, or crimes against humanity. However, in a court of law, one needs to prove rather than assume such moral and legal failure.

Still, one can argue that the presumption of innocence takes precedence over the ascription of enmity to persons or groups except when people engage in formal military combat where the distinction between enemy soldiers, namely combatants, is clearly established and the concept of innocence is virtually inane. In international law and in many nations' domestic law persons or groups are presumed innocent until proven otherwise. Since opponents' presupposition of innocence, unlike apologists' presupposition of enmity, coheres with our moral and legal intuitions, it follows that, other things being equal, the first presupposition is weightier than the latter. Nevertheless, the permissibility of terrorist violence needs to be addressed by reasonable arguments rather than by appealing to people's intuitions alone.

1. Is War Justified?

War is a rather devastating enterprise, resulting as it does in the killing, maiming, and harming physically and psychologically of vast numbers of people, including impeccably innocent civilians. Such widespread suffering provides a legitimate reason for pacifists and their sympathizers to argue in principle and sometimes in practice against war whether we conceive of it as just or unjust, and regardless of whether such a practice refers to an interstate or intrastate armed conflict.[24] Actually, intrastate armed conflicts, such as civil wars, tend to be frequently bloodier than interstate wars.

Nations go to war for different reasons. Some of them might be just, such as those based on self-defense, on preventing genocide, or on punishing those who engage in aggression. Other reasons might be simply unjust, such as imperial ambitions, engaging in crimes against humanity, or numerous self-serving motivations.

Nations seem justified in going to war to protect the impeccably innocent and to punish the aggressors, namely, those who planned, initiated, and conducted an aggressive war of conquest. In so doing, however, they end up harming the aggressors but also countless impeccably innocent persons. That is the inexorable and paradoxical nature of war. And yet, if we were to insist on the categorical immunity of the impeccably innocent, even if the heavens might fall, no war would ever be justified. Still, when facing great evil, pacifism might be a worse option than the unavoidable widespread suffering that might be inflicted on the impeccably innocent during a just war.

If we conceive of war as an existing but difficult evil to eradicate, such as homicide, then it can be justified or unjustified. Similarly, to the extent that nations have adopted domestic social and legal policies to deal with homicide, they have also adopted domestic and international legal policies to deal with war. These legal policies, however, are not based solely on protecting the rights of those who are innocent of wrongdoing beyond reasonable doubt but also on punishing those who are responsible for the aggression. Such punishment is based on the aggressor's guilt and on the human and other costs inflicted on their victims.

The justification for going to war, such as when an aggressive nation attacks another nation, might be based on a morally and legally recognized right of self-defense that has been violated or, at times, on our natural positive duty of beneficence to protect those who are being unjustifiably harmed. Nevertheless, that might be a necessary but insufficient reason for going to war. Nations need also to consider the actual overall cost of the war. That is why the notion of mutual assured destruction (MAD) during the so-called Cold War between the former Soviet Union and its satellites and the United States and its allies was and is a morally questionable notion.

Because nuclear weapons are aimed at mostly civilian populations, the policy of MAD is morally flawed. The belief that one can achieve an effective deterrence by threatening mayhem on one's opponents, especially innocent noncombatants, violates our compelling duty of nonmaleficence, which the PNCI is based on. Since respect for PNCI is a necessary condition for engaging in a just war, and the policy of MAD violates the spirit and the letter of the PNCI, it follows that those who might choose to implement MAD could not engage in a just war.

A nuclear confrontation among nations would be apocalyptic. The widespread destruction of life in general and human life in particular would be so astronomically high that a victory by one of the parties involved in the armed conflict could be seen as a pyrrhic victory. If a party were to insist on defeating an enemy, such as an aggressor, at any cost, what might have been conceived of as a just war could turn into an unjust war resulting in mutual annihilation.

As traditionally used, the expression "just war" comes from the Latin meaning *bellum iustum*. Moreover, the expressions "just war theory" and "just war tradition" refer to a heterogeneous body of works and authors who have reflected on the justifiability and restrictions of war understood as armed conflict between belligerent groups conceived of as public enemies. Some of these authors have been pagan, such as Cicero, a prominent Roman statesman, jurist, and philosopher. Others have been prominent Christian theologians and philosophers, such as St. Augustine and St. Thomas Aquinas, whose views influenced late medieval canonists and theologians. Some of the most prominent names from the late medieval period that contributed to the development of a Christian just war tradition—a tradition I turn to most often because it has substantively influenced international law as represented in UN treaties and protocols, which I will discuss later—are Spanish Catholic theologians and jurists, such as Francisco de Vitoria and Francisco Suárez, and the Dutch Protestant theologian, statesman, and jurist Hugo Grotius.

Similar to the expressions "just war theory" and "just war tradition," one could use expressions such as "just war approach" or "just war thinking" to denote the pastiche of pagan and Christian ideas that grapple with issues of war prior to, during, and after armed conflicts have ended. These ideas emerged to justify and restrict the use of force against one's public enemy by offering reasoned judgments based on some of the following moral criteria: assuming a collective right of self-defense, punishing evildoers, defending the innocent, or protecting the common good.

Since the expression "just war" reflects a rich and constantly evolving approach to dealing with armed conflicts, I prefer to use the expressions "just war approach" or "just war thinking" interchangeably when discussing authors whose views one can interpret as defending a version of just war. Authors who use such an approach are not necessarily concerned with developing a theory, but they are rather trying to develop a view of practical reason to help public officials and ordinary citizens develop sound arguments and judgments while evaluating the beginning and conduct of war.[25]

Contemporary writers who use a just war approach generally appeal to a combination of *jus ad bellum* and *jus in bello* considerations. Both *jus ad bellum* and *jus in bello* refer to a set of criteria, norms, or principles that have evolved from antiquity to the present to try to justify and constrain armed conflicts and the atrocities associated with them. However, an elaborate just war approach containing both *jus ad bellum* and *jus in bello* considerations, as we understand it nowadays, appears to be a product of the late Middle Ages. According to James Turner Johnson, before the 1500s there were two doctrines: a theological and canonical one based on *jus ad bellum* considerations and a secular one based on the Law of Arms or *jus in bello* considerations.[26] While these expressions, especially *jus in bello*, seem to be a product of contemporary international law, concerns for a just war as a way of seeking peace can be traced to the Greeks.[27]

For Aristotle, war is not a positive end but a means of seeking peace.[28] It is with the Romans, however, that *jus ad bellum* norms began to crystallize and *jus in bello* considerations emerged (if not in name, at least in practice) as reasons for respecting one's opponents' personal integrity, especially after hostilities have ended. For example, Cicero, having been influenced by the Stoics, argues that "wars, then, ought to be undertaken for this purpose, that we may live in peace, without injustice."[29] Moreover, he adds several conditions that must be satisfied if a war is to be considered just: (1) it must be a last resort, (2) it must be declared by a proper authority beforehand, and (3) a formal demand for restoration has failed.[30] In addition, one must show mercy for those who have been conquered and spare the lives of those who have surrendered.[31] Similarly, in classic Chinese martial text from the sixth century BC, Sun Tzu, a reputable military general, recommends that captured soldiers must be treated mercifully.[32]

For Cicero, either in times of peace or war, there are moral values that one ought to respect, such as promise keeping. For him, this basic duty constitutes an important part of the law of war. A promise to an enemy even under duress carries significant moral weight.[33] However, a promise to pirates carries no moral weight because, unlike an enemy in war with whom an agreement might be reached, pirates are defined as unjust enemies or enemies of humanity (i.e., *hostis humani generis*) with whom no agreement is possible.[34] This is so because they represent nobody but themselves. They are only concerned with promoting their own welfare with no regard for domestic or international norms. Hence, they have no right to make war or peace on behalf of others.

Grotius, however, disagrees with Cicero's view regarding the possible validity of promise keeping or of making an oath to pirates or tyrants. For him, a promise or an oath to pirates or tyrants generates a moral obligation to discharge it.[35] Yet he concedes that breaking a promise or an oath to a robber carries no legal liability in international law.[36]

While Cicero conceives of a duty of fidelity or promise keeping as an important moral value, he does not consider this duty to be absolute. For him, there is no single absolute duty that will trump other duties all the time and under all circumstances. According to him, justice is found on two fundamental moral values: doing no harm to others and promoting the general welfare. Sometimes these values pull in opposite directions. So when a promise does not promote the welfare of a promisee or it harms the promisor more than it helps the promisee, it must give in to that which promotes the general welfare.[37]

There is thus a tension in Cicero's conception of fundamental moral values, such as his conception of the duty of fidelity or promise keeping and his conception of beneficence. While he vehemently argues for respecting the duty of fidelity in times of war so that even under duress a promise to one's enemy ought to be kept, he admits that promises under circumstances other than war should not be honored if by honoring them one would undermine the general welfare. Therefore, his conception of duty is weaker than it appears. He assumes that acting according to duty, or that which he describes as honorable, and acting according to that which he describes as beneficial are necessarily related. So for him, "whatever is honorable is beneficial."[38] But that need not be so unless one defines the honorable so broadly as to include the beneficial. Still, doing so would simply conflate two different moral concepts representing different moral values.

Despite the already mentioned tension in Cicero's conception of fundamental moral values, his reflections on war have contributed to the development of the just war tradition. But when scholars talk about the just war tradition, they usually refer to the Christian just war tradition going back to St. Augustine and his polemic against pacifist interpreters of Christianity. According to Augustine, one needs to understand Jesus's words in Matthew 5:39–41 and Luke 6:29 as a disposition of the heart to avoid acting on vengeance so, by forbearing the hardships imposed by the wrongdoer, the latter might repent from his evil acts. Moreover, Jesus addressed his words to individual persons rather than to public servants.[39]

For almost two hundred years Christians were committed pacifists.[40] Prior to the Roman emperor Constantine, they categorically refused to participate in military service.[41] Nevertheless, whether their pacifism was based on purely religious grounds to avoid idolatry, as practiced by the Romans, or based on love of God and one's neighbor remains controversial.

Putting aside the above-mentioned controversy, Christian pacifism seems consistent with Jesus's teaching of universal love. Yet Jesus's teaching of universal love without a commitment to justice in the world seems rather flawed. So after Constantine came to power and Christianity became the dominant religion of the Roman Empire, Christians were allowed to engage in military service based on the preservation and the promotion of justice.[42]

This change of view can make Christian doctrine seem paradoxical. Such a seemingly paradoxical shift from advocacy of pacifism to allowing serving in the military based on Jesus's doctrine of universal love and just war considerations has been explained by some scholars as a "change of tactics," given a new historical context.[43]

Augustine insists that, as a private person, one is unjustified in killing an aggressor intentionally even in self-defense because such an act would be based on lust for one's life. But as an agent of the law, a soldier may kill an enemy in fulfilling his duty without lust for his life.[44] One can plausibly argue that, for Augustine, war is not justified based simply on "the inequity of the adversary," as he at times contends.[45] For him, war is justified based on love of God and one's neighbor.[46] For this reason, he argues that if the earthly city were to respect Christian principles, it would wage war with benevolence toward the defeated "for the sake of the peaceful union of piety and justice."[47]

Augustine also argues, "The will should be concerned with peace and necessity with war." Later in the same letter he states, "Let necessity slay the warring foe, not your will."[48] He defines just wars "as those which avenge injuries" when a community or state fails to punish their citizens for having wronged others.[49] Thus, one of his main criticisms of war is based on a disposition of the will to intentionally harm others, including the cruelty of revenge and the lust for domination.[50] Those who argue that Augustine justifies war mainly on military necessity rather than on Christian love seem to offer a one-sided interpretation of his view on just war.[51] This is so because Augustine consistently shows deep and serious concern for the well-being of the vanquished, which could be seen as an incipient predisposition for *jus in bello* considerations.[52]

Because in his writings Augustine was responding to various challenges, one might explain the tension that exists among his reflections on war by appealing to different contextual considerations. To criticize Augustine for not being fully coherent in his view on just war is to fall into the trap of what Quentin Skinner aptly labels the "mythology of coherence." That is, to assume a priori that a writer intends to offer the most systematic approach that s/he can advance on a given issue in a given context.[53]

It seems hyperbolic to argue as some scholars have done, that, for Augustine, "The just war was thus total and unlimited in its licit use of violence."[54] Hence, "the just warriors could kill with impunity even those who were morally innocent."[55] Those who argue so are attributing to Augustine a modern conception of total war. Such an attribution risks the charge of anachronism—that is, ascribing to an early writer based on terminological resemblance a modern conception or view that he did not or could not have held.[56]

While one can agree with critics of Augustine's view on just war that there is a tension between upholding the principle of Christian universal love as found in the Gospel, and the justification of killing in a just war, it does not follow from this tension that "so long as the Christian kills without feelings of personal rancor or vengeance," s/he rather than violating the principle of charity actually enforces it.[57] Or that "the only factors" that constrain those engaged in a just war are their subjective considerations, namely, their intention and their assessment of military necessity.[58] If that were to be so, then Augustine would not have been concerned with the well-being of the vanquished. But he was thus concerned when he states, "as violence is returned to one who rebels and resists, so should mercy be to one who has been conquered or captured."[59]

Still, critics of Augustine's view on just war raise an important point when they underscore that one cannot find an explicit defense of the PNCI in his writings. Those who argue otherwise, such as Paul Ramsey, have offered limited and, to some extent, unconvincing textual evidence to make their case.[60] Focusing on textual evidence alone, however, is insufficient to settle the argument on whether Augustine explicitly defends the PNCI. For a reasonable answer to this challenging issue, one needs to look into the spirit animating Augustine's political writings.

If Christian universal love ultimately inspired Augustine's political writings, and no sufficient reason exists to doubt him on this point, then it would seem overstated to argue that "Any objective determination to who are innocent or guilty among the enemy is not only impossible but also irrelevant."[61] If that were to be so, then one could persuasively contend that instead of being a precursor of the Christian just war approach, Augustine could be seen as the progenitor of the modern conception of total war that makes no morally relevant distinction between combatants and innocent noncombatants.

Hence, as long as one has justice on one's side and acts from a sense of love of God and one's neighbor, including one's enemies, rather than from a sense of vengeance, Augustine would allow for targeting combatants and innocent noncombatants alike.

Imputing the above-mentioned view to Augustine would be not only anachronistic, as I have already argued, but, more importantly, inconsistent with the letter and spirit of the Gospel. He was undoubtedly a committed Christian, so despite the tensions that exist in his views on war in general and on just war in particular, such an imputation appears unconvincing.

Having been influenced by Cicero, Augustine favors peace over war. For him, war is an evil or vice that should be avoided—but not at all cost. Like Cicero, Augustine claims, "peace is not sought in order to provoke war, but war is waged to attain peace."[62] Similarly, for him, war must be declared by the proper authority of a leader.[63] He contends that war must also be a last resort because "the will should be concerned with peace and necessity with war."[64] Moreover, like Cicero, he claims that we have a duty to be merciful to those who have been defeated or captured in war, and we also have a duty of fidelity or promise keeping even to one's enemies with whom war is being waged.[65] Yet Augustine contends that those who win victory in a just war may do so by engaging in open combat or through ruses.[66] Whether Augustine's understanding of "ruse" would allow those having justice on their side to intentionally lie to their enemies seems to be underdetermined. To assume that his political realism will go thus far remains debatable.[67]

Despite Augustine's influence on Aquinas in developing a Christian just war approach, Aquinas appears to take exception with Augustine on that which is morally permissible in the actual conduct of war. While Aquinas agrees that in a just war those who are in the right have no obligation to disclose their war plans to their enemies (that would be simply foolish), he clearly and unambiguously states that they have no right to intentionally lie to them.[68] Aquinas rather than Augustine is ultimately responsible for formalizing the Christian just war tradition in the fourteenth century. However, the Dominican Francisco de Vitoria and the Jesuit Francisco Suárez are the ones responsible for developing some of the nuances of this tradition during the sixteenth and the seventeenth century.

Aquinas, expanding on Augustine's views of charity and war, offers three necessary conditions for a war to be just: (1) it must be declared by a proper or legitimate authority representing the common good of the community; (2) it must be waged against those who deserve it by virtue of having committed some wrongful acts; and (3) it must be waged with right intention to bring about some good or to avoid some evil.[69] Right intention, however, applies not only to the initiation of hostilities or *jus ad bellum*, but also to the conduct of war itself or *jus in bello*.

Aquinas assumes that private persons can vindicate their grievances in a court of law by appealing to a superior authority in the community. Hence, according to him, they have no right to wage war. His assumption, however, is questionable because he presupposes that the community is well governed. Still, that need not be so, as he admits in the case of tyranny. For him, there is no sedition in trying to overthrow a tyrannical government unless doing so brings about greater suffering to the people than they would have experienced under tyrannical rule.[70] He insists, nonetheless, that it is the community and not private individuals that has the right to try to depose a tyrant.[71]

By following the spirit of a just war approach, soft-core apologists of terrorism might try to justify the use of violence. For example, Andrew Valls states, "if war can be justified, then terrorism can be as well."[72] Similarly, Virginia Held argues, "some uses of violence may be justified, and terrorism may be not more unjustifiable than war."[73] They assume that war and terrorism can be analogous in the use of violence by aiming for morally worthy goals in morally acceptable ways. To avoid incoherence, if we justify the use of violence in the former, then we should do likewise in the latter. One might divide morally acceptable goals into two: those based on self-defense and those based on combating grave evils.

By virtue of being moral agents, people have a right to life and thus the right to protect themselves from an actual or potential aggressor. Likewise, government officials representing citizens of nation-states have a substantive duty to protect them from actual or potential aggressors; that is, from those who actually use or threaten to use violence against them regardless of whether they are states or nonstate agents. Moreover, people and government officials representing nation-states have a moral and, to some extent, a positive legal duty of beneficence based on international human rights law to try to combat grave evils, such as crimes against peace, genocide, war crimes, crimes against humanity, and gross violation of human rights. The enforcement of such an international humanitarian legal obligation has been ad hoc at best, frequently depending on the interests of great powers.

A traditional Christian just war approach justifies waging war not only in self-defense, as evidently understood in contemporary international law, but also in combating grave evils. So on moral grounds, the traditional Christian just war approach could justify humanitarian interventions based on a right to protect the innocent far more so than current international law would allow. Current international law is fundamentally based on the principle of self-defense, so sanctioning humanitarian interventions is the exception rather than the rule.

Those who accept that war and terrorism can be analogous in the use of violence might try to analyze terrorist acts in the light of a contemporary just war paradigm based on *jus ad bellum* and *jus in bello* considerations. In a just war paradigm, whether traditional or contemporary, one understands the use of violence conceived of as lethal force as a necessary evil. Contemporary scholars identify the following *jus ad bellum* conditions that are necessary to justify going to war: (1) *legitimate authority*: states rather than nonstate actors have the right to declare and wage war; (2) *just cause*: the use of force is justified based on self-defense, the protection of the innocent, or the correction of a grave wrong; (3) *right intention*: force is used according to a just cause that aims at bringing about a state of peace; (4) *last resort*: since war is such a great evil, other reasonable options should be explored before using force; (5) *reasonable hope of success*: otherwise the suffering that is brought about would be futile and hence unjustified; (6) *proportionality*: the untoward consequences that result from the use of force in trying to establish a state of peace must not exceed the calamities of the unjust state of affairs that one is trying to overcome.

Once hostilities begin, a contemporary just war paradigm requires that the following *jus in bello* conditions be fulfilled to prevent a just war from degenerating into a vicious one: (1) *proportionality*: the damage inflicted on the enemy in the actual conduct of war must not be excessive; and (2) *reasonable discrimination*: those who engage in hostilities have the responsibility to distinguish between the permissibility of targeting combatants and the respect for the immunity of noncombatants.[74] If the *jus ad bellum* and *jus in bello* conditions are reasonably fulfilled, those who defend a contemporary just war approach might then contend that the use of physical force whether lethal or not can be morally justified.

While a contemporary secular just war approach might be compatible with international law by distinguishing between combatants and noncombatants, a traditional Christian just war approach presupposes a morally relevant distinction between the combatant and the innocent. Contemporary international law assumes that noncombatants are innocent. But they might not be so. According to the traditional Christian just war approach, it is categorically impermissible to intentionally kill the impeccably innocent, namely, those who are harmless or guiltless. For example, Aquinas unambiguously states, "there is . . . simply no justification for taking the life of an innocent person."[75] In the same spirit, Vitoria writes, "it is never lawful to kill innocent people, even accidentally and unintentionally, except when it advances a just war which cannot be won in any other way."[76] Following Aquinas's and Vitoria's views, Suárez maintains, "I hold that innocent persons as such may in no wise be slain."[77]

Any moral, theological, political, or legal theory that attempts to justify inflicting significant harm on others would likely encounter serious tensions within the theory as well as its application. Since those representing a traditional Christian just war approach attempt to do just that, they will at times find tension between the theory supporting such an approach and its applicability to real-case scenarios. Some classic representatives of this traditional approach, such as Vitoria and Suárez, allow for the possibility that under "extreme necessity" people who can be conceived of as innocent noncombatants might be justifiably harmed (namely, punished) but not intentionally killed.

For example, according to Vitoria, "if a sovereign wages an unjust war against another prince, the injured party may plunder and pursue all the other rights of war against that sovereign's subjects, even if they are innocent of offence."[78] While Vitoria's view seems deplorable, in the above citation he is referring to the "rights of war," or to what was legally permissible back then by the *jus gentium*. He is not morally licensing the soldiers of the offended commonwealth or nation to inflict any type of punishment on the offending nations' subjects.

On behalf of Vitoria's view, one could argue that the subjects of a sovereign who wages an unjust war against another might be innocent in a *mens rea* sense because they do not actually and deliberately engage in waging the unjust war. Despite their innocence, however, they might be punished because they belong to the commonwealth that wages such an unjustified war. In a similar vein, Suárez argues that, in a just armed conflict, it is permissible for those who are in the right "to deprive the innocent of their goods, even their liberty. The reason is that the innocent form a portion of one whole and unjust state; and on account of the crime of the whole, this part may be punished even though it does not of itself share in the fault."[79]

Perhaps the subjects or citizens could have stopped the sovereign from engaging in the unjust war, and they chose not to. Hence, one could view them as noninnocent by failing to act as a Good Samaritan would to prevent harm to others. They might have had the possibility of escaping from the sovereign's territory to avoid being caught in the midst of the armed conflict, but they simply chose to stay. Or, even though they might be "innocent of offence," as stated by Vitoria and recognized by Suárez, they might still constitute a so-called innocent threat or involuntary objective threat. So, by depriving them of their goods and liberty, they would be unable to help their sovereign in any future threat to peace. According to Vitoria and Suárez, they can be justifiably punished, but they cannot be intentionally killed.

The ordinary subjects or citizens of an offending commonwealth or nation seem noninnocent, albeit in an elliptical sense, since they belong to the commonwealth that wages an unjust war. They can be viewed as collectively guilty by openly or tacitly consenting to entrusting or supporting an unjust sovereign, so Vitoria argues.[80] Excepting children, the elderly, the severely ill, and the mentally challenged, ordinary responsible citizens of an offending commonwealth or nation seem to share some degree of moral guilt.

Whether their degree of moral guilt is serious enough to blame them individually for their commonwealth's blameworthy behavior might be debatable. Their moral guilt or responsibility would depend on their individual motives and behavior.[81]

History informs us that in any war, those who are vanquished, including the impeccably innocent, will be deliberately punished. Once a commonwealth or nation is defeated, for example, the burden of reparation will affect innocent and noninnocent alike because they are part of the same commonwealth or nation. Since in a traditional Christian just war approach a commonwealth or nation is viewed as a moral and legal corporate body, it is conceptually and practically inconceivable to deliberately punish the corporate body without deliberately punishing its parts.[82] While Suárez proscribes "intrinsic injury to innocent persons" (presumably deliberately killing them), he argues that in a just war "if the end is permissible, the necessary means to that end are also permissible; and hence it follows that in the whole course or duration of the war hardly anything done against the enemy involves injustice, except the slaying of the innocent."[83]

Similarly, responding to the view of a contemporary Dominican theologian, Silvestro Mazzolini da Prierio, about the legality of terrorizing the enemy if necessary to conduct a just war, Vitoria concedes that while it is legally permissible to set fire to a city when there are reasons for doing so in a just armed conflict, this would likely license the soldiers to commit all kinds of atrocities, including "murdering and torturing the innocent, deflowering young girls, raping women, and pillaging churches." He continues, "in these circumstances, it is undoubtedly unjust to destroy a Christian city except in the most pressing necessity and with the gravest of causes; but if *necessity decrees it is not unlawful* [my italics], even if the probability is that the soldiery will commit crimes of this kind." Nonetheless, he underlines that officers have a duty to try to prevent these crimes.[84]

I can think of two important points about the above passage. First, Vitoria seems to acknowledge that while the soldiers' behavior is not necessarily unlawful in some sense, presumably according to the *jus gentium* back then, he still describes their acts as criminal. His description implies not only legal but also moral condemnation. So he appears to distinguish between the legality or permissibility of their acts as necessary for waging a successful just war, and the morality of their otherwise criminal acts. This distinction could be a reason why he insists that officers have a duty (not only a legal but also a moral one) to prevent their soldiers from engaging in such criminal behavior.

Secondly, Vitoria unwillingly concedes that "under the most pressing necessity and with the gravest of causes" during a just armed conflict, one might allow for the infliction of harm on innocent noncombatants. In Suárez's discussion, one finds similar views regarding exceptions to the immunity of innocent noncombatants. For example, Suárez argues that the innocent may not be deliberately killed, although they might be incidentally slain when necessary for victory, and when they cannot be distinguished from the guilty.[85]

As James Turner Johnson contends, "the arguments of Suárez and Vitoria tend to erode the rights of the innocent whenever necessity . . . requires treating them as one with the guilty."[86] Vitoria's and Suárez's views in the above-mentioned passages justify collective punishment or acts of reprisals that are forbidden by current international law. To that extent, current international law that proscribes virtually all kinds of reprisals by state and nonstate agents involved in armed conflicts appears as an improvement over a Christian just war approach that would have allowed for such morally despicable acts.[87] Yet to assess with hindsight a Christian just war approach intended to be applicable during sixteenth- and seventeenth-century understanding of the law of war by appealing to our current view of the international law of armed conflict seems anachronistic.

While being sensitive to contextual differences, one can acknowledge that current international law has improved over a sixteenth- and seventeenth-century understanding of a Christian just war approach. However, it is unconvincing to argue, as some critics of a Christian just war approach do, that such an approach seems incoherent because it allows for intentionally harming the innocent while claiming that the innocent have a categorical right not to be killed.[88] One can agree with these critics that a Christian just war approach might allow undermining the rights of the innocent under stressful circumstances, namely, under supreme or extreme necessity; however, it does not follow that it would allow deliberately doing so during all armed conflicts.

By appealing to "extreme necessity," defenders of a Christian just war tradition might undermine the spirit of their own tradition, which consists of the categorical defense of the innocent and the Pauline precept that "evil may not be done that good may ensue." Extreme necessity, however, constitutes a challenge for any moral or political theory that defends the categorical immunity of the innocent. If one takes such categorical immunity seriously, as do Vitoria and Suárez in their defense of a Christian just war approach, then allowing for actions, even under extreme necessity, that undermine the physical, psychological, and moral integrity of the innocent might raise pointed questions about the coherence of such an approach.

Like anomalies in scientific theories that test the limits of their verisimilitude, extreme or exceptional circumstances test the limits of approaches to just war thinking. If, in the face of an extreme or exceptional test, one can still find value in just war thinking, such as in a Christian just war approach, then one could argue that *exceptio probat regulam*. That is, the exception proves that the rules or norms of just war thinking are nevertheless valuable.

There are three fundamental values in a Christian just war approach that can be in tension with one another. First, as Vitoria states, "the sole and only justice for waging war is when harm has been inflicted."[89] Second, he underlines, "in the just war one may do everything necessary for the defence of the public good."[90] And third, he argues, "it is never lawful in itself intentionally to kill innocent persons."[91] These three values might pull in opposite directions under stressful circumstances, such as during a war.

Defenders of a Christian just war approach try to palliate the above tension by adopting what has become known by various names, such as the principle of double effect, the doctrine of double effect, the rule of double effect, or double effect reasoning. In the next section, I will address some of the nuances of double effect relevant for my argument. To put it simply, defenders of a Christian just war approach assume that, under stressful circumstances where one's act might have two effects, one positive and the other one negative, there is a reasonable distinction between the intended and deliberate killing of impeccably innocent people and the unintended but foreseen killing of them.

Critics of just war, such as pacifists and consequentialists, can cite passages from representatives of a Christian just war approach to illustrate the tension that exists, for example, in Vitoria's and Suárez's writings on just war. I have already done so above. A fundamental issue, however, is whether just war thinking's appeal to double effect reasoning under stressful circumstances can provide ordinary citizens, government officials, and policy makers with sufficient critical reasoning tools to make reasonable and fair decisions, or whether their appeal to double effect reasoning under stressful circumstances serves as a sham.

Being essentially a Christian just war paradigm, a traditional just war approach presupposes the categorical immunity of the innocent. Hence, it proscribes the intentional and deliberate killing of the latter. As a result, soft-core apologists of terrorism who embrace a traditional just war approach must also oppose the intentional and deliberate killing of the innocent. If not, they would not be defending a traditional just war approach.

Soft-core apologists of terrorism, however, might be trying to modify traditional just war thinking. By focusing on the contestability of the term "innocent," they might consider the concept of intentionality as being too opaque for distinguishing between permissible and impermissible acts, or they might appeal, as Vitoria and Suárez do, to the concept of "extreme necessity" to try to justify the deliberate harming of the innocent. While they could try to argue so, their arguments seem incompatible with the spirit of traditional just war thinking. They could reply that traditional just war thinking is one way among others of understanding the permissibility of war. They might, for example, try to justify war and the practice of warfare based solely on consequentialist or utilitarian considerations alone. But if they were to do so, then they would certainly not be representatives of what has been identified as a traditional just war approach.

a. Double Effect Reasoning

Traditional just war thinking typically presupposes what is commonly known as the principle of double effect (PDE), the doctrine of double effect (DDE), the rule of double effect (RDE), or double effect reasoning (DER). I prefer to use the expression double effect reasoning.[92] Calling it a "principle" seems inaccurate, since such a way of reasoning involves a set of criteria or conditions that justify an action rather than a general moral principle, such as Kant's categorical imperative or Mill's principle of utility.[93] Calling it a "doctrine" might give a misleading impression that we are referring to a set of authoritative principles, rules, and assumptions, such as those embedded in a doctrine of natural law or in a doctrine of legal positivism, rather than to a set of criteria or conditions that have been conventionally adopted to help ordinary reasonable people come up with sound moral judgments. Moreover, calling it a "rule" might convey a false impression that we are dealing with narrow and unambiguous moral situations, such as rules prohibiting murder or theft, rather than with complex moral dilemmas where unavoidably innocent people's lives will be seriously harmed.[94] These moral dilemmas require sound judgment rather than algorithmic applications of a principle, a doctrine, a rule, or a combination of any of them.

Regardless of whether one calls it PDE, DDE, RDE, or DER, a fundamental idea underlying this way of reasoning is the intuition that there exists a morally relevant distinction between intending and foreseeing the consequences of one's voluntary actions understood as deliberate free choices. One can trace this distinction to Aquinas. According to Aquinas, an act can have two effects, namely a double effect, one that is intended and the other that is incidental to the person's intention. So for him, the morality of an act depends essentially on what is intended rather than on what is incidental to the person's intention.[95] Yet while an agent's intention is necessary for gauging the morality of an action, it is insufficient for doing so. For Aquinas, a human act has the following four features: its generic quality, its objective, its circumstances, and its end.[96]

If the morality of an action were solely determined by an agent's intention, then that could lead to what Elizabeth Anscombe aptly refers to as "double thinking about double effect."[97] That is, if one accepts a Cartesian psychology that an intention is just a subjective voluntary act of the will, then an agent's intention would be whatever s/he reports it to be. Based on this purely subjective view of intentionality, one could try to change the morality of an action by changing one's intention in an ad hoc fashion.[98] If one were to do so, then one's behavior could be rightly described as arbitrary, capricious, and, at times, even duplicitous.

Consider the following example of excusing duplicitous behavior. Suppose that I intend to kill an innocent person for self-regarding reasons that need not be specified. My intention to kill him is not just the thought of getting rid of him but the goal of doing so according to a given plan of action. I concoct a plan to poison him. I am ready to use a powerful poison consisting of toxins extracted from several blue scorpions, which will presumably kill him. Suppose also that, in executing my plan, I am able to pour a sufficient amount of the poison in his coffee, intending to kill him. While having breakfast with him, I succeed in encouraging him to drink his whole mug containing the coffee.

Unbeknownst to me, he is seriously ill with cancer, and I am unaware of the possible beneficial properties that blue scorpion toxins might have in fighting certain types of cancer, provided the toxins do not kill you first. Ironically, I learned later that despite having had certain nasty side effects, such as headaches, cramps, and vomiting, the poison that I poured into his coffee intending to kill him actually helped him to prolong his life by stopping the spread of his cancer. So I learned retroactively that the victim is seriously ill with cancer, and I also learned about the curative properties of blue scorpion toxins.

Suppose that the police discovered compelling evidence of my criminal scheme to kill the victim. During cross-examination, I cynically lie, pretending that I never intended to kill the person. Actually, I admit that I did pour blue scorpion toxins into his coffee without informing him about it. However, I offer the following excuse. Since I have known that he was rather skeptical about alternative medicine, I expected that, even if I had informed him about the curative properties of blue scorpion toxins, he would have refused to try it. So I would have been unable to help him! That was precisely the reason for my secrecy in carrying out my "beneficent plan."

I try to explain to the officers involved in the criminal investigation that my intention was always to help the person fight his cancer rather than to poison him. I thereby lie to them by claiming that I have been informed by reliable sources about the possible beneficial properties of these toxins to help cancer patients go into remission. Moreover, I pretend to have been aware of his illness but unaware of the possible deadly side effects of blue scorpion toxins. Hence, even though my intention has been criminal all along in a *mens rea* sense, I try to convince the officers that my intention was commendable.

Given the beneficial but unintended concomitant consequences of my act of trying to poison the victim, some people might view the act as a positive act of helping someone in need rather than as a negative act of attempted murder. But that would be pure sophistry. All the time I intended to kill him. It fortuitously happened that, inadvertently, my criminal act helped to improve his precarious health, hence my duplicity in confessing to the officers about what I intended.

An agent's intention is insufficient to establish the morality of an action. Similarly, the outcome of an action independent of an agent's intention is insufficient to establish its morality. Otherwise, my intrinsically wrong act of attempted murder that, contrary to my malicious intention, actually improved the victim's life could be considered a good deed or a morally permissible act. But that again would be pure sophistry, since I implemented my malicious plan because of and in order to kill him. Hence, mine was an evident act of attempted murder, namely, a *mala in se* act. That is, an intrinsically wrong act.

For Aquinas, "intention denotes an act of will, the ordinance of reason directing a means to an end being presupposed."[99] On Aquinas's account of intentionality, an intention is not just an internal voluntary act of the will (for example, just a thought aiming at something), but also a disposition to act according to practical reason using effective means to realize a desirable end or goal. Intentionality may be described as having a pro-attitude.[100] That is to say, having a desire or want for a particular end or goal, and a belief or set of beliefs that certain means could be effectively used to achieve such a desirable end or goal.

Aquinas's account of intentionality presupposes that one can assess the morality of a desire as well as the morality of an end or goal independently from their causal relationship. For example, when discussing self-defense, Aquinas argues that a person's act of defending himself from an unjust aggressor might result in having two effects: the saving of one's life and the killing of the aggressor. Still, while the act might have two effects, the aim or goal of the act is one, namely, to defend one's self from the aggressor. The desire and the object of my desire are morally worthy—trying to defend myself from an unjust aggressor.

An act of self-defense that results in the killing of an unjust aggressor is justified, so Aquinas argues, assuming that one's intention is directed at saving one's life rather than at killing the aggressor, one does not use excessive force in doing so, and no other reasonable options are available to prevent killing the aggressor. A person, in defending his life from an unjust aggressor, has the right to knowingly risk the aggressor's life while protecting his own, but he has no right to intentionally kill him. He foresees that by acting in self-defense he could bring about serious harm to the aggressor, including the aggressor's possible death, but his aim or goal is never to kill him.[101] Yet the act of saving one's life and the killing of the aggressor is the same act that can be described in two different ways.

So if the act of saving one's life is justified, then the act of killing the aggressor is also justified as a reasonable way to saving one's life. Still, if one were to use disproportionate force to save one's life, then that would be wrong, so Aquinas implies. He explains, "An act that is properly motivated may, nevertheless, become vitiated if it is not proportionate to the end intended."[102] Therefore, those who embrace a traditional conception of DER argue that while one can be held morally responsible for intentionally perpetrating an act, one need not be held so for the foreseen untoward consequences of the same act.[103] Nevertheless, those who defend versions of consequentialism would dismiss this way of reasoning as being rather Byzantine for establishing the moral justifiability of an act.

Consequentialist critics of DER, such as utilitarians, typically accept that a person's intention is necessary for evaluating her moral character as virtuous or vicious. They, however, typically contend that the consequences of her action alone or the consequences of the rule or set of rules that sanction her action help differentiate between right and wrong conduct. One can classify utilitarians into two types: act-utilitarians and rule-utilitarians. Act-utilitarians maintain that the consequences of a person's action alone determine the rightness or wrongness of her action. However, rule-utilitarians maintain that the consequences of the rule or set of rules sanctioning a person's action determine the rightness or wrongness of her action.[104]

For example, if an act or a rule that sanctions a given action brings about a net value of good over evil for those affected by it, then it is morally justifiable and, hence, permissible. By contrast, if an act or a rule that sanctions the action brings about a net value of evil over good for those affected by it, then it is morally unjustifiable and, hence, impermissible. Still, for consequentialists, how one defines good and evil remains an open question. In addition, since rule-utilitarians focus on the consequences of a rule or a set of rules rather than on the consequences of an action, as act-utilitarians do, it is plausible that people holding these different consequentialist positions might hold inconsistent beliefs about the rightness or wrongness of a given action. If that occurred, then utilitarians in general would face a challenging question. Given their inconsistent beliefs about the rightness or wrongness of an action, what is to determine the rightness or wrongness of such an action? Should we focus solely on the consequences of the action itself, as act-utilitarians typically do? Or should we focus solely on the consequences of the rule or set of rules, as rule-utilitarians typically do? There are no simple answers to these questions. This, however, is an issue beyond my present purpose.

According to consequentialist critics of DER, such as act-utilitarians, my act of attempted murder already described, which accidentally helped the victim to improve and prolong his life, would be conceived of by them as morally right. Therefore, according to them, my intention was vicious, but my act was morally right. Such a conclusion seems vexing and possibly incoherent. How can a vicious intention bring about a morally right act?

To avoid the above conclusion, consequentialist critics of DER could resort to rule-utilitarianism rather than to act-utilitarianism. In addition to my intention's being vicious, they could argue that my act of attempted murder, which accidentally helped the victim to improve and prolong his life, was a *malum in se* act and, therefore, intrinsically wrong. Despite its felicitous outcome, my act violated the rule against attempted murder. Moreover, violating the rule of attempted murder is morally and legally wrong. Since for consequentialists, such as utilitarians, what determines the rightness or wrongness of an action is generally its felicitous or infelicitous outcomes rather than the intention of those who perpetrate the action, it seems that they have a one-sided view of morality. They seem to allow, at times, for the possibility of ascribing moral responsibility based on kismet rather than on people's purposive behavior. As a result, their notion of moral responsibility seems rather ad hoc.

There are not only consequentialist critics but also nonconsequentialist critics of PDE, DDE, RDE, or DER. Some contemporary nonconsequentialist critics of DDE, such as Francis Kamm, still support the priority of our duty of nonmaleficence to avoid harming others who do not deserve to be harmed and do not consent to be so harmed over our positive duty of beneficence to help others. Unlike traditional deontologists, such as Joseph Boyle Jr., who defends a categorical interpretation of our duty of nonmaleficence, she favors a stringent but nonetheless prima facie conception of our duty of nonmaleficence from a less stringent but still prima facie positive duty of beneficence to help those who need it. Since for Kamm both duties are prima facie, the stringency of our duty of nonmaleficence would generally depend on either contextual considerations or reasonable people's intuitions rather than on people's intentions alone.

Contrary to traditional deontologists, Kamm contends that intentionality plays no significant role or perhaps at most a subsidiary role in distinguishing the rightness or wrongness of an action. She argues that usually the impermissibility or wrongness of that person's intentionally evil act is because of "some characteristics of the act or its effects independent of his intention."[105] To circumvent the role that intentionality plays in traditional interpretations of the PDE or DER, such as the one offered by Aquinas, developed by Gury, and adopted by Boyle Jr., she offers the following distinction. For her, there is a significant moral distinction between doing something because one has reasons for doing it, whether the reasons be morally worthy or not, and doing something in order to causally bring about a given outcome, be the outcome morally worthy or not.[106] It seems that, for Kamm, a person's intention is just one reason, and oftentimes not necessarily a weightier one among many other reasons, in trying to distinguish the rightness or wrongness of an action.

Kamm challenges the correctness of DDE by offering, for instance, the bad person counterexample. The bad person sees a loose trolley speeding toward five people that he foresees will certainly be killed if he does not divert the trolley to a different track. He has the capacity of diverting the trolley to a different track where only one person, namely, his nemesis, will be killed. While he does not care much about the five people whom he can potentially save, he has an ideal opportunity to kill his nemesis without being suspected of a crime. So he gladly diverts the trolley in order to kill him. However, he does so because he can always claim that his action of diverting the trolley actually saved five people and thereby promoted a greater good.[107] According to Kamm, regardless of the bad person's criminal intention when he diverted the trolley in order to kill his nemesis rather than to save the five, his action is justified and, therefore, permissible. According to her, this example "raises doubt about the correctness of principles such as DDE, if they determine that an act is impermissible on the basis of the presence of bad intentions in the agent."[108]

One can offer several reasons in reply to Kamm's bad person counterexample whereby she presumably challenges the correctness of DDE or any of its cognates. First, as Aquinas explains, an agent's intention is necessary but insufficient for gauging the morality of an action. In addition to the intention of the agent, one needs other conditions for assessing the morality of an action, such as its objective (Is it to promote a greater good or just a vicious aim?), its circumstances (Is it a complex moral dilemma?), and its end (Is it a morally worthy end, such as saving the five? Or is it a vicious end, such as killing your nemesis?). Similarly, as Judith Jarvis Thomson explains, the permissibility of whether to divert the trolley would depend in part on "how the six came to be where they are on the tracks." So under some descriptions the trolley might be justifiably diverted, but that would not be so under different descriptions.[109]

Second, as I have already assumed, one is to interpret DDE or any other of its cognates as a way of reasoning when facing complex moral dilemmas where inevitably innocent people's lives will be seriously harmed rather than as a principle, a doctrine, or a rule. Evidently, one can gauge people's ways of reasoning as correct or incorrect depending on whether their way of reasoning is necessary or sufficient for helping them come up with sound judgments in the face of complex moral dilemmas. By sound judgment, I mean those judgments that cohere with ordinary reasonable people's fundamental moral intuitions and that can be justified based on other-regarding reasons rather than on self-regarding reasons alone.

As Kamm's counterexample demonstrates, sometimes DDE or DER, as I prefer to call it, might be irrelevant to determining the permissibility of an action. As my original example demonstrates, however, at other times DER is relevant for ascribing responsibility, whether moral or legal, in blaming or praising someone for his or her action.[110] Moreover, even if we were to treat double effect as a doctrine, a rule, or a principle, we have reason to believe that all doctrines, rules, or principles have exceptions, especially during extraordinary or extenuating circumstances, as Kamm's counterexample demonstrates. If so, then it would be simply a category mistake to predicate truth or falsity to DDE or DER or any of its cognates.[111]

And third, even in Kamm's counterexample and despite the extenuating circumstances, if one can demonstrate that the bad person had criminal intent, namely *mens rea*, when he diverted the trolley in order to kill his nemesis, he could be charged with murder. True, it might be difficult to demonstrate that he is guilty because he can always claim that he did it because he wanted to promote a greater good, namely, to save the five persons. So his action could be conceived of as excusable homicide. Nevertheless, if, for example, he were to confess or we were able to establish beyond reasonable doubt in a court of law that he diverted the trolley with the intent of killing his enemy, he could be tried and found guilty of murder regardless of the fact that his action saved five people.

Let us consider an example different from my attempted murder example already described above and from Kamm's bad person counterexample to illustrate the necessary role that people's intentions play in distinguishing morally permissible from morally impermissible acts. Suppose that I am a physician and I had a fallout with a frail old man whom I hate for having discovered his dark past. Contrary to my first example, this time I know that he is suffering from cancer. Unbeknownst to him, I found out that he is Josef Mengele (a.k.a. the Angel of Death), the infamous Nazi physician who performed despicable experiments on innumerable inmates of the Auschwitz extermination camp during World War II.

Mengele had performed cruel and inhumane experiments in Auschwitz that resulted in the killing and maiming of numberless inmates. In my case, I am performing an experiment on him in order to try to collect empirical evidence to prolong and improve the life of cancer patients, including possibly his life, or to kill him if my experiment fails. Thus if he were to survive my experiment, he could be tried and thereby justice would be done. Moreover, I am aware that the toxins extracted from blue scorpions are highly toxic. Also, I am aware of relevant evidence that when one uses these toxins on cancer patients, as I intend to do on Mengele, the toxins could kill them. Sometimes, if they do not kill the patients, they help them prolong and improve their lives.

I concoct my plan to attempt to perform my experiment on Mengele. I have mixed reasons for carrying out my experiment, among which one can enumerate the following in no particular order: (1) improving and prolonging cancer patients' lives, (2) killing Mengele so as to inflict revenge on him, or (3) a desire for bringing Mengele to justice. If my experiment succeeds, it is likely to bring about felicitous consequences for him and for other cancer patients by prolonging and improving their lives. In addition, Mengele could be brought to justice. On the contrary, if my experiment fails and Mengele dies, I will feel no regrets because he is a despicable person. So I can fulfill my feeling of revenge. In any case, the world would be a better place without Josef Mengele in it. While performing my experiment, I intend that Mengele dies. Mengele, however, serendipitously survives my experiment. As a result, I succeed in collecting further evidence so future cancer patients, including Mengele, could benefit from the curative properties of blue scorpion toxins in fighting their cancer.

It seems that, on Kamm's account, my risky experiment need not be conceived of as morally impermissible, since some of my plausible reasons for performing the experiment are morally worthy, and presumably Mengele survived the experiment. Some of my other reasons are morally suspect, namely, I might be trying to inflict revenge on Mengele with the intent of killing him, since I know that the survival rate of those who have been exposed to blue scorpion toxins therapy has been unpredictable. Moreover, since, in my hypothetical example, I stipulate that Mengele survived the experiment, my act had a felicitous outcome because not only Mengele but future cancer patients could be helped with the new therapy. Therefore, the felicitous outcome of my experiment promoted a greater good. Since Mengele survived, he can be brought to justice and one can help prolong and improve future cancer patients' lives.

Despite the felicitous outcome, the problem that one faces is how to determine which of my reasons, if any, takes precedence over the other ones. If my first-order intention is to inflict revenge on Mengele by torturing and possibly inflicting an agonizing death on him, then my intention and behavior are not that different from Mengele's past wicked behavior. If my first-order intention, however, is to collect evidence for prolonging and improving cancer patients' lives, including Mengele's, perhaps my act could be conceived of as morally permissible.

Nevertheless, it seems that my premeditated decision, namely, my intention to perform a risky experiment on a person without his or her consent, is sufficient to conceive of my act as being morally and legally impermissible despite its felicitous outcome. By not requesting his consent, I am showing no respect for Mengele as a person whom I could seriously harm. I seem to be treating him as a means only or equivalent to the way that we treat laboratory animals when we perform experiments on them.[112] As a result, I am treating Mengele as a commodity rather than as a moral agent.

Contrary to Kamm, I am inclined to side with Aquinas, Gury, Boyle Jr., and others in supporting the view that intentions generally matter to distinguish right from wrong actions and, hence, morally permissible from morally impermissible actions.[113] If that were not the case, then nonconsequentialist theories, such as Kamm's, would risk being indistinguishable from consequentialist theories. Our reasons for acting one way or another matter, but our intentions also matter. Our intentions are not only part of our chain of reasons leading to a given outcome, which may or may not be justified, but, more importantly, our intentions are necessary for initiating such a way of reasoning.

One could argue that rather than distinguishing between acting because of a given set of reasons and acting in order to bring about a given outcome, as Kamm contends, one could instead focus on which ones of our reasons, including our intentions, constitute first-order or second-order beliefs in trying to justify our behavior regarding means or ends. Despite Kamm's neglect of intentionality in her modified nonconsequentialism, she underscores an important point that traditional deontologists, such as Boyle Jr., seem to ignore, namely, that the consequences of an action could, at times, determine its permissibility regardless of a person's intentions. Whether it is preferable to understand such permissibility as a justification, as Kamm suggests, or as an excuse remains an open question, nonetheless.

b. Double Effect Reasoning: An Interpretation

Opponents of terrorism (either hard core or soft core), in principle, embrace the categorical immunity of the innocent. That is, they typically accept a strict interpretation of the PNCI—assuming that noncombatants are impeccably innocent, namely, innocent beyond reasonable doubt. Since hard-core opponents of terrorism defend the thesis that under no circumstances is terrorism justified, they seem committed to interpreting the PNCI categorically and hence unconditionally. But since soft-core opponents of terrorism defend the thesis that, in practice, sometimes terrorism is justified or permissible, they seem committed to interpreting the PNCI conditionally. Still, since both hard core and soft core opponents of terrorism defend, in principle, a stringent limitation on the use of political violence, they are likely to embrace a deontological or nonconsequentialist interpretation of double effect reasoning (DER).

By contrast, apologists of terrorism (either hard core or soft core) typically refuse to acknowledge a stringent limitation on the use of political violence. Since hard-core apologists of terrorism justify terrorism if and only if it improves humanity, they are likely to evaluate the use of political violence only on consequentialist considerations. Nevertheless, since some soft-core apologists of terrorism justify terrorism by appealing, for example, to just war considerations, they are likely to evaluate the use of political violence not only on consequentialist considerations but also on considerations of justice. Still, since both hard-core and soft-core apologists of terrorism typically assume that the term "innocent" is oftentimes conceptually opaque, they would likely reject the categorical immunity of the innocent embedded in a deontological or nonconsequentialist interpretation of DER.

Even if some of them were to embrace a proportionalist or consequentialist interpretation of DER, they would still reject the categorical immunity of the innocent. For example, while Sterba defends the traditional distinction between intending and foreseeing used in DER, he rejects the categorical immunity of the innocent if the intentional infliction of harm to them is "(1) trivial; (2) easily repairable; or (3) greatly outweighed by the consequences of the action."[114]

Since there is so much controversy regarding DER, one needs to have a clear understanding of what a commitment to it might entail. I will follow Joseph Boyle Jr.'s interpretation of what he refers to as the principle of double effect (PDE), but I prefer to call it DER. I will, however, underscore when I find his interpretation of the PDE controversial. Putting labels aside, Boyle Jr. uses Jean-Pierre Gury's classic interpretation of the PDE.[115] According to Boyle Jr., Gury's conception of the PDE contains four conditions, each of which is necessary, and all of them together are sufficient for an act to be morally permissible: "(1) the agent's end must be morally acceptable, (2) the cause must be good or at least indifferent, (3) the good effect must be immediate, and (4) there must be a grave reason for positing the cause."[116]

According to Boyle Jr., the first condition refers to a person's choice, the morality of which one can gauge independently of the good or evil effects. That is, one can evaluate a person's intention in abstraction from the actual outcome of his or her action. For example, my intention to save an innocent person's life or to prevent her suffering is usually conceived of as good independently of my act. That is because I am so predisposed to act compatibly with my prima facie natural duty of beneficence to help those in need, provided I do not neglect a weightier obligation to help others in greater need or avoid harming others who do not deserve to be harmed and do not consent to be so harmed. By contrast, my intention to inflict unmerited and needless suffering on an innocent person is generally conceived of as evil independently of whether I act on my intention. This is so because I am voluntarily and freely predisposed to knowingly violate my compelling natural duty of nonmaleficence by threatening to inflict or actually inflicting substantive harm on those who do not deserve it and do not consent to be so harmed.

The second condition refers to the cause that might bring about two effects. One, however, can morally assess the cause apart from the effects. The classic case is Aquinas's deliberation on self-defense. If a presumably unjust aggressor attacks an innocent person and in the process of defending herself she unintentionally kills the aggressor, her act of killing the aggressor would be justified, provided that in doing so she intends to protect herself rather than to kill the aggressor; her act is proportionate to the end intended, namely, she does not use excessive force; and there is no other reasonable way to prevent the unfortunate outcome of killing the aggressor to achieve her morally desirable goal.

One needs to understand the use of excessive force contextually. Given its perspectival nature, the use of excessive force could be highly contentious. For example, some people believe that the practice of area bombing adopted by the Allies against German and Japanese cities during World War II where thousands of innocent noncombatants were intentionally targeted was morally justified and, hence, not excessive. Others believe that the practice of area bombing was excessive and, hence, morally unjustified. Therefore, their beliefs are mutually exclusive. So, in principle, it is conceptually impossible for apologists and critics of area bombing to achieve consensus on such a debatable practice.

The third condition rules out the possibility that the evil effect of the means used will causally bring about the good effect. So the evil effect may not be a means to the good effect. If, by contrast, the evil effect were a means to the good effect, then it would violate the Pauline principle that evil may not be sought so good can ensue. From a traditional deontological perspective, whether Christian or not, that would be categorically impermissible because it would be treating some people only as means for trying to achieve a presumably morally worthy end or goal—as, for example, if one were to justify intentionally killing a few innocent people in order to improve the life of many innocent ones. If a deontologist were to typically and consistently justify the above-mentioned action, then his or her deontological conception of morality would be indistinguishable from a consequentialist one.

An extreme example of the above consequentialist way of thinking was the dropping of the atomic bombs on Hiroshima on August 6 and on Nagasaki on August 9 in 1945 at the end of World War II, which indiscriminately killed thousands of innocent Japanese noncombatants. Presumably, those who argued in favor of dropping the atomic bombs assumed that by targeting combatants and innocent noncombatants alike, the war would have ended sooner, which it did. By doing so, more lives were potentially saved than if the war had been prolonged.

The third condition is nonconsequentialist. The moral permissibility of an act would supervene upon the agent's intention rather than on the net value of its consequences alone. Yet Boyle Jr. allows that the evil effect could follow from the good effect, or that the evil effect and the good effect could follow independently from the cause. The fourth condition depends upon the necessary fulfillment of the previous three conditions. We must be facing a "grave reason for positing the cause." For example, we confront a complex moral dilemma where innocent people's lives would be seriously harmed, whether by commission or by omission, no matter which way we act.

According to Boyle Jr., if one wants to present a fully coherent view of the Catholic natural law tradition, one should interpret the PDE as a principle of justification rather than as a principle of excuse.[117] Putting aside Boyle Jr.'s concerns about developing such a coherent view, I would add that if one wants to present a coherent deontological view of DER, one will need to interpret it as a way of justifying rather than excusing certain acts, such as those typically involving double effect.

From a purely deontological position, one could agree with Boyle Jr.'s reasons supporting his interpretation of the PDE. First, the foreseen but unintended evil effect permitted by the PDE is imputable to the agent. The agent knowingly and willingly brings it about by commission, namely, by voluntarily contributing to such an outcome, or by omission, namely, by voluntarily permitting such an outcome, even though the agent had the ability to prevent it without unreasonable cost to him or to others. And second, his account is compatible with Aquinas's view of human action and intention. Boyle Jr., following Aquinas and the scholastics, argues that the moral character of an act is determined by the following three conditions: (1) the end or goal of the act, (2) the object of the act, and (3) the circumstances under which it is performed.[118]

The first condition forbids acts aiming at that which is morally impermissible even though the means used might be conceived of as morally permissible or simply morally neutral. For example, suppose we provide someone with knowledge about WMD, assuming the person will use such knowledge to prevent the spread of these weapons. Instead, she chooses to develop and ultimately use the weapons to engage in terrorism. The knowledge acquired is not immoral per se, but the purpose or aim for which she uses her acquired knowledge of WMD, namely, for the indiscriminate killing of the noninnocent and the innocent alike, is morally objectionable. The second condition forbids acts that are intrinsically immoral, such as the killing of an innocent person for improving one's economic standing or for purely sadistic pleasure. And the third condition forbids using immoral means for morally permissible ends, such as intentionally killing a few innocent people to save the lives of many innocent ones when other reasonable options exist to save the latter.

Boyle Jr. views the PDE as a deontological rather than as a consequentialist principle of justification. While those who uphold some version of the PDE or DER are sympathetic to deontological considerations, some acknowledge a difficulty with the fourth of Gury's conditions. That is, even though Boyle Jr. does not elaborate on what Gury means by the expression "grave reason," he seems to read the fourth condition that "there must be a grave reason for positing the cause" as contributing to deontological limitations in the light of what the PDE allows. Other scholars, such as Cavanaugh, read Gury's interpretation of the fourth condition in a proportionalist or consequentialist way by stating, "there is a proportionately grave reason for causing the evil effect."[119]

If we read Gury's fourth condition as Cavanaugh and others have suggested, then we would need to balance the good effect that we are trying to bring about with the incidental concomitant evil consequences that might result from our action. Hence, the role that proportionality plays in determining the rightness or wrongness of an action in addition to the intention that brings it about. This way of reasoning finds support in Aquinas's formulation of DER when he writes, "an act that is properly motivated may, nevertheless, become vitiated if it is not proportionate to the end intended."[120] *Jus ad bellum* and *jus in bello* considerations share the principle of proportionality embedded in contemporary international law under the LOAC or IHL.

For an action to be justified by DER, all four of Gury's conditions must be met which, according to Boyle Jr.'s interpretation of DER, seems to exclude consequentialist or proportionalist considerations. And yet if the human cost of the action were grossly disproportionate to the morally good end that we are trying to bring about, then we might have to reconsider whether our intended action would be morally permissible. Despite the debate on whether one should interpret the fourth condition as a deontological limitation or as a consequentialist or proportionalist limitation, one can reasonably argue that when applying the PDE or DER to a moral dilemma, the number of people who can be substantively harmed plays a role in determining whether a given act is justified or morally permissible.

Boyle Jr. argues that it is morally permissible for one to undertake an action that brings about a good and an evil effect if and only if (1) the evil effect is not intrinsic to such action, namely, it is not intended, and (2) one has a "serious reason for undertaking the action."[121] Apparently, for Boyle Jr. the phrases "serious reason" and "grave reason" are morally equivalent. Unlike consequentialist critics, when evaluating the rightness or wrongness of an action, Boyle Jr. focuses primarily on the agent's intention rather than on the net consequences of her action. That is, according to him, the morality of an action is essentially related to the intention of the agent who undertakes the action. Nevertheless, he admits that the foreseen consequences of the intended action might be relevant for ascertaining the rightness or wrong-ness of the agent's behavior, "but only in a subsidiary way." So for him, if an action is morally permissible, and if one has serious reason for doing it, then "it may be done morally no matter what the foreseen consequences may be."[122]

Boyle Jr., however, overstates his deontological limitation of the PDE. He seems committed to the view that we ought to do right even if the heavens might fall. That is, "no matter what the foreseen consequences may be." But if we have reason to believe that the foreseen untoward consequences of our action were grossly disproportionate with our intended morally permissible goal, then the morality of our action would seem at least questionable, if not wrong.

Still, Boyle Jr. could argue that if that were to be so, then our intended action would have been wrong from the beginning. Moreover, if a person intends to accomplish a goal knowing or believing that accomplishing it could foreseeably bring about grossly disproportionate untoward effects on those who do not deserve it and do not consent to be so affected, then his or her action is unjustified and, therefore, morally wrong. Boyle Jr. then seems to allow for the possibility that consequentialist considerations could play a role, even if a subsidiary one, in gauging the rightness or wrongness of an action. By allowing so, he appears to weaken his deontological interpretation of the PDE.

Regardless of Boyle Jr.'s interpretation of the PDE, the PDE has always been and still is highly controversial. The PDE is not a universally valid moral principle of action. If that were to be the case, then it could be easily refuted, as consequentialists and some nonconsequentialists typically do by offering reasonable counterexamples, such as Kamm's bad person counterexample. As I have already argued, I prefer to view the PDE as a way of reasoning, namely, as DER when we face complex moral dilemmas as a result of which, no matter how we act, innocent people's lives will be ineluctably harmed. One morally important contribution of DER is to help us develop sound moral judgments in the face of uncertain but likely seriously harmful consequences of our actions.

c. Critics of Double Effect Reasoning: Terror Bombing vs. Tactical Bombing

Consequentialist critics of DER, such as Jonathan Bennett, would contend that one need not appeal to DER to justify the morality of actions. For them, the traditional scholastic distinction between intending and foreseeing is morally opaque. According to Bennett and consequentialist critics in general, the consequences or outcomes of an action solely determine its moral justifiability. Hence, for them, the rightness or wrongness of an action depends solely on whether it brings about a net value of good over evil for those affected by it.

Unlike Bennett, defenders of DER are likely to argue that, for example, there exists a morally illuminating distinction between "terror bombing" and "tactical bombing." In their argument, they assume that tactical bombing is necessarily nonterrorist bombing. So Bennett seems to miss the point when he assumes that those who argue in favor of the distinction between terror and tactical bombing would argue that the first is worse than the second.[123] His assumption seems unwarranted. Those who support the distinction are likely to contend that the practice of terror bombing is, in principle, morally impermissible while the practice of tactical bombing need not be so. Those who engage in terror bombing deliberately target innocent people, which, according to traditional defenders of DER, is equivalent to murder. Murder, however, is intrinsically wrong. Therefore, for them, terrorism is also intrinsically wrong. As a result, the practice of terror bombing violates the letter and spirit of DER.

Consider the following two scenarios that illustrate the differences between tactical and terrorist bombings. The assumption in both scenarios is that those who undertake the action of bombing, whether tactical or terrorist bombing, do so in a just war intending to defeat an unjust aggressor. In the light of *jus ad bellum* considerations within the LOAC, the aim of those who engage in tactical and terrorist bombing might be morally commendable, since they both intend to defeat an unjust aggressor.

In the light of *jus in bello* considerations within contemporary IHL, however, the behavior of those who engage in tactical bombing is legally justified, while the behavior of those who engage in terrorist bombing is not.[124] Yet we can always bracket the legality of terrorist bombing and ask the following question: Is there a legitimate moral distinction between tactical and terror bombing even when they both aim at a morally commendable goal, namely, to defeat an unjust aggressor? To answer this question, we need to understand the nature of tactical and terror bombing.

Those who, for example, undertake tactically to bomb a munitions factory aim at destroying it as a means of defeating the enemy or the unjust aggressor so they can win a just war. They know, however, or at least have reason to believe, that innocent noncombatants will die as a result of their action. They foresee the deaths of innocent noncombatants, but they do not strictly speaking intend, in the primary sense of intention, their deaths. That is, they do not voluntarily and knowingly freely choose to kill innocent noncombatants as a means to accomplish their otherwise commendable goal. The deaths of innocent noncombatants play no part in their process of deliberation before undertaking their action. Still, the foreseen deaths of innocent noncombatants is imputable to those who bring it about. But the reason for tactically bombing the munitions factory is to try to defeat the enemy who initiated an unjust war of aggression. If they could have undertaken the operation without killing innocent noncombatants, they would have done so.

By contrast, those who undertake terror bombing aim at killing, maiming, and thereby terrorizing innocent noncombatants because of and in order to defeat the enemy who initiated an unjust war of aggression. As a result of intentionally killing, maiming, and terrorizing innocent noncombatants, they aim at demoralizing the populace. They do so in the hope of speeding up the defeat of the unjust aggressor, which is a commendable goal. By ending the war sooner, they would save more innocent people's lives. In their process of deliberation before they carry out their terror bombing missions, they intend, in the primary sense of intention, to seriously harm innocent noncombatants. As a matter of policy, they voluntarily and knowingly freely choose to kill, maim, and terrorize innocent noncombatants.

For terrorist bombers, the killing, maiming, and terrorizing of innocent noncombatants is not just foreseen, as in the case of the tactical bombers, but it is an immediate part of their action in trying to defeat the unjust aggressor. Presumably, if they could have accomplished their commendable goal of defeating the unjust aggressor without seriously harming innocent noncombatants, they would have done so. Hence, the terrorist bombers are not necessarily sadists. They do not particularly enjoy killing, maiming, and terrorizing innocent noncombatants for the fun of it.

In the light of the presumed differences that exist between tactical and terrorist bombing, Bennett asks the following rhetorical question: Is tactical bombing easier to excuse than terror bombing?[125] Contrary to deontological critics, and to some people's basic intuitions, he thinks there are no substantive moral differences between them. Evidently, one can object that his rhetorical question is misleading because defenders of DER, such as Boyle Jr., conceive of it as a way of reasoning to justify rather than to excuse behavior when ordinary reasonable people face complex moral dilemmas. When offering an excuse, we generally appeal to reasons that we might not have had control over, such as benign ignorance, accidental and hence unintentional behavior, or perhaps avoiding a catastrophe not created by one's own fault.

By contrast, when offering a justification for our behavior, we generally appeal to reasons that we have some control over, such as having knowledge or warranted beliefs that motivate us to act as we do.[126] But regardless of this objection, Bennett tries to reveal the intentions of tactical and terror bombers by asking the following counterfactual question: If they had believed that there would be no civilian deaths (namely, innocent noncombatant deaths), would they have been less likely to execute their raids?[127]

Because their raids would not result in demoralizing the enemy, terror bombers would likely answer "yes" to the above-mentioned question.

By contrast, tactical bombers would answer "no" because their primary aim was never to seriously harm innocent noncombatants. Bennett, however, argues that *both* tactical bombers and terror bombers would answer "yes" because they both have reason to believe that for their raids to succeed, they must result in seriously harming innocent noncombatants.[128] But his seems a hasty conclusion.

We can agree with Bennett's stipulation that if terrorist and tactical bombers had believed that for their raids to succeed, they must have resulted in seriously harming innocent noncombatants, then they would have probably answered "yes" to his counterfactual question. But in the face of uncertainty prior to the actual bombing, tactical bombers need not hold such a belief. Such a belief is not necessarily part of their deliberation process prior to the actual bombing. By the nature of their intention, however, terror bombers must hold such a belief prior to the actual bombing.

In the face of uncertainty prior to the actual bombing, tactical bombers intend, in the primary sense of intention, to voluntarily and freely choose to target combatants and designated military targets that contribute to the war effort, such as munitions factories, ammunition depots, military industrial complexes, command and control centers, and laboratories engaged in the development of weapons, to mention only a few legitimate targets. As a result of their intended goals, they are likely to indirectly but seriously harm innocent noncombatants, including killing them. By contrast, in the face of uncertainty prior to the actual bombing, terror bombers intend, in the primary sense of intention, to voluntarily and freely choose to target innocent non-combatants, which is morally and legally unjustified as an act of unlawful killing or murder. As a result of their intended goal, they directly aim at seriously harming innocent noncombatants, including killing them.

But, according to Bennett, the terror bombers do not necessarily intend to kill innocent noncombatants. They need only that their bodies remain "inoperative" as if they were dead to speed the end of the war. Once the war is over, if they were miraculously resurrected, the terror bombers would have no objection to their being alive, since presumably the terror bombers have already accomplished their goal of speeding up the end of the war.[129] Such a counterfactual scenario, although conceivable, sheds little if any light for ascribing responsibility.

One can always think of counterfactual situations as possible justifications or false excuses for one's immoral or criminal behavior. Suppose I deliberately kill someone in order to rob him. However, in Bennett's account, I can always claim that I never really intended to kill him. I only intended to rob him because if he were to survive, I might not object to it. Whether I might or might not object to the counterfactual situation is beside the point. He simply did not survive. And as a result, I am responsible for his death.

Rather than Bennett's counterfactual question, one can offer in its place a counterfactual test to distinguish between an intended means and an unintended but foreseen concomitant effect. For example, if the unjust aggressor could have been defeated without concomitantly killing innocent noncombatants, would the tactical bombers have voluntarily and freely chosen to act the way they did? Presumably the tactical bombers would have answered "yes" because they never intended to kill innocent noncombatants. Moreover, they would have tried to minimize as much as possible the killing of innocent noncombatants without unreasonably risking their lives in carrying out their mission.

Their response, however, is unconvincing for distinguishing between intending and foreseeing because the terror bombers would have answered "yes" too. That is, the primary goal of both terror and tactical bombers is to defeat the unjust aggressor, which is morally and legally permissible under *jus ad bellum* considerations. So if they could have accomplished their primary goal, namely, defeating the unjust aggressor without killing innocent noncombatants, they would have done so. Thus, we need to come up with a better morally relevant explanation between intending a means and foreseeing a concomitant effect.

One can argue that there is a significant moral difference between intending an action conceived of as a pro-attitude and our foreseeing probable concomitant effects related to our intended action. The following conditions are necessary and sufficient for explaining an intended action conceived of as a pro-attitude: there is a preconceived plan to accomplish a given goal, we necessarily have some control in executing the preconceived plan to accomplish such a given end or goal, and we deliberately execute such a plan. By contrast, the following condition is just sufficient to explain foreseeing probable concomitant effects contingently related to our intended action: We can expect that our intended action will have probable concomitant effects.

So we can provide a reasonable description explaining the tactical bombers' action prior to executing the preconceived plan without necessarily referring to the expected probable concomitant side effects of their action. That is, the evil concomitant side effects of their action, while foreseeable, are neither necessary nor sufficient for explaining the reasons why they initiated their action. In contrast, the evil concomitant side effects of the terrorist bombers' action, namely, aiming at killing or seriously harming innocent noncombatants, are necessary for explaining the reasons why they initiated their action.

Sterba, for example, proposes what he refers to as the "Nonexplanation Test." He asks, "Does the bringing about of the evil consequences help explain why the agent undertook the action as a means to the good consequences?" In the case of tactical bombers, the answer is no. So the evil consequences of killing innocent noncombatants were just foreseen rather than intended. Such an explanation is sufficient to account for their intended action. By contrast, in the case of terrorist bombers, the answer would be yes because the evil consequences of killing innocent noncombatants were intended rather than just foreseen.[130]

Even though tactical and terror bombers' actions result in killing or seriously harming innocent noncombatants, tactical bombers' actions seem to be morally justified, while terrorist bombers' actions do not seem to be so. Despite Bennett's and consequentialist critics' objections, we typically have a stronger moral presumption against actions intended to bring about substantive harm on innocent people than against actions that result in the merely foreseen bringing about of concomitant substantive harm on them. This is because when we intend to inflict substantive harm on the innocent, we voluntarily and freely choose to directly violate our compelling natural duty of nonmaleficence to avoid bringing about substantive harm to the innocent by commission or omission.

Our goodwill to accomplish a morally desirable goal, such as defeating an unjust aggressor, is canceled by our vicious intention to bring about substantive harm on the innocent, as terror bombers intend to do. But when our intended morally worthy action brings about concomitant evil effects, we are doing so indirectly or subsidiarily, as tactical bombers foresee but do not intend to do. Our goodwill to accomplish a morally desirable goal, such as defeating an unjust aggressor, is not necessarily canceled by any prior vicious intention. Our goodwill remains intact despite our recognition that a concomitant evil effect might unavoidably result from it.

Let us consider a relevant example of contemporary threats of terrorism. Suppose informants alert the US central command in Afghanistan that the leadership of Al-Qaeda, the terrorist organization founded and directed by the late Osama bin Laden and his associate Ayman al-Zawahiri, has been located in a cave on the border with Pakistan. They also inform the US central command that Al-Qaeda's leaders have an undetermined number of innocent American hostages to be used as human shields, if necessary, to try to prevent a US attack on them. In addition, the informants have reliable evidence that some of Al-Qaeda's cadres have managed to obtain a powerful nuclear weapon to carry out a nuclear attack in an undisclosed foreign capital.[131] They also have reliable evidence that Al-Qaeda's cadres are simply waiting for orders from the top to detonate their powerful weapon in the undisclosed foreign capital. So there is reason to believe that the nuclear attack is imminent.

Let us also assume that those in charge of the US central command briefed President Obama on the situation on the ground. Moreover, they asked him whether they should go ahead and attack the terrorists' lair by using an unmanned aerial vehicle (a.k.a. UAV or drone) to carry out a so-called signature strike or a terrorist-attack-disruption strike (a.k.a. TADS) on the designated target. Suppose the president authorizes the missile attack on the cave, intending to prevent Al-Qaeda's leaders from giving the order for detonating a nuclear weapon in a foreign capital. As a result of the missile attack, not only all members of Al-Qaeda's leadership but also all innocent American hostages are killed.

Subsequently, the president informs the nation and the international community that Al-Qaeda's leadership has been decimated but that, regrettably, an undetermined number of the innocent hostages have also been killed. Rather than justifying his action by appealing to DER, the president excuses himself by appealing to extenuating circumstances. He informs the American public and the international community that, although he deplores the killing of the innocent American hostages, he could not have acted in any other way to prevent Al-Qaeda's leaders from giving the order to detonate a nuclear weapon in a foreign capital. By having approved the mission against the terrorists, the president succeeded in preventing a nuclear catastrophe where thousands of innocent people would have perished.

Some consequentialist critics, like Bennett, might argue that the president, rather than excusing his decision by appealing to extenuating circumstances, could have appealed to utilitarian calculations and, therefore, consequentialist considerations. If he had done so, however, he would not have offered an excuse but a justification for his decision. Unlike a justification, a person's behavior might be reasonably excused by appealing to extenuating circumstances, such as benign ignorance, accidental and hence unintentional behavior, being under duress, or avoiding a catastrophe (whether imminent or not) not created by one's own fault.

One can justify President Obama's choice by appealing to consequentialist reasoning, or one can excuse it by appealing to extenuating circumstances. That is, he was justified or excused for having chosen to target Al-Qaeda's leadership to prevent a nuclear catastrophe. Once we appeal to consequentialist reasoning, as Bennett does, the distinction between justification and excuse seems rather nebulous. The bottom line is that, whether we justify or excuse the president's behavior, the innocent American hostages would still have been killed. Hence, there is no felicitous outcome from this moral dilemma—either way innocent people would have been seriously harmed.

In the above scenario numbers seem to count. An undetermined number of American hostages would have been killed as a result of the attack to save the life of thousands of innocent people. Nevertheless, the intention of the president and his advisers has been to prevent a looming nuclear catastrophe rather than to deliberately kill the innocent hostages. To begin with, the life of the hostages was already precarious. So it seems that President Obama's choice could have been justified by appealing to consequentialist reasoning, or he could have been excused for having no other reasonable option to prevent a nuclear catastrophe. Anyone who was in a similar position and had chosen to act the way the president did would also have been justified or excused for having authorized such an attack.

In the potentially catastrophic scenario that I have described, one can argue that Boyle Jr. and those who think like him about DER would likely justify rather than excuse the president's decision in approving the drone attack against Al-Qaeda's leaders despite foreseeing the deaths of the innocent hostages. The president's decision would be morally justified according to DER for the following reasons: (1) the president's aim is morally permissible, namely, preventing the deaths of thousands of innocent people; (2) the attack will bring about two effects, namely, the deliberate killing of Al-Qaeda's leaders and the foreseen although unintended concomitant killing of the innocent American hostages; (3) rather than the concomitant killing of the innocent hostages, the deliberate killing of Al-Qaeda's leaders brings about the good effect; and (4) there is certainly grave reason for positing the cause of the attack. The president's decision could have prevented the virtually certain death of thousands of innocent people whose lives were imminently threatened.

Moreover, in this scenario the president's decision is morally justified "no matter what the foreseen consequences may be." The death of the innocent American hostages is still imputable to the president. His first-order intention, however, is to prevent the deaths of thousands of innocent people by authorizing the deliberate killing of the terrorists. The resulting deaths of the innocent American hostages would be an unfortunate concomitant effect of the president's decision. Presumably, the president did not have other reasonable choices in trying to prevent the deaths of thousands of innocent people.

If the president could have accomplished the mission of killing the terrorists without killing the innocent hostages, he would have had a moral obligation to do so. Such a possibility, however, would have been unrealistic because the terrorists' deaths and the deaths of the hostages were physically necessitated. Would the president have been duplicitous if he had tried to justify rather than excuse his action against the terrorists foreseeing that the innocent hostages would in all likelihood have been killed too? He does not seem to be duplicitous at all. When faced with a catastrophe, numbers do count. To deny that would demonstrate a callous indifference for human suffering. And yet our deontological obligations do not just evaporate under stressful circumstances such as the one described.

By virtue of being a moral agent first, the president has a compelling natural duty of nonmaleficence to try to prevent by commission or omission substantive harm on innocent people in general, including the innocent American hostages. By virtue of his office, the president of the United States, however, has a weightier professional duty to protect the lives of American citizens, more so than the lives of people in general. Under the present scenario, the president faces a collision of duties: his natural duty to prevent harm to innocent people in general, and his professional duty to prevent harm to American citizens in particular. No matter which way the president chooses to act, some people will inevitably be harmed. Can the president in good conscience allow the terrorists to kill thousands of innocent people while allowing the terrorists to keep the innocent American hostages as human shields? This is a thorny question.

Some could argue that American citizens elect the president to protect their lives rather than to protect the lives of people in general. While this argument carries some weight, it does not appear convincing. Being a moral agent first, the president's compelling natural duty of nonmaleficence to try to prevent by commission or by omission substantive harm befalling innocent people in general does not cease to exist because he has taken an oath to protect American lives first. Nor does it mean that the president has an absolute obligation to protect American lives at any cost. Such an argument could lead to absurd and thereby morally suspect conclusions.

Suppose the Iranian government were to unlawfully incarcerate a few American citizens and the only way to gain their release is to drop an atomic bomb on its capital, Tehran, which will inevitably kill thousands of innocent Iranian citizens. Would any reasonable person argue that the US president has an obligation or even a right to authorize such an attack? The answer is categorically no. To argue otherwise is to try to justify or excuse mayhem on a grand scale. No one has an obligation or a right to bring about such an inexcusably disproportionate amount of suffering and destruction regardless of his or her oath.

Reverting to the above-mentioned dilemma, the problem is that if the president had authorized targeting the terrorists, he would have authorized deliberately killing them, but, as a result of the attack, the innocent American hostages would also have been killed. By having authorized the attack, the president seems to have violated not only his compelling natural duty of nonmaleficence but also his professional duty to protect the lives of American citizens. And yet at some point during exceptional circumstances, the number of innocent people's lives, regardless of those people's nationality, should tilt the scale, especially when the hostages' lives were already precarious, as I have already stipulated.

Consequentialist critics of DER, such as Jonathan Bennett, would contend that one need not appeal to DER to justify the president's decision, since for them the distinction between intending and foreseeing is simply otiose. They would justify the president's decision in approving the drone attack against Al-Qaeda's leadership by appealing to utilitarian and, hence, consequentialist considerations. For Bennett, and those who think like him, the foreseen deaths of the hostages, although unfortunate, does not affect the morality of the action. The bottom line is that, despite the unfortunate deaths of the hostages, the president's decision would have saved thousands of innocent lives. So while the president's intention in approving the missile attack can be relevant for assessing his moral character, the end result of his decision determines the morality of the action.

While one can grant to Bennett and consequentialist critics in general that sometimes the intending/foreseeing distinction might be futile, that need not always be so. For example, suppose that in approving the drone attack against Al-Qaeda's leadership, President Obama, instead of foreseeing that the innocent hostages will in all likelihood be killed in the attack, orders the attack intending to kill everyone—the terrorists and the innocent hostages too.

The president's intention in launching the attack is rather malfeasant and selfish. He wants to get rid of Al-Qaeda's leadership not because he cares about saving thousands of innocent people's lives, but rather because doing so would virtually guarantee his reelection, or so he believes. Killing the terrorists will be a masterstroke of publicity for his reelection. Moreover, he intends that all hostages be killed because he has learned that they suspect the president is having an extramarital affair, and presumably they have evidence to prove it. If any of the hostages were to survive the attack, s/he could ruin the president's plan for reelection by informing the American public about his affair. Hence, if any of the hostages were saved, the president's reelection hope would be jeopardized.

Bennett would likely argue that as long as the president's decision saves thousands of innocent people's lives, his intention is irrelevant for gauging the morality of his action. For Bennett and consequentialist critics, the moral character of the president should not alter the morality of his action. But is it really the case that the president's intention does not matter in assessing the morality of his action? To argue, as consequentialists do, that a person's intention is not necessary for ascertaining the morality of her action, seems counterintuitive. To try to separate a person's intention from her action is to think of her intention as just a state of mind necessary for describing her moral character as virtuous or vicious. Such an explanation, however, is insufficient and one-sided for explaining a person's intention. In explaining a person's intention, one is presupposing the person has a pro-attitude to try to accomplish a given goal. A person's pro-attitude is necessary for acting the way she does, for providing a reasonable explanation for having acted so, and for assigning moral responsibility for her action.

Moreover, we tend to assign degrees of responsibility to people in general and in this case to the president in particular by ascertaining whether his action is voluntary in a generic sense, namely, a deliberate choice. A person's action is deliberate if he is aware of it and he ponders on the desirability of different outcomes. A person's action reflects a free choice if he had the possibility of acting otherwise, but his choosing so is necessary for explaining a given outcome. Can we reasonably ascertain that there are no significant moral differences between deliberately approving an attack intending to save the life of thousands of innocent people and foreseeing that not only the terrorists but also their innocent hostages will likely die, and deliberately approving an attack with ulterior motives by intending to kill indiscriminately terrorists and innocent hostages alike even though as a result of the attack thousands of innocent people are saved?

Unlike Boyle Jr. and similar defenders of DER, Bennett will likely argue that there is no significant moral difference between the two actions, since for him the distinction between intending and foreseeing is rather arcane. Still, for people who defend some version of traditional just war thinking based in part on DER, there is a substantive moral distinction between the above-mentioned actions. For them, the first action is morally justified. So the president would have regretted the death of the innocent hostages. The second action is unjustified because, despite saving the lives of thousands of innocent people, the president intended, in the primary sense of intention, the deaths of the innocent hostages. So he would have rejoiced in bringing about their deaths.

In both actions the innocent hostages are killed. While in the first action, the president is not necessarily morally or legally culpable for the hostages' deaths, in the second action, he is morally and legally culpable for their deaths. He intended to kill the innocent hostages, he knew or had reason to believe that he knew how to accomplish his intended goal, and he deliberately and freely chose to do so. By the way, in the previous example, Bennett's counterfactual move would not work because the first-order intention of the president is to kill everyone—terrorists and innocent hostages alike. It is not that the president would like them to be "inoperative"; he wants them to be actually dead. Despite the president's action preventing the death of thousands of innocent people, if we were to determine that the president acted from the ulterior motives described above, he could be impeached and probably prosecuted for attempted murder.

d. Avoiding Misunderstanding Double Effect Reasoning

One can avoid a simplistic and, hence, skewed interpretation of DER by keeping in mind the following three points. First, DER is not applicable to any situation of moral ambiguity but only to situations where innocent people's lives can be seriously harmed.[132] Second, people's actions can be understood in an ordinary sense by referring to a means-end relationship. So in general, if one intends a given end, one also intends the means to bring it about.[133]

And third, one can avoid being duplicitous about double effect by conceiving of intentionality as an objective pro-attitude, namely, a state of mind aiming at a goal rather than as a purely subjective state of mind.

Since the first and second points are not as controversial as the third, I will focus on the third. Consider the following hypothetical example that illustrates how duplicity about DER might occur. Suppose a similar scenario as the one originally described in the previous section about a terrorist threat. Unlike the original scenario, however, this time there is no imminent threat to anyone. Given the rugged region and the strategic location of the cave where Al-Qaeda's leaders are hiding, the informants have explained that no one could approach the cave without being detected by Al-Qaeda's militants.

Suppose also that the informants have reliable evidence that Al-Qaeda's leadership has issued an order to immediately kill all the hostages if anyone outside their circle of known comrades-in-arms were to approach the cave or any suspicious communication regarding a rescue plan were discovered. So the informants recommend and the US central command agrees that the only effective way to make sure the terrorists are killed is by executing a surprise signature strike or terrorist-attack-disruption strike (TADS) using a drone to fire a missile on the cave. Given the internal structure of the cave, a missile attack would certainly kill not only the terrorists but also the innocent hostages.

Let us also assume that the US central command briefed President Obama on the situation on the ground and asked him whether they should go ahead and attack the terrorists' lair. Suppose the president authorizes the TADS on the cave knowingly or believing that not only the terrorists but also the innocent hostages will be killed. As a result of the attack, everyone is killed— terrorists and innocent hostages alike. Subsequently, the president informs the nation and the international community that Al-Qaeda's leadership has been decapitated but that an undetermined number of the innocent American hostages have also been killed in the surprise attack.

Many would be relieved because, by killing the top echelon of Al-Qaeda's leadership, Al-Qaeda's threat to the international community, and especially to the United States, would have been significantly diminished. Others, however, might be outraged by the glaring disregard for innocent people's lives, since the hostages were also killed in the attack. Moreover, the assumption is that their lives were not imminently threatened.

Putting aside the question of how many innocent people were actually killed, some of the president's advisers might suggest to him to try to justify the attack ex post facto by appealing to DER, since such a way of reasoning has a venerable pedigree in traditional just war thinking and it is embedded in contemporary international law.[134] In so doing, the president could attempt to disarm his critics. Thus, the president could try to justify his decision according to the four necessary conditions of DER.

First, the president argues that his goal was to kill the leaders of Al-Qaeda, which is a legally and morally desirable goal. A world without Al-Qaeda's leaders would be a better world than one with them in it. Second, the cause, namely, the missile attack on the cave, had two effects: the killing of Al-Qaeda's leadership and the simultaneous killing of the innocent American hostages. Third, regrettably the killing of Al-Qaeda's leadership necessitated the killing of the American hostages—one could not have occurred without the other. And fourth, there is "grave reason for positing the cause." Al-Qaeda's leadership represents a threat to the United States and its allies. Is the president's decision justified according to DER? Or is his decision just duplicitous, since he knew that the decimation of Al-Qaeda's leadership necessitated the deaths of the innocent American hostages even though in this scenario there was no imminent threat to third parties?

From the perspective of those who defend a traditional interpretation of DER, such as Elizabeth Anscombe and Joseph Boyle Jr., the president's appeal to DER would seem a duplicitous move about double effect. The president's explanation that his intention was to kill Al-Qaeda's leaders seems disingenuous at best for the following reasons. Like the original scenario, the president knew or believed that the attack was virtually certain to kill the terrorists but also the innocent hostages. That is, the attack and its infelicitous outcome are causally necessitated, since it is inconceivable that one could have physically occurred without the other. The president had been briefed about such causal necessity prior to the attack taking place. In addition, he voluntarily and freely chose to authorize the attack. Hence, the president is responsible not only for the deaths of the terrorists but also for the deaths of the innocent hostages.

Critics of DER could argue that if the president engaged in a duplicitous move about double effect in the scenario just described, then he was duplicitous in the original scenario too. In both scenarios, the decimation of Al-Qaeda's leadership necessitates the simultaneous killing of the innocent American hostages. However, that is a rushed conclusion, since the analogy is inaccurate. True, in both scenarios the killing of Al-Qaeda's leaders necessitates the killing of the innocent American hostages. (In the original scenario, the killing of the innocent hostages is not necessary for stopping the threat of a nuclear catastrophe.) Moreover, unlike the original scenario where the lives of thousands of innocent people are imminently threatened, it is stipulated that in the latter scenario nobody's life is imminently threatened.

One could reason that so long as the innocent hostages are alive, there is room for possible negotiations to win their freedom. The US central command and the president can also wait for a better opportunity to attempt a rescue mission, provided that, in the meantime, no emergency exists. In any case, since no looming catastrophe is in sight, the president must honor his compelling natural duty of nonmaleficence and avoid authorizing the deliberate killing of innocent people, especially the killing of the innocent American hostages.

Whether the president could have justified his decision from a consequentialist perspective seems debatable. From a traditional understanding of DER, however, his decision authorizing the surprise TADS attack seems controversial too. The attack appears to violate two fundamental norms frequently associated with DER: the categorical norm against the intentional killing of the innocent, whose violation is equivalent to murder, and therefore categorically impermissible, and the Pauline principle that evil may not be done that good may ensue.[135] Hence, from a traditional DER perspective, the president's decision to launch the missile attack in the scenario just described was unjustified and, hence, plausibly duplicitous.

Some could argue that while the president's decision might not have been justified according to a traditional conception of DER, it could certainly have been excused. If the president during this scenario were to try to excuse the attack on the cave that indiscriminately targeted the terrorists and the innocent hostages alike, those who argue in favor of interpreting DER as a means of justification would also maintain that the president's action would have transgressed DER.

According to some defenders of DER, to present a coherent interpretation of a Christian natural law tradition it is preferable to understand DER as a means of justifying rather than as a means of excusing behavior under extenuating circumstances.[136] I would add that to present a coherent interpretation of DER, either from a Christian natural law tradition or from a deontological secular tradition, it is preferable to understand DER as a means of justification. As Quinn underscores, "The Doctrine of Double Effect thus gives each person some veto power over a certain kind of attempt to make the world a better place at his expense."[137] That veto power, however, is to be understood as justified rather than excused. Moral agents are not to be treated only as means for other people's ends, even when they are presumably trying to make the world a better place. Still, whether one should interpret DER as a means of justification or excuse remains debatable.

We can modify the scenario one more time offering still a different nuanced description of it. Under the new modified scenario, there is a real possibility for a successful commando rescue operation. Suppose President Obama has been informed that instead of a surprise TADS attack, there is a real but risky probability that a commando operation might be successfully executed for liberating the American hostages. As a result of the operation, it is likely that most if not all of the terrorists will be killed or captured. Is the president, according to DER, justified in risking the hostages' lives by trying to save them?

People might be ambivalent answering the above question. Their answer will likely depend on the level of risk involved in carrying out the operation. But how can we measure risk in the face of uncertainty? Is the risk acceptable or unacceptable? That is, is the risk reasonable or unreasonable? While the end of the operation is morally praiseworthy, namely, to release and bring back the hostages safely, the level of risk for bringing the operation to fruition seems questionable.

On the one hand, the foreseen consequences of doing nothing to try to release the innocent hostages put them at risk as long as their lives remain at the whim of the terrorists. At any given time, the terrorists might change their minds and decide to kill some or to kill them all. On the other hand, if the rescue operation goes awry, the hostages are virtually guaranteed to be killed together with some or all members of the commando operation who are trying to rescue them. Even though the risk of the operation could be minimal, the end result could be fatal. Assuming that the rescue operation is likely to succeed, its failure, although unlikely, will result in bringing certain death to the hostages. So families and friends could argue that as long as the hostages are alive, there is hope for some kind of negotiated settlement with their captors. The president's advisers would probably argue likewise. Hence, they are likely to advocate circumspection in light of a potentially fatal outcome.

The scenario, however, could change dramatically if Al-Qaeda's leaders threaten to kill the hostages. Under those circumstances, one can offer a persuasive case that the president enjoys moral and legal latitude in risking the hostages' lives, since they are likely to be killed if the president does not act. By sending a commando operation, the president is at least trying to rescue them from an inevitable death. So if the operation fails, the president is not guilty of moral or legal failure. Even though the hostages' death is in some sense imputable to the president because he voluntarily and freely authorized the commando operation, he is not necessarily morally or legally blameworthy for such a regrettable outcome.

Under DER, the president could be justified in having given his approval for the rescue operation, since his intention was morally transparent, he presumably chose a morally acceptable course of action, and he had grave reason for acting. No matter which course of action he had chosen, he confronted a moral dilemma where innocent people's lives were at serious risk of harm.

On the one hand, if the president had chosen not to act, his omission would have been fatal to the American hostages. Presumably, he could be criticized for having violated his prima facie natural duty of beneficence to helping those in need, but, more importantly, for failing to act according to his professional duties as the president and commander-in-chief of the US Armed Forces, whose obligation is to protect the lives and well-being of American citizens domestically and abroad. On the other hand, if the president had approved the rescue operation, he would have risked the hostages' lives in trying to save them from a virtually certain death. Nonetheless, he could argue that in risking the hostages' lives, he was trying to act not only compatibly with his prima facie natural duty of beneficence, but, more importantly, with his professional duties as the president and commander-in-chief of the US Armed Forces to which office he was elected.

e. Summary

In this section, I discussed some of the nuances associated with double effect reasoning (DER). I argued that Aquinas's exposition of double effect can still be meaningful for developing good judgments in the face of complex moral dilemmas where innocent people's lives will be inevitably and seriously harmed. I demonstrated that consequentialist critics of double effect, such as act- and rule-utilitarians, provide a one-sided view of moral responsibility. Nonconsequentialist critics of double effect, such as Francis Kamm, underestimate the central role that oftentimes intentionality plays in determining the rightness or wrongness and, hence, the permissibility or impermissibility of an action. I followed Joseph Boyle Jr.'s interpretation of Jean-Pierre Gury's understanding of the principle of double effect (PDE). While I am sympathetic to Boyle Jr.'s deontological view of PDE, I also think that a proportionalist or consequentialist understanding of PDE is compatible with Aquinas's understating of double effect. I underscored that since opponents of terrorism, be they hard core or soft core, in principle support the categorical immunity of the innocent, they are likely to embrace a deontological version of DER. By contrast, apologists of terrorism, be they hard core or soft core, are unlikely to do so. Even if they were to embrace a proportionalist or consequentialist version of DER, they would likely reject the categorical immunity of the innocent because, for them, the term "innocent" is oftentimes opaque. Nevertheless, the bottom line is that sometimes, when using lethal force, deontological restrictions seem reasonable but so are consequentialist considerations, even when innocent people's lives are at stake. Despite consequentialist critics, such as William Bennett and those who think like him, I have offered a series of examples to illustrate how important intentionality, understood in the primary sense as an objective pro-attitude, is for distinguishing between justified and unjustified moral actions.

2. Consequentialism vs. Deontology

Ethicists, social and political scholars, and ordinary reasonable people usually contrast consequentialist or teleological theories with nonconsequentialist or deontological theories of morality. Unlike consequentialist theories, deontological theories typically define that which is morally right when people deliberately act compatibly with their duties and wrong when they deliberately violate their duties, regardless of the consequences of their actions. For deontologists, the recognition of people's duties takes priority over the consequences of people's actions for determining the morality of their actions. As a result, deontologists are rather critical of the so-called Robin Hood syndrome, such as deliberately taking the rightful property of a few rich people in order to improve the life of the indigent many. Similarly, they object to deliberately violating the fundamental human rights of life, liberty, or property of a few innocent people in order to improve the life of the innocent many. For deontologists, people's individual fundamental human rights generally defeat other people's attempt to improve humanity at the expense of violating such individual rights.

By contrast, consequentialist theories typically define that which is morally right or wrong by adopting two different approaches: by weighing the consequences of people's actions or by weighing the consequences of implementing the rules whereby they try to justify their actions. Those who adopt the first approach are known as act-consequentialists. However, those who adopt the second approach are known as rule-consequentialists. For them, if an action or an application of a rule brings about a net balance of good over evil to those affected by it, then it is morally right, and wrong if the opposite is the case.[138] Therefore, act- and rule-consequentialists alike sometimes attempt to justify some version of the Robin Hood syndrome by couching their reasoning in support of improving humanity. Whether they require that their act or rule actually improves humanity or we can reasonably expect it to do so remains an open question.

Orthodox deontologists and orthodox consequentialists construe their moral theories as being mutually exclusive. But moral theories need not be so construed. Ordinary reasonable people's moral views are frequently heterodox rather than orthodox. So for them, duties and rights are important but so are consequences. Acting compatibly with our duties, which entails respecting people's corresponding rights, and weighing the consequences that our actions or rules might have on other people's well-being, provides reasonable ways for judging whether our actions are right or wrong. Acting according to duty for duty's sake even when the heavens might fall seems as one-sided as acting according to consequences alone regardless of people's intentions and who are affected by their actions.

We can reasonably assume that by fulfilling our duties, we would thereby promote our own good or happiness and also the good or happiness of others. By contrast, if more often than not by deliberately fulfilling our duties we were to thereby bring about evil or unhappiness to a great number of people, including ourselves and those we care for, we would then need to reconsider our conduct in the light of such unwelcome evidence. Refusing to do so would be dogmatic. Since it is reasonable to believe that consequences matter too, our intention to do what is right is necessary but insufficient to justify or excuse our conduct. Morality is not necessarily about dogmas but rather about developing good judgments in the light of possible harms or benefits that we can bring about to others by commission or omission.

To act morally, we need not only discharge our compelling natural duty of nonmaleficence, namely, to avoid harming others who deserve no harm, but we also need to discharge our prima facie natural duty of beneficence, namely, to help others who are in need, especially when doing so involves no serious risk of harm to ourselves or to others. Oftentimes, however, a collision of duties is unavoidable. For example, our duty of fidelity to keep our promise might collide with our duty of beneficence to help others, and vice versa. When a collision of duties occurs, we need good judgment, namely, a predisposition to fulfill our weightiest obligation according to what we can reasonably be expected to believe and how reliable the evidence available is.

Roughly speaking, a judgment is a good judgment if it is universalizable, and if its veracity or moral import can, in principle, be well established. That is, a good judgment would apply to anyone in a relevantly similar situation, and its veracity or moral import would be beyond reasonable doubt. Evidently, such a conception of a good judgment is an ideal one. When confronted with complex moral dilemmas, reasonable people oftentimes disagree about whether they are in a similar situation or whether the veracity or moral import of a given judgment is beyond reasonable doubt. Hence, when applied to real but complex moral dilemmas, disputes about whether a given judgment is a good judgment are the norm rather than the exception.

Whether people's collision of duties could be overcome by appealing to weightier obligations, broader normative rules, or maximizing good over evil consequences remains controversial. As a result, the contestability of moral judgments per se seems unavoidable. Such contestability, however, is insufficient to establish that all moral judgments are equally reasonable. Their reasonableness would depend on the evidence and the soundness of the arguments supporting them.

Occasionally, there is tension between discharging our duties and producing a net balance of good over evil in the world. As a result, deontological and consequentialist reasoning might pull in opposite directions. Consider, for example, the killing of the late Osama bin Laden. On May 2, 2011, in the Abbottabad city of Pakistan, a team of about twenty-five US Navy Seals engaged in what is known as Operation Neptune Spear.[139] Reportedly, the Navy Seals landed on bin Laden's compound and killed five people, including bin Laden. From a deontological perspective, the killing of bin Laden could have been in principle justified because of his alleged role masterminding indiscriminate terrorist acts against Al-Qaeda's declared enemies and innocent noncombatants worldwide, including the 9/11 attacks against US citizens.

Al-Qaeda's actions, promoted and planned by bin Laden and his cohorts against their declared enemies, are evident violations of international law. For example, if we take a nonpurist approach to international law and allow that an international organization, such as Al-Qaeda, may declare war against nation-states, we can describe Al-Qaeda's 9/11 attacks against the World Trade Center and the Pentagon as war crimes or as grave breaches of IHL. War crimes are acts of commission or omission that can be imputed to states or individuals for having violated international legal duties in armed conflicts as codified in international legal instruments.[140] The Geneva Conventions identify as grave breaches the following acts committed against protected persons, namely, civilians and/or property: willful killing; torture or inhuman treatment, including biological experiments; willfully causing great suffering or serious injury to body or health; and extensive destruction of property not justified by military necessity and carried out unlawfully and wantonly.[141]

By contrast, if we insist on being purists in our conception of international law and argue that one needs to understand war as an armed conflict between nation-states, then we can still describe Al-Qaeda's attacks against the World Trade Center and the Pentagon as crimes against humanity. Crimes against humanity are defined, for example, by the 1993 Statute of International Criminal Tribunal for the Former Yugoslavia (ICTY) in Article 5 and by the 1994 Statute of International Criminal Tribunal for Rwanda (ICTR) in Article 3 as those acts perpetrated against any civilian population whether in an international or in a domestic armed conflict including murder; extermination; enslavement; deportation; imprisonment; torture; rape; persecution on political, racial, and religious grounds; and other inhumane acts.[142] It is important to underscore that the ICTY and the ICTR arrived at the same list of crimes independently of each other. Such congruence provides evidence that international law seems to accept the proscription of such crimes based on peremptory norms or *jus cogens* that bind all members of the international community, including individuals.

Despite some controversies regarding whether there must be a nexus between crimes against humanity and armed conflicts, the ICTY and the ICTR seem to presuppose such a nexus.[143] However, Article 7 of the ICC does not seem to require any connection between crimes against humanity and any kind of armed conflict. Hence, individuals who perpetrate these crimes based on a systematic policy targeting civilians can be charged with crimes against humanity.[144] As a result, one can describe Al-Qaeda's actions against the World Trade Center and the Pentagon as war crimes or crimes against humanity. Since Osama bin Laden was allegedly responsible for planning and financially supporting the above-mentioned operation, he was rightly declared an international outcast and, especially, an enemy of the United States.

Someone could object that, as an allegedly international criminal organization, Al-Qaeda and its international affiliates have no legal standing and, hence, no legal obligation under IHL or the law of armed conflict (LOAC). One can argue, however, that war crimes, understood as grave breaches of IHL or crimes against humanity, are recognized as customary international law based on universally accepted peremptory norms or *jus cogens*. Peremptory norms are binding among all members of the international community, including not only states but also individuals as demonstrated, for example, by the Nuremberg Charter in 1945 after World War II for prosecuting war criminals, the establishment of the International Criminal Tribunals for the former Yugoslavia and Rwanda authorized by Chapter VII of the UN Security Council, and the establishment of the ICC.

Moreover, by having allegedly committed war crimes or crimes against humanity, bin Laden became an international pariah whose crimes might be viewed as imprescriptible and thereby having no statute of limitation. That is, jurists who favor a broad interpretation of IHL have been cautiously but progressively moving toward an understanding of war crimes and crimes against humanity as having no statute of limitation. Their views are reflected in the Convention on the Non-Applicability of Statutory Limitations to War Crimes and Crimes against Humanity of 26 November 1968.[145] Regrettably, most of the major powers, including the United States, have failed to ratify this convention, and a few nations have acceded to it with reservations.

One can persuasively argue that the US government had the right and the duty under domestic and international law to bring bin Laden and members of his Al-Qaeda organization to justice. Since bin Laden allegedly committed war crimes or crimes against humanity, not only the United States but any government had the right and the duty under ICL to help bring him to justice. Still, ICL does not grant a *carte blanche* right for any government to kill those who have allegedly committed the above-mentioned crimes or any other crime for that matter. By guaranteeing the presumption of innocence and the right of *habeas corpus* to alleged criminals, ICL provides a legal framework for prosecuting them according to the rule of law.

One might argue that bin Laden's killing could have been morally and legally justified on self-defense grounds if it is true that bin Laden resisted being arrested, or that the Navy Seals had reason to believe that their lives were in danger at the time of Operation Neptune Spear. Moreover, his killing could have also been morally and legally justified on the grounds of justice, provided it would have been too risky to try to apprehend him. Assuming the proviso true, the duty of justice would have been discharged. Still, for those who advocate respect for the rule of law, morality and legality dictate that, rather than killing bin Laden, he should have been apprehended and prosecuted in an international tribunal for war crimes and crimes against humanity. Or, at least, he could have been tried as a terrorist in a US federal court or in a US military tribunal.

Yet since the beginning of Operation Neptune Spear, it seems that bin Laden's fate was sealed.[146] There is reason to believe that all along the intention was to kill him. The possibility of capturing him alive was not seriously considered, or so it seems. If that was the case, then, from a deontological perspective, the morality of the operation was compromised. Even the legality of the operation within domestic and/or international law remains controversial.[147] For example, President Obama's executive order to assassinate an alleged international terrorist who was declared an enemy or an unlawful combatant in the ongoing armed conflict between the United States and the international community against a designated international terrorist organization, such as Al-Qaeda, might seem to contravene the letter and the spirit of Executive Order 12333, which bans the assassination of individuals, including foreign leaders.

The executive order unambiguously states, "No person employed by or acting on behalf of the United States Government shall engage in or conspire to engage in assassination."[148] Nevertheless, how narrowly or broadly one interprets the term "assassination" remains an open question because it is not defined in the executive order. Is it killing someone for political, religious, or personal reasons? Or is the killing equivalent to murder and, therefore, morally and legally wrong?

Whether one should conceive of Osama bin Laden as a foreign leader remains questionable, and so is the idea that the United States can be at war with an international terrorist organization, such as Al-Qaeda. He was certainly not a foreign leader representing a nation-state. Still, the leaders of Al-Qaeda assume that they have a right to represent the *umma*, namely, the international Islamic community. Their assumption, however, remains opaque, since no one has granted them such a right. Moreover, who the rightful members of the *umma* are seems elusive. Would moderate and even radical Islamic scholars, politicians, and moderate Islamists worldwide who are opposed to Al-Qaeda's militant interpretation of the Quran be considered by Al-Qaeda's leaders as genuine members of the *umma*?

For those who take Al-Qaeda's leaders at their word, the answer to the above question is evident. They conceive of those who oppose their militant interpretation of the Quran as their enemies. Therefore, in Al-Qaeda's grand eschatological and political scheme, they become fair game. Moreover, whether one agrees to grant Osama bin Laden the status of a foreign leader or not, Executive Order 12333 clearly forbids the assassination of individuals by persons employed or acting on behalf of the US government.

Operation Neptune Spear seemed to have infringed on the territorial sovereignty of Pakistan. If so, that would have been a violation of international law. For those who fall back on Article 51 of the UN Charter, which stipulates a right of self-defense to justify bin Laden's killing, one might reply that such a right is not absolute. It is doubtful that a right of self-defense would justify the killing of an alleged terrorist if he can be apprehended without unreasonably risking the lives and well-being of those involved in the operation unless the alleged terrorist has already been identified as a combatant.

Combatants are "members of the armed forces of a Party to a conflict (other than medical personnel and chaplains)."[149] Bin Laden was a member of a designated terrorist organization, but not a combatant as this term is typically used in LOAC. Some might argue that once a government designates an organization as a terrorist organization, all members, especially its leaders, can be conceived of as enemy or unlawful combatants or as enemy belligerents. Still, the terms "enemy or unlawful combatants" and "enemy belligerents" are not recognized in international law. The term "belligerent" as recognized in LOAC applies to members of the armed forces, militias, and volunteer corps.[150] Therefore, neither the right of self-defense nor LOAC as they have been traditionally understood in international law would have justified or excused killing bin Laden, if he could have been apprehended without unreasonably risking the lives and well-being of those involved in the operation.

If one can apprehend a suspect, domestic and international law demand that his or her right to a fair trial be respected. Respect for the presumption of innocence is the backbone of the rule of law and, hence, it is necessary for justice rather than vengeance to prevail. Once we ignore the presumption of innocence until proven guilty in a fair court of law, the difference between our conception of justice and Al-Qaeda's conception of justice becomes nebulous. The so-called "vigilante's justice" is no justice at all but vengeance.

Some people might think that such a formalistic and procrustean legal demand in the face of evil would be morally insensitive to those who were victims of bin Laden's and Al-Qaeda's macabre policies of targeting their alleged enemies and innocent noncombatants alike. Others might see the above criticisms of bin Laden's killing as undermining the courage of those who valiantly put their lives in harm's way to bring their mission to fruition. Many rightfully admire the courage of those who successfully executed the operation on behalf of a constitutional democracy whose citizens have been deliberately killed and are under a constant threat of reprisals by a transnational criminal organization such as Al-Qaeda and its affiliates.

However, neither the courage of those who participated in the operation nor people's gratitude to them is in question. They voluntarily chose to play that role. Nevertheless, risking their lives on behalf of a respect for democratic values is admirable. My point is different. If the president and government officials who presumably act on behalf of a constitutional democracy based on respect for the rule of law, having the possibility to apprehend and, hence, try an alleged terrorist instead order to kill him in cold blood, they have a substantive burden of proof to explain how their order is compatible with respect for the rule of law and justice.

An executive order to deliberately kill an alleged terrorist resembles an act of vengeance rather than an act of justice regardless of how good people might feel about it.[151] Justice is not about feelings and, hence, appealing to people's emotions. People's feelings and emotions are unreliable for bringing about justice because these can easily change depending on a person's experience or mood. Instead, justice is about respecting people's rights, including the rights of alleged criminals and terrorists to a fair trial.

From an act-consequentialist perspective, however, bin Laden's killing seems to have been morally justified. Only five people were reportedly killed in the operation, including one of his sons and other collaborators. Moreover, one can reasonably assume that, by killing bin Laden and some of his collaborators, many innocent lives have been saved. Hence, overall, one can defend the view that the killing of bin Laden was morally right because his death and those of his collaborators brought about a net balance of good over evil in the world. The world is a better place without bin Laden and some of his collaborators than with them. And yet from a similar act-consequentialist perspective, one might see it as a rushed conclusion.

Suppose instead that bin Laden's killing had set off a worldwide massive terrorist campaign by his global jihadist acolytes against the citizens of Western democracies and their allies, resulting in the death of hundreds or perhaps even thousands of innocent victims. Under those circumstances, act-consequentialist considerations would seem to tilt the scale against bin Laden's killing because it resulted in a net balance of evil over good in the world. Moreover, from a rule-consequentialist perspective, one could argue that a rule allowing for what one can describe as vigilante's justice might bring about a net balance of evil over good in the long run, especially when one considers that the implementation of such a rule might affect innumerable innocent people.

One could offer similar consequentialist reasons if rather than killing bin Laden he had been apprehended and tried, for example, in a US federal court, in a US military tribunal, or in an international tribunal. Paradoxically, by trying to respect the rule of law, bin Laden's trial could have instigated a worldwide massive terrorist campaign by his global jihadist acolytes against citizens of Western democracies and their allies, resulting in the death of hundreds or perhaps even thousands of innocent victims. Hence, under those circumstances, act-consequentialist reasoning would seem to tilt the scale against trying bin Laden in a court of law. Rule-consequentialist reasoning, however, need not agree with act-consequentialist reasoning. Although, occasionally, an act of violating the rule of law might seem to bring about a net balance of good over evil, such as in the case of killing bin Laden, in the long run to do so could have the opposite effect. One can make a reasonable case that civilized societies have chosen to respect the rule of law precisely because acting accordingly is likely to bring about a net balance of good over evil in the long run.[152]

Deontological and consequentialist reasoning seem to be pulling in different directions. Would bin Laden's trial have been worth risking the lives of hundreds or perhaps thousands of innocent people? I am afraid that one could raise the same question about his killing. Prior to his death, one had reason to expect that bin Laden's killing was going to set off a worldwide rampage of terrorist attacks by members of Al-Qaeda and its international affiliates against citizens of Western democracies and their allies. Fortunately, such a Cassandra prophecy never materialized.

Apologists of terrorism who adopt a consequentialist moral framework could argue that bin Laden's killing was an assassination rather than an act of justice. If so, they would argue that his assassination undermined the rule of law. Thus, in the long run, such a precedent could bring about more harm than good for everyone, assuming that respect for the rule of law, unlike political assassinations, generally promotes justice. Still, apologists of terrorism who define people's rights and obligations based on minimizing harm or improving the lives of the many frequently embrace some version of the so-called Robin Hood syndrome, which seems an anathema to the rule of law.

Some hard-core apologists of terrorism argue that the well-being of the innocent many might at times trump the right of the innocent few not to be deliberately harmed. For example, Ted Honderich argues for a "principle of humanity" based on recognizing a positive obligation to extend and improve human lives, or as he puts it, "we are to save people from bad lives."[153] If that is so, then Honderich and those who argue like him must accept the view that the well-being of the innocent many at times trumps the rights of the presumably guilty few not to be deliberately harmed, as in the case of bin Laden, who seems to have been deliberately killed when he could have been apprehended and tried in a court of law.

While Honderich's principle of humanity might seem benign and even admirable to some, it could, in principle, justify the deliberate use of terrorist violence against the innocent few to improve the lives of the innocent many, provided one can reasonably expect to succeed in such an endeavor. Therefore, in principle, Honderich and similar hard-core apologists of terrorism justify the deliberate use of terrorism on consequentialist grounds.[154]

Still, if targeting the presumably guilty when they can be apprehended and tried in a court of law so justice can be served seems morally and legally objectionable, deliberately targeting the presumably innocent seems even worse. The first is an act of vengeance while the second is an evident act of murder. Unlike vengeance that might or might not be excused, murder is categorically wrong.

a. Summary

In this section, I explained the contrast between consequentialist or teleological theories of morality and nonconsequentialist or deontological theories of morality. Deontological theories define that which is morally right or wrong by focusing on people's duties. As a result, deontologists typically reject the so-called Robin Hood syndrome. Unlike consequentialists, deontologists typically defend the categorical immunity of the innocent. By contrast, consequentialist theories define that which is morally right or wrong by weighing the consequence of people's actions or the consequences of implementing the rules whereby they try to justify their actions. For them, if an action or application of a rule brings about a net balance of good over evil to those affected by it, then it is morally right, and wrong if the contrary is the case. Hence, consequentialists typically embrace some version of the Robin Hood syndrome. I argued that orthodox deontologists and orthodox consequentialists construe their theories as being mutually exclusive. Ordinary reasonable people, however, generally accept that both duties and consequences are important for determining the morality of an action, especially when dealing with complex moral dilemmas where innocent people's lives will be unavoidably harmed, such as in war. Occasionally, there is tension between discharging our duties and the detrimental consequences of doing so. Therefore, deontological and consequentialist reasoning could pull in opposite directions. I explored some of the nuances regarding the killing of Osama bin Laden in Operation Neptune Spear to illustrate the tension that exists between those two different theories of morality. Unlike deontologists who defend the categorical immunity of the innocent, I underscored that consequentialists who adopt some version of the Robin Hood syndrome to attempt to justify, in principle, the deliberate use of terrorist violence against the innocent few to improve the lives of the innocent many. I argued that more often than not that seems to be not only morally but also legally impermissible.

3. Moral Relativism

As I have already argued, apologists of terrorism can defend their view of political violence by appealing to just war considerations, consequentialist reasons, or a combination of these two approaches. In addition, I will argue that some of them might try to defend their view of political violence based on some kind of moral relativism, such as the one found in the "terrorist/ freedom fighter" dichotomy embedded in the slogan "one man's terrorist is another man's freedom fighter." Other apologists of terrorism, such as nihilists, might view the use of political violence as being beyond moral evaluation. So for them nothing is morally right or wrong.

Reasonable people, be they opponents or apologists of terrorism, might differ on how they interpret the terrorist/freedom fighter dichotomy. However, for some apologists of terrorism, namely moral relativists, no matter which side of this dichotomy a given act falls on, it could be equally classified as an unjustifiable or a justifiable act of political violence. But such a perspectival classification might seem, at times, arbitrary.

If the justification of political violence were to be perspectival, as some who uphold the terrorist/freedom fighter dichotomy suggest, then they could also argue that the principles of the presumption of innocence and noncombatant immunity (PNCI), in addition to our natural duties of nonmaleficence and beneficence, could be conceived of as being similarly perspectival too. Therefore, for them, these principles and duties would have no transcultural value. But a society, culture, or community that does not recognize these principles and duties seems to be morally impoverished.

In what follows, I will try to explain different versions of moral relativism, including nihilism. Moral relativism is a widespread but contestable view. Many people believe that morality is just a matter of opinion. So what is right for one person in a given culture or community is wrong for another person in a different culture or community despite their being similarly situated. Even within the same culture or community people disagree vehemently about fundamental moral and political issues. As a result, there is no universal consensus on these issues, including those related to terrorism. In addition, people who use the label "moral relativism" like those who use the label "terrorism" do not always agree on its meaning or referent.

Moral relativism is frequently contrasted with ethical universalism. Unlike moral relativists, ethical universalists argue that some moral values need not vary from culture to culture, from community to community, or from person to person. They defend the view that there are either transcultural moral values or at least transcultural moral judgments that can be true, right, or at least reasonable for everyone at all times.

I do not pretend to defeat all conceivable arguments for moral relativism, because that is virtually impossible. Nor do I pretend to establish that ethical universalism is true. Nevertheless, I will try to show that some comparative normative judgments, such those evaluating physical harm, are more reasonable than others because one can show them to be justified beyond reasonable doubt across cultures. In doing so, I will disarm on practical grounds the typical arguments offered by some moral relativists.

To accomplish my task, I will explore different meanings of the terrorist/ freedom fighter dichotomy. The relativity conveyed by this expression illustrates how people's perspectives and their oftentimes conflicting moral values have conditioned their views of terrorism. Nevertheless, one might argue that their disagreement on whether someone is a terrorist or a freedom fighter need not be the result only of their conflicting moral values. Their disagreement could also be the result of their cynicism or expediency.

I conceive of moral relativism as a species of perspectivism. Perspectivists defend some version of skepticism or relativism in epistemology or morality. Since I am dealing with morality, I will focus on moral relativism. Moral relativists deny that we can have universal moral knowledge. They might adopt three different perspectives: individual, cultural, or contractual. Those who adopt an individual perspective support some version of subjectivism. Their subjectivism, however, could manifest as nihilism. I identify two different versions of nihilism: solipsist and moral.

Those who adopt a cultural perspective defend what is known as descriptive relativism. Descriptive relativists maintain that, based on empirical observations of different people in different cultures or communities, there seem to be no universally recognized moral values.[155] Moreover, those who adopt a contractual perspective defend some version of moral relativism, namely, contractual relativism. For contractual relativists, moral judgments are right or wrong according to people's open or tacit agreement in a given culture or community.

Moral subjectivists, such as Mackie, and moral contractualists, such as Harman, both deny that there are objective transcultural moral values or moral judgments.[156] By contrast, ethical universalists, such as Kant and Mill, argue for strong versions of objectivity in trying to defend the view that there are either transcultural moral values or at least transcultural moral judgments whose reasonableness can be objectively gauged independent of how one subjectively feels about them and independent of any open or tacit agreement.

For Mackie, the terms "good," "bad," "right," and "wrong" do not refer to any moral properties or relations that exist independently of our beliefs.[157] For him and those who share his view, moral claims are neither true nor false. Therefore, these claims have no truth value.

If knowledge requires truth and, according to Mackie and those who share his view, moral claims have no truth value, then people cannot have moral knowledge. Yet their lack of moral knowledge would not preclude them from expressing approval or disapproval of controversial moral and political issues, nor would it preclude them from trying to justify their approval or disapproval on different grounds, such as the possible benefit of upholding their beliefs.

Once we accept moral subjectivism, arguments about controversial moral and political issues seem intractable. Terrorism is a good case in point. Consider again the hackneyed expression "one person's terrorist is another person's freedom fighter." For some reasonable people, such as hard-core opponents of terrorism, terrorism is equivalent to murder, and since murder is always wrong, it follows that terrorism for them is absolutely wrong. Other reasonable people, such as hard- or soft-core apologists of terrorism, might embrace the expression as a legitimate criticism of cynicism and double standard in politics or as an illustration of moral relativism.

Apologists of terrorism, though not only them, might argue that those who use the controversial expression are oftentimes privileging the use of political violence by powerful states in detriment to the use of political violence by nonstate agents. Those who privilege state-sanctioned violence label as terrorists only nonstate agents. They, nonetheless, refuse to apply the same label to states, even when the political violence used on behalf of states resembles and oftentimes is more lethal than the political violence committed by nonstate agents. Their refusal, therefore, seems one-sided.

One might also use the terrorist/freedom fighter dichotomy as a disguise for political expediency. People can use the dichotomy depending on their ideological proclivities. They identify those whom they conceive of as their friends as freedom fighters, while they identify those whom they conceive of as their enemies as terrorists. Their alleged friends and enemies, however, might engage in analogous despicable acts. If so, their impartiality is questionable.[158] Evidently, for cynics impartiality might be a hollow concept. They might just be motivated by whatever it takes to achieve their goals.

Since the dichotomy is ambiguous, I offer the following interpretation of it. Some people might believe that a set of individuals or groups are terrorists and others might believe that the same set of individuals or groups are freedom fighters. For example, the jihadists who attacked the World Trade Center and the Pentagon are considered terrorists by some, namely, their critics, and the same jihadists are considered freedom fighters by others, namely, their apologists. Hence, the proposition or judgment "The jihadists who attacked the World Trade Center and the Pentagon were terrorists" is believed to be true by their critics who disapprove of their action, and the proposition or judgment "The jihadists who attacked the World Trade Center and the Pentagon were freedom fighters," namely not terrorists, is believed to be true by their supporters who approve of their action.

The two propositions or judgments need not be contradictory. But they seem to generate contrary propositions or judgments based on different and mutually exclusive beliefs. These propositions or judgments cannot both be true, but they might both be false.

Despite the opacity of the terms "terrorist" and "freedom fighter," one might argue that the term "terrorist" refers to individuals or groups who use political violence deliberately or recklessly to inflict substantive undeserved harm or to threaten doing so on those who are innocent noncombatants beyond reasonable doubt, namely, the impeccably innocent. By contrast, one might argue that the term "freedom fighter" refers to individuals or groups who use political violence deliberately to inflict substantive harm or to threaten doing so on combatants or noninnocent people for justifiable political goals, such as defending or establishing a free democratic society based on respect for the rule of law.

If one accepts the above interpretations of the terms "terrorist" and "freedom fighter," one cannot truthfully describe the jihadists who carried out the 9/11 attacks in New York City and Washington, DC; the 11-M attacks in Madrid; and the 7/7 attacks in London as having been terrorists and freedom fighters at the same time. They might have been none of the above. Perhaps one might describe them as common criminals or as nihilist fanatics. Still, these descriptions seem inaccurate. The jihadists did not behave as common criminals usually behave because they acted based on a political agenda. Moreover, unlike common criminals, they acted for other-regarding rather than for self-regarding reasons, the latter of which is a trademark of common criminals.

In addition, the jihadists did not seem to be nihilists either because they were motivated by a militant interpretation of the Quran, which they believed to be true.[159] If they believed in the Quran and we have no reason to think otherwise, they necessarily believed in an objective distinction between morally right and morally wrong actions. Nihilists, however, do not believe that there is such a distinction. Hence, the jihadists cannot be nihilists.

One could argue that the terrorist/freedom fighter dichotomy might also express some kind of relativism based on people's different perspectives, including their conflicting moral values. A challenging issue, however, is whether they can justify such perspectives. I argue that if we can determine that a person is a terrorist because he voluntarily engaged in a terrorist act, namely deliberately and inexcusably targeting or recklessly harming innocent noncombatants for political goals, then that person is just a terrorist because of what he has done. Evidently, such a description would not exclude the possibility that under different conditions (namely, different contexts), the same person might be described as a freedom fighter. Being a freedom fighter in a different context, however, need not excuse anyone for having committed or having conspired to commit terrorist acts.

Some former terrorists or freedom fighters have become heads of state. Moreover, some have even won the Nobel Peace Prize, such as the late

Menachem Begin, former prime minister of Israel, the late Anwar Sadat, former president of Egypt, the late Yasser Arafat, former president of the Palestinian National Authority, and the late Nelson Mandela, former president of South Africa, to mention four notable contemporary examples. The international community, including the Norwegian Nobel Committee, is willing to ignore some individuals' violent pasts if, once they are in power or in an influential position, they are willing to promote a peace initiative. Frequently, many of yesterday's terrorists become tomorrow's peacemakers, especially if they become heads of state.

The Norwegian Nobel Committee has also awarded the Nobel Peace Prize to individuals who have been associated with a great deal of unlawful violence, such as the former secretary of state Henry Kissinger. Oddly enough, the Norwegian Nobel Committee seems to have rushed to judgment awarding the Nobel Peace Prize to President Obama based on what he might do in the future on behalf of peace rather than on his past accomplishments on behalf of it.[160]

As I have already stated, apologists of terrorism might view the terrorist/ freedom fighter dichotomy as an illustration of moral relativism. Moral relativists deny that there exists a universal moral point of view. For some, value judgments can be a matter of subjective approval or disapproval. Consequently, they can accept or reject a given value judgment depending on their perspectives, their attitudes, and their beliefs about the world.[161]

They can adopt a nihilist point of view, either solipsist or moral. Regardless of their point of view, for them, no significant moral difference exists between deliberately killing the impeccably innocent, which is considered murder by most civilized people, and killing in self-defense. For nihilists, arguing about morality is just inane.

For solipsist nihilists, such as Max Stirner, terms such as "truth," "good," and "evil" have no objective referent independently of their own convictions—whatever their convictions might be. Thus, he writes, "My concern is neither the divine nor the human, not the true, good, just, free, etc., but solely what is *mine*, and it is not a general one, but is—*unique*, as I am unique. Nothing is more to me than myself!"[162] As a result, for Stirner and those who think like him, comparative judgments of worth offered and defended by different people would be pointless. It is only what a person believes that matters to him.

According to moral nihilists, nothing is morally right or wrong. Ivan Fyodorovitch's argument in Fyodor Dostoyevsky's novel *The Brothers Karamazov* offers a classic example of moral nihilism. Ivan contends that without believing in a transcendent being, such as God, who could ultimately establish right and wrong, everything would be morally and legally permissible. He states, "if you were to destroy in mankind the belief in immortality . . . nothing then would be immoral, everything would be lawful, even cannibalism."[163] We might add that, according to Ivan's pro-nihilistic attitude, even the practice of terrorism resulting in the deliberate killing of innocent noncombatants could be permissible too; so would any holocaust for that matter. For Ivan, the notion of evil without God is inadmissible.

Still, I venture to contend that most ordinary people, including theists, atheists, or agnostics, find nihilism appalling. To argue, as nihilists do, that no significant moral difference exists between, for example, the life of a criminal sadist and the life of an innocent child is to commit oneself to a futilitarian view of the world. In such a futile world, no significant moral differences would exist between life and death, between good and evil, between guilt and innocence, and between human existence and nothingness.

Nihilists are indifferent about choosing life over death or vice versa. So for ordinary reasonable people the nihilists' motives for acting might seem absurd and hence arbitrary. Still, by choosing to stay alive, most people arguably reject the absurdity of nihilism. Even for many who have experienced extreme situations, such as inmates in concentration and death camps, their painful daily lives were good enough for them to keep on living.[164] Despite infrahuman conditions such as those experienced in Nazi concentration and death camps, most inmates found reasons for continuing living. Others, however, found their experiences in these hellish camps so humiliating and unbearable that years after their liberation they committed suicide.[165]

Suppose we were to challenge the nihilists about why they have a given pro- or con-attitude about terrorism, and they could provide two possible answers. They might answer that this is how they actually feel, in which case they would be begging the question because they refuse to offer any further justification or explanation for their feelings and convictions that motivate their actions. Or they could claim that they feel the way they do because people generally feel like them, in which case they would not be begging the question. They would rather be offering an empirical hypothesis about people's feelings and convictions.

In the latter case, however, the burden of proof would be on the nihilists to demonstrate that reasonable people actually feel that way. Regardless of which answer they provide, they deny that there are moral facts that we can appeal to in trying to settle our deep moral disagreements. For them, morality is just another way of expressing their subjectivism, or their will to power, or perhaps it is simply an empirical description of how people act rather than how they ought to act. Such a view of the world is consistent with the infamous expression that "might makes right," which has had a somber legacy in human history.[166]

More often than not, terrorists are not nihilists. Genuine nihilists are indifferent to how other people view the use of political violence, including terrorism. By contrast, for terrorists, political violence or the threat of it does matter. It is their preferred tool to try to achieve their political goals. So, for them, political violence has first and foremost a redeeming value.

The main point of contention between terrorists and their opponents is about the conditions under which political violence might be justified. Terrorists typically have a political agenda. They use terrorism either to undermine an established political order, to protect an established political order, or to try to establish a new political order. Perhaps some might use terrorism as revenge against powerful enemies who have wronged them or have wronged members of their community thereby shaming them. Their resentment could explain why they have opted for terrorism as a way to redeem themselves and their people. Such resentment, however, neither justifies nor excuses their use of violence against impeccably innocent people.

Those who defend the terrorist/freedom fighter dichotomy might conceive of it as having other possible meanings. For example, they can adopt a descriptive or a normative relativist view. Descriptive relativism seems empirically unassailable. It states what is evidently true, namely, that people from different cultures or communities and even within the same culture or community oftentimes hold inconsistent value judgments regarding the same controversial issue, such as whether the practice of terrorism is right or wrong. They harbor seemingly inconsistent value judgments based on different sets of beliefs. Therefore, for them moral judgments are perspectival. For example, some might believe that the killing of Osama bin Laden was right, while others might believe that it was wrong.

Those who claim that the killing of Osama bin Laden was wrong can try to justify their judgment based on the following set of beliefs. They, echoing bin Laden's reasons for engaging in a jihad against the United States and its allies, believe that the United States and its allies have been supporting despotic and nepotic regimes in the Middle East for quite some time. They believe that the United States has been one-sidedly supporting the State of Israel at the expense of establishing an independent and viable Palestinian state. They might also believe that the United States and its allies maintain their military presence in Islamic States, especially on the Holy Land of Islam, which, according to them, violates the Quran.[167] So they view the late Osama bin Laden as a hero or *shaheed* who courageously fought the imperial ambitions of non-Muslims and the imperialists' Muslim lackeys who have been desecrating their religion and oppressing members of the *umma*, namely, the international Islamic community.

By contrast, those who argue that the killing of Osama bin Laden was right can try to justify their judgment based on the following set of beliefs. They believe that bin Laden and his acolytes in Al-Qaeda and its international affiliates have engaged in a global jihad, deliberately and indiscriminately targeting without compunction combatants and innocent noncombatants alike. Moreover, they believe that even though bin Laden, his associates, and his global apologists complain about US support for despotic and nepotic Islamic regimes, since the beginning bin Laden and his associates have intended to establish a worldwide caliphate where sharia law will prevail, jeopardizing the lives and freedoms of those who do not embrace their conception of Islam. In addition, they believe that bin Laden's global jihad threatens the lives of non-Salafi Islamic people, including the lives of Salafi and non-Salafi Islamic women who are treated as second-class citizens under the type of Salafism embraced by him and his associates.[168]

For supporters of bin Laden and his associates his being killed was wrong because they believe that he was a hero or *shaheed* who sacrificed his life and that of other pious Muslims fighting against Western imperialism in order to protect the *umma*. By contrast, for opponents of bin Laden and his associates his being killed was right because he was an international outlaw and a criminal. Even moderate Islamists might argue that, by intentionally or recklessly killing or seriously harming innocent noncombatants, including fellow Muslims, bin Laden and his associates have desecrated the letter and spirit of the Quran. Therefore, they deserve to be punished. According to moderate interpreters of the Quran, such as Ziauddin Sardar, the only justification for war is self-defense, and the only legitimate enemy is one who wages war against you.[169] That is, of course, one interpretation among others. For example, according to Majid Khadduri, the jihad has been used on behalf of "the universalization of religion and the establishment of an imperial world state."[170]

Rather than holding a descriptive relativist view, those who use the adage "one person's terrorist is another person's freedom fighter" might be defending a view based on a normative perspective, such as the one adopted by contractual relativists. For them, the same judgment that is openly or tacitly agreed upon to be right by people living in a given culture or community is openly or tacitly agreed upon to be wrong by people living in a different culture or community.[171]

Unlike descriptive relativism that is evidently true, normative relativism is controversial. For normative relativists, the notion of transcultural moral facts would be just a fiction. Some of them contend that not only moral facts but also scientific facts are value-laden. But instead of depending on a scientific theory, moral facts are dependent upon their recognition by a culture or a community as being valuable.[172]

According to normative relativists of the contractualist kind, for example, the following value judgments: "the practice of global jihad against the infidels is right in culture A" (for example, Saudi Arabia) and "the practice of global jihad against the infidels is wrong in culture B" (for example, France) are not necessarily contradictory. Unlike ethical universalists, normative relativists deny the existence of universal transcultural moral principles, rules, standards, mind-independent objective values, or moral facts that reasonable people can invoke in trying to settle their intractable moral disputes. So they believe and in some cases argue that ethical universalism is false.

When we challenge moral relativists who support an open or tacit agreement, they need to justify it. For them, to argue that whatever they agree on is either right or wrong is to beg the question. If moral relativists justify openly or tacitly an agreement, they are also committed to the judgments that follow from such an agreement within a given culture or community. Nothing would prevent them from honoring relevantly similar agreements and the judgments that follow from such agreements in other cultures or communities. Otherwise, they would seem to be arbitrary and possibly incoherent.

In principle, their agreements could have objective moral import in the strong sense of objectivity as having transcultural value. For example, agreeing to the claim that deliberately inflicting undeserved suffering on the innocent is wrong in a given culture or community does not rule out that the same judgment can be accepted as wrong in other cultures or communities. Hence, moral relativists have not proved that ethical universalism is false.

Moral relativists of the subjectivist kind might argue that ethical universalism is false based on the metaethical claim that "all moral judgments are subjective," including this claim. So objectively their claim is neither true nor false except in the subjective sense of "being true for them." If so, they face the following challenging question: Why should we accept that the expression "being true for them" makes sense? If they were to answer that that is what they believe, they would be begging the question. As a result, we could disregard their position as unfounded because we are not only concerned with their beliefs but with the reasons for holding such beliefs.

People's beliefs might change in a rather ad hoc way. If so, our beliefs, though necessary, are insufficient for defending a given claim as true or false. On the contrary, if they were to offer another nonmoral objective reason for an answer, such as that they have agreed that "all moral judgments are subjective," we can always ask: why should we in the first place accept their agreement? If they were to answer that that is what they have agreed upon, they would be begging the question too. As a result, we could disregard their position as unfounded because we are concerned not only with their agreement but also with the reasons for making the agreement.

Those who use the terrorist/freedom fighter dichotomy might be nihilist, either solipsist or moral. For example, since nihilists deny that moral values exist, they could possibly mean the following: a first group of nihilists might have a set of beliefs and, hence, a pro-attitude supporting the struggle of those whom they view as freedom fighters, yet a second group of nihilists might think otherwise. They might view those whom the first group conceives of as freedom fighters as terrorists instead. So the second group of nihilists might have a set of beliefs and, hence, a con-attitude against those whom the first group of nihilists identifies as freedom fighters.

People's pro- or con-attitudes, however, can change at any moment if their beliefs change. Since they believe in no values independent from their own convictions, including the values of coherence and justification, they can arbitrarily change their attitudes without having to justify them. Hence, nihilists' views are rather fluid in ad hoc fashion. As a result, they could change capriciously the referent of the terms "freedom fighter" and "terrorist."

When one challenges moral relativists, including nihilists but not only them, they frequently revert to descriptive relativism. But, as I have already stated, descriptive relativism only highlights the obvious, namely, that sometimes individuals harbor inconsistent moral judgments regarding the same contestable issue based on different sets of beliefs. The point, however, is whether their beliefs are justified. Discovering people's beliefs could be as simple as asking them about their beliefs or observing their interaction among others to determine whether their answers are truthful. Nevertheless, justifying their beliefs is more challenging. Justification depends on the reasons one can offer to support one's beliefs, and whether those reasons are based on reliable empirical observations and sound arguments.

When making judgments, including moral judgments, our reasons in favor of or against these judgments could be well founded, namely, based on epistemically or morally justified beliefs, or they could be ill-founded, namely, based on epistemically or morally unjustified false beliefs. For example, I believe that the following value judgment can be reasonably and objectively defended based on epistemically or morally justified beliefs: "Martin Luther King Jr.'s way of life is better than Osama bin Laden's way of life."

I have reason to believe that the sentence "Martin Luther King, Jr.'s way of life is better than Osama bin Laden's way of life" expresses a value judgment that is propositional. That is, the judgment is either true or false. However, I accept the judgment as true not only because I have a pro-attitude in favor of Martin Luther King Jr.'s way of life and a con-attitude against Osama bin Laden's way of life. Nor do I accept the judgment as true because there has been an open or tacit agreement among members of my community and only my community about its truth conditions. Such an open or tacit agreement may not exist.

I accept the above judgment as true because I find it sufficiently justified, namely, justified beyond reasonable doubt. People with relatively normal and reliable belief systems who are reasonable and understand the possible transcultural objective nature of harm might accept the judgment as being sufficiently justified too. Reasonable persons, I would argue, have not only a right but also a duty to accept any judgment that is justified beyond reasonable doubt, provided the judgment has not already been proven false and they are aware of its falsity. Otherwise a person's reasonableness is questionable.

Roughly speaking, one can describe reasonable persons as those who are intellectually virtuous, namely, those who are intelligent, accept the value of doxastic coherence, and have a properly function belief system that generally aims and is conducive to truth in some meaningful sense of the term "truth." That is, a system that excludes expressions such as "true for me" and "true now" as incoherent conceptions of truth or as an argument stopper. Moreover, a reasonable person is justified in accepting a belief or a judgment "beyond reasonable doubt" if accepting it is more reasonable than accepting its contrary. That is, there is presently sufficient evidence for the belief or judgment being probably true. Moreover, there is presently insufficient evidence for its contrary being probably true.

For example, there is presently sufficient evidence for the belief or judgment that "Osama bin Laden ordered the 9/11 attacks," and there is presently insufficient evidence for its contrary, namely, that "Osama bin Laden did not order the 9/11 attacks." It is conceivable, and therefore possible, that Osama bin Laden never ordered the 9/11 attacks. But given the actual evidence available, it is beyond reasonable doubt to believe that he did give the order. In other words, while one could conceive of a plausible scenario under which one's belief or judgment could be challenged, there is presently insufficient evidence to challenge its veracity or its justification.

A reasonable person can offer agent-neutral rather than agent-relative reasons to defend the objectivity of the above-mentioned judgment. An agent-neutral reason is one that is not necessarily self-regarding. For example, to acknowledge having a natural duty of nonmaleficence is to acknowledge that people in general have a reason, namely, an obligation, to avoid harming those who deserve no harm. By contrast, an agent-relative reason is necessarily self-regarding. For example, to admit having a craving for chocolate lava cake is to admit having a reason, namely, an interest in satisfying my personal desire.[173] Needless to say, agent-neutral and agent-relative reasons can both be objective but in a different sense of "objectivity." While agent-neutral objectivity is based on reasons other than people's interests, agent-relative objectivity depends solely on people's interests.

One might challenge the meaning of term "better" in the value judgment "Martin Luther King, Jr.'s way of life is better than Osama bin Laden's way of life." One could argue, however, that the term "better" in this context means "improving at least as much innocent people's lives as any of its alternatives would or avoiding harming them as little as possible as any of its alternatives would." Martin Luther King Jr., who was awarded the Nobel Peace Prize in 1964, devoted part of his life to improving the lives of African-Americans by adopting nonviolent civil disobedience to combat racial inequality and to promote the civil rights of African Americans. In doing so, he voluntarily put himself in harm's way to try to accomplish a morally worthy goal. Therefore, one can describe Martin Luther King Jr.'s actions as supererogatory. His actions on behalf of the African American community in the United States were right, and he voluntarily risked his own life in acting so. As a result, his conduct was beyond the call of duty and, hence, admirable.

Unlike Martin Luther King Jr., bin Laden dedicated his life to a violent campaign trying to expel the alleged infidels from the Holy Land of Islam. In addition, he was trying to establish a new global caliphate under sharia law by indiscriminately targeting combatants and innocent noncombatants alike. Moreover, unlike Martin Luther King Jr.'s actions that one can aptly describe as supererogatory, his are morally suspect. He brought mayhem not only to the so-called infidels but also to members of his Islamic community or *umma*, which is forbidden by the Quran.

It would be conceptually and practically incoherent to defend the view that bin Laden has helped to improve the lives of innocent people without intending to harm others who deserve no harm and did not consent to risk being harmed. Even if one were to argue on consequentialist grounds that bin Laden was acting on some version of the Robin Hood syndrome by intending to harm the life of a few alleged enemies or infidels to improve the lives of the many members of the *umma*, the consequences of his actions were contrary to such a far-fetched intention. This is because Al-Qaeda's campaign of terror has killed or seriously harmed more Muslims than non-Muslims.[174]

Nihilists are likely to deny that the judgment "Martin Luther King Jr.'s way of life is better than Osama bin Laden's way of life" has truth value or moral import independent from people's preferences or attitudes. For them, the predicates true or right simply mean that some people have a pro-attitude in favor of Martin Luther King Jr.'s way of life, and the predicates false or wrong simply mean that some people have a con-attitude against bin Laden's way of life.

If we were to blame the nihilists for the above-mentioned denial, they could explain that, according to their worldview, there are no moral values independent from their pro- or con-attitudes about their experiences. Good and evil or right and wrong are just labels that describe their individual feelings and emotions about their diverse experiences. For them nothing is morally wrong. So nihilists could simply state that their behavior is beyond good and evil and, hence, beyond moral praise or blame. Still, people's behavior does not seem to be beyond being worthy of moral praise or blame. Hence, the way nihilists behave is not beyond good and evil. One could praise or blame them depending on how their behavior affects other people's well-being, especially those who are impeccably innocent.

Moral relativists do not need to conceive of value judgments as having no truth value or moral import. They could instead interpret value judgments as supervening upon the preferences and attitudes of a culture or a community. For them, the predicate true or right could simply mean that people living in a given culture or community have a pro-attitude favoring Martin Luther King Jr.'s way of life. By contrast, people living in a different culture or community might have a con-attitude against Martin Luther King Jr.'s way of life. Hence, the same judgment that is conceived of as true or right in one culture or community is conceived of as false or wrong in a different culture or community.

The blasé attitude of nihilists and moral relativists alike is incompatible with the attitude of some ethical universalists who defend a transcultural basic sense of human dignity or at least a minimal sense of human decency based on the objective nature of harm. There are acts or practices that are beyond the pale, such as the deliberate targeting of the impeccably innocent, the torturing of people (especially the impeccably innocent), the practice of genocide and ethnic cleansing, and the raping of individuals, especially when these acts or practices are deliberately adopted as a matter of policy. Nihilists and moral relativists have a substantial burden of proof to provide reasonable and convincing arguments to demonstrate that the predicates true and false and right and wrong do not have transcultural value.

If people were to accept that nihilism is true, they would probably not waste their time by trying to justify a global condemnation of terrorism. For them, doing so would be pointless. The same, however, is not true of moral relativists. People might accept that moral relativism could be true. That is, that there are no transcultural moral facts, and since moral facts are context dependent so are the value judgments depending on these facts. Unlike nihilists, moral relativists will not rule out seeking a global consensus denouncing terrorism.

Still, since moral relativists reject the view that there are transcultural moral facts and corresponding transcultural moral judgments depending on these facts, it would be rather challenging for them to achieve a global consensus on controversial issues, such as agreeing on a universally binding definition of international terrorism. While several member states in the UN have been endlessly debating a possible compromise on a universally bind-ing definition of international terrorism, the vast majority of member states have become signatories and many have even ratified several legal instru-ments identifying specific acts as terrorist acts. Hence, despite their moral and political differences and their reservations about a binding definition of international terrorism, they have chosen to criminalize these acts.[175]

We have reason to believe that people in general, especially leaders of nation-states whose citizens have faced or might face serious and real threats of bodily and psychological harms, frequently tend to move away from moral relativism and most definitely from nihilism. Still, they might do so without necessarily embracing any specific kind of ethical universalism. They could, however, embrace some kind of global legalism. That is, leaders of the global community of nations might achieve consensus on global issues that they have reason to believe could benefit all or most nations and their citizens.

I have already granted that totally defeating all conceivable philosophical arguments for moral relativism would, in principle, be virtually impossible. But one can always try to disarm some of these arguments on practical grounds. For example, suppose that in the face of what one could contend is a preventable evil act, such as the 1994 Rwanda genocide, moral relativists, having the possibility to prevent this evil act without unreasonably risking harming their lives or harming other people's lives who neither deserve to be harmed nor consent to be so harmed, choose not to prevent it.

If they were challenged for their failure to prevent the act, they could try offering several justifications or excuses. They could argue that the term "genocide" is not part of their vocabulary and, therefore, not part of their cultural or community tradition. In addition, they could argue that, in their culture or community, the concept of a preventable evil act and its corresponding concept of a duty to rescue do not exist. So they could also argue that those who criticize their moral relativism are begging the question against them.

One can argue, pace moral relativists, that the issue is not whether the term "genocide" exists in their vocabulary, but whether it is permissible to harm, namely, to kill and torture innocent noncombatants based on certain morally irrelevant characteristics, such as their race, ethnic, gender, or religion. One could raise a similar argument about moral predicates such as right, wrong, good, or evil. Whether the terms exist in a given culture or community and are meaningful there is not what matters. But preventing evil acts does matter. If people were to allow these actions to occur, those responsible for such actions would inflict significant unmerited suffering and detrimentally affect the lives of impeccably innocent people who never consented nor expected to be so treated.

Once we allow that there are preventable actions in one culture or community, there is no reason why we should not accept on analogical grounds that similar actions could exist in a different culture or community regardless of the labels that we might use to describe them. So we can argue that there are transcultural preventable actions. Yet moral relativists might reply that in their culture or community there is no obligation to rescue. They might admit without incoherence that they could prevent a given action, for example, an act similar to the Rwanda genocide, but they have no obligation to do so. In their culture or community, if they are not causing the killing or the harming, they need not be distressed about it. Consequently, according to them, to raise the issue of blame for failing to rescue would be pointless.

But is it pointless? One can argue that there is a minimal sense of solidarity with other people's undeserved suffering or a minimal sense of human decency that impels us to act in the face of preventable evil acts. Even the late Richard Rorty, who conceived of himself as a liberal ironist and whose foundationless liberalism committed him to a version of moral relativism, acknowledged the possibility of moral progress based on our identification and, hence, solidarity with others who could feel pain and suffering as we do.[176]

One can grant that, at times, such a minimal sense of solidarity or human decency could be contestable, but oftentimes what needs to be done is evident despite moral relativists' concerns. Suppose that a person is in a café in Kandahar, Afghanistan, and a suicide bomber blows himself up, killing and maiming several people. The person is fortunate enough to escape with just a few bruises and scratches. Next to him lies a child badly hurt and crying for help. The person has the strength to carry her. So we can reasonably expect that someone in his position would carry the child on his arms to a safe haven, or at least he would call for help. But he chooses to do naught. He deliberately ignores her distress and allows her to bleed to death.

Suppose we challenge the above person to justify or at least excuse his questionable behavior in allowing a child to die when he could have easily prevented it. Acting as a good moral relativist would, he could argue that the term "rescue" does not exist in his culture or community. In his culture or community, there is no such thing as a duty to rescue. Moreover, the notion of preventable evil is also nonexistent. One could also add, for example, that, in the alleged person's culture or community, the child's bleeding to death was conceived of as an act of Nature or God. So her death was neither noncontextually good nor evil, and his failure to act was neither right nor wrong. As a result, he accepts no responsibility for the child's death.

Given the person's ignorance and assuming that most if not all the people living in such a primitive community feel the same way he does, one can understand his act of omission as not being morally bad. So he is not blameworthy for his act.[177] However, one could argue that trying to justify or excuse his omission in the face of what appears as a preventable evil is likely to be seen by ordinary people in civilized societies as an insufficiently justified or inexcusable act. Despite his ignorance, one can still think of his omission as a serious failure to rescue those who are in need of help and, hence, as an act of callous indifference in the face of undeserved human suffering. Evidently, he can be excused for his omission because he did not know any better and, as a member of his community, he could not have been expected to behave differently. Nevertheless, one can always question the moral development of what appears as a rather morally impoverished community.

168 Chapter 4

Moral relativists could reply that their critics are begging the question against them, since they are assuming what needs to be proved, namely, that there are such things as preventable evil acts and a corresponding duty to rescue people from these acts. We can agree that those who criticize them are indeed begging the question against them. However, we can note instead that the following question needs an answer: Which culture or community is preferable? One where, other things being equal, people acknowledge a minimal threshold of human solidarity or human decency with a corresponding duty to rescue people from preventable evil acts? Or one where, other things being equal, the notions of preventable evil and its corresponding duty to rescue is nonexistent? Perhaps the answers to these questions are underdetermined from a moral relativist point of view. Yet there is ample historical evidence to support the view that indifference to human suffering has contributed a great deal to evil that it seems reasonable to believe could have been prevented before it unfolded.

Moral relativists might contend that to speculate on what people could have done in a given situation is not illuminating because one would never know with any degree of certainty the answer to hypothetical questions. We can grant them that too. Still, our reasoning is partly based on hypothetical conjectures. If we were unable to reason hypothetically, we would not be able to reason well. That is partly the reason why we oftentimes pass judgment on people's behavior because we think that they could and should have acted otherwise. If we were to think that they could not have acted otherwise, it would be pointless for us to pass those judgments. So if we were living in a futilitarian universe, we would not be passing those judgments. Since we are passing those judgments, we therefore have reason to believe that we are not living in a futilitarian universe.

We can always raise the question: Is it really the case that the evil could have been prevented? When dealing with complex historical events, the answers to hypothetical conjectures are debatable. For example, was the Armenian genocide perpetrated by the Ottoman Empire, nowadays the Republic of Turkey, during and after World War I a reasonably preventable evil? Were the Stalinist purges and kangaroo trials of the 1930s reasonably preventable evils? One might ask a similar question about the Soviet Gulag, the infamous Rape of Nanking and other atrocities committed by the Japanese in Manchuria during the late 1930s, the British area bombing of German civilians during World War II, the US dropping of the atomic bombs on Hiroshima and Nagasaki at the end of World War II, Mao's Cultural Revolution during the late 1960s, Pol Pot's genocide in Cambodia during the 1970s, the Rwanda genocide in 1994, and the epitome act of infamous evil—the Nazi Holocaust during World War II.

We are generally distressed about these and other infamous historical events because people deliberately perpetrated them, and we believe that the local communities where these events occurred and the global community too failed to stop the perpetrators from committing these evil acts. We usually believe that some people could have prevented the perpetrators from committing such evil acts, but they chose not to do anything or they did not try hard enough when they could have done something to prevent these acts. Perhaps we are deceiving ourselves. If so, then these acts were not after all really preventable evil acts.

Some might even believe that these acts had to occur. Such fatalism, however, is baffling at best because it entails a physical or metaphysical necessity that is difficult to comprehend. One can wonder about why so many of us are still distressed about past evil acts. Are we distressed because people actually perpetrated these evil acts? Are we distressed because nobody prevented these evil acts? Or are we distressed because people actually perpetrated these evil acts, and we believe that others could have done something about it to prevent them, but they either did not do anything or they did not try hard enough?

Let us put aside for a moment complex historical events, and let us revert to my pedestrian example about allowing the child to bleed to death when the person could have saved her without unreasonable cost to himself and others. It seems that we could have expected him to save the child if he were a member of any civilized society. The bleeding unto death of the child was a preventable evil, which he had the possibility of stopping but failed to do so. For him to argue, as some moral relativists might argue, that the concepts of preventable evil and a duty to rescue do not exist in his culture or community and, hence, it is pointless to talk about his failure to rescue the child seems unconvincing.

Despite moral relativists' concerns, the alleged person's omission can be seen as an excusable but still preventable evil. His appeal to ignorance and moral relativism are unpersuasive. One can conceive of a culture or community that lacks the concept and understanding of a duty to rescue and allows for such insensitive behavior as a rather primitive culture or community whose moral worth is questionable.

a. Summary

In this section, I explored the challenge that relativism in general and moral relativism in particular offers to traditional moral theories. A good illustration of this challenge is shown by the hackneyed expression "one person's terrorist is another person's freedom fighter." I offered different interpretations of this expression. Those who use this expression might use it to criticize cynicism or expediency in politics or to defend some kind of perspectivism and thereby relativism. They are either nihilists or moral relativists. For nihilists, there are no moral facts. Hence, for them there are no transcultural moral values that correspond to those facts. According to them, people just have pro- or con-attitudes about their experiences. For moral relativists, value judgments have no objective universal truth value. Nor do they have universal moral import. Rather than offering an empirical hypothesis of how people actually behave, as descriptive relativists do, moral relativists offer a normative principle, namely that the same judgment that is openly or tacitly agreed upon to be true or right by people living in a given culture or community is openly or tacitly agreed upon to be false or wrong by people living in a different culture or community. Hence, like nihilists, moral relativists contend that there are no transcultural moral facts. Despite rejecting the existence of transcultural moral facts, they allow for the possibility of achieving consensus on specific contestable issues, such as terrorism. I acknowledged that totally defeating all conceivable arguments for moral relativism would, in principle, be a virtually impossible task. Instead, I offered plausible reasons to try to disarm on practical grounds some typical arguments of moral relativism. I argued that if we accept that there are transcultural preventable acts, then we have sufficient reason to believe on analogical grounds that there are transcultural preventable evil acts with a corresponding duty to rescue innocent people from these acts. I showed that some comparative normative judgments based on the objectivity of physical harm are more reasonable than others. I offered several examples that could be conceived of as preventable evil acts, such as the 1994 Rwanda genocide. Moreover, if we accept that it is possible in a practical sense to think that there are transcultural preventable evil acts, then the burden of proof is on moral relativists who deny such a possibility based on their appeal to ignorance and contextual considerations. A culture or community that lacks a duty to rescue and allows for the callous behavior that I have already described can be conceived of as a rather primitive culture or community whose moral worth is questionable.

4. Supreme Emergency

Apologists of terrorism, but not only them, can try to justify or excuse terrorism by appealing to a supreme emergency. A call to supreme emergency resembles a call to last-resort policies or actions whose morality or legality under normal circumstances one could question, but that under stressful circumstances, such as war, one might justify or excuse; for example, using massive lethal force against an unjust enemy after one exhausts all reasonably conceivable peaceful means to solve a political impasse. Since for ordinary reasonable people the use of lethal force should be the last option, a call to supreme emergency to justify or excuse the use of morally suspect policies or actions is likely to generate moral distress to those who are ready to make such a call.

Despite our fallibility and uncertainty, sometimes we must act in light of what we perceive as a morally or legally suspect decision, such as deliberately targeting innocent noncombatants to try to prevent a catastrophe and, hence, to promote a greater good. Supreme emergency is an instance of such a morally or legally questionable decision. As Michael Walzer argues, supreme emergency is a matter of life and death.

Oftentimes, however, a call to supreme emergency is a call to defend a certain *Weltanschauung*, such as the principles of liberal democracy or a nation's independence. Presumably, the nation whose independence one is trying to defend embodies a morally worthwhile way of life. In choosing to defend such a morally worthwhile way of life, one deliberately puts innocent people's lives in harm's way. As a result, leaders and representatives of a political community can face an ineluctable moral dilemma: either they deliberately kill innocent noncombatants to try to salvage their political community, or the latter will perish, so they may believe.

As individuals, Walzer argues, we can opt to sacrifice ourselves rather than to violate the moral law by deliberately killing innocent noncombatants. As representatives of a political community, he argues, we must do what is necessary to save it.[178] Still, our natural moral duties as individuals do not vanish just because, as representatives of a given political community, we might acquire certain self-assumed duties, such as a patriotic duty to defend the independence of our political community.

Serious doubts exist about Walzer's description of supreme emergency. One can argue that a political community must be a morally worthy community to deliberately sacrifice innocent people's lives on its behalf. People have no collective or individual moral obligation to defend a morally unworthy community regardless of whether or not they have promised to do so. A promise to do that which is morally suspect is not morally binding on the promisee. In trying to defend the notion of supreme emergency, Walzer conflates the notions of regime, state, and nation. Rodin pointedly contends that one ascribes the right of national self-defense to states rather than to nations or communities, as Walzer assumes. The notions of nations or communities are too amorphous to ground the aforementioned right. So no necessary overlapping exists among a community, a nation, and a state.[179]

The punishment that befalls on innocent noncombatants as a result of belonging to an aggressive or a tyrannical regime, which might or might not represent the wishes and needs of a political community, thus seems morally dubious. So it is also Walzer's assertion that "citizenship is a common destiny."[180] And yet, as an empirical statement, his assertion is regrettably accurate. In stressful situations, such as war and *post bellum* reparations imposed on the vanquished, the destiny of combatants and innocent noncombatants is frequently intertwined.[181]

Walzer focuses on Winston Churchill's behavior at the beginning of
World War II to illustrate what he means by the expression "supreme emergency." During the early days of the war, when the German armed forces
seemed unstoppable and the possibility of a British defeat seemed real,
Churchill, the prime minister of Great Britain, used a cri de coeur of supreme
emergency to justify or excuse suspending or ignoring temporarily the law of
war in trying to forefend the Nazi aggression. In so doing, he was also trying
to prevent what might have appeared to him as a possible catastrophic and
shameful British defeat at the hands of Nazi Germany.

According to Churchill, "Our defeat would mean an age of barbaric violence, and would be fatal, not only to ourselves, but to the independent life
of every small country in Europe." He continued, "The letter of the law must
not in *supreme emergency* [my italics] obstruct those who are charged with
its protection and enforcement. . . ." Under supreme emergency, he argued,
"humanity rather than legality must be our guide."[182]

Apparently, for Churchill, one's moral compass during supreme emergency should be the survival and well-being of humanity rather than
the protection and enforcement of law—either domestic or international.
He assumed that the use of law would be futile if those who are conquered
by a vicious aggressor, such as the Nazis, were forced into an undignified
way of life that might include the arbitrary destruction of certain groups of
people or the enslavement of a whole population. However, was there any
credible evidence in 1940 that, despite their xenophobic anti-Semitic ideology and aggressive behavior, the Nazis were going to destroy and enslave
every nation they would have conquered, including the British? An affirma-
tive answer is dubious.

In the above-mentioned context, Churchill appealed to supreme emergency to stop the delivery of iron ore from Norway to Germany by laying
minefields in Norwegian territorial waters. Norway, however, was a friendly
country. Hence, Churchill's act was an evident violation of the law of war.[183]
So Walzer acknowledges that Churchill's act was far from a supreme emergency.[184] Churchill's call of supreme emergency at the time was simply an
inexcusable call on behalf of British expediency at the expense of Norway's
neutrality. The British behavior subsequently seemed to have provided an
excuse for Nazi Germany to invade Norway. It is precisely the Churchillian
plasticity of the concept of supreme emergency that renders it not only
vacuous but also most dangerous.

Subsequently, by using his cri de coeur of supreme emergency, Churchill
tried to justify or excuse bombing German cities as a result of which thousands of innocent civilians were deliberately and systematically killed or
maimed. According to him, he violated the law of war to save "humanity."
His view of humanity, however, is arguably skewed. According to him, not

only the Nazis and their acolytes, but also all Germans, including the impeccably innocent, such as infants, the mentally and physically challenged, the elderly, and the chronically ill, were excluded from his conception of humanity. Hence, Churchill had a one-sided view of humanity.

Even the French, erstwhile Britain's allies, were the victims of Churchillian supreme emergency. Fearing that the French fleet could have fallen into Germany's hands after France signed the 1940 armistice with Germany, and despite an explicit promise by France's naval minister Admiral Darlan never to surrender the French fleet to the Nazis, Churchill offered a humiliating ultimatum to the French government. He demanded that the French fleet join the British to fight the Nazi regime, which the French could not have done without violating their already signed armistice with Germany. If not, Churchill demanded instead that the French fleet could have sailed to British ports, which again would have violated the armistice.

Barring the above-mentioned options, Churchill offered the French fleet the possibility of sailing away to other French ports somewhere in the world or even to the United States, if they so desired. If the French did not comply with his ultimatum, he ordered the British Royal Navy to scuttle the French vessels, thereby preventing them from falling into Germany's hands. Thereafter the British Royal Navy executed Churchill's ultimatum.

A telling example was the British attack on French vessels stationed at the harbor of Mers-el-Kébir, Algeria. British vice admiral Sir James Summerville, complying with Churchill's ultimatum, reluctantly ordered on July 3, 1940, an attack on the vessels, killing over one thousand French sailors and officers and wounding numberless others. The French felt betrayed. They were justifiably incensed by the British action. Whether Churchill's extreme measure against a former ally was justified or excused by supreme emergency was questionable then and still remains debatable nowadays.[185]

Not only the British Royal Navy, but especially the British Royal Air Force, adopted a morally dubious strategy based on Churchill's call of supreme emergency. Instead of traditional tactical bombing aimed at the enemy's military targets, such as enemy combatants, military installations, munitions factories, and control and command centers, Churchill approved the infamous implementation of strategic or area bombing aimed at the enemy's civilian population. In his reflections on World War I, Churchill had ominously augured the possibility of adopting area bombing as a policy in future wars.[186] The labels "strategic" or "area" bombing are just euphemisms for the terrorist bombing of civilians. How else can one describe a policy of deliberately and systematically targeting innocent civilians?

While prior to 1940 no specific international legally binding instruments existed outlawing the practice of area bombing, one might argue that the spirit animating international law could have been broadly construed as forbidding such a deplorable practice. For instance, Article 25 of the 1907 Annex to the Convention (Hague IV) Regulations Respecting the Laws and Custom of War on Land is unambiguously clear about prohibiting targeting civilian towns, which entails a prohibition against targeting innocent civilians. The article states, "The attack or bombardment, by whatever means, of towns, villages, dwellings, or buildings which are undefended is prohibited." It is casuistry to argue that these prohibitions are applicable only to war on land and not necessarily to aerial bombardments.

The analogy between the regulations of war on land and aerial warfare appears to be strong, especially in the light of the relevant parts of the Hague Conventions that are conceived of as *jus cogens* or peremptory norms binding on all states.[187] The International Military Tribunal at Nuremberg in 1946 and the International Criminal Tribunal for the former Yugoslavia in 1993 acknowledge the existence of such peremptory norms.[188] Even if the legality of area bombing was legally opaque prior to 1940, its immorality was certainly pellucid. Ordinary reasonable people considered back then as well as nowadays the deliberate and systematic killing of innocent civilians to be murder.

One can argue that the practice of area bombing prior to and during the 1940s could have been interpreted as a criminal act, namely, a war crime, regardless of the motives and ideological reasons expressed by those who perpetrated these acts. Since people who engage in the practice of area bombing deliberately and systematically target innocent civilians, and doing so is proscribed by IHL, it necessarily follows that such a practice is unambiguously conceived of as a war crime nowadays.[189]

Still, the ratification of international legal instruments after 1945, such as the Geneva Conventions, cannot change the nature of the acts committed prior to the ratification of these conventions. If that were not to be so, then the legality and, more importantly, the morality of the International Military Tribunal at Nuremberg (a.k.a. the Nuremberg Trials) and the International Tribunal for the Far East (a.k.a. the Tokyo Trials) after World War II would have been suspect. The tribunals violated the legal principle of *nullem crimen, nulla poena sine lege* according to which no crime and, hence, no punishment is warranted without the prior existence of law. To that extent the tribunals were legally anomalous. Hence, their legality was and still remains highly debatable. Despite the above anomaly, however, the justification of these tribunals seems morally compelling.

Human decency could not have allowed the exceptional nature of Nazi crimes to go unpunished. And yet back then there were no legal precedents for such international tribunals under international law. Thereafter, the tribunals have become an integral part of current ICL. Despite the questionable legality of the International Military Tribunal at Nuremberg and at

Tokyo, one can argue with hindsight that as a result of these trials international law has been improved, for example, by criminalizing genocide and aggressive war and by recognizing individual responsibility for these and other heinous crimes.[190] Still, it is revealing that during the trials the Allies did not indict the Nazis for having initiated the practice of area bombing, which it is arguably a war crime. If the Allies had done so, they could have been charged with double standard.[191] The specter of victor's justice still lingers on.[192]

Apparently, people who appeal to a supreme emergency, as Churchill did back then and Walzer defends nowadays, believe that their appeal somewhat miraculously changes the nature of abominable acts. They might believe that their motives justify or at least excuse those acts. Perhaps they believe that, during a state of emergency, utilitarian reasoning can justify the practice of area bombing because allegedly such practice succeeded in ending the war sooner. Assuming so, they might argue that with area bombings more lives were potentially saved. However, their argument is inconclusive, since there is no way to verify or falsify such a claim. Moreover, Walzer seems unpersuaded by utilitarian calculations. He writes, "to kill 278,966 civilians (the number is made up) in order to avoid the deaths of an unknown but probably larger number of civilians and soldiers is surely a fantastic, godlike, frightening, and horrendous act."[193]

We will never know whether more actual lives were saved by the practice of area bombing. We do know, however, that such an insidious practice destroyed the lives of tens of thousands of innocent noncombatants.[194] Deliberately killing innocent noncombatants by appealing to one's survival or the survival of one's community is neither a courageous act nor a heroic act. It is a tragic and shameful act. In addition, doing so on behalf of lofty ideals, such as defending "humanity," and doing the same in the name of morally questionable ideas, such as defending the myth of an Aryan race or the Thousand Year Reich, provides no consolation for those on the receiving end.

Churchill, however, was on the victor's side of the war. Still, if the Allies had lost the war, their political and military leaders who had sanctioned systematic area bombing against innocent noncombatants would likely have been prosecuted for war crimes. Or, given the vicious nature of the Nazi regime and Imperial Japan, probably they would have been executed with no legal recourse. Legality then seems capricious depending on who has the power to enforce it.

What makes it criminal to deliberately kill or seriously harm innocent civilians if one loses a war and legal if one wins it? Or, more pointedly, as Robert McNamara underscores in the film The *Fog of War*, "what makes it immoral if you lose and not immoral if you win?"[195] Regardless of the fog of war, morality and legality are not about winning but about respecting people's rights while acknowledging our duties to them. In trying to win a presumably just war at virtually any cost, we might end up losing our souls, namely, our own humanity.

If we want our moral, legal, and political views to be credible rather than vulnerable to being considered ideologically spurious, we must apply them consistently. We are not, however, referring to a foolish consistency whatever might come. Instead, we are referring to a consistency based on relevantly similar evidence. In war, as in politics, moral and legal consistency is the exception rather than the norm. Unfortunately, political expediency camouflaged as morality or legality creates havoc before the imminence of war, during war, and immediately after war.

The victor can always try the vanquished for war crimes, but not conversely. There might not be a neutral third party one can appeal to in trying the victor for having committed similar crimes. Even if there were a neutral third party, more likely than not the victor would refuse to accept it. Francisco de Vitoria suggested back in the sixteenth century that the laws of war require that "The victor must think of himself as a judge sitting in judgment between two commonwealths . . . he must not pass sentence as the prosecutor, but as a judge."[196] Despite Vitoria's suggestion, not only the enforcement of *jus post bellum* but also the enforcement of *jus ad bellum* and *jus in bello* are frequently partial because powerful nations impose their will on the less powerful ones.

The enforcement of *jus post bellum* is especially one-sided because the vanquished has no political power to try the victor for similar crimes. Hence, the widespread use of the adage "victor's justice." The victor, who has won political power over the vanquished, always speaks with a louder voice on behalf of humanity than does the vanquished. It is only after the dust has settled and sufficient time has passed for taming people's passions that we can reflect with hindsight not only on the victor's virtues but also on their vices.

Walzer not only borrowed the expression "supreme emergency" from Churchill, but he also condones, although reluctantly, the British area bombings of German cities at the beginning of the war, from 1940 to 1941, by appealing to a supreme emergency. In doing so, he seems to lionize Churchill's approval of area bombings. At the time, according to Walzer, the Nazi threat was imminent and the possibility of a British defeat at the hands of the Nazis was real. Thereafter, so he argues, the practice of area bombing was unjustified because "it had become clear that Germany could no longer win the war."[197]

As I have already noted, when Churchill used the expression "supreme emergency," as quoted by Walzer, he tried to justify or excuse violating international law by laying minefields in Norwegian territorial waters to intersect the delivery of iron ore from Norway to Germany. In so doing, he expected to slow down and, hence, to undermine Germany's war efforts. Yet there is a substantive moral difference between illegally laying minefields in a friendly nation's territorial waters and deliberately killing innocent civilians. The first is an act of war while the latter is arguably a war crime.

Walzer's defense of supreme emergency is puzzling because he is also a hard-core opponent of terrorism. He offers at least two different definitions of terrorism. For him, terrorism "is the random murder of innocent people."[198] He also characterizes terrorism "as an attack upon the innocent."[199] Both definitions refer to the deliberate or reckless killing of the innocent. Since the deliberate or reckless killing of the innocent is equivalent to murder, and murder is always wrong, it necessarily follows that, according to Walzer, "every act of terrorism is a wrongful act."[200]

What is paradoxical is that Walzer's support of the doctrine of supreme emergency allows for the intentional killing of innocent noncombatants. According to him, "supreme emergency is a time for heroic decision." He explains, "A supreme emergency exists when our deepest values and our collective survival are in imminent danger."[201] His paradigmatic example of supreme emergency is Churchill's approval of area bombing against the civilian German population at the beginning of the war.

Churchill expected the Germans to be so horrified and intimidated by the carnage resulting from the area bombing campaign that they would have tried to overthrow the Nazis, or at least they would have forced them to stop their aggression. In the spirit of Churchill, Walzer considers Nazism "a threat to human values so radical that its imminence would surely constitute a supreme emergency; and this example can help us understand why lesser threats might not do so."[202]

As noted by others, Walzer's views on terrorism and supreme emergency seem not only puzzling but possibly inconsistent.[203] He is an absolutist when repudiating terrorism. For him, terrorism is always wrong. Under a supreme emergency, however, he allows for the intentional killing of innocent non-combatants, which is how he defines terrorism. Walzer argues that a supreme emergency is an exceptional situation. He could argue that, under a supreme emergency, he does not really justify the intentional killing of noncombatants, but rather he just excuses such behavior. It is doubtful, however, that the distinction between justification and excuse would avoid Walzer's incoherent position.

The following conditions are relevant for morally evaluating a supreme emergency. First and foremost, the community being attacked must be represented by a relatively morally worthy or at least a minimally decent political regime. Second, according to Walzer, the threat to the community's existence, presumably represented by a morally worthy political or at least a minimally decent regime, must be imminent. That is, the aggressor is about to vanquish it. Third, the threat must also be grave or catastrophic. That is, one expects the aggressor not only to defeat the defending state but also to massacre and enslave its citizens. Fourth, there is no reasonable alternative means to ward off the aggression. That is, one might conceive of supreme emergency as the reasonable last resort. And fifth, suspending the PNCI, as Churchill suggested, and thereby targeting the innocent noncombatants of the offending state is likely to stop the threat to the offended state.

A regime is relatively morally worthy if and only if it respects the dignity of its individual citizens by protecting their fundamental human rights and equal right to help shape not only their destinies as individuals but also the destiny of their community according to the rule of law more so than other existing regimes do. A regime is minimally decent only if it does not systematically torture, incarcerate, intimidate, or discriminate against citizens in general and peaceful political opponents in particular. For example, Western constitutional democracies are relatively morally worthy regimes or at least minimally decent ones. A regime that systematically violates the above-mentioned conditions is neither morally worthy nor minimally decent. The Democratic People's Republic of North Korea, the People's Republic of China, the Republic of Cuba, the Republic of Zimbabwe, the Syrian Arab Republic, and the Kingdom of Saudi Arabia are just a few examples of repressive and, hence, indecent regimes.

During a supreme emergency, those who are being attacked must have the *jus ad bellum* principle of just cause on their side, such as the British did during World War II. An indecent and, hence, morally unworthy political regime, such as the former Nazi regime in Germany or the former Imperial regime in Japan did not impose a moral obligation on their citizens to defend these regimes because their leaders deliberately and systematically engaged in substantive violation of fundamental human rights, including the practice of aggression and genocide. By virtue of their abominable behavior, these political regimes forfeited their right to rule over their citizens. Hence, the citizens of morally suspect political regimes have a right to disobey their unjust laws and a right to overthrow them if possible, assuming they can do so without unreasonably harming others who neither deserve to be harmed nor consent to be so harmed.

The same way that a murderer cannot be conceived of as a minimally decent person, thereby forfeiting his right to liberty and possibly his right to life if convicted, a political regime that engages in substantive and systematic violation of fundamental human rights, including the practice of aggression, genocide, or democide, cannot be conceived of as a minimally decent regime, thereby forfeiting its right to exist as a sovereign member of a civilized international community. Morally unworthy political regimes ought not to exist. Their citizens and the international community of nations would be better off if tyrannical regimes were not around. Regrettably, their existence is an anomaly that sometimes is too costly to fix, especially when tyrannical regimes are powerful. So the world community engages with some of these regimes based on considerations of expediency to benefit other members of the world community or to prevent a worse state of affairs.

Morally unworthy political regimes engage in morally and legally despicable behavior, such as adopting a policy of aggression; practicing genocide, democide, or ethnic cleansing; or systematically implementing brutal and inhumane policies. Their odious practices, however, do not provide a license for morally worthy political regimes or at least minimally decent ones to deliberately violate the *jus in bello* PNCI when defending themselves from the aggression of a morally unworthy political regime. The aggression of a morally unworthy political regime, such as the former Nazi regime, against a relatively decent regime, such as the British parliamentary democracy, did not license the latter to adopt a systematic policy of area bombing targeting innocent noncombatants to try to stop or defeat the aggressor. That is considered reprisals. Regrettably, the British engaged in reprisals not only at the beginning but also during and at the very end of the war.

Reprisal against belligerents was not against IHL per se prior to 1939.[204] As Ingrid Detter acknowledges, "Reprisals as a means of warfare were forbidden by the Four Geneva conventions."[205] Hence, one can convincingly argue that reprisals against protected persons, such as civilians and civilian objects, are forbidden in present-day IHL.[206] Although the practice of reprisals was not legally forbidden back then, it was certainly morally questionable. By treating people simply as means only rather than as ends, the practice of reprisals is against human dignity and human decency.

Churchill's insistence on supreme emergency established a dangerous snowballing effect resulting in the practice of total war whereby the law of war (LOAC) was simply ignored or just temporarily suspended, especially by the Allies. The German Luftwaffe had already carried out area bombing attacks against the civilian population in Warsaw on September 25, 1939, and in Rotterdam on May 14, 1940.[207] Thereafter the distinction between combatants and innocent civilians was blurred during the war. As a result, the Allies tried to justify their area bombing campaign of German cities at the end of the war when Nazi Germany was virtually defeated.[208]

Since the Nazis initiated a war of aggression by using area bombing first against the British, albeit as a rather ad hoc practice, Walzer excuses the deliberate and systematic retaliatory targeting of German cities by the British at the beginning of the war because the war's outcome, at the time, was uncertain. Moreover, a Nazi victory would have been catastrophic for Europe. Hence, Walzer's supreme emergency allows for the deliberate and systematic targeting of innocent civilians under conditions of uncertainty as a way of trying to accomplish a morally worthy goal, such as fending off an aggression or defeating a vicious regime, thereby avoiding a possible catastrophe.

One might excuse a person's behavior by appealing to extenuating circumstances. For example, one might appeal to benign ignorance, to accidental and, therefore, unintentional behavior, or to the desire to prevent a catastrophe not brought about by one's own fault.[209] There is, however, something seriously wrong with trying to excuse the deliberate and systematic harming of the innocent under conditions of uncertainty. Such behavior comes across as gambling with innocent people's lives and, hence, treating them only as means for an uncertain end. Walzer admits to this moral quandary. Still, under supreme emergency the stakes are so high that he reluctantly opts for such a gambit.[210]

There might be exceptional circumstances under which one excuses morally abhorrent behavior during a war. For example, when the following conditions are met: (1) the nation being attacked is represented by a morally worthy political regime or a minimally decent one; (2) the offended nation must have been unjustly attacked or seriously threatened; (3) a reasonable expectation must exist that a morally worthy goal can be accomplished, for example, fending off or defeating the aggressor or neutralizing their threat of aggression; (4) no other reasonable peaceful or coercive measures exist to try to accomplish the goal; and (5) a victory by the aggressor would be catastrophic.

Even if one assumes that (1), (2), (4), and (5) were met at the beginning of the war, (3) was certainly unmet. First, as Walzer admits, the outcome of the war was uncertain. Still, the outcome of the British policy of indiscriminately and systematically targeting innocent civilians was most certain. They deliberately inflicted death and suffering on a significant number of innocent noncombatants. Second, the assumption that an appeal to supreme emergency and, therefore, temporarily ignoring LOAC was a reasonable option in trying to prevent the aggression or to defeat the aggressor seems to have been flawed. Was there sufficient evidence to believe in the effectiveness of a massive area bombing campaign to bring about the capitulation of an enemy nation that has been subjected to it? Or perhaps, as Walzer suggests, the appeal to supreme emergency was just a gamble. The extent to which one might gamble with innocent people's lives under conditions of uncertainty is morally questionable.

Rather than ignoring LOAC, the British could have chosen to fight in accordance to such law. They could have chosen to target combatants and legitimate military objectives rather than deliberately and systematically targeting innocent noncombatants. If one were to argue that the British adopted a policy of targeting innocent noncombatants in retaliation for similar behavior by the Germans, one could counter that two or more wrongs do not make a right. By adhering to LOAC, the British could have tried to act compatibly with the rule of international law. To try to excuse the suspension and deliberate violation of the PNCI contingent on an uncertain outcome seems rather Machiavellian.

Whether we represent ourselves or others as in the case of a statesman, we have no right to do wrong. Even if as a leader and representative of a morally worthy or a minimally decent community one were to publicly consent to do whatever it takes to protect it, one could only consent to doing that which is morally permissible. In principle, we could consent to doing even that which is morally wrong, but our consent would carry no moral weight. That is, we would not be necessarily bound by it. A deliberate promise to do wrong is void *ab initio* regardless of the outcome. Without justice, as St. Augustine implied, there would not be any difference between a morally worthy community and a criminal gang that manages to win recognition with impunity.[211]

Walzer's defense of supreme emergency and his absolute criticism of terrorism seem incoherent at two different levels. On the one hand, he appeals to supreme emergency at the beginning of the war. He tries to justify or excuse the British area bombing campaign against the German civilian population because the outcome of the war was uncertain. But he opposes a similar campaign by the Allies toward the end of the war because Nazi Germany and Imperial Japan were virtually defeated. An Allied victory was almost certain. Hence, according to him, there was no need for an area bombing campaign. Such an area bombing campaign can be aptly described as reprisals or as a terrorist campaign against enemies who were practically defeated.

If Walzer denounced the indiscriminate targeting of innocent civilians at the end of the war because an Allied victory was almost certain, then moral consistency requires that he should have denounced similar behavior at the beginning of the war when its outcome was uncertain. Uncertainty of outcome, even in a just war, is insufficient to justify or excuse violating the PNCI, which is based on people's compelling natural duty of nonmaleficence. This duty is so fundamental for valuing people's physical, psychological, and moral integrity that those who deliberately violate it and the community that condones such behavior are blameworthy of serious moral failure.

Walzer's defense of supreme emergency and his absolute criticism of terrorism seem incoherent at another level. His justification or excuse of supreme emergency at the beginning of the war contributed to an unwelcome precedent that led to the practice of total war. One could argue that the Nazis' aggression and their deliberate violation of LOAC promoted the practice of total war. The moral issue, however, is not who initiated a given practice but whether such practice is morally justified or at least excused. There seems to be no moral justification or excuse for the practice of total war. Total war, like nuclear war, is mayhem on a grand scale.

One could reasonably argue that an appeal to supreme emergency at the beginning of the war opened up the floodgate that led to the Allied area bombing campaigns. Operation Gomorrah is a good example of what one might aptly describe as a deliberate and systematic policy of indiscriminate killing of German civilians during the bombing of Hamburg in 1943 as a result of which thousands of civilians were burned to death.[212] Likewise, the senseless bombing of Dresden in 1945 where thousands of innocent civilians were deliberately and systematically killed, even when the Nazis were virtually defeated and there were no major strategic targets in the city.[213]

One might describe these area bombing campaigns as senseless reprisals. It is likely that these questionable bombing campaigns established the precedents that led to the infamous firebombing of Japanese cities, including the catastrophic firebombing of Tokyo from March 9 to March 10, 1945. Since there was no likelihood in sight that Imperial Japan would surrender, and it was unclear if or when the Soviets were going to declare war on Japan, the United States decided to use atomic weapons for the first time in history.

Without previous warning and in daylight, to remind the Japanese of their surprise attack on Pearl Harbor, two atomic bombs were dropped on two different Japanese cities: one on Hiroshima, August 6, and the other on Nagasaki, August 9 of 1945, at the very end of the war when Imperial Japan was no longer a real threat. The magnitude of these two explosions, the widespread carnage, and the number of people who perished and suffered were unprecedented.[214] And yet, given the viciousness of Japanese officers and soldiers during the war, very few people or nations publicly objected to such moral Armageddon.

Once we try to justify or excuse deliberately and systematically killing innocent noncombatants for the sake of preserving our community or defending fundamental moral and political values, we are simply trying to justify or excuse wicked behavior: calling it "supreme emergency" is just a euphemism for camouflaging behavior that can be aptly described as criminal. The statement "a terrorist is just a terrorist" while being self-evident is morally illuminating. That is, a terrorist is one who deliberately or recklessly inflicts serious harm on people regardless of their innocence for political goals. Trying to excuse people's behavior by appealing to Churchillian supreme emergency would not change the immorality or the illegality of execrable actions.

Depending on the values one is defending and the actual outcome of armed conflicts, some people might be willing to forgive execrable actions, including Walzer. Nevertheless, the choice to forgive the perpetrators is only up to those who have suffered the consequences of such actions, namely the victims. The perpetrators can only apologize to the victims.

Walzer, and those who share his view, could assume that during a supreme emergency the contending parties return to a Hobbesian state of nature, which is a state of war. In this state, so Hobbes argues, "nothing can be Unjust. The notions of Right and Wrong, Justice and Injustice have there no place." He continues, "Where there is no common Power, there is no Law: where no Law, no Injustice. Force, and Fraud, are in warre the two Cardinal virtues."[215] And yet it seems that this assumption helps to defeat Walzer's view because he morally justifies or at least tries to excuse Churchill's declaration of supreme emergency. Moreover, he supports his justification or excuse of supreme emergency not only on the imminence of defeat, but, more importantly, on his judgment about the unique evil of Nazism and the presupposition that the community being defended is represented by a morally worthy political regime or at least a minimally decent one.

As a result, Walzer is committed to the general view that when any community represented by a morally worthy political regime or a minimally decent one faces an imminent and unusual evil threat similar to the Nazi threat during 1940–1941, those representing the morally worthy regime or minimally decent one have the right to use not only illegal but also immoral means to ward off such a threat. That is, they have the right to violate not only the fundamental legal PNCI shared by *jus ad bellum* and *jus in bello* considerations that are integral components of a well-established just war approach, but also their compelling natural duty of nonmaleficence to avoid deliberately or recklessly harming the innocent by commission or omission.

As Coady argues, Walzer's justification or excuse of Churchill's "supreme emergency" in the early 1940s seems ex post facto. [216] Since the beginning of National Socialism, Hitler used xenophobic and anti-Semitic rhetoric. It was known at the time that National Socialism was based on anti-Semitism, anticommunism, and antiliberalism. But the trademark of National Socialism was its anti-Semitism.[217] So it was lamentable but not unforeseen that Jews and political enemies were persecuted and prosecuted since Hitler came to power in 1933.[218] In 1940–1941, however, there were no known specific and actual programs for the extermination of the Jews and other designated enemies of National Socialism. Moreover, the international community was rather indifferent to the enactment of the 1933 and 1935 deplorable anti-Semitic Nuremberg Laws stigmatizing Jews and people of Jewish ancestry as second-class citizens.[219]

Thus Walzer's appeal to the unique evil of Nationalism Socialism in 1940–1941 is at best inaccurate. It is only after 1942 that the Holocaust unfolded in crescendo.[220] Nazi Germany from 1940 to 1941 was no worse than the Soviet Union, Fascist Italy, or Imperial Japan. These were tyrannical militaristic regimes that appeal to jingoism in trying to justify imperial expansion abroad and domestic oppression at home. Even British parliamentary democracy's moral pedigree was tainted, since the same parliamentary democracy that has been used to defend the rights of British citizens at home had chosen to approve, establish, and expand the British Empire abroad.

As a colonial power, the British established and defended their colonies by implementing xenophobic policies and by using violence against the natives.[221] Despite Churchill's Eurocentric conception of humanity, he nonetheless augured the ominous threat that Nazism represented for the rest of the world. He could have chosen to ignore such a threat, since Nazi Germany had never declared war on Great Britain, but Churchill stood up to the threat. Still, in light of his defense of British imperialism and his paternalism toward non-Europeans, one can legitimately question his mixed motives for having stood up to the threat of Nazism.[222]

Perhaps at the time the interests of the British Empire and the interests of a substantive portion of humanity coincidentally overlapped.[223] Churchill might have been merely trying to prevent the collapse of the British Empire vis-à-vis the challenges offered by new empires in the making, such as the Nazi Third Reich and the Japanese Empire. In doing so, however, Great Britain paid dearly. Regardless of his one-sided Eurocentric view of humanity, his paternalism toward non-Europeans, and some of his morally questionable war polices, such as his appeal to supreme emergency to protect the British Empire, he was instrumental in defeating the Axis powers. Therefore, Churchill helped save humanity from the scourges of Nazi and Japanese imperialism.

Coady underscores how Walzer's recognition and defense of supreme emergency against Nazi Germany is based on the evil nature of Nazism, but his somewhat less critical view of the nature of Imperial Japan's aggressive policies seems ad hoc.[224] During the late 1930s and early 1940s, the Japanese armed forces adopted a policy of total war against both China and the Allies, including the terrorist bombing of Chinese cities, indiscriminate implementation of biological warfare against combatants and innocent noncombatants, and experimentation on prisoners of war (POWs) that was as gruesome as the experimentations conducted by Nazi Germany.[225]

Unlike the atrocities of the Nazis that were not fully known at the time, the Japanese war crimes were well publicized, especially those that occurred during the battle of Nanking, the former capital of the Republic of China, on December 13, 1937, and thereafter.[226] In her work, Iris Chang argues that "the Rape of Nanking was front-page news across the world, and yet most of the world stood by and did nothing while an entire city was butchered."[227]

Coady's point is well taken. If one accepts that the British would have been justified or excused in targeting innocent German civilians by appealing to supreme emergency in the early stages of the war, then the Chinese had an even more compelling case for doing the same against innocent Japanese civilians. And so would any oppressed group whose members believe that their survival is being seriously threatened by others, such as the Palestinians by the Israelis, the Chechnyans by the Russians, the Kurds by the Turks, and the Tibetans by Communist Chinese. Supreme emergency seems too plastic of a concept. As Coady contends, "whenever you are engaged in legitimate self-defense and seem to be losing, you will be able to produce plausible reasons of supreme emergency for attacking the innocent."[228]

a. Supreme Emergency vs. State of Exception

Walzer's conception of supreme emergency, as an exception rather than as a norm, faces similar challenges to those associated with Carl Schmitt's infamous concept of the state of exception.[229] He defends Churchill's supreme emergency against the Nazi aggression. Schmitt published his defense of the state of exception during the early 1920s before the Nazis came to power. Nevertheless, he was a leading Nazi collaborator known as "the crown jurist of the Third Reich."[230]

Walzer and Schmitt share a similar pro-state bias. For Schmitt, the state of exception resembles the role of a miracle in natural theology. A miracle represents a rupture in the laws of nature. Similarly, the state of exception represents a rupture in the juridical continuity of an established legal order.[231] When an established legal order is threatened, either domestically or internationally, the sovereign has the power to suspend it.[232] In the spirit of Churchill, Walzer argues that when an established legal order is threatened during a supreme emergency, the letter of the law must be suspended. Unlike Schmitt, however, Walzer presupposes that the established legal order must be morally worthy and, hence, morally defensible.

During a supreme emergency, as well as during a state of exception, there is no third neutral party one can invoke in trying to solve a given conflict peacefully. A state of emergency suspends law in the name of "humanity," or so Churchill argued, while a state of exception suspends law in the name of a political order, or so Schmitt contended. The terms "humanity" and "political order," however, are hallowed concepts. It is what people do on behalf of these concepts that makes their behavior susceptible to moral appraisal. The deliberate and systematic killing of innocent noncombatants is intolerable whether in the name of a given conception of humanity or in the name of a given conception of a political order.

A war on behalf of humanity could be more vicious than a war on behalf of a given political order. Frequently, those who wage war on behalf of humanity paradoxically tend to dehumanize their opponents. As Carl Schmitt acknowledges, those who appropriate the term "humanity" are effectively "denying the enemy the quality of being human and declaring him to be an outlaw of humanity; and a war can thereby be driven to the most extreme inhumanity."[233] The atrocities committed during World War II by the Axis powers and the Allies are a vivid testimony of such a possibility.

The concepts of supreme emergency and the state of exception demonstrate the limits of politics and law but not necessarily the limits of morality. Schmitt, however, is a moral relativist. His belief in the state of exception commits him to the view that a sovereign's decision during such a situation is beyond good and evil. For him, the decision occurs in a moral vacuum, or so he assumed. Needless to say, his assumption is as controversial as the decision itself.

Yet Walzer is no moral relativist. By taking the PNCI seriously, he is sympathetic to deontological or nonconsequentialist limitations. His belief in a supreme emergency presupposes that people who appeal to such an emergency are doing so on behalf of a morally worthy political community or a minimally decent one whose existence is threatened by an aggressive and presumably vicious enemy. As a result, their appeal to supreme emergency does not occur in a moral vacuum. On the contrary, they make their appeal to begin with because of moral considerations. Hence, their appeal is morally bound. They have a right to defend themselves.

As Walzer admits, one might retroactively learn that the decision to deliberately violate the PNCI during a supreme emergency could have been mistaken. Given the moral gravity of the threat facing one's political community, he reluctantly gambles with innocent people's lives. Despite their differences, Walzer and Schmitt allow those representing the state to make this gamble.

One might interpret Walzer as arguing that when the representatives of a morally worthy political community or a minimally decent one face a supreme emergency, they replace their deontological scruples with utilitarian and, therefore, consequentialist considerations. He contends that when the existence of a morally worthy political community, presumably one represented by a morally worthy political regime, is at stake "the restraint on utilitarian calculation must be lifted."[234] From which it follows, or so it seems, that "Perhaps it is only a matter of arithmetic: individuals cannot kill other individuals to save themselves, but to save a nation we can violate the rights of a . . . smaller number of people."[235]

Walzer seems committed to the view that during supreme emergencies utilitarian calculations take precedence over deontological scruples against deliberately targeting innocent noncombatants. According to him, representatives of a morally worthy political community or a minimally decent one have a right to deliberately and systematically target innocent noncombatants living under an aggressive political regime whose success will be catastrophic to the citizens of the defending state if they were vanquished by the aggressive state.

Notwithstanding what Walzer says, one need not describe his way of reasoning as utilitarian. A utilitarian defines right, wrong, and obligatory based on the principle of utility. This principle entails that if an action or rule promotes a net balance of good over evil for those affected by it, then a person is not only allowed but he ought to fulfill his obligation. Yet according to Walzer, an appeal to a supreme emergency is not mandatory but only allowed, which goes against the notion of a utilitarian obligation.[236]

Since for Walzer a supreme emergency is simply allowed but not obligatory, then it is better understood as a right rather than as a utilitarian obligation. When an offending state unjustly attacks a morally worthy political community or a minimally decent one, the members of these communities have the right to defend themselves. Therefore, one can better understand a supreme emergency as a deontological right of self-defense rather than as a utilitarian duty to protect.

By allowing, as Walzer seems to suggest, that supreme emergency depends on utilitarian calculations, a defending community could never rightly try to fend off the unjust aggressor by killing more people than the ones they are trying to defend. That is so because from a utilitarian perspective numbers rather than intentions count for distinguishing right from wrong.

Assuming that a supreme emergency depends on the right of self-defense, the members of a morally worthy political community or a minimally decent one that is being attacked have a right to defend themselves. They, however, have the right to defend their community by targeting only those responsible for the unjust aggression. Members of the defending community have no right to deliberately attack innocent noncombatants belonging to the community represented by the unjust aggressor.

When a person threatens my life, I have the right to defend myself from the aggressor, but I have no right to use an innocent third party as a shield to protect me from the aggressor. Least of all, I have no right to kill deliberately an innocent third party to save me from the aggressor. I have only the right to defend myself from the aggressor or those who directly contribute to the aggression. So it seems that when Walzer asks the rhetorical question "Can one do *anything*, violating the rights of the innocent, in order to defeat Nazism?" and he answers, "I am going to argue that one can do what is necessary,"[237] he is overstating his case. For example, if defeating Nazism or any other vicious political regime were to require that we intentionally kill millions of innocent noncombatants, and we were to do so, then we would not be morally better than the vicious enemy we are trying to defeat. By Walzer's own definition of terrorism, we, as a matter of fact, would have become terrorists too. Like our vicious enemy, we would have descended into hell. And if I may be allowed some poetic license, in hell the concept of accountability might be simply moot.

Chapter 5

"Whatever It Takes"

Since oftentimes statesmen and terrorists invoke the ambiguous expression "whatever it takes" to try to accomplish their goals, I would like to explore the following question: Can statesmen or terrorists justifiably invoke such an ambiguous expression to achieve their goals? The answer to this question would depend to a large extent on what people who use it mean by it and contextual considerations.

As I have underscored throughout, hard-core opponents and hard-core apologists of terrorism hold contradictory beliefs regarding the justifiability of political violence, especially regarding the practice of terrorism. While hard-core opponents of terrorism would under no circumstances justify a terrorist act, hard-core apologists of terrorism sometimes would justify such an act. If my argument defending the view of hard-core opponents of terrorism is compelling, then under no circumstances can those who endorse this view answer affirmatively to the above question. By contrast, those whom I describe as apologists of terrorism might sometimes answer affirmatively to the same question. Hence, hard-core opponents and apologists of terrorism hold contradictory beliefs regarding the reasons for invoking the expression "whatever it takes."

The expression "whatever it takes" implies using all the necessary means to achieve a given goal. Insofar as its meaning is concerned, there seems to be a prima facie universal agreement on what the expression means. However, the universal agreement soon vanishes depending on whether one interprets the expression absolutely or conditionally. For example, whether a morally worthy goal would justify absolutely "all the necessary means" to obtain it is frequently questionable depending on the following conditions: (1) the intention or pro-attitude of those using the means to obtain the goal; (2) whether the means are necessary to obtain the goal (namely, no other reasonable means exist to obtain the same goal with a lesser cost); and (3) the number of people positively or detrimentally affected by the actions of those seeking to obtain the goal.

Those who are attempting to achieve a morally worthy goal, such as either stopping an aggressor or preventing a systematic campaign to exterminate political opponents, could risk engaging themselves in vicious behavior by deliberately or recklessly targeting the innocent and the noninnocent alike in trying to achieve their goal. They might end up deliberately harming an excessive number of people who ought not to be harmed and never consented to be harmed nor expected to be so harmed, such as those who are impeccably innocent.

To illustrate the above risk, one might consider the following scenario. For quite some time, the international community has been aware that the North Korean government and its officials have been deliberately torturing, starving, and executing those whom they designate as political opponents. So the North Korean government and its officials have engaged and continue to engage in a systematic campaign to exterminate their alleged political opponents. This systematic campaign of extermination is virtually a genocide— if not in name, at least in practice, the end result being the same.[1] However, given the closed nature of the North Korean regime, it is rather challenging to provide accurate estimates of how many of its citizens have been seriously harmed or killed and continue to be harmed within such a tyrannical regime.

If some people have qualms about applying the term "genocide" to the above-mentioned extermination campaign, perhaps one can use a different label to describe this state of affairs. For example, since government officials have approved this extermination campaign, we can label it a democide rather than a genocide.[2] Some people might still have reservations using either of the terms "genocide" or "democide" to describe what the North Korean government and its officials have been practicing for quite some time.

Despite their reservations, there is sufficient evidence that North Korean government officials have been actively committing crimes against humanity.[3] They have been using and continue to use the naked power of the state to accomplish their morally reprehensible goal, namely, silencing their opponents by any means and at virtually any cost. Consequently, these officials have practiced and continue to practice state terrorism against those whom they view as their alleged political enemies. Whether they are real political enemies remains an open question, since the North Korean government refuses to allow them the opportunity of defending themselves in an impartial court of justice.

Those who are skeptical of singling out North Korea for committing crimes against humanity and state terrorism could argue that most if not all nations have committed crimes against humanity and state terrorism, including liberal democratic countries, such as the United States, Great Britain, and France, to mention only a few.[4] Two points are worth mentioning. First, contemporary liberal democratic countries generally, although not exclusively, tend to commit these crimes during extraordinary circumstances, such as during armed conflicts. Oftentimes, however, they are the ones responsible for creating these extraordinary circumstances to obtain self-serving goals, such as the US invasion of Iraq. And second, once the extraordinary circumstances are over, they are likely to reestablish a genuine respect for the rule of law.

I have argued that certain acts, such as terrorist acts, are morally wrong and, therefore, intolerable—whether one commits any of these acts during an armed conflict or not. Moreover, it is important to underscore that the North Korean government is presumably in a "state of peace" in its relationship to its citizens. That is, no civil war exists in the country. Also, one or more wrongs do not make a right. So even if those representing liberal democracies that have committed gross violation of fundamental human rights were to be hypocritical in their judgment describing North Korea's violations of such fundamental rights, their hypocrisy would have no bearing on the veracity of their judgment. One can grant that those representing liberal democracies might not have the high moral ground that they presume to have. Still, the veracity of their judgment, if true, remains intact.

For the sake of argument, let us assume that the international community has exhausted all reasonable peaceful means in trying to persuade the North Korean government to stop their extermination campaign. Since under international law there is no automatic right or duty to humanitarian intervention or a responsibility to protect (a.k.a. R2P), it is up to the UN Security Council to decide on an ad hoc basis if, when, and how to intervene in a given conflict. So let us assume that the five permanent members of the Security Council (China, France, Russia, the United Kingdom, and the United States) are privy to reliable information that the only way the North Korean government and its officials would stop their odious campaign is if they were to suffer a catastrophic attack. One could bring about such a catastrophic attack, for example, by dropping several atomic bombs on the capital Pyongyang and its vicinity, which would result in the deaths of tens of thousands of innocent victims. I am assuming that the North Korean government would be unable to retaliate in kind. This assumption might be questionable, since they seem already to possess some nuclear weapons. Still, I am ignoring this possibility for my example.

Let us also suppose that the UN Security Council unanimously votes to engage in a humanitarian operation and, therefore, to do whatever it takes to stop the unfolding campaign of extermination. As a result, they choose to drop several atomic bombs on Pyongyang and its vicinity to force North Korean government officials to stop their extermination campaign. In my example, the first and second conditions previously mentioned are presumably met but not the third condition, because a vast number of innocent victims would be killed or seriously harmed as a result of the indiscriminate bombing.

The intention of the UN Security Council's members is to achieve a worthy goal, namely, stopping a morally abhorrent campaign of extermination. Moreover, I have stipulated that the means chosen for stopping such a vicious campaign of extermination are, in fact, necessary to accomplish the goal in question. One could not achieve this goal in any other way at a lesser cost. Nevertheless, the number of innocent victims resulting from the act of deliberately dropping several atomic bombs would be conceived of by some as an excessively high price to pay, since this act is likely to bring about devastating effects to North Korean society overall.

For example, the above use of violence might be seen as excessive and, hence, inexcusable to some, such as hard-core opponents of terrorism who adopt a stringent interpretation of the PNCI—assuming that noncombatants are innocent beyond reasonable doubt and, therefore, impeccably innocent. For them, people have a compelling natural duty of nonmaleficence to avoid deliberately or recklessly harming the innocent. By contrast, apologists of terrorism take exception with such a stringent interpretation of the PNCI. Since some apologists hold a consequentialist view, they are likely to justify the dropping of the atomic bombs if and only if more innocent people are benefited than harmed as a result of dropping the bombs. They interpret the meaning of the expression "whatever it takes" conditionally rather than absolutely.

When statesmen or terrorists invoke the expression "whatever it takes" or any of its cognates, such as extreme crisis, extreme necessity, or supreme emergency to justify or excuse morally questionable actions, they have a substantial burden of proof. In previous chapters, I have shown how dangerous an appeal to extreme necessity can be within the Christian just war approach as typically exemplified in Francisco de Vitoria's and Francisco Suárez's reflections on just war during the fifteenth and sixteenth centuries. Moreover, I have also underscored some of the dangers associated with Winston Churchill's invocation of supreme emergency at the beginning of World War II, and with Michael Walzer's contemporary defense of such a concept, despite his being a hard-core opponent of terrorism.

Some statesmen who have invoked any of the above-mentioned expressions to justify or excuse using political violence against their opponents have been responsible for the deaths of more innocent civilians than well-known terrorists have been. It is morally perplexing how the same people who lionize statesmen who have been responsible for deliberately or recklessly killing and maiming tens of thousands of innocent civilians tend to demonize terrorists for deliberately or recklessly killing and maiming a few hundred or a couple of thousand innocent civilians.

It is rather cynical how sometimes citizens in liberal democracies license their democratically elected leaders to kill or harm with impunity innocent civilians in foreign countries while simultaneously being incensed when terrorists act likewise against innocent citizens in liberal democracies. Moral consistency requires that we respect the lives and well-being of innocent civilians at home as well as abroad. By valuing the lives and well-being of innocent civilians at home while deliberately or recklessly undermining the lives and well-being of innocent civilians abroad, leaders and ordinary citizens of liberal democracies adopt a double standard. As a result, the so-called exceptionalism of liberal democracies is questionable.

Consider, for example, Winston Churchill's *cri de coeur* of supreme emergency at the beginning of World War II to justify a policy of deliberately bombing German civilians, namely, the so-called area bombing campaign, which is just a euphemism for terrorist bombing. In addition, consider former President George W. Bush's appeal to "whatever it takes" after the infamous 9/11 terrorist attack. He tried to justify not only overthrowing the Taliban in Afghanistan, who harbored those responsible for the terrorist attacks, but he also subsequently approved the invasion of Iraq and the expansion of the extraordinary practice of rendition abroad.

Former President George W. Bush's promise to the American people and his subsequent actions are good illustrations of the dangers involved in using hyperbolic language that foreshadows domestic and foreign policies. After the terrorist attack of 9/11, and while addressing the California Business Association on October 17, 2001, President Bush stated, "We will do *whatever it takes* [my italics] to protect our country, protect the good American families. And we will do whatever it takes to punish those who have attacked us."[5]

In principle, President Bush's exhortations are commendable: protecting the country from terrorist violence and bringing to justice those who perpetrated the infamous 9/11 terrorist attack. There is, however, a serious challenge in trying to understand what he meant by invoking the expression "whatever it takes" to achieve the above-mentioned goals. On the one hand, if by invoking this expression he meant using "any morally permissible means" to bring to justice those responsible for the 9/11 attacks, then his view would be morally praiseworthy, assuming his later actions were consistent with it. Otherwise he would have been hypocritical.

On the other hand, if by invoking the above expression President Bush meant approving any morally questionable means to bring to justice those responsible for the 9/11 attacks, such as torturing alleged enemy combatants, indefinitely incarcerating them without recourse to *habeas corpus*, or unilaterally declaring war based on rather questionable evidence against an alleged enemy, then his view would be morally suspect. If he had acted on this morally suspect view, he would have violated fundamental moral principles, such as our compelling natural duty of nonmaleficence. Moreover, he would have also violated the LOAC, UN treaties and protocols, and international human rights law.[6]

Peter Singer offers a nuanced and persuasive evaluation of the former president's ethical views as being either incoherent or hypocritical.[7] In fairness to the former president, however, one can argue that to expect any person to have a coherent ethical vision regarding motley challenging social and political issues is too demanding. I venture to say that if we were to uphold such an expectation, most people's ethical visions would not pass scrutiny. And yet, despite being vices rather than virtues, incoherence and hypocrisy need not be substantial moral failures. If incoherence and hypocrisy were such serious vices, the world would likely be more chaotic than it actually is, since most if not all individuals would oftentimes reason incoherently or hypocritically at different intervals during their lifetime.

A fundamental moral failure is when a person's incoherence or hypocrisy results in serious harm to those who do not deserve it and do not consent to it. So when the decisions of a person in a leadership position detrimentally affect the lives of combatants and innocent noncombatants alike, we have not only a right but also a duty to question those decisions and to hold accountable those who claim to represent us, especially, although not exclusively, elected officials who are also bound to protect us.

It is difficult to believe that a democratically elected president, such as former President George W. Bush, who had sworn to honor the US Constitution and thereby the rule of law, would have understood the expression "whatever it takes" in an absolutely literal and, hence, morally dubious sense. If he had done so, then his view on justifying political violence would have been not much different from the view of those who carried out the infamous 9/11 terrorist attack and those who have perpetrated and continue to perpetrate similar attacks elsewhere around the globe.

Reasonable critics of President Bush's policies could underscore that he has been responsible for killing and seriously harming more innocent people than the Al-Qaeda cadres who carried out the 9/11 attacks. In fairness to the president it should be noted that we have no reason to believe that he approved deliberate attacks against innocent noncombatants. Still, the killing and harming of a disproportionate number of innocent noncombatants as a result of his questionable policies are imputable to the president. By contrast, Al-Qaeda's core policy has been and remains aimed at killing as many innocent Americans and alleged infidels as possible. So while numbers matter, intentions matter too. The fact that members of Al-Qaeda are fighting an asymmetrical war against more powerful enemies does not license them to deliberately kill or seriously harm those who can be conceived of as impeccably innocent.

Thus, I am assuming that President Bush's view on justifying political violence is different from the view of those who carried out the infamous 9/11 terrorist attacks and those who continue to execute similar attacks elsewhere. Presumably, he did not use the expression "whatever it takes" in an absolutely literal and, therefore, morally dubious sense. And yet, while his motives might have been praiseworthy, his behavior thereafter remains controversial.

If President Bush did not use the above expression in an absolutely literal sense, in what sense did he use it? Some might argue that he used this expression as a purely rhetorical device to show, for example, determination in the face of a serious challenge or to appeal to citizens' emotions. Or perhaps by using this expression, he meant only to show his moral clarity and his inexorable conviction in trying to achieve the desirable goals, namely, finding the culprits and bringing them to justice. Having such moral clarity and inexorable conviction could be admirable if the person who holds these beliefs knows how to achieve the desirable goals without creating equal or greater injustices while doing so.

President Bush might have assumed, nonetheless, that reasonable people can differ on how to achieve desirable goals, such as the ones already mentioned, depending on our knowledge of the unfolding events on the ground. So even though he might have had some clear threshold in mind when he originally invoked the expression "whatever it takes," he probably realized that the threshold might change according to the changing needs on the ground for achieving the desirable goals. Hence, the moral threshold that he started with and the threshold that his subsequent domestic and foreign policies brought about could be seen as inconsistent.

For example, at first, President Bush might have been convinced that his foreign policies, such as his decision of invading Iraq to topple Saddam Hussein's ruthless dictatorship and presumably prevent the spread of terrorism, were not going to result in the deliberate or reckless killing or harming of a disproportionate number of Iraqi civilians and the widespread torturing of Iraqi prisoners. So, presumably, his initial moral threshold could have been morally worthwhile. Unfortunately, as we realize with hindsight, his policies violated such a morally worthwhile threshold.

For ordinary people who are aware of their fallibility, it is just perplexing that President Bush did not admit to any mistakes in his policies or to having had any moral uncertainties while implementing his policies.[8] He could have believed that the above-mentioned shifting and thereby inconsistent moral thresholds was unfortunate but not necessarily undesirable if he succeeded in accomplishing a desirable goal, such as the overthrowing of Saddam Hussein's ruthless dictatorship. If he had done so, he would have been neither the first nor the last statesman to disregard consistency in politics.

According to Winston Churchill, for example, consistency in politics is simply foolish. The virtue of a true statesman "in contact with the moving current of events and anxious to keep the ship on an even keel and steer a steady course may lean all his weight now on one side and now on the other. . . . We cannot call this inconsistency. In fact it may be claimed to be the truest consistency."[9] Regrettably, such latitude in politics oftentimes results in questionable practices.

So even if President Bush meant to use the expression "whatever it takes" as suggested above, it was an ominous sign given what followed. It was unfortunate because his words and his subsequent behavior detrimentally affected combatants and innocent noncombatants alike. The invasion of Iraq is an evident reminder of such adverse consequences.[10] People in leadership positions who are responsible for domestic or foreign policies have no excuse for using hyperbolic language, especially when putting the lives and well-being of those whom they have sworn to protect in harm's way. Under those circumstances, they have a substantive obligation to mean what they say and, henceforth, to act accordingly. Having moral clarity of a desirable end is no justification or excuse for using vicious means in trying to bring it about.[11]

Others could argue that President Bush might have used the expression "whatever it takes" conditionally. That is, he might have meant all necessary actions consistent with domestic and international law, although not necessarily consistent with fundamental moral principles, to defeat and bring to justice the culprits for the 9/11 attacks. However, this interpretation is challengeable in the face of his subsequent behavior.

By committing himself to do whatever it takes to protect the US national security, President Bush adopted unilateralism and preemption in foreign policy. As a result, he decided to invade Iraq based on spurious data, namely, that Saddam Hussein was harboring WMD and was ready to use them against the United States and its allies. It is unfortunate that the invasion had the blessing of the US Congress and the consent and, hence, complicity of government officials and the majority of the American public. According to a Gallup poll right after the hostilities began, 70 percent favored the war with Iraq and only 25 percent opposed it.[12]

The decision to go to war with Iraq, it seems, was not based solely on the presence and threat of WMD but on other geopolitical considerations, such as trying to promote democracy in the region.[13] One could cite numerous legitimate reasons, including right to protect reasons or traditional just war considerations, for going to war against a ruthless and aggressive dictator, such as the late Saddam Hussein. For example, Condoleezza Rice, former national security adviser and secretary of state, mentions some of these reasons in her memoir.[14] However, that was not the strategy that President Bush and his chief advisers, including Ms. Rice, chose to try to persuade the American public and the international community of the need for regime change in Iraq. Instead they settled on the issue of WMD and the imminent threat that those weapons posed to the United States and its allies.

President Bush, his chief advisers, government officials and analysts, and some foreign leaders used the presence and threat of WMD as their main public justification for invading Iraq.[15] They also alluded to an alleged connection between Al-Qaeda operatives and Saddam Hussein for which they had no compelling evidence.[16] Still, for President Bush and his supporters, Saddam was an imminent threat to the United States and its allies.[17] Needless to say, the existence of such an imminent threat has been debunked—the alleged link between Al-Qaeda operatives and Iraq was never proved nor were the infamous WMD ever found.[18]

In addition, President Bush's commitment to do "whatever it takes to punish those who have attacked us" created a culture of unaccountability that was instrumental in expanding the extraordinary practice of rendition abroad, thereby secretly sending alleged terrorists to other countries to be interrogated harshly, tortured, and imprisoned. This culture of unaccountability established a dangerous precedent by allowing for the widespread practice of torture euphemistically called by the CIA "enhanced interrogation techniques," such as the cases in the infamous Abu Ghraib prison in Iraq, and the alleged practice of torturing enemy combatants in Guantánamo Bay prison, Cuba.[19]

For example, according to former assistant attorney general Jay S. Bybee, for an act to constitute torture under Title 18 U.S.C. Section 2340, "it must inflict pain that is difficult to endure. Physical pain . . . equivalent in intensity to the pain accompanying serious physical injury, such as organ failure, impairment of bodily function, or even death." Furthermore, for mental pain or suffering "to amount to torture . . . it must result in significant psychological harm of significant duration, e.g., lasting for months or years." But, according to him, the president could simply ignore the above-mentioned restrictions because "under the current circumstances, necessity or self-defense may justify interrogation methods that might violate Section 2340A."

Bybee offers a broad reading of presidential executive power that during wartime allows the president to do virtually anything to defeat the enemy. He writes, "In war time, it is for the President alone to decide what methods to use to best prevail against the enemy."[20] One could argue that such broad and thereby questionable interpretation of executive power during wartime allowed for morally and legally questionable practices that violated not only fundamental moral principles but also domestic and international law, both of which proscribe torture.[21]

It is precisely the disposition of statesmen or nonstate agents, including terrorists, to invoke ambiguous expressions, such as "extreme crisis," "extreme necessity," or "supreme emergency," that might allow them to try to justify or excuse a "whatever it takes approach" when faced with an allegedly extreme situation. They may use morally opaque language to engage in deplorable actions. For example, they might deliberately or recklessly target innocent noncombatants, or they might unilaterally and with suspect evidence declare war on a nation whereby innocent and noninnocent citizens alike are seriously harmed.

Ordinary citizens, including those living in liberal constitutional democracies, usually have no effective means to prevent or stop their leaders from adopting morally suspect policies that will result in abominable actions, such as the ones already mentioned. Nevertheless, ordinary citizens can at least publicly demand that those who claim to act on their behalf behave responsibly. That is, they can insist that when their leaders use ambiguous expressions to try to justify or excuse morally controversial actions, they have a substantial burden of proof to present a public non-question-begging argument providing an account of why they are opting for such controversial actions.

As responsible citizens, it is important to make our leaders aware that an appeal to ambiguous expressions to achieve a morally worthy goal is insufficient to justify using morally questionable means to achieve such a goal. If so, they would need to provide compelling evidence that no other reasonable course of action exists to achieve such a morally worthy goal and that one can reasonably expect to achieve it. If after presenting what they believe to be compelling evidence to support their course of action they are unable to persuade ordinary citizens, especially those with whom they share similar values, that they are in the right, our leaders could perhaps avoid great injustices by reconsidering their reasoning leading to their questionable decision.

Oftentimes statesmen or nonstate agents use morally questionable means to achieve morally worthy goals during so-called extreme circumstances. When they do so, ordinary responsible citizens should insist that, before their leaders act on their behalf, they, the leaders, are to think of themselves "as if" they were reasonable and fair-minded persons who would be willing to view themselves on the receiving end of their questionable actions. One could argue that if statesmen or nonstate agents were to reason accordingly, they would be more likely to render a reasoned and level-headed judgment regarding their controversial action under an allegedly extreme situation. They might still be unable to justify their action. But, assuming they were to take seriously the already mentioned hypothetical conditions, they might be excused for having tried to act responsibly.

Some might argue that it is unrealistic to expect people who confront an extreme situation to fulfill hypothetical conditions prior to choosing a course of action. Those who so argue could underscore that such an expectation represents an ideal rather than a practical approach. They might add that when facing an extreme situation, people in general and those who are in a position of leadership in particular have no time to ponder hypotheticals. In addition, even if they were to pretend to act according to these hypotheticals, nothing could prevent them from acting from expediency alone. They might just equate extreme situation with expediency. Perhaps one could grant that occasionally such an equation could be partly sound when, for example, one faces a life or death situation, assuming that one has not been responsible for bringing about this stark choice.

It is important to note that ideal theories help to inform us about the excesses of acting from expediency, even during an allegedly extreme or stressful situation. An extreme situation could be a matter of life and death but not necessarily a matter of life or death. A classic example of a matter of life and death is when soldiers face their adversaries in an armed conflict. By being soldiers engaged in an armed conflict, they are putting their lives at risk. A matter of life or death, however, is when people confront a stark moral dilemma. Either they save their lives and, in order to do so, they deliberately kill others who might or might not be threatening them, or they are killed. No third option is available.[22]

Consider the following conceivable matter of life or death example. Suppose that I am an American teacher who has volunteered to do pro bono work in Kabul, Afghanistan, to help Afghani students improve their lives. While walking to school, I see an Afghani woman running toward me. I am startled when I realize that she is wearing a suicide vest and that she is ready to set it off. Given that people who live in Kabul, especially foreigners, are under a constant threat of violence by the Taliban, I am licensed to carry a weapon in case I need to defend myself. So I am faced with a stark moral dilemma: either I choose to kill the woman in order to stop her from carrying out her suicide mission or she will kill me instead. In order to defend myself, I choose to kill her first. Because I am exercising my right of self-defense, I can justifiably kill her. As demonstrated by the above-mentioned example, acting on the presumption of life *and* death and acting on the presumption of life *or* death under stressful conditions would justify different actions. But under most circumstances, including stressful ones, I am not allowed to do whatever it takes to save my life. For example, I am not allowed to kill deliberately an innocent bystander to save my life.

One can argue that a generic relationship seems to exist between the expressions "whatever it takes" and those that denote exceptional circumstances, such as "extreme crisis," "extreme necessity," and "supreme emergency." One can view the latter expressions as species of the first. So those who invoke any of these expressions frequently have a disposition to do whatever it takes to accomplish their goals. Hence, when a statesman who claims to represent the interests of ordinary citizens of a nation or nonstate agents, such as a terrorist group who claims to act on behalf of other people's grievances, invoke one of the already mentioned expressions, they are often willing to do "whatever it takes" to achieve their goals. This is because they typically hold the following two beliefs: they believe themselves to be in the right, and they believe themselves to be confronted with a matter of a life or death situation. Nonetheless, their beliefs might, at times, be unwarranted. More importantly, since they are fallible, their beliefs might be unjustified or simply false.

By attempting to justify their actions, those who invoke the concept "whatever it takes," such as those who invoke the expressions "extreme crisis," "extreme necessity," or "supreme emergency," seem to adopt a consequentialist way of reasoning. They evaluate actions as right, wrong, or obligatory depending on their outcome. So they assume that those who try to achieve a given morally worthy goal are predisposed to justifying using the necessary means to achieve it, even when the means used in trying to achieve the goal are arguably morally dubious or intrinsically wrong.

Consequentialist ways of reasoning seem oftentimes to allow for the violation of the following three important deontological moral principles: Socrates's principle of no harm, St. Paul's principle of avoiding evil means, and Kant's categorical imperative. According to Socrates, under "no circumstances must one do wrong," not "even when one is wronged."[23] According to St. Paul, "evil may not be done so that good may ensue."[24] And according to Kant, morality requires that people act primarily motivated by their unconditional respect for the moral law. He contends that people have an absolute obligation to act consistently with the categorical imperative. According to his second formulation of the categorical imperative, we ought to "Act in such a way that you always treat humanity, whether in your own person or in the person of any other, never simply as a means, but always at the same time as an end."[25] Generally speaking, allowing for the violation of any of these principles could jeopardize people's physical, psychological, and moral integrity.[26]

By respecting our compelling natural duty of nonmaleficence, we are simultaneously honoring the physical, psychological, and moral integrity of those who can be conceived of as innocent noncombatants beyond reasonable doubt. That is, in this book, I have assumed a stringent interpretation of the PNCI. Neither an appeal to extreme crisis nor to extreme necessity nor to supreme emergency can justify acts that are categorically wrong. Those who interpret the PNCI categorically believe that the use of terrorism, regardless of its geographical context or seemingly lofty goals, is not morally justified under any circumstances. Thus, hard-core opponents of terrorism's negative answer to the original question is consistent with the Socratic principle of no harm, the Pauline principle of avoiding evil, and the Kantian categorical imperative.

I grant, however, that sometimes the number of people affected by our actions or inactions does matter. When considering an appeal to do whatever it takes to try to overcome an allegedly extreme crisis, extreme necessity, or supreme emergency to achieve a morally worthy goal, a clash between our categorical and, hence, compelling natural duty of nonmaleficence and consequentialist considerations seems, at times, unavoidable. Statesmen who represent citizens of a liberal constitutional democracy or terrorists who claim to act on behalf of oppressed groups might use the expression "whatever it takes" when they face a moral dilemma. They believe that no matter which option in their dilemma they choose, their action or inaction will likely result in serious harm to innocent people. An important issue, however, is not whether their action or inaction will incidentally harm innocent people because during an armed conflict that seems inevitable, but rather whether they will deliberately or recklessly harm them, which might be avoidable.

Whether we are able to excuse using whatever it takes, including morally suspect means under exceptional circumstances to achieve a morally worthy goal, is a different matter. Even during exceptional circumstances, the wrongness of certain acts, such as terrorist acts, remains. Deliberately or recklessly inflicting substantive undeserved harm on those who can be conceived of as impeccably innocent is categorically wrong.

A plea for being excused from using terrorism as a lesser evil, for example, during a supreme emergency in a just war, does not make terrorism right. It might be a way of not holding accountable and, hence, liable those who, for example, have committed a terrorist act to avoid a greater evil that we have reason to believe could not have been prevented by morally acceptable means. Some might try to preserve their good conscience by calling such a terrorist act a lesser evil or a permissible harm. Nevertheless, a lesser evil remains evil, and a permissible harm remains a harm. To allow statesmen or terrorist groups to do absolutely whatever it takes to accomplish their goals, even when their goals are lofty ones, is to sanction at times not only terrorism but murder.

Postscript

In this book, I have taken exception with apologists' arguments supporting terrorism. I defend a view analogous to the one defended by hard-core opponents of terrorism. They, in principle, uphold the PNCI unconditionally. Some hard-core opponents, such as Michael Walzer, in practice justify violating the PNCI under a "supreme emergency," making his hard-core opposition to terrorism challengeable. Apologists of terrorism, however, understand the PNCI conditionally, so that under some circumstances they would justify deliberately using violence against innocent noncombatants. They offer numerous reasons to justify doing so, arguments that I discussed in detail above and summarize below.

I roughly divide apologists' arguments supporting terrorism as follows: those based on an analogy between a justification of terrorism and a justification of war as conceived of in traditional just war thinking—whether Christian or secular, those based on consequentialist considerations, those based on relativism, and those based on invoking exceptional circumstances, for example, a supreme emergency or any of its cognates. I argue that an analogy between a justification of terrorism and a justification of war as conceived of in Christian just war thinking is questionable, since the latter is committed to the Pauline principle that evil may not be done that good might ensue. Moreover, an analogy between a justification of terrorism and a justification of war as conceived of in a secular just war approach is also questionable, since current international law justifies the use of violence only in self-defense or as a last resort. Yet last resort arguments justifying or excusing violence against the innocent are usually suspect. Oftentimes perpetrators of terrorist acts, at least those living in liberal constitutional democracies, do not exhaust all reasonable viable options that exist within domestic or international law for pursuing their grievances peacefully. As a result, they unjustifiably and inexcusably risk innocent people's lives.

Arguments supporting terrorism based on consequentialist considerations are objectionable for the following reasons: first, consequentialists allow, at times, for deliberately killing the innocent if and only if one can reasonably expect that a net balance of good over evil will result from it; second, they allow for treating people as means only; and third, they disregard double effect reasoning, since they exclude the intentions of moral agents from their consequentialist calculus. Arguments based on relativism and some of its cognates tend to blur the distinction between the innocent and the noninnocent because they presuppose that the justification of terrorism is just perspectival. So apologists who defend this approach seem committed to the view that a person's innocence is in the eyes of the beholder, whether the beholder be a person, a community, or a culture. Lastly, arguments supporting terrorism based on exceptional circumstances, such as supreme emergency or some of its cognates, seem to fail because they attempt to justify the killing of the innocent on consequentialist considerations or expediency.

I have defended a working definition of terrorism that supports the view of hard-core opponents of terrorism, who refuse to justify using terrorism under any circumstances. I view terrorism as the use of political violence by people who deliberately or recklessly inflict or threaten to inflict substantive undeserved harm on those who can be conceived of as impeccably innocent, aiming at influencing a domestic or an international audience. Still, I do not pretend that my definition of terrorism will be universally accepted. I hope, nevertheless, that I have succeeded in making the definition philosophically sophisticated and politically acceptable to those who share certain basic moral intuitions. That is, those who view morality primarily as determined by agents' intentions and subsidiarily by the consequences of their actions. For them, the rightness or wrongness of people's actions supervenes primarily upon their intentions rather than upon the consequences of their actions.

Those who share different basic moral intuitions, such as consequentialists, will find my suggested definition of terrorism unacceptable or will likely have serious reservations about it. For consequentialists, the result of an agent's action determines the morality of his or her action regardless of the agent's intentions. For them, agents' intentions are necessary for evaluating people's moral character as virtuous or vicious, but not necessarily their actions.

My stipulated working definitions ascribed to opponents and apologists of terrorism presuppose different moral intuitions. Still, hard-core opponents of terrorism might agree that while terrorism can never be justified, sometimes but rarely might it be excused. I argue so in this book. Soft-core opponents and apologists of terrorism, however, agree that sometimes but rarely can terrorism be justified. Hence, the soft-core opponents' view and the soft-core apologists' view regarding the possible justification of terrorism might, at times, be consistent. Nevertheless, given the different moral intuitions that undergird their mostly incompatible views of terrorism, they would probably disagree on the conditions for its justification.

While I contend that terrorism is never justified, if we want our view of terrorism to be practical rather than ideal, we would need to allow for the possibility that terrorism might sometimes but rarely be excused, such as during a catastrophic situation. As I have argued in the book, the catastrophic is just one among other necessary conditions for excusing a terrorist act. Two further necessary conditions must be met for the terrorist act to be excused, namely, there is no other reasonable way to prevent or stop the catastrophe, and it is reasonable to expect that the terrorist act will be efficacious in preventing or stopping such a catastrophe. It is important to underscore that the conception of the catastrophic is rather unsettled. There is no settled answer to the following question: How many people need to be seriously harmed for an act to be described as catastrophic? Certainly many, but how many remains an open question.

Hard-core opponents of terrorism presuppose a fundamental normative distinction between excusing and justifying an act. They might excuse or permit the practice of terrorism when the individuals who deliberately engage in a terrorist act face an extraordinary or catastrophic situation not created by their fault, such as an unfolding genocide. Moreover, the individuals also know that they can stop the unfolding genocide by deliberately targeting the impeccably innocent few to save the lives of the impeccably innocent many. Given such an extraordinary tragic state of affairs, those who are in a position to stop the unfolding genocide, even though they can do it only by deliberately violating the PNCI, seem to have a right instead of a duty to do so. However, they enjoy this right in the weak sense of being excused or permitted to violate the PNCI rather than in the strong sense of having a right with a corresponding duty to target impeccably innocent people. No one can have a duty to do a categorically wrong act, such as deliberately inflicting undeserved substantive harm on the impeccably innocent.

In the spirit of hard-core opponents of terrorism, I contend that the number of innocent people affected by people's act of commission or omission during a catastrophic situation could count as a plausible ground for excusing their action. Still, that would not necessarily make the practice of terrorism right during such a catastrophic situation. Being conceived of as the exception rather than the norm, a catastrophic situation is likely to demonstrate the limits of our ordinary and, therefore, conventional moral judgments about right and wrong conduct. Those who knowingly harm impeccably innocent people during a catastrophic situation might sometimes be legally and perhaps even morally excused for having done so.

Nevertheless, excusing those who knowingly harm impeccably innocent people during catastrophic events could be insufficient for them to avoid experiencing a heavy conscience and, therefore, avoid feeling remorse for their actions. For example, being in a situation under which we have no choice but to deliberately kill or seriously harm a few impeccably innocent persons to save or prevent harm to many impeccably innocent others can be seen as a tragic situation. Under such a situation, our heavy conscience and remorse might only be tamed by the forgiveness of the relatives and friends of the impeccably innocent person whom we killed or seriously harmed as a result of our actions. However, that might be too much to ask from them.

Our conventional ordinary judgments of right, wrong, or obligatory are frequently insufficient to palliate the heavy conscience of those who knowingly kill or seriously harm the innocent. To preserve their good conscience, they might need to appeal to forgiveness rather than to ordinary moral judgments. Regardless of how catastrophic a situation might be, knowingly or deliberately killing or seriously harming an impeccably innocent person is "as if" we have deliberately killed or harmed every innocent person.[1]

During ordinary and relatively normal circumstances, we frequently come up with sound moral judgments that ordinary reasonable people can agree with, such as noncontroversial cases of murder, theft, or breach of contract, to mention only a few cases. But that is not so during exceptional or catastrophic circumstances where no matter which way we act, innocent people's lives will be seriously harmed. Under the above-mentioned situations, serious harm might be allowed—either excused or permitted. Whether a harm is excused or permitted, a harm remains nonetheless.

As a result, those who engage either in an excusable or a permissible harm have a substantial burden of proof. They need to demonstrate the reasons for the harm to be either excused or permitted so they will not be morally or legally blameworthy for bringing about such harm. They would need to show that the alleged harm is necessary to accomplish a worthy goal—meaning that there is no other reasonable way to obtain the same worthy goal without deliberately harming the impeccably innocent.

Since I have stipulated that terrorism might rarely be excused, it follows that an excused terrorist act is an anomalous act. As a result, such an act belongs to the realm of the exception rather than the norm. Whether one might excuse terrorism will depend not only on how exceptional the situation might be but, more importantly, on the intentions of those who engage in it and on its result. Intentions matter but, of course, numbers matter too. Regrettably, those who invoke an allegedly anomalous catastrophic situation to justify or excuse engaging in the practice of terrorism oftentimes hide behind the façade of improving or salvaging humanity. Nevertheless, we frequently learn ex post facto that they were instead concerned with expedient considerations. They might have used elliptical language to hide their real intentions. Such a hypocritical view applies to both state and nonstate agents.

By allowing such a hypocritical view to prevail during allegedly anomalous catastrophic conditions, we are allowing statesmen, as well as terrorists, to treat people only as a means for their self-serving political scheme. Hence, sometimes there is virtually no distinction between the behavior of statesmen and the behavior of terrorists. That is why citizens must scrutinize the political rhetoric used by those who act on their behalf. Even representatives of liberal constitutional democracies can be at fault for spinning the meaning of political expressions such as "the war on terrorism" and "defeating terrorism."

One would be rushing to judgment to believe that the international community, especially those countries representing liberal constitutional democracies, would succeed in "defeating terrorism," whatever that expression might mean. The meaning of expressions such as "the war on terrorism" and "defeating terrorism" is rather elusive. It seems odd to make war on or to defeat a noun, especially when the noun refers to a tactic rather than, for example, an ideology such as the one embodied in Fascism, Nazism, or Communism. So both expressions seem to be improperly conceived and phrased.[2]

Individual nations and the international community as a whole, however, can fight against certain groups and defeat them, such as those designated by domestic or international law as terrorist groups. As a result, some of these groups have been defeated at great human and financial cost, for example, the guerrilla group Sendero Luminoso (a.k.a. Shining Path) in Perú and the separatist group the Liberation Tigers of Tamil Elam (a.k.a. LTTL) in Sri Lanka. Unfortunately, war and terrorism have been staples of humanity since ancient times. Therefore, it is not only possible but likely that terrorism, like war, will be with us in the foreseeable future.[3]

There is, however, room for cautious optimism. Despite the Sisyphean controversy regarding the subject of terrorism, there is an international consensus around outlawing some morally despicable acts, such as the ones designated by the UN's legal instruments as terrorist acts.[4] Unfortunately, powerful countries at times exhibit a rather selective interpretation and enforcement of these legal instruments. Still, despite their occasional double standard, it is better to have these legal instruments than to have none at all.

While the threat of terrorism is real, we need to learn how to live with this menace without succumbing to an unreasonable fear of it that could permanently undermine our civil and political rights. The probability of being a victim of a terrorist attack outside interstate or intrastate armed conflict zones is rather low or virtually negligible. So we need to be vigilant to avoid compromising some of our hard-won civil and political rights because of an unreasonable fear of terrorism. That would be too high a price to pay in the so-called "war on terrorism."

Notes

CHAPTER 1

1. Walter Laqueur, *A History of Terrorism*, with a new introduction (New Brunswick, NJ: Transaction Publishers, 2002), p. 6; henceforth Laqueur, *A History of Terrorism*. See also Bruce Hoffman, *Inside Terrorism*, revised and expanded edition (New York: Columbia University Press, 2006), pp. 3–4; henceforth Hoffman, *Inside Terrorism*.

2. David Andress, *The Terror: The Merciless War for Freedom in Revolutionary France* (New York: Farrar, Straus and Giroux, 2005), especially chs. 7–9.

3. David C. Rapoport, "The Four Waves of Rebel Terror and September 11," in Charles W. Kegley Jr. (ed.), *The New Global Terrorism: Characteristics, Causes, Controls* (Upper Saddle River, NJ: Prentice Hall, 2003), p. 37; henceforth Rapoport, "The Four Waves of Rebel Terror and September 11." See also Gérard Chaliand and Arnaud Blin, "Zealots and Assassins," in Gérard Chaliand and Arnaud Blin (eds.), *The History of Terrorism: From Antiquity to Al Qaeda* (Los Angeles: University of California Press, 2007), ch. 3.

4. Abdel Bari Atwan, *The Secret History of Al Qaeda* (Berkeley: University of California Press, 2006), pp. 67–70.

5 Walter Laqueur (ed.), *Voices of Terror: Manifestos, Writings and Manuals of Al Qaeda, Hamas, and Other Terrorists from Around the World and Throughout the Ages* (New York: Reed Press, 2004), pp. 8–10; henceforth Laqueur, *Voices of Terror*. For the relationship between terror and tyrannicide before the French Revolution, see Randall D. Law, *Terrorism: A History* (Malden, MA: Polity Press, 2010), pp. 1–56; henceforth Law, *Terrorism*.

6. Max Weber, "Politics as a Vocation," in H. H. Gerth and C. Wright Mills (eds.), *From Max Weber: Essays in Sociology* (New York: Oxford University Press, 1958), p. 78.

7. Louise Richardson, *What Terrorists Want: Understanding the Enemy, Containing the Threat* (New York: Random House, 2007), p. xx; henceforth Richardson, *What Terrorists Want*.

8. Rapoport, "The Four Waves of Rebel Terror and September 11," p. 37.

9. The term "guerrilla" comes from Spanish and it means "small war." The term was used for the first time to describe the partisan or irregular groups fighting the Napoleonic invasion of Spain from 1808 to 1813. See Carl Schmitt, *Theory of the Partisan*, trans. by G. L. Ulmen (New York: Telos Press, 2007), especially pp. 3–23.

10. Adam Roberts and Richard Guelff (eds.), *Documents of the Laws of War*, 3rd ed. (New York: Oxford University Press, 2004); henceforth Roberts and Guelff (eds.), *Documents of the Laws of War*.

11. Law, *Terrorism*, pp. 203–6.

12. Robert A. Pape, *Dying to Win: The Strategic Logic of Suicide Terrorism* (New York: Random House, 2005), pp. 139–40; henceforth Pape, *Dying to Win*.

13. Ibid., pp. 14–15.

14. Laqueur, *A History of Terrorism*, p. x.

15. Pape, *Dying to Win*, p. 4.

16. Ibid., p. 4.

17. Ibid., pp. 14–15.

18. Ibid., p. 139.

19. Richardson, *What Terrorists Want*, especially ch. 5.

20. Angus McDowall, "Saudi Arabia's top clerics speak out against militancy," *Reuters*, September 17, 2014. Available from http://www.reuters.com/article/2014/09/17/us-saudi-islam-security-idUSKBN0HC0XD20140917 (accessed 9/19/2014).

21. See, e.g., Douglas Johnston and Cynthia Sampson (eds.), *Religion, the Missing Dimension of Statecraft* (New York: Oxford University Press, 1994); see also the sequel to this work by Douglas Johnston (ed.), *Faith-Based Diplomacy: Trumping Realpolitik* (New York: Oxford University Press, 2003).

22. There are encouraging signs from different religious communities that are trying to undermine and delegitimize the practice of terrorism. For example, participants from about eighty nations have agreed to reject religious terrorism; see "UN Interfaith conference rejects religious terrorism," *yaLibnan*, November 14, 2008. Available from http://yalibnan.com/site/archives/2008/11/un_interfaith_c.php (accessed 1/31/2009). See also Richard Owen, "Catholic Muslim forum condemns religious terrorism," *TimesOnline.* November 6, 2008. Available from http://www.timesonline.co.uk/tol/comment/faith/article5100320.ece? (accessed 1/31/2009). See Geraldine Baum and Richard Boudreaux, "Terror victims recount stories for U.N. forum," *Los Angeles Times*, September 10, 2008. Available from http://articles.latimes.com/2008/sep/10/world/fg-victims10 (accessed 1/31/2009).

23. Osama bin Laden, "Terror for Terror, October 21, 2001" in Bruce Lawrence (ed.), *Messages to the World: The Statements of Osama Bin Laden* (New York: Verso, 2005), especially p. 121; henceforth Lawrence (ed.), *Messages to the World.*

24. Ramzy Mardini, "The Islamic State threat is overstated," *Washington Post*, September 12, 2014. Available from http://www.washingtonpost.com/opinions/the-islamic-state-threat-is-overstated/2014/09/12/acbbebb2-33ad-11e4-8f02-03c644b2d7d0_story.html (accessed 9/12/2014).

25. W. G. Dunlop, "IS jihadists urge killing of citizens from US-led coalition," *AFP*, September 22, 2014. Available from http://news.yahoo.com/jihadists-urge-killing-citizens-us-led-coalition-102650763.html (accessed 9/22/2014).

26. See, e.g., "Sunni rebels declare new 'Islamic caliphate,'" *Aljazzera*, June 30, 2014. Available from http://www.aljazeera.com/news/middleeast/2014/06/isil-declares-new-islamic-caliphate-201462917326669749.html (accessed 8/28/2014). See also Stephanie Nebehey and Ahmed Rasheed, "U.N. accuses Islamic State of mass killings," *Reuters*, August 25, 2014. Available from http://www.reuters.com/article/2014/08/25/us-iraq-security-idUSKBN0GP0L020140825 (accessed 8/29/2014).

27. For those who are skeptical about this view, see Antony Field, "The 'New Terrorism': Revolution or Evolution?" *Political Studies Review* 7 (2009): 195–207.

28. Alan M. Dershowitz, *Why Terrorism Works: Understanding the Threat, Responding to the Challenge* (New Haven, CT: Yale University Press, 2002), p. 31 and ch. 2. See also Jakana Thomas, "Actually, sometimes terrorism does work," *Washington Post*, April 22, 2014. Available from http://www.washingtonpost.com/blogs/monkey-cage/wp/2014/04/22/actually-sometimes-terrorism-does-work/ (accessed 4/23/2014).

29. Bruce Hoffman, "The awful truth is that terrorism works," *The Daily Beast*, March 14, 2015. Available from http://www.thedailybeast.com/articles/2015/03/14/the-awful-truth-is-that-terrorism-works.html (accessed 3/14/2015].

30. For the historical and legal nuances of using this term, see, e.g., W. Seth Carus, *Defining "Weapons of Mass Destruction,"* revised and updated, *Center for the Study of Weapons of Mass Destruction Occasional Paper, No. 8* (Washington, DC: National Defense University Press, 2012). Available from http://www.ndu.edu/press/lib/pdf/CSWMD-OccasionalPapers/CSWMD_OccationalPaper-8.pdf (accessed 5/14/2013).

31. For the risks involved regarding the use of WMD and chemical, biological, radiological, and nuclear weapons by terrorist groups in general and religiously inspired terrorist groups in particular, see Jeffrey M. Bale and Gary A. Ackerman, "Profiling the WMD Terrorist Threat," in *WMD Terrorism: Science and Policies*, ed. Stephen M. Maurer (Cambridge, MA: The MIT Press, 2009), pp. 11–45, especially pp. 36–40.

32 For the threat of nuclear terrorism, see Matthew Bunn and William Tobey, "The Nuclear Terrorism Threat—And Next Steps to Reduce the Danger," Presentation, United Nations Headquarters, New York City, October 7, 2013. Available from http://belfercenter.ksg.harvard.edu/publication/23484/nuclear_terrorism_threat_and_next_steps_to_reduce_the_danger.html?breadcrumb=%252Fpublication%252F23879%252Fnuclear_terrorism_threat (accessed 4/13/2014). See also the remarks by Yukiya Amano, director general of the UN International Atomic Agency (IAEA) about how real the threat of nuclear terrorism is nowadays, UN News Center, 7/1/2013. Available from http://www.un.org/apps/news/story.asp?NewsID=45311&Cr=iaea&Cr1=nuclear (accessed 7/15/2014). See "Fukushima a "blueprint" for terrorists, IAEA warns," *Japan Times,* July 3, 2013. Available from http://www.japantimes.co.jp/news/2013/07/03/national/fukushima-a-blueprint-for-terrorists-iaea-warns/ (accessed 7/15/2014).

33. Rollie Lal, "Terrorists and organized crime join forces," *New York Times*, May 12, 2005. Available from http://www.nytimes.com/2005/05/23/opinion/23iht-edlal.html?_r=0 (accessed 7/14/2014).

34. Gus Martin, "Terrorism and Transnational Organized Crime," in Jay L. Albanese and Philip L. Reichel (eds.), *Transnational Organized Crime: An Overview from Six Continents* (Thousand Oaks, CA: SAGE, 2014), pp. 165–92. See also John Rollins and Liana Sun Wyler, "Terrorism and Transnational Crime: Foreign Policy Issues for Congress," *Congressional Research Service*, June 11, 2013. Available from http://fas.org/sgp/crs/terror/R41004.pdf (accessed 7/15/2014).

35. For an argument supporting the view that the expression "state terrorism" has had and still has clear referents, see Jonathan Glover, "State Terrorism," in R. G. Frey and Christopher W. Morris (eds.), *Violence, Terrorism, and Justice* (New York: Cambridge University Press, 1991), ch. 10; henceforth Frey and Morris (eds.), *Violence, Terrorism, and Justice*; see also Igor Primoratz, "State Terrorism and Counter-Terrorism," in Igor Primoratz (ed.), *Terrorism: The Philosophical Issues* (New York: Palgrave Macmillan, 2004), ch. 9; henceforth Primoratz (ed.), *Terrorism: The Philosophical Issues*.

36. See Ben Kiernan, *Blood and Soil: A World History of Genocide and Extermination from Sparta to Darfur* (New Haven, CT: Yale University Press, 2007), p. 8; see also R. J. Rummel, *Death by Government* (New Brunswick, NJ: Transaction Publishers, 1997), especially ch. 1; henceforth Rummel, *Death by Government*.

37. John Mueller and Mark G. Stewart, *Terror, Security, and Money* (New York: Oxford University Press, 2011), pp. 40–53.

38. According to a newly released report by the RAND Corporation's National Defense Research Institute, the number of Salafi-jihadist groups similar to Al-Qaeda and its affiliates has increased since 2010. Similarly, the number of attacks by these groups since 2010 has also increased. See Seth G. Jones, *A Persistent Threat: The Evolution of Al Qa'ida and Other Salafi Jihadists* (Santa Monica, CA: RAND Corporation, 2014). Available from http://www.rand.org/content/dam/rand/pubs/research_reports/RR600/RR637/RAND_RR637.pdf (accessed 7/22/2014).

39. My conception of state terrorism overlaps with Rummel's conception of democide. See Rummel, *Death by Government*, pp. 36–37.

40. For an argument against the justification of modern war and in support of pacifism, see Robert L. Holmes, *On War and Morality* (Princeton, NJ: Princeton University Press, 1989), p. 17 and pp. 183–213. Also for an argument against most wars and in favor of what he calls "defensive deterrence" in resisting aggression, see Richard Norman, *Ethics, Killing and War* (New York: Cambridge University Press, 1995), p. 1 and pp. 242–53; henceforth Norman, *Ethics, Killing and War*.

41. Cicero, *On Duties*, M. T. Griffin and E. M. Atkins (eds.) (New York: Cambridge University Press, 1991), bk. I, sec. 34, p. 14; henceforth Cicero, *On Duties*.

42. Charter of the United Nations. Available from https://www.un.org/en/documents/charter/. See especially the preamble, ch. 1 and 2, arts. 2 and 3 (accessed 4/8/2014).

43. International humanitarian law is part of international law that governs relations among states. See ICRC, "What is international humanitarian law?" Available from http://www.icrc.org/eng/resources/documents/legal-fact-sheet/humanitarian-law-factsheet.htm (accessed 4/8/2014).

44. See, e.g., Robert Young, "Political Terrorism as a Weapon of the Politically Powerless," in Primoratz (ed.), *Terrorism: The Philosophical Issues*, ch. 5, especially pp. 58–61.

45. For some of the problems associated with asymmetric conflicts, see Shannon E. French, "Murderers, not Warriors: The Moral Distinction between Terrorists and Legitimate Fighters in Asymmetric Conflicts," in James P. Sterba (ed.), *Terrorism and International Justice* (New York: Oxford University Press, 2003), pp. 31–46, especially pp. 34–35; henceforth Sterba (ed.), *Terrorism and International Justice*.

46. Michael Ignatieff, *The Lesser Evil: Political Ethics in an Age of Terror* (Princeton, NJ: Princeton University Press, 2004), ch. 4, especially p. 91; henceforth Ignatieff, *The Lesser Evil*.

47. Islamic extremists who claim to be following sharia ignore that Muslim jurists defend the presumption of innocence. See, e.g., Khaled Abou El Fadl, *Islam and the Challenge of Democracy*, Joshua Cohen and Deborah Chasman (eds.) (Princeton, NJ: Princeton University Press, 2004), p. 24; henceforth El Fadl, *Islam and the Challenge of Democracy*. In addition, the Quran forbids killing people unless one does it as retribution for murder or for spreading corruption in the land. See Ziauddin Sardar, *Reading the Qur'an: The Contemporary Relevance of the Sacred Text of Islam* (New York: Oxford University Press, 2011), p. 258; henceforth Sardar, *Reading the Qur'an*. See also, e.g., Abdullah Yusuf Ali, *The Holy Qur'an: Text, Translation and Commentary* (Elmhurst, NY: Tahrike Tarsile Qur'an, 2005), 6:151 and 17:33; henceforth A. Y. Ali, *The Holy Qur'an*.

48. Available from http://www.un.org/Docs/journal/asp/ws.asp?m=s/res/1373(2001) and http://www.un.org/Docs/journal/asp/ws.asp?m=s/res/1535(2004) (accessed 9/27/2008).

49. See, e.g., Giles Fraser, "If we can have just war, why not just terrorism?" *Guardian*, 25 July 2014. Available from http://www.theguardian.com/commentisfree/belief/2014/jul/25/just-war-then-why-not-just-terrorism (accessed 7/23/2014).

50. See, e.g., F. M. Kamm, "Terrorism and Intending Evil," *Philosophy and Public Affairs*, 36, no. 2 (2008): 157–86, especially 157–58; Virginia Held, "Legitimate Authority in Non-State Groups Using Violence," *Journal of Social Philosophy*, vol. 36, no. 2 (Summer 2005): 175–93, especially 180; henceforth Held, "Legitimate Authority in Non-State Groups Using Violence"; Alison Jaggar, "What Is Terrorism, Why Is It Wrong, and Could It Ever Be Morally Permissible?" *Journal of Social Philosophy*, vol. 36, no. 2 (Summer 2005): 202–17, especially 213; henceforth Jaggar, "What Is Terrorism, Why Is It Wrong, and Could It Ever Be Morally Permissible?" See also James P. Sterba, "Terrorism and International Justice," in Sterba (ed.), *Terrorism and International Justice*, p. 211; henceforth Sterba, "Terrorism and International Justice"; Andrew Valls, "Can Terrorism be Justified?" in Andrew Valls (ed.), *Ethics and International Affairs* (Lanham, MD: Rowman & Littlefield, 2000), p. 78; henceforth Valls, "Can Terrorism be Justified?"

51. Bin Laden, "Terror for Terror," in Lawrence (ed.), *Messages to the World*, p. 120.

52. Ted Honderich, *After the Terror* (Great Britain: Edinburgh University Press, 2002), p. 100; henceforth Honderich, *After the Terror*; see also Tomis Kapitan, "Terrorism in the Arab-Israeli Conflict," in Primoratz (ed.), *Terrorism: The Philosophical Issues*, ch. 13, especially pp. 181–82, and p. 187.

53. For Bin Laden's declaration of war against the United States and its allies, see "Declaration of *Jihad*, August 23, 1996," p. 29; his interview, "From Somalia to Afghanistan, March, 1997," p. 46; and Bin Laden et al., "The World Islamic Front, February 23, 1998," p. 61 in Bruce Lawrence (ed.), *Messages to the World*.

54. Carl von Clausewitz, *On War*, Michael Howard and Peter Paret (eds.) (Princeton, NJ: Princeton University Press, 1976), bk. I, ch. 1, sec. 2, p. 75.

55. See, e.g., "1977 Geneva Protocol I Additional to the Geneva Conventions of 12 August 1949, and Relating to Victims of International Armed Conflicts," in Roberts and Guelff (eds.), *Documents of the Laws of War*, Art. 52 (2), p. 450; henceforth 1977 Geneva Protocol I.

56. Helen Duffy, *The "War on Terror" and the Framework of International Law* (New York: Cambridge University Press, 2005), footnote 63, p. 84; henceforth Duffy, *The "War on Terror."*

57. This speech was published in the *Ohio State Journal* of August 12, 1880. See Lloyd Lewis, *Sherman: Fighting Prophet* (New York: Harcourt, Brace and Company, 1958), pp. 635–37.

58. For Thucydides's view, see the famous Melian Debate in Thucydides, *The Peloponnesian Wars*, trans. with introduction and notes by Steven Lattimore (Indianapolis: Hackett, 1998), bk. V, sec. 89, p. 295. For Thrasymachus's view, see Plato, *The Republic* in *The Collected Dialogues of Plato*, Edith Hamilton and Huntington Cairns (eds.) (Princeton, NJ: Princeton University Press, 1978), bk. I, sec. 338c, p. 588.

CHAPTER 2

1. Raymond Aron, *Peace and War: A Theory of International Relations*, 2nd ed. (New York: Frederick A Praeger, 1968), p. 169; henceforth Aron, *Peace and War*.

2. In the 109 definitions the terms "violence" and "force" appear 83.5 percent, while the term "political" appears 65 percent. See Alex P. Schmid and Albert J. Jongman, *Political Terrorism* (New Brunswick: Transaction Publishers, 2005), p. 5.

3. For a chronological list of these legal instruments, see the UN Action to Counter Terrorism. Available from http://www.un.org/en/terrorism/instruments.shtml (accessed 7/11/2013).

4. For a brief explanation of the notions of customary international law and *opinio juris*, see Michael Byers, *War Law: Understanding International Law and Armed Conflict* (New York: Grove Press, 2005), pp. 3–4; henceforth Byers, *War Law*. See also Duffy, *The 'War on Terror,'* pp. 277–78.

5. For criticisms against the injustices committed by the Allies during World War II, see G. E. M. Anscombe, "The Justice of the Present War," in G. E. M. Anscombe, *The Collected Philosophical Papers of G. E. M. Anscombe, Vol. 3: Ethics, Religion and Politics* (Minneapolis: University of Minnesota Press, 1981), pp. 72–81; henceforth Anscombe, "The Justice of the Present War."

6. James G. Blight and Janet M. Lang, *The Fog of War: Lessons from the Life of Robert S. McNamara* (Lanham, MD: Rowman & Littlefield, 2005), p. 8; henceforth Blight and Lang, *The Fog of War*.

7. Ibid., pp. 122–23.
8. Roberts and Guelff (eds.), *Documents on The Laws of War*, p. 2; see also Byers, *War Law*, p. 9.
9. See 1977 Geneva Protocol I, Arts. 50 and 43; and 1949 Geneva Convention III, Art. 4 A (1), (2), (3), and (6) in Roberts and Guelff (eds.), *Documents on the Laws of War*.
10. For international criminal law against genocide, see 1948 United Nations Convention on the Prevention and Punishment of the Crime of Genocide in Roberts and Guelff (eds.), *Documents of the Laws of War*, pp. 180–94. For international criminal law against war crimes and crimes against humanity, see Charter of the International Military Tribunal at Nuremberg, August 8, 1945, in Michael Reisman and Chris T. Antoniou (eds.), *The Laws of War: A Comprehensive Collection of Primary Documents on International Laws Governing Armed Conflict* (New York: Vintage Books, 1994), pp. 318–22; henceforth Reisman and Antoniou (eds.), *The Laws of War*. For recent enforcement and expansion of international criminal law, see Statute of the International Tribunal for the Prosecution of Persons Responsible for Serious Violations of International Humanitarian Law Committed in the Territory of the Former Yugoslavia since 1991, May 25, 1993, in Steven R. Ratner and Jason S. Abrams (eds.), *Accountability for Human Rights Atrocities in International Law: Beyond the Nuremberg Legacy* (New York: Oxford University Press, 2001), Appendix 16, pp. 365–71; henceforth Ratner and Abrams (eds.), *Accountability for Human Rights Atrocities*. See also 1994 Statute of International Criminal Tribunal for Rwanda: Extract, in Roberts and Guelff (eds.), *Documents of the Laws of War*, pp. 618–21; Rome Statute of the International Criminal Court, July 17, 1998 in William A. Shabas, *An Introduction to the International Criminal Court*, 2nd ed. (New York: Cambridge University Press, 2004), appendix 1.
11. UN Action to Counter Terrorism: Available from http://www.un.org/en/terrorism/instruments.shtml (accessed 4/9/2014).
12. 1977 Geneva Protocol I, Art. 51; see also 1977 Geneva Protocol II Additional to the Geneva Conventions of 12 August 1949, and Relating to the Protection of Victims of Non-International Armed Conflicts , Art. 13., in Roberts and Guelff (eds.), *Documents of the Laws of War*.
13. Ratner and Abrams, *Accountability for Human Rights Atrocities*, p. 331.
14. Duffy, *The 'War on Terror,'* pp. 18–19.
15. See League of Nations Convention for the Prevention and Punishment of Terrorism (adopted November 16, 1937) in Ben Saul, *Terrorism* (Portland, OR: Hart Publishing, 2012), p. 1. See also Amrith Rohan Perera, "Response to Global Terrorism: UN Initiatives to Enhance International Cooperation in Combating Terrorism," *International Institute for Middle East and Balkan Studies*. Available from http://www.ifimes.org/en/researches/response-to-global-terrorism-un-initiatives-to-enhance-international-cooperation-in-combating-terrorism/ (accessed 4/9/2014); Andrea Gioia, "The UN Conventions on the Prevention and Suppression of International Terrorism," in *International Cooperation in Counter-Terrorism: The United Nations and Regional Organizations in the Fight Against Terrorism*, Giuseppe Nesi (ed.) (Burlington, VT: Ashgate, 2005), pp. 3–23, especially pp. 3–4.

16. Antonio Cassese, *International Law*, 2nd ed. (New York: Oxford University Press, 2005), pp. 449–50; henceforth Cassese, *International Law*. See also Duffy, *The 'War on Terror,'* pp. 19–20.

17. UN A/RES/49/60 December 9, 1994. Available from http://www.un.org/documents/ga/res/49/a49r060.htm (accessed 9/27/2009).

18. Cassese, *International Law*, pp. 449–50.

19. See "China passes law to help fight 'acts of terror,'" *Reuters*, October 29, 2011. Available from http://in.reuters.com/article/2011/10/29/idINIndia-60189920111029 (accessed 4/16/2014). See also Human Rights Watch, "China: Draft Counterterrorism Law a Recipe for Abuses," January 20, 2015. Available from http://www.hrw.org/news/2015/01/20/china-draft-counterterrorism-law-recipe-abuses (accessed 3/5/2015); Simon Denyer, "China's new terrorism law provokes anger in U.S., concern at home," *Washington Post*, March 5, 2015. Available from http://www.washingtonpost.com/world/asia_pacific/china-invokes-terrorism-as-it-readies-additional-harsh-measures/2015/03/04/1e078288-139c-497e-aa8a-e6d810a5a8a2_story.html (accessed 3/5/2015).

20. See, "China accuses Dalai Lama of encouraging suicide by fire," *BBC News*, October 19, 2011. Available from http://www.bbc.co.uk/news/world-asia-pacific-15372731 (accessed 4/17/2014).

21. "Saudi Arabia: New Terrorism Regulations Assault Rights," *Human Rights Watch*, March 20, 2014. Available from http://www.hrw.org/news/2014/03/20/saudi-arabia-new-terrorism-regulations-assault-rights (accessed 4/2/2014). See also Areej Abuqudairi, "Jordan anti-terrorism law sparks concern," *Aljazeera*, April 25, 2014. Available from http://www.aljazeera.com/news/middleeast/2014/04/jordan-anti-terrorism-law-sparks-concern-201442510452221775.html (accessed 4/28/2014).

22. Hoffman, *Inside Terrorism*, p. 40.

23. Ibid., p. 40.

24. Ibid., pp. 15–16.

25. For example, during the Reign of Terror or the Red Terror of the French Revolution, Robespierre attempted a teleological justification of political violence conceived of as terror against the enemies of the revolution. In so doing, he conflated virtue and terror. See Maximilien Robespierre, "On the Principles of Political Morality That Should Guide the National Convention in the Domestic Administration of the Republic," in *Virtue and Terror: Maximilien Robespierre*, Slavoj Žižek (ed.), (New York: Verso, 2007), p. 115. For a similar attempt at a teleological justification of terror conceived of as revolutionary or progressive violence, see Maurice Merleau-Ponty, *Humanism and Terror: An Essay on the Communist Problem*, trans. by John O'Neill (Boston: Beacon Press, 1969). For an argument against such a teleological justification of political violence conceived of as both individuals terror and state terrorism, see Albert Camus, *The Rebel: An Essay on Man in Revolt*, trans. Anthony Bower (New York: Vintage Books, 1956), especially pp. 125–32.

26. See, e.g., Rémi Brulin, "Terrorism Is Terrorism," *Foreign Policy*, August 20, 2012. Brulin justifiably criticizes Hoffman's conception of terrorism as violence committed by nonstate agents because it neglects state-sponsored terrorism, such the Salvadoran right-wing death squads during El Salvador's civil war in the 1980s.

The fact that Hoffman explicitly labels the violence perpetrated by death squads as "terror" rather than as "terrorism" does not address that which is most objectionable to the practice of terrorist violence, namely, the deliberate targeting of impeccably innocent civilians. Available from http://www.foreignpolicy.com/articles/2012/08/20/terrorism_is_terrorism?page=0,1 (accessed 8/22/2012).

27. Held, "Legitimate Authority in Non-State Groups Using Violence," p. 178.

28. Roberts and Guelff (eds.), *Documents on the Laws of War*, pp. 1–46, especially pp. 1–10.

29. Aron, *Peace and War*, p. 326.

30. See 1949 Geneva Convention I for the Amelioration of the Condition of the Wounded and Sick in Armed Forces in the Field, Art. 3, pp. 198–99 in Roberts and Guelff (eds.), *Documents of the Laws of War*. In the case of noninternational armed conflict, Article 3 states that parties involved in the conflict are bound to minimally apply the following provisions: (1) Persons taking no active part in the hostilities, including members of the armed forces who have laid down their arms and those placed *hors de combat* by sickness, wounds, detention, or any other cause, shall in all circumstances be treated humanely. To this end, the following acts are and shall remain prohibited at any time and in any place whatsoever with respect to the above-mentioned persons: (a) violence to life and person, in particular murder of all kinds, mutilation, cruel treatment, and torture; (b) taking hostages; (c) outrages upon personal dignity, in particular humiliating and degrading treatment; (d) the passing of sentences and the carrying out of executions without previous judgment pronounced by a regularly constituted court, affording all the judicial guarantees which are recognized as indispensable by civilized peoples.

(2) The wounded and sick shall be collected and cared for. See also Protocol Additional to the Geneva Conventions of 12 August 1949, and Relating to the Protection of Victims of Non-International Armed Conflicts, in idem, pp. 483–93.

31. Theodor Meron, "International Criminalization of Internal Atrocities," *American Journal of International Law*, vol. 89, no. 3 (July 1995): 554–77, especially 554–55.

32. See 1993 Statute of International Criminal Tribunal for the former Yugoslavia: Extract, in Roberts and Guelff (eds.), *Documents on the Laws of War*, pp. 568–72. See also idem, 1994 Statute of International Criminal Tribunal for Rwanda: Extract, pp. 618–21; 1998 Rome Statute of the International Criminal Court: Extract (henceforth, ICC), pp. 671–92. The ICC entered into force on July 1, 2002, once sixty states signed it.

33. Brian M. Jenkins, "International Terrorism: The Other World War," in Charles W. Kegley Jr. (ed.), *The New Global Terrorism: Characteristics, Causes, Controls* (Upper Saddle River, NJ: Prentice Hall, 2003), p. 17.

34. M. Byers, *War Law*, p. 6.

35. See, e.g., the Vienna Convention on the Law of Treatises, 1969 (henceforth VCLT, 1969), Article 53, which defines a peremptory norm as follows: "a norm accepted and recognized by the international community of States as a whole as a norm from which no derogation is permitted and which can be modified only by a subsequent norm of general international law having the same character." Available

from https://treaties.un.org/doc/Publication/UNTS/Volume%201155/volume-1155-I-18232-English.pdf (accessed 8/13/2014). See also Duffy, *The "War on Terror,"* p. 9; Ratner and Abrams, *Accountability for Human Rights Atrocities*, p. 20.

36. U.S.C. Title 22, Section 2656f(d). Foreign Relations and Intercourse. Available from http://www.gpo.gov/fdsys/pkg/USCODE-2010-title22/html/USCODE-2010-title22.htm (accessed 4/17/2014).

37. See, e.g., the controversial decision by the International Court of Justice (ICJ) in the case concerning military and paramilitary activities in and against Nicaragua: Nicaragua v. United States of America [1986 ICJ 1(June 27, 1986)] in Reisman and Antoniou (eds.), *The Laws of War*, pp. 12–19. The United States simply withdrew from the case. A majority of the judges voted twelve votes to three that the United States had violated customary international law by using force against Nicaragua.

38. Michael Walzer, *Just and Unjust Wars*, 2nd ed. (New York: Basic Books, 1977), p. 146; henceforth Walzer, *Just and Unjust War*; see also G. E. M. Anscombe, "War and Murder," in Anscombe, *The Collected Philosophical Papers of G. E. M. Anscombe, Vol. 3*, p. 53.

39. See the preamble of the OIC Convention to Combat Terrorism (1999-1420H), Part I, Art. I, sec. 2. Available from http://www.oicun.org/7/38/ (accessed 9/7/2013). See also the preamble of the OAU Convention on the Prevention and Combating of Terrorism, 1999, Part I, Art. 1, sec. 3. Available from http://treaties.un.org/doc/db/Terrorism/OAU-english.pdf (accessed 9/7/2013).

40. See OIC Convention to Combat Terrorism, Part I, Art. 1, sec. 3.

41. Ibid., see the preamble.

42. El Fadl, *Islam and the Challenge of Democracy*, pp. 12–16.

CHAPTER 3

1. John Rawls, *A Theory of Justice*, revised ed. (Cambridge, MA: Harvard University Press, 1999), pp. 98–99.

2. St. Augustine, *The City of God*, bk. 19, ch. 14, p. 157 in Oliver O'Donovan and Joan Lockwood O'Donovan (eds.), *From Irenaeus to Grotius: A Sourcebook in Christian Political Thought*, (Grand Rapids, MI: William B. Eerdmans Publishing Co., 1999); henceforth O'Donovan and O'Donovan (eds.), *From Irenaeus to Grotius*.

3. St. Thomas Aquinas, *Summa Theologiae, Vol. 28, Law and Political Theory* (Ia2a. 90–97) (New York: Cambridge University Press, 2006), Q. 94, art. 2, p. 81.

4. Abdullah Yusuf Ali, *The Qur'an: Text, Translation and Commentary* (New York: Tahrike Tarsile Qur'an, Inc., 2005), 3:104; see also 7:157; hereafter A. Y. Ali, *The Qur'an*.

5. For a classic exposition of a forfeiture theory of natural rights, see John Locke, *Two Treatises of Government*, 2nd ed. (New York: Cambridge University Press, 1980), ch. 15, sec. 170 and ch. xvi, secs. 180–83.

6. The presumption of innocence principle is part of international customary law as it is recognized, e.g., in Article 11 of the Universal Declarations of Human

Rights. Available from http://www.un.org/en/documents/udhr/ (accessed 8/9/2014). Moreover, this principle is also unambiguously recognized in Article 14 (2) of the International Covenant on Civil and Political Rights (ICCPR) of the UN. Unlike the Universal Declaration of Human Rights, this treaty is binding among the 152 nations that have already ratified it. Available from http://www.ohchr.org/en/professionalinterest/pages/ccpr.aspx (accessed 4/9/2014); see also Article 6 (2) of the European Convention for the Protection of Human Rights and Fundamental Freedoms that has been ratified by forty-six states. Available from http://conventions.coe.int/treaty/en/treaties/html/005.htm (accessed 4/9/2014).

7. Kenneth Pennington, "Innocent Until Proven Guilty: The Origins of a Legal Maxim," in Patricia M. Dugan (ed.), *The Penal Process and the Protection of Rights in Canon Law* (Montreal, CA: Wilson & Lafleur, 2005), p. 45; henceforth Pennington, "Innocent Until Proven Guilty."

8. William Blackstone, *Commentaries on the Laws of England* (Oxford: Clarendon Press, 1765–1769), bk. 4, ch. 27. Available from http://avalon.law.yale.edu/subject_menus/blackstone.asp (accessed 9/12/2012). The spirit of Blackstone's statement is found in the Bible when Abraham intercedes on behalf of the innocent citizens of Sodom. See *The New American Bible* (New York: Catholic Book Publishing Co., 1970), Genesis 18: 23–32; henceforth *The New American Bible*.

9. See *Coffin v. United States*, 156 US 432 (1845). Available from: http://constitution.org/ussc/156-432.htm. While admiring Justice White's use of legal history, Kenneth Pennington underscores the historical inaccuracies of Justice White's interpretation of "innocent until proven guilty." See Pennington, "Innocent Until Proven Guilty," pp. 48–49. According to Pennington, the origin of the principle is explicitly found in a French canonist, Johannes Monachus (1250–1313). The sources of the principle, however, can be traced back to Roman law, canon law, and the *ius commune*, see idem, pp. 55–57.

10. Andrew Stumer, *The Presumption of Innocence: Evidential and Human Rights Perspectives* (Portland, OR: Hart Publishing, 2010), pp. 27–40.

11. Ibid., pp. 40–48.

12. Richard A. Posner, *Law, Pragmatism, and Democracy* (Cambridge: Harvard University Press, 2003), pp. 63–65; henceforth Posner, *Law, Pragmatism, and Democracy*.

13. Geoffrey R. Stone, *Perilous Times: Free Speech in Wartime* (New York: W. W. Norton & Company, 2005), pp. 297–302; henceforth Stone, *Perilous Times*. For a pragmatist defense of the infamous ruling of *Hirabayashi* and *Korematsu*, see Posner, *Law, Pragmatism, and Democracy*, pp. 293–95.

14. Stone, *Perilous Times*, p. 307.

15. According to the late John Ashcroft, former attorney general, they only detained "close to 750 people, all based on violations, and most of them were held for short duration." See John Ashcroft, *Never Again: Securing America and Restoring Justice* (New York: Center Street, 2006), p. 125; henceforth Ashcroft, *Never Again*. For a different account of what transpired right after the 9/11 attacks, see Jodi Wilgoren, "Swept Up in a Dragnet, Hundreds Sit in Custody, and Ask 'Why?'" *New York Times*, November 25, 2001. Available at http://www.nytimes.com/2001/11/25/national/25DETA.html (accessed 7/24/2014).

16. Richard A. Posner, *Not a Suicide Pact: The Constitution in a Time of National Emergency* (New York: Oxford University Press, 2006), p. 9.

17. Ashcroft, *Never Again*, pp. 120–30.

18. Ronald Dworkin, *Is Democracy Possible Here? Principles for a New Political Debate* (Princeton, NJ: Princeton University Press, 2006), pp. 24–51, especially p. 50.

19. Amnesty International, People's Republic of China Submission to the UN Universal Periodic Review Fourth Session of the UPR Working Group of the Human Rights Council February 2009. Available from http://lib.ohchr.org/HRBodies/UPR/Documents/Session4/CN/AI_CHN_UPR_S4_2009_AmnestyInternational.pdf (accessed 7/23/2010).

20. See UN E/CN.4/1995/52. Report on the situation of human rights in Cuba, prepared by the Special Rapporteur, Mr. Carl-Johan Groth, in accordance with Commission resolution 1994/71. Available from http://www1.umn.edu/humanrts/commission/country51/52.htm (accessed 4/18/2014).

21. Charter of the United Nations, art. 1 (3) and art. 2 (4). Available from https://www.un.org/en/documents/charter/ (accessed 4/10/2014).

22. Jessica Stern, *Terror in the Name of God* (New York: HarperCollins, 2003), pp. 40 and 57.

23. Giora Eiland, "In Gaza, there is no such a thing as 'innocent civilians,'" *Ynet News*, July 4, 2014. Available from http://www.ynetnews.com/articles/0,7340,L-4554583,00.html (accessed 8/5/2014).

24. See, e.g., the Amnesty International (AI) report, *Israel/Gaza Operation 'Cast Lead':22 days of death and destruction*, where AI charges the State of Israel with committing war crimes by indiscriminately targeting Palestinian civilians. AI is also critical of Hamas's policies of launching rockets into Israel. Available from http://www.amnesty.org/en/library/asset/MDE15/015/2009/en/8f299083-9a74-4853-860f-0563725e633a/mde150152009en.pdf (accessed 7/21/2009). See also Paul Wood, "Breaking silence on Gaza abuses," *BBC News*, July 15, 2009. Available from http://news.bbc.co.uk/2/hi/middle_east/8151336.stm (accessed 7/21/2009).

25. See, e.g., United Nations Fact Finding Mission on the Gaza Conflict, Press Release 29 September 2009. Available from http://www.ohchr.org/EN/HRBodies/HRC/SpecialSessions/Session9/Pages/FactFindingMission.aspx (accessed 4/17/2014). See also Statement by Richard Goldstone on behalf of the Members of the United Nations Fact Finding Mission on the Gaza Conflict before the Human Rights Council, September 29, 2009. Available from http://www.ohchr.org/EN/HRBodies/HRC/SpecialSessions/Session9/Pages/FactFindingMission.aspx (accessed 4/17/2014). While other members of the fact finding mission of the Goldstone Report did not retract from their findings, Goldstone retracted from the allegation that Israel had deliberately targeted civilians; see Richard Goldstone, "Reconsidering the Goldstone Report on Israel and War Crimes," *Washington Post*, April 1, 2011. Available from http://www.washingtonpost.com/opinions/reconsidering-the-goldstone-report-on-israel-and-war-crimes/2011/04/01/AFg111JC_story.html (accessed 4/17/2014).

26. Isabel Kershner, "Israel Braces for War Crimes Inquiries on Gaza," *New York Times*, August 14, 2014. Available from http://www.nytimes.com/2014/08/15/world/middleeast/israel-braces-for-war-crimes-inquiries-on-gaza.html?_r=0

(accessed 8/15/2014). Amnesty International has released a report denouncing that Palestinian armed groups, including the armed wing of Hamas, of committing war crimes during the 2014 Gaza/Israel conflict. See AI, "State of Palestine: Unlawful and Deadly: Rocket and mortar attacks by Palestinian armed groups during the 2014 Gaza/Israel conflict," March 26, 2015. Available from https://www.amnesty.org/en/documents/mde21/1178/2015/en/ (accessed 4/4/2015).

27. Golda Meir, *A Land of Our Own: An Oral Autobiography*, edited by Marie Syrkin (New York: G. P. Putnam's Sons, 1973), p. 242.

28. See, e.g., Hamas Charter (1988), Selected Documents Regarding Palestine. Available from http://www.thejerusalemfund.org/www.thejerusalemfund.org/carryover/documents/charter.html?chocaid=397 (accessed 8/20/2014). Still, some world leaders and even former heads of state publicly advocate recognizing Hamas as a legitimate political actor. See, e.g., Jimmy Carter and Mary Robinson, "How to Fix It: Ending this war in Gaza begins with recognizing Hamas as a legitimate political actor," *Foreign Policy*, August 4, 2014. Available from http://www.foreignpolicy.com/articles/2014/08/04/how_to_fix_it_jimmy_carter_mary_robinson_israel_palestine_gaza_hamas (accessed 8/30/2014).

29. For the excessive and, at times, indiscriminate use of force by Israel Defense Forces (IDF), see B'Tselem, *Death Foretold: The inevitable outcome of bombing homes and inhabited areas in Gaza*, August 12, 2014. Available from http://www.btselem.org/gaza_strip/20140811_a_death_foretold (accessed 8/21/2014). For further criticisms of Israel's policies within the Jewish community, see *BBC News Middle East*, "Holocaust families criticize Israel over Gaza," August 24, 2014. Available from http://www.bbc.com/news/world-middle-east-28916761 (accessed 8/24/2014). Those critical of Israel's policies claimed that they drafted the above statement as a response to Elie Wiesel's accusation against Hamas's alleged practice of child sacrifice. Patrick Martin, "Elie Wiesel accuses Hamas of child sacrifice in news ad," *Globe and Mail*, August 6, 2014. Available from http://www.theglobeandmail.com/news/world/elie-wiesel-accuses-hamas-of-child-sacrifice-in-news-ad/article19944809/ (accessed 8/24/2014).

30. See, e.g., William Booth, "The UN says 7 in10 Palestinians killed in Gaza were civilians. Israel disagrees," *Washington Post*, August 29, 2014. Available from http://www.washingtonpost.com/world/middle_east/the-un-says-7-in-10-palestinians-killed-in-gaza-were-civilians-israel-disagrees/2014/08/29/44edc598-2faa-11e4-9b98-848790384093_story.html?wpisrc=nl_hdtop (accessed 8/30/2014).

31. Immanuel Kant, "Perpetual Peace: A Philosophical Sketch," in *Kant: Political Writings* Hans Reiss (ed.) (New York: Cambridge University Press, 1999), pp. 93–96.

32. Ibid., p. 96.

33. See Sartre's preface to Frantz Fanon, *The Wretched of the Earth* (New York: Grove Press, 2004), p. lvi; henceforth Fanon, *The Wretched of the Earth*. It is painfully ironic that Fanon, who exposes the Manichaean nature of colonialism, ends up embracing this either/or mentality to justify the indiscriminate use of violence against colonialists. See, idem, ch. 1. Manichaeism on the left has its counterpart on the right. One finds such a sophism on ideologues on the left and the right alike.

34. George W. Bush's Address to a Joint Session of Congress and the American People, September 20, 2001. Available from http://georgewbush-whitehouse.archives. gov/news/releases/2001/09/20010920-8.html (accessed 4/17/2014).

35. Leon Trotsky, *Marxism and Terrorism* (New York: Pathfinder Press, 1995), especially pp. 9–10 and pp. 16 and 23.

36. Leon Trotsky, *Terrorism and Communism: A Reply to Karl Kautsky* (New York: Verso, 2007), p. 58.

37. Che Guevara, *Guerrilla Warfare* (Lincoln: University of Nebraska Press, 1998), pp. 21–22.

38. Che Guevara, "Message to the Tricontinental," in Guevara, *Guerrilla Warfare*, p. 173.

39. Abraham Guillén, "Urban Guerrilla Strategy," in Laqueur (ed.), *Voices of Terror*, pp. 377–83, especially p. 38.

40. See Paul Wilkinson, *Terrorism Versus Democracy: The Liberal State Response*, 2nd ed. (New York: Routledge, 2006), pp. 17–18. Once they obtained political power, however, both Che and Mao practiced what can be arguably described as state terrorism against their enemies. While Mao's reputation has been generally discredited, some people, including serious scholars, still have an idealized view of Che Guevara. See, e.g., Ignatieff, *The Lesser Evil*, pp. 95–96.

41. C. A. J. Coady, "Defining Terrorism," in Primoratz (ed.), *Terrorism: The Philosophical Issues*, p. 5. See also Anne Schwenkenbecher, *Terrorism: A Philosophical Inquiry* (New York: Palgrave Macmillan, 2012), p. 38; henceforth Schwenkenbecher, *Terrorism: A Philosophical Inquiry*.

42. Title 18 U.S.C 2332B-Acts of Terrorism Transcending National Boundaries. Available from http://www.gpo.gov/fdsys/granule/USCODE-2011-title18/USCODE-2011-title18-partI-chap113B-sec2332b (accessed 4/18/2014). For a similar wide range definition of terrorism, see UK Terrorism Act 2000. Available from http://www. opsi.gov.uk/acts/acts2000/ukpga_20000011_en_2#pt1-l1g1 (accessed 8/20/2009).

43. Ignatieff, *The Lesser Evil*, especially ch. 5.

44. For the notion of militant intolerant people, see Vicente Medina, "Militant Intolerant People: A Challenge to John Rawls' Political Liberalism," *Political Studies*, vol. 58 (2010): 556–71, especially 558.

45. Three years later, bin Laden finally assumed responsibility for the 9/11 attacks. See Osama bin Laden, "The Towers of Lebanon," in Lawrence (ed.), *Messages to the World*, pp. 239–40.

46. For the prohibition of suicide, including suicide bombing, in the Quran, see Sardar, *Reading the Qur'an*, pp. 345–49. See also A. Y. Ali, *The Holy Qur'an*, 6:151 and 2:195.

47. See, e.g., F. M. Kamm, *The Moral Target: Aiming at Right Conduct in War and Other Conflicts* (New York: Oxford University Press, 2012), pp. 167–216; henceforth Kamm, *The Moral Target*; Haig Khatchadourian, "Terrorism and Morality," *Journal of Applied Philosophy* 5, no. 2 (1988): 131; henceforth Khatchadourian, "Terrorism and Morality"; Tamar Meisels, *The Trouble with Terror: Liberty, Security, and The Response to Terrorism* (New York: Cambridge University Press, 2007), pp. 52–53; Igor Primoratz, "Terrorism in the Israeli-Palestinian Conflict:

A Case Study in Applied Ethics," *Iyyun/The Jerusalem Philosophical Quarterly* 55 (January 2006): 27–48; henceforth Primoratz, "Terrorism in the Israeli-Palestinian Conflict"; Michael Walzer, *Just and Unjust Wars*, p. 197. See also Michael Walzer, *Arguing about War* (New Haven: Yale University Press, 2004), ch. 4, especially p. 51; henceforth Walzer, *Arguing about War*.

48. See Primoratz, "Terrorism in the Israeli-Palestinian Conflict," p. 34; see also Kamm, *The Moral Target*, p. 168 and pp. 207–10.

49. Igor Primoratz, "Civilian Immunity," *Philosophical Forum*, vol. 36, no. 1 (Spring 2005): 58.

50. Carl Wellman, "On Terrorism Itself," *Journal of Value Inquiry*, vol. 13, no. 4 (Winter 1979): 250.

51. Virginia Held, *How Terrorism Is Wrong* (New York: Oxford University Press, 2008), p. 75; henceforth Held, *How Terrorism Is Wrong*.

52. Schwenkenbecher, *Terrorism: A Philosophical Inquiry*, p. 38.

53. See the Executive Summary of the ICJ, *Assessing Damage, Urging Action: Report of the Eminent Jurists Panel on Terrorism, Counter-terrorism and Human Rights*, 2009, p. 3. Available from http://www.un.org/en/sc/ctc/specialmeetings/2011/docs/icj/icj-2009-ejp-execsumm.pdf (accessed 4/8/2014).

54. C. A. J. Coady, *Morality and Political Violence* (New York: Cambridge University Press, 2008), p. 162; henceforth Coady, *Morality and Political Violence*.

55. Glen Chapman, "Bill Gates playfully frees swarm of mosquitoes," Yahoo News, February 4, 2009. Available from http://www.binrev.com/forums/index.php/topic/40268-bill-gates-unleashes-a-swarm-of-mosquitoes-at-a-tech-conference/ (accessed 1/12/2014).

56. Claudia Card, "Making War on Terrorism in Response to 9/11" in Sterba (ed.), *Terrorism and International Justice*, pp. 171–85, especially pp. 178–81.

57. Jaggar, "What Is Terrorism, Why Is It Wrong, and Could It Ever Be Morally Permissible?" p. 209.

58. Ibid., p. 211.

59. For some of the nuances involved in classifying rape as a crime against humanity, see Larry May, *Crimes Against Humanity: A Normative Account* (New York: Cambridge University Press, 2005), pp. 96–111.

60. Véronique Zanetti, "Women, War, and International Law," in Igor Primoratz (ed.), *Civilian Immunity in War* (New York: Oxford University Press, 2007), pp. 217–38, especially p. 219; henceforth Primoratz (ed.), *Civilian Immunity in War*.

61. Lewis Carroll, *Through the Looking-Glass and What Alice Found There* (New York: Random House, 1946), especially pp. 94–95.

62. Joel Feinberg, *Harm to Others: The Moral Limits of the Criminal Law* (New York: Oxford University Press, 1984), pp. 31–36.

63. For a classic moving account of Western indifference to the unfolding genocide in Rwanda, see L Gen. Roméo A. Dallaire, *Shake Hands with the Devil: The Failure of Humanity in Rwanda* (Toronto: Random House Canada, 2003), p. xvii; henceforth Dallaire, *Shake Hands with the Devil*. For the failure of UN peacekeeping operation in Rwanda, see also Joshua S. Goldstein, *Winning the War on War* (New York: Dutton, 2011), pp. 78–87. For an account confirming most of Dallaire's

assessment on the ground and the lack of will of the members of the Security Council to stop the Rwandan genocide, see Kofi Annan and Nader Mousavizadeh, *Intervention: A Life in War and Peace* (New York: The Penguin Press, 2012), pp. 46–59; henceforth Annan and Mousavizade, *Intervention*.

64. See Samantha Power, "Bystanders to Genocide," *Atlantic*, September 2001. Available from http://www.theatlantic.com/doc/200109/power-genocide (accessed 6/12/2009).

65. William Schabas, "The Genocide Convention at Fifty," *United States Institute of Peace*, Special Report No. 41, January 7, 1999. Available from http://www.usip.org/sites/default/files/sr990107.pdf (accessed 4/10/2014).

66. For the negative effects experienced by those who have been subjected to prolonged periods of solitary confinement, see Sharon Shalev, *A Sourcebook on Solitary Confinement* (London: Mannheim Center for Criminology, 2008). Available from http://solitaryconfinement.org/uploads/sourcebook_web.pdf (accessed 8/23/2014).

67. This seems to be the letter and the spirit of the UN Charter. For example, Article 2 (4) rules out the arbitrary use of force by one state against another. The Charter allows two exceptions to the prohibition against resorting to force: self-defense and authorization by the Security Council under Chapter VII. See Charter of the United Nations, available from https://www.un.org/en/documents/charter/ (accessed 4/10/2014).

68. For Cicero's recognition of human dignity or worthiness, see Cicero, *On Duties*, bk. I, secs. 105 and 106. For Kant's second formulation of the categorical imperative, see Immanuel Kant, *Groundwork of the Metaphysic of Moral*, trans. H. J. Paton (New York: Harper and Row, 1964), p. 96; henceforth Kant, *Groundwork*.

69. See the Universal Declaration of Human Rights, especially the preamble, arts. 1, 22, and 23. Available from http://www.un.org/en/documents/udhr/ (accessed 8/19/2013). See also International Covenant on Civil and Political Rights, the preamble and art. 10. Available from http://www.ohchr.org/en/professionalinterest/pages/ccpr.aspx (accessed 8/19/2013); Basic Law for the Republic of Germany, art. 1:1. Available from http://www.gesetze-im-internet.de/englisch_gg/ (accessed 8/19/2013).

70. For example, consider the allegorical sense used in Genesis 1:27: "God created man in his image; in the divine image he created him; male and female he created them."

71. A. Y. Ali, *The Qur'an*, 17:70. It seems that the terms "honor" and "dignity" are used interchangeably in different translations of the Quran. Despite semantic considerations, the important point is that those who are honored or who are bestowed dignity have special status in God's creation.

72. See John Rawls, "Two Concepts of Rules," in *John Rawls: Collected Papers*, Samuel Freeman (ed.) (Cambridge, MA: Harvard University Press, 1999), p. 27; henceforth Rawls, *Collected Papers*.

73. Plato, *Crito*, in Plato, *The Collected Dialogues of Plato*, Edith Hamilton and Huntington Cairns (eds.), (Princeton, NJ: Princeton University Press, 1978), p. 34, 49b; henceforth Plato, *The Collected Dialogues*.

74. Plato, *Gorgias*, *The Collected Dialogues*, p. 251, 469b.

75. Ibid., p. 252, 469c.

76. Paul, "The Epistle of Paul to the Romans," *The New American Bible, Romans* 3:8, p. 183.

77. Kant, *Groundwork*, p. 96.

78. For an argument against proportionalism and a defense of the Socratic and Pauline principle, see John Finnis, *Fundamentals of Ethics* (Washington, DC: George-town University Press, 1983), pp. 110–33; henceforth Finnis, *Fundamentals of Ethics.*

79. Stephen Nathanson, *Terrorism and the Ethics of War* (New York: Cambridge University Press, 2010), p. 291.

80. John Rawls, *Justice as Fairness: A Restatement*, Erin Kelly (ed.), (Cambridge, MA: Harvard University Press, 2001), especially part III, secs. 23, 25, and 26.

81. For a classic consequentialist argument supporting a substantive duty of beneficence to help the needy, see Peter Singer, "Famine, Affluence, and Morality," in Steven M. Cahn and Peter Markie (eds.), *Ethics: History, Theory, and Contemporary Issues* (New York: Oxford University Press, 2006), pp. 789–96; henceforth Cahn and Markie (eds.), *Ethics*. See also, idem, "A life to save: direct action on poverty." Available from http://www.opendemocracy.net/article/a-life-to-save-direct-action-on-poverty (accessed 5/14/2009).

82. See, e.g., John Arthur, "Famine Relief and the Ideal Moral Code," in Cahn and Markie (eds.), *Ethics*, pp. 797–808. Arthur argues against Peter Singer's substantive duty of beneficence by defending a more complex view of morality that also includes entitlements, desert, and a less demanding duty of beneficence. But, like Singer, he justifies his ideal conception of morality on consequentialist considerations.

83. Thomas Hobbes, *Leviathan*, Richard Tuck (ed.), (New York: Cambridge University Press, 1991), ch. 13, p. 89; henceforth Hobbes, *Leviathan*.

84. Klaus Dahmann, DW, *Terrorism trumps military taboos in Germany*, 8/18/2012. Available from http://www.dw.de/dw/article/0,,16177278,00.html (accessed 8/20/2012). For some of the constitutional challenges leading to such an unprecedented legal decision, see Nils, *Targeted Killing in International Law* (New York: Oxford University Press, 2008), pp. 15–18; henceforth *Targeted Killing in International Law.*

85. For the notion of "permissible harm," see Francis Kamm, "Toward the Essence of Nonconsequentialist Constraints on Harming: Modality, Productive Purity, and the Greater Good Working Itself Out," in Francis Kamm, *Intricate Ethics: Rights, Responsibilities, and Permissible Harm* (New York: Oxford University Press, 2007), pp. 130–89, especially pp. 135–135.

86. Averroes, "The Legal Doctrine of Jihad," in Rudolph Peters, *Jihad in Classical and Modern Islam* (Princeton, NJ: Markus Wiener Publishers, 1996), p. 33. A Christian just war approach rejects such a doctrine. See Francisco de Vitoria, "On the Law of War," in Francisco de Vitoria, *Political Writings*, Anthony Pagden and Jeremy Lawrance (eds.), (New York: Cambridge University Press, 1991), sec. 38, p. 316; henceforth Vitoria, "On the Law of War." Vitoria writes, "It is never right to commit evil, even to avoid greater evil. It is quite unacceptable that a person should be killed for a sin he has yet to commit." This prohibition applies to both fellow citizens and foreigners alike.

87. Osama bin Laden et al., "The World Islamic Front," in Osama bin Laden, Lawrence (ed.), *Messages to the World*, pp. 58–62, especially p. 61.

88. Muhammad Abdel Haleem, *Understanding the Qur'an: Themes and Style* (New York: I. B. Turis, 2011), pp. 65–66.

89. See Jean-Paul Sartre's preface to Fanon, *The Wretched of the Earth*, p. lv. There is a contemporary trend to interpret Sartre's views on violence in light of his oeuvre. See Jennifer Ang Mei Sze, *Sartre and the Moral Limits of War and Terrorism* (New York: Routledge, 2010). Such a trend seems questionable. First, despite Mei Sze's argument, Sartre advocates unbridled violence in the preface. Second, nowhere in his oeuvre does he explicitly adopt a critical view of terrorism, as Mei Sze argues on p. 189. Her contention that Sartre does not approve of violence that breeds more violence or the use of violence for its own sake is a straw man argument, p. 2. Not only Sartre but I doubt any ordinary reasonable person would argue so. And third, in the absence of solid textual evidence, to assume that Sartre had a coherent view of violence is unconvincing.

90. Fanon, *The Wretched of the Earth*, pp. 44 and 51.

91. Kent Greenawalt, *Conflicts of Law and Morality* (New York: Oxford University Press, 1987), p. 258.

92. Hannah Arendt, "On Violence" in *Crises of the Republic* (New York: Harcourt Brace Jovanovich, 1972), p. 122. For a sympathetic and more nuanced contemporary interpretation of Sartre's view on violence, see Marguerite La Caze, "Sartre Integrating Ethics and Politics: The Case of Terrorism," *Parrhesia*, no. 3 (2007), pp. 43–54. Yet La Caze's argument that Sartre was trying to understand rather than condone terrorist violence is unpersuasive. It would be rather odd to try to understand violence by advocating it as Sartre did in his preface to Fanon, *The Wretched of the Earth*. For Sartre's admiration and support of proletarian violence, see Tony Judt, *Past Imperfect: French Intellectuals, 1944–1956* (Berkeley: University of California Press, 1992), pp. 125–26.

93. Carlos Marighella, excerpt from the "Minimanual" in Walter Laqueur (ed.), *Voices of Terror*, p. 374.

94. Mwaura Samora, "Carlos de Jackal: Terrorist and revolutionary to some," *Saturday Monitor*, November 20, 2011. Available from http://www.monitor.co.ug/News/Insight/-/688338/1275892/-/rq2o30/-/index.html (accessed 10/20/2011).

95. The former president of Venezuela, the late Hugo Chávez, praised Carlos as a freedom fighter. See Rory Carroll, "Hugo Chávez courts outrage with praise for Carlos, Mugabe and Amin," *Guardian*, Sunday, November 22, 2009. Available from http://www.theguardian.com/world/2009/nov/22/hugo-chavez-defence-carlos-jackal (accessed 1/5/2014).

96. Ann Louise Bardach, *After Fidel: A Death Foretold in Miami, Havana, and Washington* (New York: Scribner, 2009), p. 99. In the same chapter, Luis Posada Carriles, another well-known anticommunist militant long associated with Orlando Bosh, defends a similar view of political violence.

97. Walzer, *Arguing about War*, p. 130; see also Walzer, *Just and Unjust Wars*, p. 197.

98. Michael Walzer, "Terrorism: A Critique of Excuses," in Steven Luper-Foy (ed.), *Problems of International Justice* (Boulder, CO: Westview Press, 1988), p. 238; henceforth Luper-Foy (ed.), *Problems of International Justice*.

99. Robert K. Fullinwider, "Understanding Terrorism" in Luper-Foy (ed.), *Problems of International Justice*, p. 250.

100. Walter Benjamin, "Critique of Violence," in Walter Benjamin, *Selected Writings*, Vol. 1 1913–1926, Marcus Bullock and Michael W. Jennings (eds.), (Cambridge, MA: Harvard University Press, 1996), p. 252.

101. See, e.g., Slavoj Žižek, *Violence: Six Sideways Reflections* (New York: Picador, 2008), pp. 178–205; especially pp. 196–99.

102. Khatchadourian, "Terrorism and Morality," 139.

103. President Obama has conceded that the CIA tortured some people in the after aftermath of the 9/11 attacks and that it was wrong to have done so. See Paul Lewis, "Obama admits CIA 'tortured some folks' but stands by Brennan over spying," *Guardian*, August 1, 2014. Available from http://www.theguardian.com/world/2014/aug/01/obama-cia-torture-some-folks-brennan-spying (accessed 8/30/2014). For compelling evidence corroborating not only the use of torture and other morally and legally questionable practices committed by some members of the CIA and its associates, see the report by the United States Senate Select Committee on Intelligence forwarded by Senator Dianne Feinstein with the Senate Floor Statement by Senator John McCain, *The Official Senate Report on Torture: Committee Study of the Central Intelligence Agency's Detention and Interrogation Program* (New York: Skyhorse Publishing, 2015).

104. For some of the lingering moral, political, and legal problems associated with the incarceration and treatment of so-called "enemy combatants" at Guantánamo, see Charlie Savage, "Decaying Guantánamo Defies Closing Plans," *New York Times*, September 1, 2014. Available from http://www.nytimes.com/2014/09/01/us/politics/decaying-guantanamo-defies-closing-plans.html?emc=edit_th_20140901&nl=todays headlines&nlid=13987239&_r=0 (accessed 9/12/2014).

105. This writ is guaranteed by the suspension clause of art. 1, sect. 9 of the US Constitution, which states, "The Privilege of the Writ of Habeas Corpus shall not be suspended, unless when in Cases of Rebellion or Invasion the Public Safety may require it."

106. *Boumediene v. Bush*, 553 U.S. (2008), pp. 69–70. Available from http://www.law.cornell.edu/supct/pdf/06-1195P.ZO (accessed 7/21/2009).

107. Lakhdar Boumediene, "My Guantánamo Nightmare," *New York Times*, January 7, 2012. Available from http://www.nytimes.com/2012/01/08/opinion/sunday/my-guantanamo-nightmare.html?pagewanted=print (accessed 1/9/2012).

108. Jeff McMahan, *Killing in War* (New York: Oxford University Press, 2009), p. 8.

109. Ibid., p. 11.

110. Ibid., 33–34.

111. Jeffrie Murphy, "The Killing of the Innocent," *The Monist*, 57: 531–32.

112. It might be worthwhile distinguishing, as Judith Jarvis Thomson does, between the concept of a Good Samaritan who in going out of his way to help others incurs some cost to himself, and a Minimally Decent Samaritan whom one can reasonably expect to help those in distress with insignificant cost to himself or to others affected by his actions. See Judith Jarvis Thomson, "A Defense of Abortion," *Philosophy and Public Affairs*, vol. 1, no. 1 (Fall 1971): 62–64.

113. T. A. Cavanaugh, *Double-Effect Reasoning: Doing Good and Avoiding Evil* (New York: Oxford University Press, 2006), xv–xvi; henceforth Cavanaugh, *Double-Effect Reasoning.* Cavanaugh proposes a similar typology based on the concept of formal and material innocence. Regardless of one's typology, an important moral issue is whether those who pose an innocent threat should also enjoy categorical immunity.

114. For the development of this taxonomy of the innocent, see Vicente Medina, "The Innocent in the Just War Thinking of Vitoria and Suárez: A Challenge Even for Secular Just War Theorists and International Law," *Ratio Juris*, vol. 26, no. 1 (March 2013): pp. 47–64, especially pp. 50–51.

115. Michael R. Gordon and General Bernard E. Trainor, *The Generals' War: The Inside Story of the Conflict in the Gulf* (New York: Little, Brown & Co., 1995), pp. 324–26.

116. Thomas Nagel, "Moral Luck" in Thomas Nagel, *Mortal Questions* (New York: Cambridge University Press, 1991), pp. 24–38. For Nagel, the traditional view of ascribing moral praise or blame based on whether there was good will or not is philosophically perplexing. For a recent defense of the traditional view of moral responsibility, see Harry G. Frankfurt, "Inadvertence and Moral Responsibility," *The Amherst Lecture in Philosophy* 3 (2008), pp. 1–15. Available from http://www.amherstlecture.org/frankfurt2008/frankfurt2008_ALP.pdf (accessed 7/25/2009).

117. Whether the appraisal of justification should aim at the act rather than the agent's mental state remains debatable. Likewise, whether the excuse of an agent pertains to her mental state or to her environment also remains debatable. For an argument exploring the limits of this distinction in criminal law, see Kent Greenawalt, "The Perplexing Borders of Justification and Excuse," *Columbia Law Review*, vol. 84, no. 8 (December 1984): 1897–927. For a rejection of the analogy between the traditional moral distinction of justification and excuse and the distinction in criminal law, see Mitchell N. Berman, "Justification and Excuse, Law and Morality," *Duke Law Journal*, vol. 53, no. 1 (October 2003): 1–43. For some of the nuances about justifications and excuses in moral and legal theory, see Marcia Baron, "Justifications and Excuses," *Ohio State Journal of Criminal Law*, vol. 2, no. 2 (Spring 2005): 387–406.

118. Alan Donagan, for example, argues otherwise. In the case of a fetus that threatens the mother's life, he agrees with Maimonides that the fetus might be conceived of as "an involuntary pursuer." So he views the fetus as formally innocent but materially guilty. Hence, the fetus can be justifiably destroyed. So, in principle, he justifies the intentional destruction of innocent threats. See Alan Donagan, *The Theory of Morality* (Chicago: The University of Chicago Press, 1977), pp. 162–63. For objections against Donagan's view, see Cavanaugh, *Double-Effect Reasoning*, pp. 51–52.

119. See note 40 above.

120. R. G. Frey and Christopher W. Morris, "Violence, Terrorism, and Justice," in Frey and Morris (eds.), *Violence, Terrorism, and Justice*, p. 7.

121. Virginia Held, "Terrorism and War," *Journal of Ethics*, vol. 8, no. 1 (2004): 66.

122. Held, *How Terrorism Is Wrong*, pp. 32–33.

123. See, e.g., Knut Ipsen, "Combatants and Non-Combatants," in Dieter Fleck (ed.), *The Handbook of Humanitarian Law in Armed Conflict*, (New York: Oxford University Press, 2004), ch. 3, p. 66.

124. See, e.g., 1977 Geneva Protocol I, sec. II, art. 43 (2) in Roberts and Guelff (eds.), *Documents of the Laws of War*, p. 444; Combatant or belligerent status is also granted to militia and volunteer corps who are party to an armed conflict and even to inhabitants of an unoccupied territory who spontaneously use armed resistance against invading troops, provided they respect the laws of war and carry arms openly. See 1907 Hague Convention IV Respecting the Laws and Custom of War on Land, Annex to the Convention, sec. I, ch. 1, art (1), idem, p. 73.

125. See, e.g., Ingrid Detter, *The Law of War*, 2nd ed. (New York: Cambridge University Press, 2004), p.140; henceforth Detter, *The Law of War*.

126. For a classification of those who are considered civilians and, hence, non-combatants within the confines of international law, see 1977 Geneva Protocol I, ch. 2, arts. 50 and 51 in Roberts and Guelff (eds.), *Documents of the Laws of War*, pp. 448–49.

127. See 1977 Geneva Protocol I, ch. 2, arts. 50 and 51 in Roberts and Guelff (eds.), *Documents of the Laws of War*, pp. 448–49.

128. Igor Primoratz, "Civilian Immunity in War: Its Grounds, Scope, and Weight," in Igor Primoratz (ed.), *Civilian Immunity in War*, p. 29; henceforth Primoratz, "Civilian Immunity in War: Its Grounds, Scope, and Weight."

129. Norman, *Ethics, Killing and War*, pp. 167–68.

130. Cicero, *On Duties*, bk. III, secs. 19 and 20, p. 107, and sec. 32, p. 111. See also John of Salisbury, *Policraticus*, bk. III, ch. 15; bk. VIII, chs. 17–18, 20 in Gregory M. Reichberg (ed.), et al., *The Ethics of War: Classic and Contemporary Readings* (Malden, MA: Blackwell Publishing, 2006), pp. 128–30; henceforth, Reichberg (ed.), *The Ethics of War*; see Thomas Aquinas, *On Law, Morality and Politics*, W. P. Baumgarth and R. J. Regan (eds.) (Indianapolis: Hackett, 1988), ST II-II, Q. 42, p. 232; henceforth Aquinas, *On Law, Morality and Politics*; see also Thomas Aquinas, *On Kingship*, in Aquinas, *On Law, Morality and Politics*, ch. 6, p. 269.

131. See Executive Order 12333 United States Intelligence Activities, Part 2, sec. 2.11. Available from: http://www.fas.org/irp/offdocs/eo/eo-12333-2008.pdf (accessed 3/30/2012).

132. Melzer, *Targeted Killing in International Law*, p. 10

133. See 1907 Hague Convention IV Respecting the Laws and Customs of War on Land, in Roberts and Guelff (eds.), *Documents of the Laws of War*, II, art. 23 (b), p. 77.

134. See 1977 Geneva Protocol I in Roberts and Guelff (eds.), *Documents of the Laws of War*, art. 37, p. 442. The following are examples of perfidy: "(a) the feigning of an intent to negotiate under a flag of truce or of a surrender; (b) the feigning of an incapacitation by wounds or sickness; (c) the feigning of civilian, non-combatant status; and (d) the feigning of protected status by the use of signs, emblems or uniforms of the United Nations or of neutral or other States not Parties to the conflict."

135. See Detter, *The Law of War*, p. 307.

136. See 1977 Geneva Protocol I, sec. II, art. 43(2) in Roberts and Guelff (eds.), *Documents of the Laws of War*, p. 444.

137. Zanetti, "Women, War, and International Law," p. 226. For the definition of grave breaches in the Geneva Conventions and 1977 Geneva Protocol I, see http://www.icrc.org/Web/Eng/siteeng0.nsf/html/5ZMGF9 (accessed 6/15/2009).

138. The following taxonomy can illuminate the ambiguity of the term "noninnocent." A person can be considered noninnocent in the following senses: (1) *Moral sense*: one is noninnocent in the moral sense only if one deliberately and unjustifiably infringes on someone's rights by omission or commission; (2) *Legal sense*: one is noninnocent in the legal sense only if one violates domestic or international law; (3) *Political sense*: one is noninnocent in the political sense only if one is perceived or designated as such by state or nonstate agents who claim to represent others; (4) *Agonistic sense*: one is noninnocent in the agonistic sense only if one deliberately harms or threatens to harm someone.

139. Walzer, *Just and Unjust Wars*, p. 43.

140. John A. Vasquez, *The War Puzzle* (New York: Cambridge University Press, 1993), pp. 66–68. For a more nuanced typology of total war, see Hans J. Morgenthau, *Politics among Nations: The Struggle for Power and Peace*, 6th ed. revised by Kenneth W. Thomson (New York: Alfred A. Knopf, Inc., 1985), pp. 392–413. For Morgenthau, a war can be total in four different ways: (1) the number of people one identifies with the war, (2) the number of people who participate in the war, (3) the number of people affected by the war, and (4) the aim of the war.

141. C. A. J. Coady, "Terrorism, Just War and Supreme Emergency," in Tony Coady and Michael O' Keefe (eds.), *Terrorism and Justice: Moral Argument in a Threatened World* (Melbourne: Melbourne University Press, 2002), p. 13.

142. Alan Ryan, "State and Private; Red and White," in Frey and Morris (eds.), *Violence, Terrorism, and Justice*, p. 251.

CHAPTER 4

1. See, e.g., Held, "Legitimate Authority in Non-State Groups Using Violence," 180; Jaggar, "What Is Terrorism, Why Is It Wrong, and Could It Ever Be Morally Permissible?" p. 209; Sterba, "Terrorism and International Justice," p. 211; Honderich, *After the Terror*, pp. 150–51; Valls, "Can Terrorism Be Justified?" p. 78.

2. The notion of "grave breaches" is found in 1949 Geneva Convention I, Art. 50; Geneva Convention II, Art. 51; Geneva Convention III, Art.130; and Geneva Convention IV, Art. 147. It is also found in Art. 85 of Protocol Additional to the Geneva Conventions of 12 August 1949, and Relating to the Protection of Victims of International Armed Conflicts (Protocol I), 8 June 1977. Available from http://www.icrc.org/eng/resources/documents/misc/5zmgf9.htm (accessed 1/10/2014).

3. See War Crimes, Art. 8, Rome Statute of the International Criminal Court, 17 July 1998. Available from http://www.icrc.org/ihl/WebART/585-08?OpenDocument (accessed 4/10/2014).

4. For the distinction between grave breaches and war crimes, and how the first has been progressively subsumed under the latter, see Marko Divac Öberg, "The Absorption of Grave Breaches into War Crimes Law," *International Review of the Red Cross*, vol. 91, no. 873 (March 2009): 163–83. Available from http://www.icrc.org/eng/assets/files/other/irrc-873-divac-oberg.pdf (accessed 1/9/2014).

5. Misperception and overconfidence are subjective biases that are not mutually exclusive; hence, at times, they might overlap. For the role of perception in foreign policy, see Robert Jervis, *Perception and Misperception in International Politics* (Princeton, NJ: Princeton University Press, 1976), especially ch. 1. See also idem, "War and Misperception," *Journal of Interdisciplinary History*, vol. 18, no. 4 (Spring 1988): 675–700. For the role of overconfidence in foreign policy, see Steve A. Yetiv, *National Security through a Cockeyed Lens: How Cognitive Bias Impacts U.S. Foreign Policy* (Baltimore, MD: Johns Hopkins University Press, 2013), pp. 49–70.

6. For the illegality of the US invasion of Iraq, see Kofi Annan and Nader Wousavidazadeh, *Interventions*, pp. 344–54.

7. Plato, *Republic*, in The *Collected Dialogues*, bk. v, 470c and 470d, p. 709. For a contemporary elaboration of this view, see Carl Schmitt, The *Concept of the Political*, translated and with an introduction by George Schwab with a new foreword by Tracy Strong (Chicago: The University of Chicago Press, 1996), pp. 28–29; henceforth Schmitt, The *Concept of the Political*.

8. For Cicero's view on pirates as enemies of humanity, see Cicero, *On Duties.*, III, sec. 107, p. 141. For a contemporary definition of piracy as "any illegal acts of violence or detention, or any act of depredation, committed for private ends by the crew or the passengers of a private ship or a private aircraft against other ships, air-crafts, persons or property," see United Nations Convention on the Law of the Sea (UNCLOS) Convention on the High Seas, December 10, 1982, part VII, art. 101. Available from http://www.un.org/Depts/los/convention_agreements/texts/unclos/closindx.htm (accessed 3/11/2009).

9. Cicero, *On Duties*, I, sec. 37, p. 16.

10. Ibid., I, secs. 35–38, pp. 14–17.

11. Ibid., I, sec. 108, p. 142.

12. See, e.g., Alberico Gentili, *On the Law of* War, "Chapter II: The Definition of War," in Reichberg (ed.), The *Ethics of War,* pp. 373–74; see also Hugo Grotius, The *Rights of War and Peace*, Richard Tuck (ed.), (Indianapolis, IN: Liberty Fund, 2005), bk. III, ch. 3, sec. 1, p. 1246; henceforth Grotius, The *Rights of War and Peace*.

13. For the first time the UN has collected compelling evidence of the atrocities that have been committed and continue being committed in the Democratic People's Republic of North Korea. Those atrocities are classified as crimes against humanity. See *Report of the Detailed Finding of the Commission of Inquiry of Human Rights in the Democratic People's Republic of North Korea,* February 7, 2014. Available from http://www.ohchr.org/EN/HRBodies/HRC/CoIDPRK/Pages/CommissionInqui-ryonHRinDPRK.aspx (accessed 2/21/2014). See also Roberta Cohen, "Preventing a massacre in North Korea's gulags," *Washington Post*, July 25, 2014. Available from http://www.washingtonpost.com/opinions/preventing-a-massacre-in-north-koreas-gulags/2014/07/25/b9d6a3fe-1284-11e4-9285-4243a40ddc97_story.html?wpisrc=nl_headlines (accessed 7/25/2014). See Victor Cha, The *Impossible State: North Korea Past and Future* (New York: HarperCollins Publishers, 2013), especially pp. 162–211. R. J. Rummel offers a rough estimate of the North Korean democide from 1948 to 1987 at about 1,663,000. See R. J. Rummel, *Death by Government*, pp. 365–79, especially p. 377.

14. Immanuel Kant, The *Metaphysics of Morals*, Introduction, translation, and notes by Mary Gregor (New York: Cambridge University Press, 1991), p. 156.

15. Ibid., p. 155.

16. Ibid., p. 155.

17. For a transcultural and interreligious foundation of the principle *Pacta sunt servanda* or the sanctity of contracts in international law, see Hans Wehberg, "Pacta Sunt Servanda," American *Journal of International Law*, vol. 53, no. 4 (October 1959): pp. 775–86, especially p. 775.

18. For some of the problems associated with Kant's conception of the unjust enemy, and the inapplicability of such a conception to international law, see Carl Schmitt, The *Nomos of the Earth in the International Law of the Jus Publicum Europeum*, trans. by G. L. Ulmen (New York: Telos Press Publishing, 2006), pp. 168–71; henceforth Schmitt, The *Nomos of the Earth in the International Law of the Jus Publicum Europeum*. Schmitt conceives of the friend-enemy distinction as a concrete political choice rather than as an a priori moral judgment, as Kant argues. See, e.g., Carl Schmitt, The *Concept of the Political*, especially pp. 28–29.

19. ICC-02/05-01/09. Available from http://www.icc-cpi.int/iccdocs/doc/doc639078.pdf (accessed 4/21/2014).

20. For a characterization of a state as a decent society, see John Rawls, The *Laws of People* (Cambridge, MA: Harvard University Press, 1999), p. 88.

21. For an article arguing for the possibility of a universal definition of terrorism conceived of as piracy, see Douglas R. Burgess Jr., "The Dread Pirate Bin Laden," *Legal Affairs*, July/August 2005. Available from http://www.legalaffairs.org/issues/July-August-2005/feature_burgess_julaug05.msp (accessed 3/11/09).

22. See, e.g., the following UN multilateral conventions in United Nations Action to Counter Terrorism: Convention on Offences and Certain Other Acts Committed on Board Aircraft, signed at Tokyo on September 14, 1963; Convention for the Suppression of Unlawful Seizure of Aircraft, signed at the Hague on December 16, 1970; International Convention against the Taking of Hostages, adopted by the General Assembly of the United Nations on December 17, 1979; Convention for the Suppression of Unlawful Acts against the Safety of Maritime Navigation, done at Rome on March 10, 1988. Available from http://www.un.org/en/terrorism/instruments.shtml (accessed 4/11/2014).

23. See, e.g., the following UN multilateral conventions in United Nations Action to Counter Terrorism: Convention on the Prevention and Punishment of Crimes against Internationally Protected Persons, including Diplomatic Agents, adopted by the General Assembly of the United Nations on December 14, 1973; International Convention for the Suppression of Terrorist Bombings, adopted by the General Assembly of the United Nations on December 15, 1997; International Convention for the Suppression of the Financing of Terrorism, adopted by the General Assembly of the United Nations on December 9, 1999; International Convention for the Suppression of Acts of Nuclear Terrorism, New York, April 13, 2005. Available from http://www.un.org/en/terrorism/instruments.shtml (accessed 4/11/2014).

24. See note 40, ch. 1 above.

25. Oliver O'Donovan, The *Just War Revisited* (New York; Cambridge University Press, 2003), pp. 6–7; henceforth O'Donovan, The *Just War Revisited*.

26. James Turner Johnson, *Ideology, Reason, and the Limitation of War* (Princeton, NJ: Princeton University Press, 1975), p. 8; henceforth Turner Johnson, *Ideology, Reason, and the Limitation of War*.

27. Robert Kolb, "Origin of the Twin Terms Jus ad Bellum/Jus in Bello," *International Review of the Red Cross*, no. 320 (1997): 553–62. According to Kolb, prior to 1930 the terms *jus ad bellum* and *jus in bello* were not widely used. Available from http://www.icrc.org/eng/resources/documents/misc/57jnuu.htm (accessed 4/21/2014).

28. Aristotle, *Nicomachean Ethics* in Richard McKeon (ed.), The *Basic Works of Aristotle* (New York: Random House, 1941), bk. X, ch. 7 (1177^{b}5–14). See also Aristotle, *Politics*, idem, bk. VII, ch. 15 (1334^a-15).

29. Cicero, *On Duties*, bk. I, secs. 35 and 80.

30. Ibid., bk. I, sec. 36.

31. Ibid., bk. I, secs. 35 and 80.

32. Sun Tzu, The *Art of War*, Dallas Galvin (ed.), trans. Lionel Giles (New York: Barnes & Noble, 2003), ch. II, par. 17, p. 13.

33. Cicero, *On Duties*, bk. I, sec. 39.

34. Ibid., bk, III, sec. 107

35. Grotius, The *Rights of War and Peace*, bk. II, ch. 13, sec. 15, pp. 788–89.

36. Ibid., bk III, ch. 19, sec. 5, pp. 1538–39.

37. Cicero, *On Duties*, bk. III, secs. 94 and 95, pp. 136–37. For a discussion of Cicero's duty of promise keeping and his conception of justice in international relations, see Thomas L. Pangle and Peter J. Ahrensdorf, *Justice among Nations: On the Moral Basis of Power and Peace* (Lawrence: University Press of Kansas, 1999), pp. 68–69; henceforth Pangle and Ahrensdorf, *Justice among Nations*.

38 Cicero, *On Duties*, bk. III, sec. 35, pp. 112–13.

39. For Augustine's arguments against Christian pacifism, see Augustine, *Letter 138, to Marcellinus*, especially pp. 205–9 in *Augustine Political Writings*, Ernest L. Fortin and Douglas Kries (eds.), (Indianapolis: Hackett, 1994), henceforth Augustine, *Political Writings*; see also Augustine, *Against Faustus the Manichean XXII.* 73–79, p. 223 in idem.

40. For an argument against those who defend Christian pacifism, see Grotius, The *Rights of War and Peace*, bk. I, ch. 2, secs. 8–10, pp. 208–39.

41. See, e.g., Tertullian, *On Idolatry*, ch. 19 and Tertullian, *On the Crown*, ch. 11 in Reichberg (ed.), The *Ethics of War*, pp. 63–64; see also Origen, *Against Celsus*, bk. 8, ch. 73, and Origen, *Homilies on Joshua*, bk. 15, ch. 1, Ibid., pp. 64–65 in idem.

42. St. Ambrose was one of the earliest supporters of this view. See, e.g., Ambrose, *On the Duties of the Clergy*, bk. 1, ch. 28, 139–41 in Reichberg (ed.), The *Ethics of War*, p. 67.

43. Paul Ramsey, *War and the Christian Conscience* (Durham, NC: Duke University Press, 1961), pp. xv–xviii; henceforth Ramsey, *War and the Christian Conscience*.

234 *Notes*

44. Augustine, *On Free Choice of the Will* (Indianapolis: The Bobbs-Merrill Company, 1979), bk. 1, V, pp. 10–12.

45. Augustine, *Political Writings*, The *City of God*, bk. XIX, ch. 7, p. 149.

46. For an elaboration of this view, see Ramsey, *War and the Christian Conscience*, p. 37.

47. Augustine, *Letter 138, to Marcellinus*, in Augustine, *Political Writings*, p. 209.

48. Augustine, *Letter 189, to Boniface*, in Augustine, *Political Writings*, p. 220.

49. Augustine, *Questions on the Heptateuch*, bk. VI, ch. 10, in Reichberg (ed.), The *Ethics of War*, p. 82.

50. Augustine, *Against Faustus the Manichaean* XXII. 73–79, in Augustine, *Political Writings*, pp. 221–22.

51. Richard Shelly Hartigan, "Saint Augustine on War and Killing: The Problem of the Innocent," *Journal of the History of Ideas*, vol. 27, no. 2 (April–June, 1966): 201–3; henceforth Hartigan, "Saint Augustine on War and Killing." See also Hugo Slim, "Why Protect Civilians? Innocence, Immunity and Enmity in War," *International Affairs*, vol. 79, no. 3 (2003): 492. As Hartigan, Slim overstates his case against Augustine's view of war and the immunity of the innocent.

52. Augustine, *Letter 189, to Boniface*, p. 220; see also Augustine, *Letter 138, to Marcellinus*, p. 209.

53. Quentin Skinner, "Meaning and Understanding in the History of Ideas," in Quentin Skinner, *Visions of Politics, Vol. I: Regarding Method* (New York: Cambridge University Press, 2002), ch. 4, especially pp. 66–67; henceforth Skinner, "Meaning and Understanding in the History of Ideas."

54. Frederick H. Russell, The *Just War in the Middle Ages* (New York: Cambridge University Press, 1977), p. 19.

55. Ibid., p. 20.

56. Quentin Skinner, "Meaning and Understanding in the History of Ideas," ch. 4, p. 60.

57. Hartigan, "Saint Augustine on War and Killing," p. 201.

58. Ibid., p. 203.

59. Augustine, *Letter 189, to Boniface*, in Augustine, *Political Writings*, p. 220.

60. Ramsey, *War and the Christian Conscience*, pp. 35–36.

61. Hartigan, "Saint Augustine on War and Killing," p. 203.

62. Augustine, *Letter 189, to Boniface*, p. 220; see also Augustine, *City of God*, bk xix, ch. 12, in Augustine, *Political Writings*, p. 150.

63. Augustine, *Against Faustus the Manichean* XXII. 73–79, in Augustine, *Political Writings*, p. 222.

64. Augustine, *Letter 189, to Boniface*, in Augustine, *Political Writings*, p. 220.

65. Ibid., p. 220.

66. Augustine, *Questions on the Heptateuch*, bk. vi, ch. 10, in Reichberg (ed.), The *Ethics of War*, p. 83.

67. For Augustine's conception of political realism, see Reinhold Niebuhr, "Augustine's Political Realism," in Robert M. Brown (ed.), The *Essential Reinhold Niebuhr* (New Haven: Yale University Press, 1986), pp. 123–41.

68. Thomas Aquinas, The *Cardinal Virtues: Prudence, Justice, Fortitude, and Temperance*, translated and edited, with introduction and glossary by Richard J. Regan (Indianapolis, IN: Hackett, 2005), ST II-II, Q. 40, A. 2, p. 70.

69. Ibid., ST II-II, Q. 40, A. 1, 69–70.

70. Aquinas, *On Law, Morality and Politics*, ST II-II, Q. 42, p. 232.

71. Aquinas, *On Kingship*, in Aquinas, *On Law, Morality and Politics*, ch. 6, p. 269.

72. Andrew Valls, "Can Terrorism Be Justified?" p. 78.

73. Held, "Legitimate Authority in Non-State Groups Using Violence," p. 180. See also Sterba, "Terrorism and International Justice," especially p. 211; Jaggar, "What Is Terrorism, Why Is It Wrong, and Could It Ever Be Morally Permissible?" p. 213.

74. For similar versions of a contemporary just war paradigm based on *jus ad bellum* and *jus in bello* considerations, see, e.g., Coady, *Morality and Political Violence*, pp. 63–67 and pp. 110–11; see also Nicholas Fotion, *War and Ethics: A New Just War Theory* (New York: Continuum International Publishing Group, 2007), pp. 10–23; James Turner Johnson, *Morality and Contemporary Warfare* (New Haven: Yale University Press, 1999), pp. 28–29.

75. St. Thomas Aquinas, *Summa Theologiae, vol. 38, Injustice* (2a2ae. 63–79) (New York: Cambridge University Press, 2006), Q. 64, A. 6, p. 39; henceforth Aquinas, *Summa Theologiae, vol. 38, Injustice*; the United States Conference of Catholic Bishops (USCCB) defends the traditional view of innocence in The *Challenge of Peace: God's Promise and Our Response, A Pastoral Letter on War and Peace* (Washington, DC: United States Catholic Conference, 1983), art. 104, where they argue against "total war," and art. 286, where they contend that "nothing . . . can justify direct attack on innocent human life." For a contemporary defense of the Catholic just war tradition and the traditional conception of innocence, see John Finnis, "Ethics of War and Peace in the Catholic Natural Law Tradition," in Terry Nardin (ed.), *Ethics of War and Peace: Religious and Secular Perspectives* (Princeton, NJ: Princeton University Press, 1996), pp. 15–39.

76. Vitoria, "On the Law of War," Q. 3, art. 1.2, sec. 35, p. 316.

77. Francisco Suárez, "On War," in Francisco Suárez, *Selections from Three Works of Francisco Suárez* , translated by Gwladys L. Williams (Buffalo: William S. Hein & Co., 1995), sec. vii, art. 15, p. 845; henceforth Suárez, *Selections from Three Works*.

78. Vitoria, "On Civil Power," in Vitoria, *Political Writings*, Q. 1, art. 9, p. 21.

79. Suárez, "On Charity," in Suárez, *Selections from Three Works*, sec. vii, art. 12, p. 843.

80. Vitoria, "On Civil Power," Q. 1, art. 9, p. 21.

81. For a classic argument against collective responsibility or collective guilt, see H. D. Lewis, "Collective Responsibility," in L. May and S. Hoffman (eds.), *Collective Responsibility: Five Decades of Debate in Theoretical and Applied Ethics* (Lanham, MD: Roman & Littlefield, 1991), pp. 17–34. For Lewis, moral responsibility belongs "essentially to the individual." While Margaret Gilbert argues that the notion of collective responsibility can be meaningful, she seems to agree with Lewis that the blameworthiness of a collective act does not imply individual blameworthiness.

See Margaret Gilbert, "Who's to Blame? Collective Moral Responsibility and the Implication for Group Members," in P. A. French and H. K. Wettstein (eds.), *Midwest Studies in Philosophy: Shared Intentions and Collective Responsibility* (Malden, MA: Blackwell, 2006), pp. 94–114, especially p. 109.

82. This position is not only peculiar to traditional Christian just war theorists, such as Vitoria and Suárez. Secular just war theorists such as Michael Walzer admit as much. See Walzer, *Just and Unjust Wars*, p. 297.

83. Suárez, "On War," in Suárez, *Selections from Three Works*, 7.6, p. 840.

84. Vitoria, "On the Law of War," Q. 3, art. 7, sec. 52, p. 323.

85. Ibid., sec. VII, art. 15, p. 845.

86. Turner Johnson, *Ideology, Reason, and the Limitation of War*, p. 200.

87. See, e.g., Detter, The *Law of War*, pp. 299–303. Detter distinguishes between the concept of general reprisal as a right of a state to resort to force, and the concept of belligerent reprisal that generally designates individuals who commit hostile acts against innocent civilians in an interstate or intrastate conflict. The 1977 Geneva Protocol I and II to the Geneva Conventions attempt to rule out reprisals during armed conflicts against civilians, protected persons, protected objects, and the natural environment. See, e.g., Edward K. Kwakwa, The *International Law of Armed Conflict: Personal and Material Fields of Application* (Boston: Kluwer Academic Publishers, 1992), ch. 6, pp. 129–58.

88. See, e.g., Pangle and Ahrensdorf, *Justice among Nations*, pp. 104–6.

89. Vitoria, "On the Law of War," Q. 1, art. 3, sec. 10, p. 302.

90. Ibid., Q. 1, art. 4, sec. 15, p. 304.

91. Ibid., Q. 3, art. 1, sec. 35, pp. 314–15.

92. T. A. Cavanaugh, *Double-Effect Reasoning*, p. xx. I find his reasons persuasive for using the expression "double-effect reasoning" or DER rather than any of the other better-known expressions.

93. For Kant's categorical imperative, see Immanuel Kant, *Groundwork*, p. 88; for Mill's principle of utility, see John Stuart Mill, *Utilitarianism with Critical Essays edited by Samuel Gorovitz* (New York: The Bobbs-Merrill Company, 1971), ch. II, p. 18.

94. Some might describe the notion of a moral dilemma in a weaker sense. For example, P. A. Woodward conceives of a moral dilemma when people confront a situation whereby no matter which way they act they would unavoidably violate some moral precept or precepts. I think that the conception of moral dilemma that is relevant for DER seems to apply to rather stressful situations, such as those where no matter which way we act we will substantively and inevitably harm others. Still Woodward's conception and my conception of moral dilemma are consistent. For Woodward's view of moral dilemma, see his P. A. Woodward (ed.), The *Doctrine of Double Effect: Philosophers Debate a Controversial Moral Principle* (Indiana: University of Notre Dame Press, 2010), p. 2; henceforth Woodward (ed.), The *Doctrine of Double Effect*.

95. Aquinas, *Summa Theologiae, vol. 38, Injustice.* Q. 64.

96. St. Thomas Aquinas, *Summa Theologiae, vol. 18 Principles of Morality* (Ia2ae. 181–21) (New York: Cambridge University Press, 2006), Q. 18, 4.

97. Anscombe, "War and Murder," pp. 58–59.

98. G. E. M. Anscombe, *Intention*, 2nd ed. (Ithaca: Cornell University Press, 1969), p. 42.

99. St. Thomas Aquinas, *Summa Theologiae, vol. 17 Psychology of Human Acts* (Ia2ae. 6–17) (New York: Cambridge University Press, 2006), Q. 12, 1.

100. For an account of intentionality expressed in terms of having a pro-attitude, see Donald Davidson, "Intending," in Donald Davidson, *Essays on Actions and Events* (New York: Oxford University Press, 2001), pp. 83–102, especially pp. 86–87.

101. For a relevant distinction between risked homicide and accidental killing in Aquinas's conception of double effect, see Cavanaugh, *Double-Effect Reasoning*, p. 11.

102. Aquinas, *Summa Theologiae, vol. 38 Injustice*, Q. 64, 7.

103. See, e.g., Joseph M. Boyle Jr., "Toward Understanding the Principle of Double Effect," *Ethics*, vol. 90 (July 1980): 527–38; henceforth Boyle Jr., "Toward Understanding the Principle of Double Effect."

104. For the distinction between act- and rule-utilitarianism, J. J. C. Smart, "Act-Utilitarianism and Rule-Utilitarianism," in Jonathan Glover (ed.), *Utilitarianism and its Critics* (New York: Macmillan Publishing Company, 1990), p. 199.

105. Kamm, "Toward the Essence of Nonconsequentialist Constraints on Harming," p. 135.

106. Ibid., p. 132.

107. While I am paraphrasing Kamm's bad person counterexample, I am trying to be true to the letter and the spirit of her counterexample. See Kamm, "Toward the Essence of Nonconsequentialist Constraints on Harming," p. 132. Trolley scenarios have a long pedigree in moral philosophy. See, e.g., Philippa Foot, "The Problem of Abortion and the Doctrine of Double Effect," in Philippa Foot, *Virtues and Vices* (Berkeley: University of California Press, 1978), p. 23; henceforth Foot, "The Problem of Abortion and the Doctrine of Double Effect"; Judith Jarvis Thomson, "Killing, Letting Die, and the Trolley Problem," *Monist*, vol. 59 (1976), 204–17; idem, The *Realm of Rights* (Cambridge, MA: Harvard University Press, 1990), pp. 176–202; henceforth Thomson, The *Realm of Rights*; and Kwame Anthony Appiah, *Experiments in Ethics* (Cambridge, MA: Harvard University Press, 2008), especially pp. 88–92.

108. Kamm, "Toward the Essence of Nonconsequentialist Constraints on Harming," p. 132.

109. Thomson, The *Realm of Rights*, p. 180.

110. Foot, The *Problem of Abortion and the Doctrine of Double Effect*, p. 22.

111. See, e.g., Woodward's view in Woodward (ed.), The *Doctrine of Double Effect*, p. 3.

112. Warren S. Quinn, "Actions, Intentions, and Consequences: The Doctrine of Double Effect," in Woodward (ed.), The *Doctrine of Double Effect*, pp. 23–40, especially pp. 34–37; henceforth Quinn, "Actions, Intentions, and Consequences: The Doctrine of Double Effect."

113. I have already referred to Aquinas's and Boyle Jr.'s view on double effect. For Gury's view, see Joseph T. Mangan, "A Historical Analysis of the Principle of Double Effect," *Theological Studies*, vol. 10, no. 1 (1949): 41–61; henceforth Mangan, "A Historical Analysis of the Principle of Double Effect."

114. James Sterba, "Reconciling Pacifists and Just War Theorists," *Social Theory and Practice*, vol. 18, no. 1 (Spring 1992): 21–38; henceforth Sterba, "Reconciling Pacifists and Just War Theorists."

115. For a classic interpretation of Gury's view, see Mangan, "A Historical Analysis of the Principle of Double Effect:" 41–61, especially 58–61.

116. Boyle Jr., "Toward Understanding the Principle of Double Effect," especially p. 528.

117. Ibid., p. 529.

118. Ibid., p. 532.

119. Cavanaugh, *Double Effect Reasoning*, p. 22.

120. Aquinas, *Summa Theologiae*, vol. 38 *Injustice*, Q. 64, 7.

121. Boyle Jr., "Toward Understanding the Principle of Double Effect," p. 532.

122. Ibid., p. 533.

123. Jonathan Bennett, "Morality and Consequences," in Sterling McMurrin (ed.), The *Tanner Lectures of Human Values*, vol. II (Salt Lake City: University of Utah Press, 1981), p. 96; henceforth Bennett, "Morality and Consequences."

124. For the law of armed conflict or international humanitarian law that proscribes the practice of what is commonly known as area or terror bombing, see, e.g., 1907, Hague Convention IV Respecting the Laws and Customs of War and Land, Annex to the Convention Regulations Respecting the Laws and Customs of War, II, ch. 1, arts. 22, 23, 25, 26, and 27 in Adam Roberts and Richard Guelff (eds.), *Documents of the Laws of War*. See also 1923 Hague Draft Rules of Aerial Warfare, ch. 4, arts. 22, 23, 24 (3) in idem. Unfortunately, the draft rules were never ratified, hence, strictly speaking, they are not legally binding. But they seem to capture the spirit of *jus in bello* or IHL in contemporary international law; 1946 Judgment of the International Military Tribunal at Nuremberg: Extracts on Crime Against International Law, especially art. 6, (b) and (c) in idem; 1949 Geneva Convention IV Relative to the Protection of Civilian Persons in Time of War, part III, especially art. 33 in idem.

125. Bennett, "Morality and Consequences," p. 99.

126. For some subtleties between our uses of the terms "justification" and "excuse," see J. L. Austin, "A Plea for Excuses" in *J. L. Austin: Philosophical Papers*, J. O. Urmson and G. J. Warnock (eds.), (New York: Oxford University Press, 1961), pp. 124–25; henceforth Austin, "A Plea for Excuses."

127. Ibid., p. 100.

128. Bennett, "Morality and Consequences," p. 101.

129. Ibid., p. 111.

130. Sterba, "Reconciling Pacifists and Just War Theories," 21–38, especially p. 26.

131. Such a possibility might seem far-fetched to some. Others, however, conceive of such a threat as real. Even if the probability of a terrorist group's getting hold of a nuclear weapon and launching a successful attack nowadays might be rather remote, if they were able to do so in the future, the result of such an attack could be catastrophic. See the remarks of Yukiya Amano, director general of the UN International Atomic Agency, about how real the threat of nuclear terrorism is nowadays.

UN News Center. Available from http://www.un.org/apps/news/story.asp?NewsID=4 5311&Cr=iaea&Cr1=nuclear (accessed 7/2/2013). See also "Fukushima a 'blueprint' for terrorists, IAEA warns," *Japan Times,* July 3, 2013. Available from http://www. japantimes.co.jp/news/2013/07/03/national/fukushima-a-blueprint-for-terrorists-iaea-warns/ (accessed 7/3/2013).

132. O'Donovan, The *Just War Revisited,* p. 105; see also Foot, "The Problem of Abortion and the Doctrine of Double Effect," p. 22.

133. Coady, *Morality and Political Violence,* pp. 138–39.

134. President Obama has defended the just war tradition in his acceptance of the Nobel Peace Prize at Oslo. See Barack Obama, "Remarks by the President at the Acceptance of the Nobel Peace Prize." Available from http://www.whitehouse. gov/the-press-office/remarks-president-acceptance-nobel-peace-prize (accessed 12/28/2009).

135. Whether those who embrace some version of DER must be committed to exceptionless norms remains an open question. See, e.g., Cavanaugh, *Double-Effect Reasoning,* p. xxii.

136. Boyle Jr., "Toward Understanding the Principle of Double Effect." p. 529.

137. Quinn, "Actions, Intentions, and Consequences: The Doctrine of Double Effect," p. 37.

138. For the difference between act and rule consequentialism, see *Morality, Rules, and Consequences: A Critical Reader,* Brad Hooker, Elinor Mason, and Dale E. Miller (eds.), (Lanham, MD: Rowman & Littlefield, 2000), p. 1.

139. Nicholas Schmidle, "Getting Bin Laden: What Happened That Night in Abbottabad," *New Yorker,* August 8, 2011. Available from http://www.newyorker. com/reporting/2011/08/08/110808fa_fact_schmidle?currentPage=all (accessed 4/26/2014); henceforth Schmidle, "Getting Bin Laden: What Happened That Night in Abbottabad."

140 See, e.g., the Hague Conventions (1899–1907), the Charters of the Nuremberg Tribunals (a.k.a. Nuremberg Trials), and the Tribunals for the Far East (a.k.a. Tokyo Trials) for prosecuting alleged war criminals after World War II, the 1948 UN Convention on the Prevention and Punishment of Genocide, the 1949 Geneva Conventions, the 1977 Geneva Protocols I and II Additional to the Geneva Conventions. Despite the controversy regarding the expression "war crimes," these crimes could be viewed minimally as violations or "grave breaches" stipulated in the Geneva Conventions and 1977 Additional Protocols I and II. Available from http://www.icrc.org/eng/ resources/documents/misc/5zmgf9.htm (accessed 3/25/2012).

141. ICRC, How "grave breaches" are defined in the Geneva Conventions and Additional Protocols, 4/6/2004. Available from https://www.icrc.org/eng/resources/ documents/misc/5zmgf9.htm (accessed 3/25/2012).

142. See 1993 Statute of International Criminal Tribunal for the Former Yugoslavia in Roberts and Guelff (eds.), *Documents of the Laws of War,* pp. 555–72, especially p. 570. See also the 1994 Statute of International Criminal Tribunal for Rwanda in idem, pp. 615–21, especially p. 619.

143. See, e.g., Ratner and Abrams (eds.), *Accountability for Human Rights Atrocities,* p. 56

240   *Notes*

144. See, e.g., Article 7 of the Rome Statute of the International Criminal Court that enumerates the different categories of crimes against humanity. Available from http://www.icc-cpi.int/NR/rdonlyres/ADD16852-AEE9-4757-ABE7-9CDC7CF02886/283503/RomeStatutEng1.pdf (accessed 7/19/2014). See also Robert Arnold, "Terrorism as a Crime Against Humanity under the ICC Statute," in *International Cooperation in Counter-Terrorism: The United Nations and Regional Organizations in the Fight Against Terrorism*, Giuseppe Nesi (ed.), (Burlington, VT: Ashgate, 2005), pp. 121–37, especially 122–24.

145. ICRC, Convention on the Non-Applicability of Statutory Limitations to War Crimes and Crimes Against Humanity, November 26, 1968. Available from http://www.icrc.org/applic/ihl/ihl.nsf/Treaty.xsp?documentId=735456606A8F58FDC1256 3CD002D6C51&action=openDocument (accessed 4/28/2014).

146. Schmidle, "Getting Bin Laden: What Happened That Night in Abbottabad."

147. For the controversy regarding bin Laden's killing, see Aidan Lewis, "Osama Bin Laden: Legality of Killing Questioned," *BBC News*, May 12, 2011. Available from http://www.bbc.co.uk/news/world-south-asia-13318372 (accessed 4/5/2012).

148. Executive Order 12333 United States Intelligence Activities, Part 2, sec. 2.11. Available from http://www.fas.org/irp/offdocs/eo/eo-12333-2008.pdf (accessed 3/30/2012). For a view supporting the domestic legality of the president's decision, and legality of the mission under international law, see John B. Bellinger III, "Bin Laden Killing: The Legal Basis," *Council of Foreign Relations*, May 2, 2011, in http://www.cfr.org/terrorism/bin-laden-killing-legal-basis/p24866 (accessed 3/30/2012); see also Kevin H. Govern, "Operation Neptune Spear: Was Killing Bin Laden a Legitimate Military Objective?" in Claire Finkelstein, et al. (eds.), *Target Killings: Law Morality in an Asymmetrical World* (New York: Oxford University Press, 2012), pp. 347–73, especially p. 363. For an interesting conversation from a military, philosophical, and religious perspective on bin Laden's death, see Sam Jones and Owen Bowcott, "Osama bin Laden's death—killed in a raid or assassinated?" *Guardian* (UK), May 6, 2011. http://www.guardian.co.uk/world/2011/may/06/osama-bin-laden-death-assassination (accessed 5/6/2011).

149. 1977 Geneva Protocol I, II, art. 43 (2) in Roberts and Guelff (eds.), *Documents of the Laws of War*, p. 444

150. 1907 Hague Convention IV Respecting the Law and Customs of War on Land. Annex to the Convention Regulations Respecting the Laws and Customs of War on Land, I, ch. 1, art. 1 in Roberts and Guelff (eds.), *Documents of the Laws of War*, p. 73.

151. See Daniele Archibugi, "Should bin Laden have been tried?" *openDemocracy*, May 3, 2011, in http://www.opendemocracy.net/daniele-archibugi/should-bin-laden-have-been-tried (accessed 5/30/2012).

152. See, e.g., how Hume understands the natural duties of justice, fidelity, and allegiance. According to him, we are naturally predisposed to act compatibly with these duties because experience has taught us that acting so will promote the general welfare. Hence, Hume can be viewed as a defender of rule-utilitarianism. See David Hume, "Of the Original Contract," in *Hume's Moral and Political Philosophy*, Henry D. Aiken (ed.), (New York: Hafner, 1964), pp. 356–72, especially p. 367. Whether he was actually a defender of utilitarianism remains controversial; see J. L. Mackie,

Hume's Moral Theory (Boston, MA: Routledge & Kegan Paul, 1980), especially pp. 151–54.

153. Honderich, *After Terror*, p. 53.

154. Ibid., pp. 118–19 and p. 151.

155. Mackie refers to this argument as the "argument from relativity" and Williams refers to the same argument as the "anthropologist's heresy." See J. L. Mackie, *Ethics: Inventing Right and Wrong* (New York: Penguin Books, 1990), p. 36; henceforth Mackie, *Ethics*. See also Bernard Williams, *Morality: An Introduction to Ethics* (New York: Harper & Row, 1972), p. 20.

156. For Mackie's view on the subjectivity of values, see Mackie, *Ethics*, pp. 15–49. For Harman's contractualist view, see Gilbert Harman, "Moral Relativism Defended," in *Relativism: Cognitive and Moral*, Michael Kraus and Jack W. Meiland (eds.), (Indiana: University of Notre Dame Press, 1982), pp. 189–204; henceforth Harman, "Moral Relativism Defended."

157. Mackie, *Ethics*, pp. 17–18.

158. Stephen Nathanson, "Terrorism and the Ethics of War," in *Intervention, Terrorism, and Torture: Contemporary Challenges to Just War Theory*, Steven P. Lee (ed.), (Dordrecht: Springer, 2007), pp. 173–74.

159. Some scholars rushed to judgment by misrepresenting jihadists who carried out the 9/11 attacks as nihilists; see Jean Bethke Elshtain, The *Just War against Terror:* The *Burden of* American *Power in a Violent World* (New York: Basic Books, 2004), p. 124.

160. Regrettably, under President Obama's administration there has been a substantial increase of drone strikes that have allegedly killed hundreds of civilians. See Jack Serle, "Drone warfare: More than 2,400 dead as Obama's drone campaign marks five years," *Bureau of Investigative Journalism.* Available from http://www.thebureauinvestigates.com/2014/01/23/more-than-2400-dead-as-obamas-drone-campaign-marks-five-years/ (accessed 5/17/2014). For some of the legal anomalies domestically and internationally regarding President Obama's drone campaign and its questionable results, see International Human Rights and Conflict Resolution at Stanford Law School and Global Justice Clinic at NYU School of Law, *Living Under Drones: Death, Injury and Trauma to Civilians from US Drones Practices in Pakistan (2012).* Available from http://www.livingunderdrones.org/wp-content/uploads/2013/10/Stanford-NYU-Living-Under-Drones.pdf (accessed 5/17/2014).

161. Nietzsche offers an arguably challenging defense of epistemological and moral skepticism, the latter of which is sometimes used as a defense of moral relativism. See, e.g., Frederick Nietzsche, The *Will to Power*, trans. by Walter Kaufmann and R. J. Hollingdale (New York: Random House, 1967), aphorism 481, p. 267. See also Frederick Nietzsche, *Thus Spake Zarathustra* in The *Philosophy of Nietzsche*, (New York: The Modern Library, 1954), ch. 15.

162. Max Stirner, The *Ego and His Own*, trans. Steven T. Byington (New York: Modern Library, 1918), p. 5

163. Fyodor Dostoyevsky, The *Brothers Karamazov*, cited in The *Moral of the Story: An Anthology of Ethics through Literature*, Peter Singer and Renata Singer (eds.), (Malden, MA: Blackwell, 2005), pp. 436–37.

164. See, e.g., Viktor E. Frankl, *Man's Search for Meaning: An Introduction to Logotherapy*, 4th ed. (Boston: Beacon Press, 1992).
165. See, e.g., Jean Améry, *At the Mind's Limits: Contemplation by a Survivor on Auschwitz and Its Realities*, trans. Sidney Rosenfeld and Stella P. Rosenfeld (Indianapolis: Indiana University Press, 1980); see also Primo Levi, The *Drowned and the Saved* (New York: Summit Books, 1986).
166. For recent criticisms of those who embrace this infamous expression, see Simon Blackburn, *Plato's Republic: A Biography* (New York: Atlantic Monthly Press, 2006), ch. 2.
167. Chomsky, for example, is rather critical of the US government's double standard in foreign policy. While critical of bin Laden's jihad too, he acknowledges the legitimacy of most of bin Laden's grievances against the United States and its allies. But he deliberately ignores that two or more wrongs do not make a right. See Noam Chomsky, *Hegemony or Survival: America's Quest for Global Hegemony* (New York: Metropolitan Books, 2003), pp. 211–16. Similarly, while unconditionally condemning the 9/11 attacks, Derrida acknowledges that those who "tried to justify this attack saw it as a response to the state terrorism of the United States and its allies." See Giovanna Borradori, *Philosophy in a Time of Terror: Dialogues with Jürgen Habermas and Jacques Derrida* (Chicago: University of Chicago Press, 2004), p. 112; henceforth Borradori, *Philosophy in a Time of Terror*.
168. For the viral influence and the nuances of a Wahhabi-Salafi ideology embraced by bin Laden and associates, see Frédéric Volpi, *Political Islam* (New York: Columbia University Press, 2010), pp. 164–73.
169. Sardar, *Reading the Qur'an*, pp. 135–41. For quite some time, Sunni extremists have been responsible for the greatest number of terrorist attacks. In addition, Muslims are the largest group of people to be victims of terrorism. See US Department of State, Country Report on Terrorism 2012. Available from: http://www.state.gov/r/pa/prs/ps/2013/05/210103.htm (accessed 4/28/2014).
170. Majid Khadduri, *War and Peace in the Law of Islam* (Baltimore, MD: Johns Hopkins University Press, 1955; reprint, Clark, NJ: The Lawbook Exchange, 2010), p. 51 and pp. 55–73.
171. Harman, "Moral Relativism Defended," especially pp. 189–90.
172. For this type of global relativism, including ethical relativism, that denies the existence of any facts, see Richard Rorty, "Relativism: Finding and Making," in Richard Rorty, *Philosophy and Social Hope* (New York: Penguin Putnam, Inc., 1999), pp. xvi–xxxii. For an argument showing the incoherence of global relativism, see Paul Boghossian, *Fear of Knowledge: Against Relativism and Constructivism* (New York: Oxford University Press, 2006), ch. 4, especially pp. 54–56.
173. Thomas Nagel, The *View from Nowhere* (New York: Oxford University Press, 1986), pp. 152–56.
174. Yassin Musharbash, "Al-Qaida Kills Eight Times More Muslims Than Non-Muslims," *Spiegelonline*, 12/3/2009. Available from http://www.spiegel.de/international/world/surprising-study-on-terrorism-al-qaida-kills-eight-times-more-muslims-than-non-muslims-a-660619.html (accessed 9/7/2013).

175. For UN action to counterterrorism, see the thirteen major international legal instruments against terrorism. Available from http://www.un.org/en/terrorism/instruments.shtml (accessed 4/28/2014).

176. Richard Rorty, *Contingency, Irony and Solidarity* (New York: Cambridge University Press, 1989), pp. 189–98, especially p. 192.

177. Ramon M. Lemos, *Rights, Goods, and Democracy* (Cranbury, NJ: Associated University Presses, 1986), p. 185. For Lemos, a person has an obligation to help others only if he believes that they need help and he can help them. His ignorance can excuse his failure to help those who need it only if he could have not reasonably been expected to know that they needed help.

178. Walzer, *Just and Unjust Wars*, p. 254.

179. David Rodin, *War and Self-Defense* (New York: Oxford University Press, 2003), pp. 158–62.

180. Ibid., p. 297.

181. Members of the School of Salamanca in sixteenth- and seventeenth-century Spain defended similar views. For example, according to the Dominican Francisco de Vitoria, the ordinary citizens of a commonwealth who wage an unjust war against another commonwealth, although innocent of an offense, can be rightfully punished. See Vitoria, "On the Law of War," p. 21. See also the Jesuit Francisco Suárez, Disputation XIII: On War *(De bello)*, in Reichberg (ed.), The *Ethics of War*, p. 364.

182. Walzer quotes the whole passage in *Just and Unjust Wars*, p. 245.

183. See, e.g., 1907 Hague Convention VIII Relative to the Laying of Automatic Submarine Contact Mines in Roberts and Guelff (eds.), *Documents of the Laws of War*, especially art. 2, which states: "It is forbidden to lay automatic contact mines off the coast and ports of the enemy, with the sole object of intercepting commercial shipping," p. 105. Since Norway was no enemy country, but rather a friendly one, Churchill's violation of international law amounted to an act of war.

184. Walzer, *Just and Unjust Wars*, p. 249.

185. David Brown, The *Road to Oran: Anglo-French Naval Relations September 1939–July 1940* (New York: Taylor & Francis, 2004), especially pp. 171–205.

186. Winston Churchill, "Shall We All Commit Suicide?" in *Amid These Storms: Thoughts and Adventures* (New York: Charles Scribner's Sons, 1932), pp. 245–52, especially 246–47.

187. See 1907 Annex to the Convention (Hague IV) Regulations Respecting the Laws and Custom of War on Land, especially sec. II, ch. 1, arts. 25, 26, and 27 in Roberts and Guelff (eds.), *Documents of the Laws of War*, especially art. 25. See idem, p. 68.

188. Roberts and Guelff (eds.), *Documents of the Laws of War*, p. 68

189. See, e.g., Geneva Convention IV Relative to the Protection of Civilian Persons in Time of War of August 12, 1949, in Roberts and Guelff (eds.), *Documents of the Laws of War*, I, arts. 3 and 4, 302–3. See also idem, 1977 Geneva Protocol I Additional to the Geneva Conventions of 12 August 1949, and Relating to the Protection of Victims of International Armed Conflicts part IV, sec. I, ch. 1, arts. 50 and 51, 448–49; part IV, sec. I, art. 147, 352. According to Article 147, the willful

killing of protected persons, namely civilians, is conceived of as a grave breach of humanitarian law and, hence, a war crime.

190. Allan Buchanan, "From Nuremberg to Kosovo: The Morality of Illegal International Legal reform," in *Humanitarian Intervention*, edited by Aleksandar Jokic (New York: Broadview Press, 2004), pp. 123–58, especially p. 132.

191. Robert G. Moeller, "The Bombing War in Germany, 2005-1940: Back to the Future," in *Bombing Civilians: A Twentieth-Century History*, Yuki Tanaka and Marilyn B. Young (eds.), (New York: The New Press, 2009), p. 54; henceforth Tanaka and Young (eds.), *Bombing Civilians*.

192. Richard Falk, "Geopolitics and international state crime: an accountability black hole." Available from https://www.opendemocracy.net/richard-falk/geopolitics-and-international-state-crime-accountability-black-hole (accessed December 15, 2014).

193. Walzer, *Just and Unjust Wars*, p. 262.

194. For the devastating results of area or terror bombing on the German civilian population during World War II, see Jörg Friedrich, The *Fire: The Bombing of Germany, 1940–1945*, translated by Allison Brown (New York: Columbia University Press, 2002); henceforth Friedrich, The *Fire*.

195. Blight and Lang, The *Fog of War*, pp. 122–23.

196. Vitoria, "On the Law of War," sec. 60, p. 327.

197. Walzer, *Arguing about War*, p. 46.

198. Walzer, *Just and Unjust Wars*, p. 197.

199. Walzer, *Arguing about War*, p. 51.

200. Ibid., 52.

201. Ibid., 33.

202. Walzer, *Just and Unjust Wars*, p. 253.

203. See, e.g., Stephen Nathanson, "Terrorism, Supreme Emergency, and Noncombatant Immunity: A Critique of Michael Walzer's Ethics of War," *Iyyun: The Jerusalem Philosophical Quarterly*, vol. 55 (January 2006): pp. 3–25; Daniel Statman, "Supreme Emergencies Revisited," *Ethics*, vol. 117 (October 2006): pp. 58–79; henceforth Statman, "Supreme Emergencies Revisited"; Brian Orend, "Is There a Supreme Emergency Exemption?" in *Just War Theory: A Reappraisal*, Mark Evans (ed.), (New York: Palgrave, 2005), pp. 134–53.

204. See, e.g., Andrew D. Mitchell, "Does One Illegality Merit Another? The Law of Belligerent Reprisals in International Law," *Military Law Review*, vol. 170, 2001. Available from http://www.pegc.us/_LAW_/Volume170Mitchell.pdf (accessed August 23, 2011).

205. Detter, The *Law of War*, p. 301.

206. See, e.g., 1977 Geneva Protocol I, part IV, ch. 2, art. 51, 5(6). This article unambiguously state that "Attacks against the civilian population or civilians by way of reprisals are prohibited" in Roberts and Guelff (eds.), *Documents of the Laws of War*, p. 449.

207. A. C. Grayling, *Among the Dead Cities: The History and Moral Legacy of WWII Bombing of Civilians in Germany and Japan* (New York: Walker & Company, 2006), pp. 34–35; henceforth Grayling, *Among the Dead Cities*.

208. See, e.g., Jonathan Glover, *Humanity: A Moral History of the Twentieth Century* (New Haven, CT: Yale University Press, 2001), chs. 11 and 12.

209. For different uses of the terms "justification" and "excuse," see J. L. Austin, "A Plea for Excuses," pp. 124–25.

210. Walzer, *Just and Unjust Wars*, p. 260.

211. Augustine, *City of God*, in O'Donovan and O'Donovan (eds.), *From Irenaeus to Grotius*, bk. 4, sec. 4, p. 139.

212. A. C. Grayling, *Among the Dead Cities*, pp. 16–20. See also Friedrich, *The Fire*, pp. 166–68. For criticisms of Friedrich's work, especially his use of language typically reserved to describe the Holocaust for describing instead the killing and suffering deliberately inflicted on German civilians by the Allies' practice of area bombing, see Robert G. Moeller, "The Bombing War in Germany, 2005–1940: Back to the Future," in Tanaka and Young (eds.), *Bombing Civilians*, pp. 46–76.

213. For a vivid but sordid description of what transpired at Dresden from an eyewitness report, see Kurt Vonnegut, "Wailing Shall Be in All Streets," in Kurt Vonnegut, *Armageddon in Retrospect And Other New and Unpublished Writings on War and Peace* (New York: The Penguin Group, 2008), pp. 33–45. See also Grayling, *Among the Dead Cities*, pp. 72–73.

214. Yuki Tanaka, "Introduction," in Tanaka and Young (eds.), *Bombing Civilians*, pp. 1–7. See Mark Selden, "A Forgotten Holocaust: U.S. Bombing Strategy, "The Destruction of Japanese Cities, and the American Way of War from the Pacific War to Iraq," in idem, pp. 77–96. For a meticulous appraisal of whether the use of the atomic bombs and the demand for an unconditional surrender were justified, see Tsuyoshi Hasegawa, "Were the Atomic Bombs of Hiroshima and Nagasaki Justified?" Idem, pp. 97–134.

215. Hobbes, *Leviathan*, p. 90.

216. Coady, *Morality and Political Violence*, p. 288.

217. Adolf Hitler, "The Mission of the Nazi Movement," in *Fascism*, Roger Griffin (ed.), (New York: Oxford University Press, 1995), pp. 116–17. See also Alfred Cobban, *Dictatorship: Its History and Theory* (New York: Charles Scribner's Sons, 1939), pp. 142–43.

218. The Nuremberg laws of 1935 identifying Jews as second-class citizens are clear examples of bigotry in Nazi jurisprudence. See, e.g., Alan Bullock, *Hitler: A Study in Tyranny*, completely revised ed. (New York: Harper & Row, 1962), p. 339.

219. See, e.g., Karl Dietrich Bracher, *The German Dictatorship: The Origins, Structure, and Effects of National Socialism*, trans. Jean Steinberg (New York: Praeger Publishers, 1970), pp. 252–53 and pp. 365–66.

220. Ibid., pp. 420–31.

221. For a fair assessment of the pros and cons of the British Empire's actions, see Niall Ferguson, *Empire: The Rise and Demise of the British World Order and the Lessons for Global Power* (New York: Basic Books, 2002), especially ix–xxvi and ch. 6.

222. For a nuanced interpretation of Churchill's moral character, including not only his virtues but also his vices such as his diehard imperialist convictions,

paternalism, and racism, see Richard Toye, *Churchill's Empire: The World That Made Him and the World He Made* (New York: St. Martin's Press, 2010).

223. Ibid., pp. 310–11.

224. Coady, *Morality and Political Violence*, p. 289.

225. Yuki Tanaka, *Hidden Horrors: Japanese War Crimes in World War II* (Boulder, CO: Westview Press, 1996), ch. 5.

226. For a moving account of these execrable acts, see Iris Chang, The *Rape of Nanking:* The *Forgotten Holocaust of World War II* (New York: Penguin Books, 1997), especially pp. 81–104; henceforth Chang, The *Rape of Nanking*.

227. Chang, The *Rape of Nanking*, p. 221. It is appalling and inexcusable that in 1994, fifty-seven years after the Rape of Nanking, world leaders stood by doing little to stop extremists of the Hutu majority from massacring the Tutsi minority. They killed an estimated eight hundred thousand people in Rwanda. This genocide adds one more shameful omission by world leaders who chose not to act in the face of evil when they could have prevented the genocide. See Roméo A. Dallaire, *Shake Hands with the Devil.*

228. Coady, *Morality and Political Violence*, p. 289.

229. For a theoretical conception of Schmitt's state of exception, see Carl Schmitt, *Political Theology: Four Chapters on the Concept of Sovereignty*, translated by George Schwab (Cambridge, MA: The MIT Press, 1988), p. 36. For the concrete application of the state of exception as resembling martial law, see Carl Schmitt, The *Nomos of the Earth in the International Law of the Jus Publicum Europeaum*, pp. 98–99.

230. Ellen Kennedy, *Constitutional Failure: Carl Schmitt Weimar* (Durham, NC: Duke University Press, 2004), p. 18.

231. For an explanation of Schmitt's state of exception, see Vicente Medina, "Locke's Militant Liberalism: A Reply to Carl Schmitt's State of Exception," *History of Philosophy Quarterly*, vol. 19, no. 4 (October 2002): pp. 345–65, especially p. 348.

232. For the relationship between Schmitt's state of exception and the Roman *iustitium*, see Giorgio Agamben, *State of Exception*, trans. Kevin Attell (Chicago: University of Chicago Press, 2005), p. 59. As Agamben argues, the state of exception is not nomothetic. Hence, it is devoid of law because it occurs in a normative vacuum.

233. Schmitt, The *Concept of the Political*, p. 54.

234. Walzer, *Just and Unjust Wars*, p. 228.

235. Ibid., p. 254.

236. Statman, "Supreme Emergencies Revisited," 60.

237. Ibid., pp. 248–49.

CHAPTER 5

1. According to the 1948 Convention on the Prevention and Punishment of the Crime of Genocide, the term "genocide" means "any of the following acts committed with intent to destroy, in whole or in part, a national, ethnical, racial or religious group." Available from http://www.hrweb.org/legal/genocide.html (accessed 7/18/2013). It is

important to underscore that the term "political killings" was included in the first draft of the convention, but representatives of the former Soviet Union objected to such inclusion. The narrow legal definition of genocide came about as a compromise.

2. Theodore Abel used the term "democide" to describe what he found typical of Nazi concentration camps, namely, extermination of inmates who were chosen from particular social groups. See Theodore Abel, "The Sociology of Concentration Camps," *Social Forces*, vol. 30, no. 2 (December 1951): pp. 150–55, especially p. 150. R. J. Rummel defines the term "democide" more broadly as "murder by government agents acting authoritatively." Abel's and Rummel's definitions of democide are consistent. Democide amounts to the intentionally organized killing of noncombatants by government officials. For Rummel, genocide, mass murder, and terrorism are species of the genus democide. For the nuances involved in the meaning of democide, see Rummel, *Death by Government*, pp. 36–38.

3. The meaning of the notion of crimes against humanity has been expanded from its first recognition in international law in the Nuremberg Charter of 1945 to the Rome Statute of the International Criminal Court of 1998. Article 6 of the Charter lists as crimes against humanity, for example, murder, extermination, enslavement, deportation, etc. See the Charter and Judgment of the Nürnberg Tribunal: History and Analysis in the UN treaty collection. Available from http://legal.un.org/ilc/documentation/english/a_cn4_5.pdf (accessed 4/11/2014). Article 7 of the ICC includes all of the crimes enumerated in the charter, but adds others, such as imprisonment in violation of fundamental rules of international law, torture, and rape, to mention only a few. See the Rome Statute of the International Criminal Court. Available from http://www.icc-cpi.int/NR/rdonlyres/ADD16852-AEE9-4757-ABE7-9CDC7CF02886/283503/RomeStatutEng1.pdf (accessed 08/13/2013).

4. For a provocative but at times one-sided account of the atrocities committed by Western nations against Latin American, African, and Asian nations, including some indigenous populations, see Noam Chomsky and Andre Vltchek, *On Western Terrorism: From Hiroshima to Drone Warfare* (New York: Palgrave Macmillan, 2013).

5. George W. Bush, *We Will Prevail* (New York: The Continuum International Publishing Group Inc., 2003), p. 43. In his visit to Ground Zero right after the 9/11 attacks, rescue workers encouraged the president to do whatever it took to punish the perpetrators. See Peter Baker, *Days of Fire: Bush and Cheney in the White House* (New York: Anchor Books, 2013), p. 141; henceforth Baker, *Days of Fire*. That might explain why the president chose the elliptical expression "whatever it takes" in his speech.

6. For example, the term "enemy combatant" does not exist in international law. See the classification of prisoners of war in ch. 1, art. 3, and ch. 2 in Annex to the 1907 Hague Convention IV Respecting the Law and Custom of Law on Land in Robert and Guelff (eds.), *Documents of the Laws of War*; see also 1949 Geneva Convention III Relative to the Treatment of Prisoners of War, especially part I, art. 5, which states, "Should any doubt arise as to whether persons, having committed a belligerent act and having fallen into the hands of the enemy, . . . such persons shall enjoy the protection of the present Convention until such time as their status has been determined by a competent tribunal," idem, *Documents of the Laws of War*. In addition, the United States has also ratified the UN Convention against Torture, which is

an integral part of international human rights law. See UN Convention against Torture and Other Cruel, Inhuman or Degrading Treatment or Punishment, December 10, 1984, especially the definition of torture in art. 1.1. Available from http://www.ohchr. org/EN/ProfessionalInterest/Pages/CAT.aspx (accessed 4/11/2014).

7. Peter Singer, *The President of Good and Evil: Questioning the Ethics of George W. Bush* (New York: Plume, 2004).

8. Ibid., pp. viii–x.

9. Winston Churchill, "Consistency in Politics," in Winston Churchill, *Amid These Storms: Thoughts and Adventures* (New York: Charles Scribner's Sons, 1932), pp. 39–47, especially p. 39.

10. As a result of the US intervention in Iraq, there have been several reports offering different estimates about violent deaths of Iraqi citizens. For example, one important but controversial study estimates the number of violent deaths, including combatants and civilians, at about 600,000. See Gilbert Burnham, et al., *The Human Cost of the War in Iraq: Mortality Study 2003–2006.* Available from http://web.mit. edu/CIS/pdf/Human_Cost_of_War.pdf (accessed 7/19/2013). Other studies offer lower estimates. For example, the Iraq Body Count Project reports over 100,000 Iraqi civilian killed. Available from http://www.iraqbodycount.org/ (accessed 7/18/2013). The Brookings Institute's Iraq Index reports about 116,000 Iraqi civilians killed. Available from http://www.brookings.edu/~/media/Centers/saban/iraq%20index/index201207. pdf (accessed 07/19/2013). The Costs of War project estimates at a minimum that between 123,000 and 134,000 Iraqi civilians have died as a direct result of the war. Available from http://costsofwar.org/article/iraqi-civilians (accessed 7/19/2013). The US Department of Defense reports 4,409 US soldiers killed and 31,927 wounded in action (a.k.a. WIA). Available from http://www.defense.gov/news/casualty.pdf (accessed 7/18/2013). Like in any other war, the possibility of providing an accurate calculation of excess mortality rate is a challenging project. See, e.g., Catherine A. Brownstein and John S. Brownstein, "Estimating Excess Mortality in Post-Invasion Iraq," *New England Journal of Medicine,* vol. 358, no. 5 (January 31, 2008): 445–47. Available from http://archive.is/wpZE. (accessed 7/19/2013).

11. The classic exposition of this fallacious and dangerous reasoning is found in Anscombe's argument against granting the late President Truman an honorary degree after World War II. See G. E. M. Anscombe, "Mr. Truman's Degree," in Anscombe, *The Collected Philosophical Papers of G. E. M. Anscombe, Vol. 3,* pp. 62–71.

12. Frank Newport, "Seventy-Two Percent of Americans Support War Against Iraq," *Gallup,* March 24, 2003. Available from http://www.gallup.com/poll/8038/ seventytwo-percent-americans-support-war-against-iraq.aspx (accessed 8/27/2014).

13. George Tenet, *At the Center of the Storm: My Years at the CIA* (New York: HarperCollins, 2007), pp. 331–39.

14. Condoleezza Rice, *No Higher Honor: A Memoir of My Years in Washington* (New York: Crown Publishers, 2011), p. 197.

15. Former British prime minister Tony Blair supported the US invasion of Iraq. For his at times inconsistent views regarding the presence of weapons of mass destruction in Iraq prior to and after the US invasion, see "Timeline: Tony Blair's statements on weapons in Iraq," *BBC News,* December 12, 2009. Available from http://news.

bbc.co.uk/2/hi/uk_news/politics/8409526.stm (accessed 9/8/2014). See also former secretary of state Colin Powell's infamous presentation at the UN accusing the Iraqi government of egregious violations of UN Security Council Resolution 1441 that prohibited the development and possession of WMD. Regrettably, in so doing, he wittingly helped to galvanize public support for the US invasion of Iraq. See Colin Powell, "Remarks to the United Nations Security Council," February 5, 2003. US Department of State Archive. Available from http://2001-2009.state.gov/secretary/former/powell/remarks/2003/17300.htm (accessed 9/8/2014). Despite his misgivings prior to the US operation, Powell supported the US invasion; see Christopher D. O'Sullivan, *Colin Powell: A Political Biography* (Lanham, MD: Rowman & Littlefield, 2010), pp. 159–74.

16. Both the CIA and the British MI-6 agreed that there was no compelling evidence to link Al-Qaeda with Iraq. See Tenet, *At The Center of the Storm*, pp. 307–8. It seems that vice president Dick Cheney and the deputy secretary of state Paul Wolfowitz insisted on trying to link Saddam Hussein to Al-Qaeda operatives without having any compelling evidence. See idem, p. 302. Moreover, the vice president was convinced that not only Saddam Hussein possessed weapons of mass destruction but that he was ready to acquire nuclear weapons soon. See idem, p. 315.

17. Even assuming that former president George W. Bush and former British prime minister Tony Blair did not lie about the presence of WMD in Iraq, they certainly exaggerated the threat that the late Saddam Hussein posed to the United States and its allies. See "Saddam Hussein's weapons mirage: George Bush and Tony Blair exaggerated, but they did not lie," *Economist*, January 29, 2004. Available at http://www.economist.com/node/2384510?fsrc=email_to_a_friend (accessed 9/8/2014).

18. As established by the United Nations Monitoring, Verification and Inspection Commission (UNMOVIC), it is reasonable to accept the hypothesis that no weapons of mass destruction were found because the Iraqi government had already destroyed them in 1991 and thereafter. Hans Blix, Chair of UNMOVIC, offers a compelling case for this hypothesis. See Hans Blix, *Disarming Iraq* (New York: Pantheon Books, 2004), pp. 255–74.

19. See, e.g., Baker, *Days of Fire*, pp. 193–94.

20. Jay S. Bybee, "Memorandum for Alberto R. Gonzales, Counsel to the President, Re: Standards of Conduct for Interrogation under 18 U.S.C. 2340-2340A," August 1, 2002, in Karen J. Greenberg and Joshua L. Dratel (eds.), *The Torture Papers: The Road to Abu Ghraib* (New York: Cambridge University Press, 2005), pp. 172–214, especially pp. 172, 173, and 206; henceforth Greenberg and Dratel, *The Torture Papers*. For the statute defining "torture" in domestic US law, see Title 18 U.S.C. 2340. Available from http://www.gpo.gov/fdsys/pkg/USCODE-2011-title18/pdf/USCODE-2011-title18-partI-chap113C-sec2340.pdf (accessed 7/23/2014).

21. The Eighth Amendment of the US Constitution, which prohibits "cruel and unusual punishments," proscribes the infliction of torture. Moreover, international human rights law (IHRL) also proscribes the infliction of torture. See, e.g., the UN Universal Declaration of Human Rights, December 10, 1948. Art. 5. Available from http://www.un.org/en/documents/udhr/index.shtml (accessed 7/19/2014). See also Convention against Torture and Other Cruel, Inhuman or Degrading Treatment

or Punishment, December 10, 1984. Available from http://www.ohchr.org/EN/
ProfessionalInterest/Pages/CAT.aspx (accessed 7/19/2014). The United States ratified
the convention in 1994 but with considerable reservations including, for example, that
"the provisions of Articles 1 through 16 of the Convention are not self-executing."
See US Declarations and Reservations in UNTC. Available from https://treaties.
un.org/Pages/ViewDetails.aspx?mtdsg_no=IV-9&chapter=4&lang=en#EndDec.
(accessed 7/19/2014). For a US peculiar interpretation of torture that seems inconsistent with IHRL, see John C. Yoo, "Letter to Alberto R. Gonzales, Counsel to the
President," August 1, 2002, in Greenberg and Dratel, *The Torture Papers*, pp. 218–22.
For the controversial practice of torture and state violence in general in the history
of the United States, see Robert M. Pallitto (ed.), *Torture and State Violence in the
United States* (Baltimore, MD: Johns Hopkins University Press, 2011).

22. Consider a variation of the trolley problem that provides an example of a matter of life or death situation. Suppose that I am on the track and a runaway trolley is
speeding toward me. I have nowhere to go because I am working on a high-altitude
bridge. I, however, can hit a switch redirecting the trolley to a different track where
I foresee that five people will be killed. Am I allowed to do so? Consequentialist theorists, such as utilitarians, typically stipulate that I have no right to redirect the trolley
because, as a result of my action, more people will be killed than saved. By contrast,
nonconsequentialist or deontological theories typically stipulate that I am permitted but not obligated to redirect the trolley in order to save my life. For some of the
nuances related to traditional trolley problems, see F. M. Kamm, "Toward the Essence
of Nonconsequentialist Constraints on Harming," especially pp. 131–32.

23. Plato, *Crito, The Collected Dialogues*, p. 34, 49b.

24. Paul, "The Epistle of Paul to the Romans," *The New American Bible, Romans
3:8*, p. 183.

25. Kant, *Groundwork*, p. 96. Some authors contend that Kant's nonconsequentialist position is consistent with consequentialism. So for them the right and the good
are not necessarily mutually exclusive, as other authors argue, but rather consistent
with each other. That is to say, they presuppose that acting according to Kant's
categorical imperative does not exclude promoting the greatest happiness. On the
contrary, they argue that according to Kant's moral view, including his categorical
imperative, everyone ought to try to promote the greatest happiness. For this interesting but arguably debatable interpretation of Kant's moral theory, see Derek Parfitt,
On What Matters, vol. 1 (New York: Oxford University Press, 2011), pp. 244–57.

26. For an argument against proportionalism or consequentialism, and a defense
of the Socratic and Pauline principles, see John Finnis, *Fundamental of Ethics*,
pp. 110–33.

POSTSCRIPT

1. While the late Osama bin Laden and his acolytes appeal to all Muslims to
deliberately kill alleged infidels, especially Americans, the Quran seems to forbid the
killing of the innocent. See, e.g., A. Y. Ali, *The Qur'an*, 5:32.

2. Habermas, e.g., claimed that former President Bush's decision to call for a "war against terrorism" was a serious mistake for two main reasons: (1) such a description elevated "these criminals [the perpetrators of the 9/11 terrorist attacks] to the status of war enemies" and (2) "one cannot lead a war against a 'network' if the term 'war' is to retain any definite meaning." See Borradori, *Philosophy in a Time of Terror*, pp. 34–35.

3. The US Department of State reports a 43 percent increase in terrorist attacks between 2012 and 2013. Available from http://www.state.gov/j/ct/rls/crt/2013/224831. htm (accessed 5/6/2014).

4. See note 3, ch. 2 above.

Bibliography

Abel, Theodore. 1951. "The Sociology of Concentration Camps." *Social Forces* 30: 150–55.

Abuqudairi, Areej. 2014. "Jordan anti-terrorism law sparks concern." *Aljazeera*. Available from http://www.aljazeera.com/news/middleeast/2014/04/jordan-anti-terrorism-law-sparks-concern-201442510452221775.html.

Agamben, Giorgio. 2005. *State of Exception*. Trans. Kevin Attell. Chicago: University of Chicago Press.

AI Report. 2009. People's Republic of China Submission to the UN Universal Periodic Review Fourth Session of the UPR Working Group of the Human Rights Council. Available from http://lib.ohchr.org/HRBodies/UPR/Documents/Session4/CN/AI_CHN_UPR_S4_2009_AmnestyInternational.pdf.

AI Report. 2009. "Israel/Gaza Operation 'Cast Lead': 22 days of death and destruction." Available from http://www.amnesty.org/en/library/asset/MDE15/015/2009/en/8f299083-9a74-4853-860f-0563725e633a/mde150152009en.pdf.

AI Report. 2015. "State of Palestine: Unlawful and Deadly: Rocket and mortar attacks by Palestinian armed groups during the 2014 Gaza/Israel conflict." Available from https://www.amnesty.org/en/documents/mde21/1178/2015/en/.

Ali, Abdullah Yusuf. 2005. *The Qur'an: Text, Translation and Commentary*. New York: Tahrike Tarsile Qur'an, Inc.

Aljazzera. 2014. "Sunni rebels declare new 'Islamic caliphate.'" Available from http://www.aljazeera.com/news/middleeast/2014/06/isil-declares-new-islamic-caliphate-201462917326669749.html.

Amano, Yukiya. 2013. UN News Center. Available from http://www.un.org/apps/news/story.asp?NewsID=45311&Cr=iaea&Cr1=nuclear.

Ambrose. 2006. *On the Duties of the Clergy*. In *The Ethics of War and Peace: Classic and Contemporary Readings*. Eds. Gregory M. Reicheberg, Henrik Syse, and Endre Begsy, 67. Malden, MA: Blackwell.

Améry, Jean. 1980. *At the Mind's Limits: Contemplation by a Survivor on Auschwitz and Its Realities.* Trans. Sidney Rosenfeld and Stella P. Rosenfeld. Indianapolis: Indiana University Press.

Andress, David. 2005. *The Terror: The Merciless War for Freedom in Revolutionary France.* New York: Farrar, Straus and Giroux.

Annan, Kofi and Nader Mousavizadeh. 2012. *Intervention: A Life in War and Peace.* New York: The Penguin Press.

Anscombe, G. E. M. 1969. *Intention.* 2nd ed. Ithaca: Cornell University Press.

———. 1981. *The Collected Philosophical Papers of G. E. M. Anscombe, Vol. 3: Ethics, Religion and Politics.* Minneapolis: University of Minnesota Press.

Appiah, Kwame Anthony. 2008. *Experiments in Ethics.* Cambridge, MA: Harvard University Press.

Aquinas, Thomas. 1988. *Saint Thomas Aquinas: On Law, Morality and Politics.* Eds. W. P. Baumgarth and R. J. Regan. Indianapolis, IN: Hackett.

———. 1988. *On Kingship.* In *Saint Thomas Aquinas: On Law, Morality and Politics.* Eds. W. P. Baumgarth and R. J. Regan. Indianapolis, IN: Hackett.

———. 2005. *The Cardinal Virtues: Prudence, Justice, Fortitude, and Temperance.* Trans. Richard J. Regan. Indianapolis, IN: Hackett.

———. 2006. *Summa Theologiae, vol. 17, Psychology of Human Acts* (Ia2ae. 6-17). New York: Cambridge University Press.

———. 2006. *Summa Theologiae, vol. 18, Principles of Morality* (Ia2ae. 181-21). New York: Cambridge University Press.

———. 2006. *Summa Theologiae, vol. 28, Law and Political Theory* (Ia2a. 90-97). New York: Cambridge University Press.

———. 2006. *Summa Theologiae, vol. 38, Injustice* (2a2ae. 63-79). New York: Cambridge University Press.

Archibugi, Daniele. 2011. "Should bin Laden have been tried?" *openDemocracy.* Available from http://www.opendemocracy.net/daniele-archibugi/should-bin-laden-have-been-tried.

Arendt, Hannah. 1972. "On Violence." In Hannah Arendt, *Crises of the Republic,* 103–84. New York: Harcourt Brace Jovanovich.

Aristotle. 1941. *Nicomachean Ethics.* In *The Basic Works of Aristotle.* Ed. Richard McKeon. New York: Random House.

Arnold, Robert. 2005. "Terrorism as a Crime Against Humanity under the ICC Statute." In *International Cooperation in Counter-Terrorism: The United Nations and Regional Organizations in the Fight Against Terrorism.* Ed. Giuseppe Nesi, 121–37. Burlington, VT: Ashgate.

Aron, Raymond. 1968. *Peace and War: A Theory of International Relations.* 2nd ed. New York: Frederick A Praeger.

Arthur, John. "Famine Relief and the Ideal Moral Code." In *Ethics: History, Theory, and Contemporary Issues.* Eds. Steven M. Cahn and Peter Markie, 797–808. New York: Oxford University Press.

Atwan, Abdel Bari. 2006. *The Secret History of Al Qaeda.* Los Angeles: University of California Press.

Augustine. 1979. *On Free Choice of the Will.* Indianapolis, IN: The Bobbs-Merrill Company.

———. 1994. *Against Faustus the Manichean XXII*. In *Augustine Political Writings*. Eds. Ernest L. Fortin and Douglas Kries, 73–79. Indianapolis, IN: Hackett.

———. 1994. *Letter 138, to Marcellinus*. In *Augustine Political Writings*. Eds. Ernest L. Fortin and Douglas Kries, 205–12. Indianapolis, IN: Hackett.

———. 1994. *Letter 189, to Boniface*. In *Augustine Political Writings*. Eds. Ernest L. Fortin and Douglas Kries, 219–20. Indianapolis, IN: Hackett.

———. 1994. *The City of God*. In *Augustine Political Writings*. Eds. Ernest L. Fortin and Douglas Kries. Indianapolis, IN: Hackett.

———. 1999. *The City of God*. In *From Irenaeus to Grotius: A Sourcebook in Christian Political Thought*. Eds. Oliver O'Donovan and Joan Lockwood O'Donovan. Grand Rapids, MI: William B. Eerdmans Publishing Co.

———. 2006. *Questions on the Heptateuch*. In *The Ethics of War and Peace: Classic and Contemporary Readings*. Eds. Gregory M. Reicheberg, Henrik Syse, and Endre Begsy, 82–83. Malden, MA: Blackwell.

Austin, J. L. 1961. "A Plea for Excuses." In *J. L. Austin: Philosophical Papers*. Eds. J. O. Urmson and G. J. Warnock, 175–204. New York: Oxford University Press.

Averroes. 1996. "The Legal Doctrine of Jihad." In *Jihad in Classical and Modern Islam*. Ed. Rudolph Peters, 27–42. Princeton, NJ: Markus Wiener Publishers.

Baker, Peter. 2013. *Days of Fire: Bush and Cheney in the White House*. New York: Anchor Books.

Bale, Jeffrey M. and Gary A. Ackerman. 2009. "Profiling the WMD Terrorist Threat." In *WMD Terrorism: Science and Policies*. Ed. Stephen M. Maurer, 11–45. Cambridge, MA: The MIT Press.

Bardach, Ann Louise. 2009. *After Fidel: A Death Foretold in Miami, Havana, and Washington*. New York: Scribner.

Baron, Marcia. 2005. "Justifications and Excuses." *Ohio State Journal of Criminal Law* 2: 387–406.

Basic Law for the Republic of Germany. 2012. Available from http://www.gesetze-im-internet.de/englisch_gg/.

Baum, Geraldine and Richard Boudreaux. 2008. "Terror victims recount stories for U.N. forum." *Los Angeles Times*. Available from http://articles.latimes.com/2008/sep/10/world/fg-victims10.

BBC News. 2009. "Timeline: Tony Blair's statements on weapons in Iraq." Available from http://news.bbc.co.uk/2/hi/uk_news/politics/8409526.stm.

BBC News. 2011. "China accuses Dalai Lama of encouraging suicide by fire." Available from http://www.bbc.co.uk/news/world-asia-pacific-15372731.

BBC News Middle East. 2014. "Holocaust families criticize Israel over Gaza." Available from http://www.bbc.com/news/world-middle-east-28916761.

Bellinger III, John B. 2011. "Bin Laden Killing: The Legal Basis." *Council of Foreign Relations*. Available from http://www.cfr.org/terrorism/bin-laden-killing-legal-basis/p24866.

Benjamin, Walter. 1996. "Critique of Violence." In Walter Benjamin, *Selected Writings*, Vol. 1 1913–1926. Eds. Marcus Bullock and Michael W. Jennings, 236–52. Cambridge, MA: Harvard University Press.

Bennett, Jonathan. 1981. "Morality and Consequences." In *The Tanner Lectures of Human Values II* Ed. Sterling McMurrin, 45–116. Salt Lake City: University of Utah Press.

Berman, Mitchell N. 2003. "Justification and Excuse, Law and Morality," *Duke Law Journal* 53: 1–43.

Bin Laden, Osama. 2005. *Messages to the World: The Statements of Osama Bin Laden.* Ed. Bruce Lawrence. New York: Verso.

Blackburn, Simon. 2006. *Plato's Republic: A Biography.* New York: Atlantic Monthly Press.

Blackstone, William. 1765–1769. *Commentaries on the Laws of England.* Oxford: Clarendon Press. Available from http://avalon.law.yale.edu/subject_menus/blackstone.asp.

Blight, James G. and Janet M. Lang. 2005. *The Fog of War: Lessons from the Life of Robert S. McNamara.* Lanham, MD: Rowman & Littlefield.

Blix, Hans. 2004. *Disarming Iraq.* New York: Pantheon Books.

Bloomberg. 2013. "Fukushima a 'blueprint' for terrorists, IAEA warns." *Japan Times.* Available from http://www.japantimes.co.jp/news/2013/07/03/national/fukushima-a-blueprint-for-terrorists-iaea-warns/.

Boghossian, Paul. 2006. *Fear of Knowledge: Against Relativism and Constructivism.* New York: Oxford University Press.

Booth, William. 2014. "The UN says 7 in10 Palestinians killed in Gaza were civilians. Israel disagrees." *Washington Post.* Available from http://www.washingtonpost.com/world/middle_east/the-un-says-7-in-10-palestinians-killed-in-gaza-were-civilians-israel-disagrees/2014/08/29/44edc598-2faa-11e4-9b98-848790384093_story.html?wpisrc=nl_hdtop.

Borradori, Giovanna. 2004. *Philosophy in a Time of Terror: Dialogues with Jürgen Habermas and Jacques Derrida.* Chicago: University of Chicago Press.

Boumediene v. Bush. 2008. 553 U.S. Available from http://www.law.cornell.edu/supct/pdf/06-1195P.ZO.

Boumediene, Lakhdar. 2012. "My Guantánamo Nightmare," *New York Times.* Available from http://www.nytimes.com/2012/01/08/opinion/sunday/my-guantanamo-nightmare.html?pagewanted=print.

Boyle Jr., Joseph M. 1980. "Toward Understanding the Principle of Double Effect." *Ethics* 90: 527–38.

Bracher, Karl Dietrich. 1970. *The German Dictatorship: The Origins, Structure, and Effects of National Socialism.* Trans. Jean Steinberg. New York: Praeger Publishers.

Brookings. 2012. *Iraq Index: Tracking Variables of Reconstruction and Security in Iraq.* Available from http://www.brookings.edu/~/media/Centers/saban/iraq%20index/index201207.pdf.

Brown, David. 2004. *The Road to Oran: Anglo-French Naval Relations September 1939–July 1940* New York: Taylor & Francis.

Brownstein, Catherine A. and John S. Brownstein. 2008. "Estimating Excess Mortality in Post-Invasion Iraq." *New England Journal of Medicine* 358: 445–47. Available from http://archive.is/wpZE.

Brulin, Rémi. 2012. "Terrorism Is Terrorism." *Foreign Policy*. Available from http://www.foreignpolicy.com/articles/2012/08/20/terrorism_is_terrorism?page=0,1.

B'Tselem. 2014. *Death Foretold: The inevitable outcome of bombing homes and inhabited areas in Gaza*. Available from http://www.btselem.org/gaza_strip/20140811_a_death_foretold.

Buchanan, Allan. 2004. "From Nuremberg to Kosovo: The Morality of Illegal International Legal Reform." In *Humanitarian Intervention*. Ed. Aleksandar Jokic, 123–58. New York: Broadview Press.

Bullock, Alan. 1962. *Hitler: A Study in Tyranny*. Completely revised edition. New York: Harper & Row.

Bunn, Matthew and William Tobey. 2013. "The Nuclear Terrorism Threat—And Next Steps to Reduce the Danger." Presentation, United Nations Headquarters, New York City. Available from http://belfercenter.ksg.harvard.edu/publication/23484/nuclear_terrorism_threat_and_next_steps_to_reduce_the_danger.html?breadcrumb=%252Fpublication%252F23879%252Fnuclear_terrorism_threat.

Burgess Jr., Douglas R. 2005. "The Dread Pirate Bin Laden." *Legal Affairs*. Available from http://www.legalaffairs.org/issues/July-August-2005/feature_burgess_julaug05.msp.

Burnham, Gilbert et al. 2006. *The Human Cost of the War in Iraq: Mortality Study 2003-2006*. Available from http://web.mit.edu/CIS/pdf/Human_Cost_of_War.pdf.

Bush, George W. 2001. Address to a Joint Session of Congress and the American People. Available from http://georgewbush-whitehouse.archives.gov/news/releases/2001/09/20010920-8.html.

———. 2003. *We Will Prevail*. New York: The Continuum International Publishing Group Inc.

Bybee, Jay S. 2005. "Memorandum for Alberto R. Gonzales, Counsel to the President, Re: Standards of Conduct for Interrogation under 18 U.S.C. 2340-2340A," August 1, 2002. In *The Torture Papers: The Road to Abu Grahib*. Eds. Karen J. Greenberg and Joshua L. Dratel, 172–214. New York: Cambridge University Press.

Byers, Michael. 2005. *War Law: Understanding International Law and Armed Conflict*. New York: Grove Press.

Camus, Albert. 1956. *The Rebel: An Essay on Man in Revolt*. Trans. Anthony Bower. New York: Vintage Books.

Card, Claudia. 2003. "Making War on Terrorism in Response to 9/11." In *Terrorism and International Justice*. Ed. James P. Sterba, 171–85. New York: Oxford University Press.

Carroll, Lewis. 1946. *Through the Looking-Glass and What Alice Found There*. New York: Random House.

Carroll, Rory. 2009. "Hugo Chávez courts outrage with praise for Carlos, Mugabe and Amin." *Guardian*. Available from http://www.theguardian.com/world/2009/nov/22/hugo-chavez-defence-carlos-jackal.

Carter, Jimmy and Mary Robinson. 2014. "How to Fix It: Ending this war in Gaza begins with recognizing Hamas as a legitimate political actor." *Foreign Policy*. Available from http://www.foreignpolicy.com/articles/2014/08/04/how_to_fix_it_jimmy_carter_mary_robinson_israel_palestine_gaza_hamas.

Carus, W. Seth. 2012. *Defining "Weapons of Mass Destruction."* Revised and updated, *Center for the Study of Weapons of Mass Destruction Occasional Paper, No. 8*. Washington, DC: National Defense University Press. Available from http://www.ndu.edu/press/lib/pdf/CSWMD-OccasionalPapers/CSWMD_Occational Paper-8.pdf.

Cassese, Antonio. 2005. *International Law*. 2nd ed. New York: Oxford University Press.

Cavanaugh, T. A. 2006. *Double-Effect Reasoning: Doing Good and Avoiding Evil*. New York: Oxford University Press.

Cha, Victor. 2013. *The Impossible State: North Korea Past and Future*. New York: HarperCollins Publishers.

Chaliand, Gérard and Arnaud Blin. 2007. "Zealots and Assassins." 2007. Eds. Gérard Chaliand and Arnaud Blin, ch. 3. *The History of Terrorism: From Antiquity to Al Qaeda*. Los Angeles: University of California Press.

Chang, Iris. 1997. *The Rape of Nanking: The Forgotten Holocaust of World War II*. New York: Penguin Books.

Chapman, Glen. 2009. "Bill Gates playfully frees swarm of mosquitoes." Yahoo News. Available from http://www.binrev.com/forums/index.php/topic/40268-bill-gates-unleashes-a-swarm-of-mosquitoes-at-a-tech-conference/.

Charter and Judgment of the Nürnberg Tribunal. 1949. UN Treaty Collection. Available from http://legal.un.org/ilc/documentation/english/a_cn4_5.pdf.

Charter of the United Nations. Available from https://www.un.org/en/documents/charter/.

Chomsky, Noam. 2003. *Hegemony or Survival: America's Quest for Global Hegemony*. New York: Metropolitan Books.

Chomsky, Noam and Andre Vltchek. 2013. *On Western Terrorism: From Hiroshima to Drone Warfare*. New York: Palgrave Macmillan.

Churchill, Winston. 1932. *Amid These Storms: Thoughts and Adventures*. New York: Charles Scribner's Sons.

———. 1948. *The Second World War: The Gathering Storm*. Vol. 1. Cambridge, MA: The Riverside Press.

Cicero. 1991. *On Duties*. Eds. M. T. Griffin and E. M. Atkins. New York: Cambridge University Press.

Clausewitz, Carl von. 1976. *On War*. Eds. Michael Howard and Peter Paret. Princeton, NJ: Princeton University Press.

Coady, C. A. J. 2002. "Terrorism, Just War and Supreme Emergency." In *Terrorism and Justice: Moral Argument in a Threatened World*. Eds. Tony Coady and Michael O' Keefe, 8–21. Melbourne: Melbourne University Press.

———. 2004. "Defining Terrorism." In *Terrorism: The Philosophical Issues*. Ed. Igor Primoratz, 3–14. New York: Palgrave Macmillan.

———. 2008. *Morality and Political Violence*. New York: Cambridge University Press.

Cobban, Alfred. 1939. *Dictatorship: Its History and Theory*. New York: Charles Scribner's Sons.

Coffin v. United States. 1845. 156 US 432. Available from http://constitution.org/ussc/156-432.htm.

Cohen, Roberta. 2014. "Preventing a massacre in North Korea's gulags." *Washington Post*. Available from http://www.washingtonpost.com/opinions/preventing-a-massacre-in-north-koreas-gulags/2014/07/25/b9d6a3fe-1284-11e4-9285-4243a40ddc97_story.html?wpisrc=nl_headlines.

Costs of War. 2013. Available from http://costsofwar.org/article/iraqi-civilians.

Council of Europe. 2010. Convention for the Protection of Human Rights and Fundamental Freedoms. Available from http://conventions.coe.int/treaty/en/treaties/html/005.htm.

Dallaire, Roméo A. 2003. *Shake Hands with the Devil: The Failure of Humanity in Rwanda*. Toronto: Random House Canada.

Dahmann, Klaus. 2012. "Terrorism trumps military taboos in Germany." *DW*, August 18, 2012. Available from http://www.dw.de/dw/article/0,,16177278,00.html.

Davidson, Donald. 2001. *Essays on Actions and Events*. New York: Oxford University Press.

Dershowitz, Alan M. 2002. *Why Terrorism Works: Understanding the Threat, Responding to the Challenge*. New Haven, CT: Yale University Press.

Detter, Ingrid. 2004. *The Law of War*. 2nd ed. New York: Cambridge University Press.

Denyer, Simon. 2015. "China's new terrorism law provokes anger in U.S., concern at home." *Washington Post*. Available from http://www.washingtonpost.com/world/asia_pacific/china-invokes-terrorism-as-it-readies-additional-harsh-measures/2015/03/04/1e078288-139c-497e-aa8a-e6d810a5a8a2_story.html.

Donagan, Alan. 1977. *The Theory of Morality*. Chicago: The University of Chicago Press.

Dostoyevsky, Fyodor. 2005. *The Brothers Karamazov*. In *The Moral of the Story: An Anthology of Ethics through Literature*. Eds. Peter Singer and Renata Singer, 436–37. Malden, MA: Blackwell.

Duffy, Helen. 2005. *The 'War on Terror' and the Framework of International Law*. New York: Cambridge University Press.

Dunlop, W. G. 2014. "IS jihadists urge killing of citizens from US-led coalition." *AFP*. Available from http://news.yahoo.com/jihadists-urge-killing-citizens-us-led-coalition-102650763.html.

Economist. 2004. "Saddam Hussein's weapons mirage: George Bush and Tony Blair exaggerated, but they did not lie." Available from http://www.economist.com/node/2384510?fsrc=email_to_a_friend.

Eiland, Giora. 2014. "In Gaza, there is no such a thing as 'innocent civilians." *Ynet News*, July 4, 2014. Available from http://www.ynetnews.com/articles/0,7340,L-4554583,00.html.

El Fadl, Khaled Abou. 2004. *Islam and the Challenge of Democracy*. Eds. Joshua Cohen and Deborah Chasman. Princeton, NJ: Princeton University Press.

Elshtain, Jean Bethke. 2004. *The Just War against Terror: The Burden of American Power in a Violent World*. New York: Basic Books.

Executive Order 12333. 2008. United States Intelligence Activities. Available from http://www.fas.org/irp/offdocs/eo/eo-12333-2008.pdf.

Falk, Richard. 2014. "Geopolitics and international state crime: an accountability black hole." Available from https://www.opendemocracy.net/richard-falk/geopolitics-and-international-state-crime-accountability-black-hole.

Fanon, Frantz. 2004. *The Wretched of the Earth*. New York: Grove Press.

Feinberg, Joel. 1984. *Harm to Others: The Moral Limits of the Criminal Law*. New York: Oxford University Press.

Ferguson, Niall. 2002. *Empire: The Rise and Demise of the British World Order and the Lessons for Global Power*. New York: Basic Books.

Field, Antony. 2009. "The 'New Terrorism': Revolution or Evolution?" *Political Studies Review* 7: 195–207.

Finnis, John. 1983. *Fundamentals of Ethics*. Washington, DC: Georgetown University Press.

———. 1996. "Ethics of War and Peace in the Catholic Natural Law Tradition." In *Ethics of War and Peace: Religious and Secular Perspectives*. Ed. Terry Nardin, 15–39. Princeton, NJ: Princeton University Press.

Foot, Philippa. 1978. *Virtues and Vices and Other Essays in Moral Philosophy*. Berkeley: University of California Press, 1978.

Fotion, Nicholas. 2007. *War and Ethics: A New Just War Theory*. New York: Continuum International Publishing Group.

Frankfurt, Harry G. 2008. "Inadvertence and Moral Responsibility." *The Amherst Lecture in Philosophy* 3. Available from http://www.amherstlecture.org/frankfurt 2008/frankfurt2008_ALP.pdf.

Frankl, Viktor E. 1992. *Man's Search for Meaning: An Introduction to Logotherapy*. 4th ed. Boston: Beacon Press.

Fraser, Giles. 2014. "If we can have just war, why not just terrorism?" *Guardian*. Available from http://www.theguardian.com/commentisfree/belief/2014/jul/25/just-war-then-why-not-just-terrorism.

French, Shannon E. 2003. "Murderers, not Warriors: The Moral Distinction between Terrorists and Legitimate Fighters in Asymmetric Conflicts." In *Terrorism and International Justice*. Ed. James P. Sterba, 31–46. New York: Oxford University Press.

Frey, R. G. and Christopher W. Morris. 1991. "Violence, Terrorism, and Justice." In *Violence, Terrorism, and Justice*. Eds. R. G. Frey and Christopher W. Morris, 1–17. New York: Cambridge University Press.

Friedrich, Jörg. 2002. *The Fire: The Bombing of Germany, 1940-1945*. Trans. Allison Brown. New York: Columbia University Press.

"Fukushima a 'blueprint' for terrorists, IAEA warns." 2013. *Japan Times*. Available from http://www.japantimes.co.jp/news/2013/07/03/national/fukushima-a-blueprint-for-terrorists-iaea-warns/.

Fullinwider, Robert K. 1988. "Understanding Terrorism." In *Problems of International Justice*. Ed. Steven Luper-Foy, 248–59. Boulder, CO: Westview Press.

Gentili, Alberico. 2006. *On the Law of War*. In *The Ethics of War: Classic and Contemporary Readings*. Eds. Gregory M. Reichberg, Henrik Syse, and Endre Begby, 371–77. Malden, MA: Blackwell.

Gilbert, Margaret. 2006. "Who's to Blame? Collective Moral Responsibility and the Implication for Group Members." In *Midwest Studies in Philosophy: Shared Intentions and Collective Responsibility*. Eds. Peter A. French and Howard K. Wettstein, 94–114. Malden, MA: Blackwell.

Gioia, Andrea. 2005. "The UN Conventions on the Prevention and Suppression of International Terrorism." In *International Cooperation in Counter-Terrorism:*

The United Nations and Regional Organizations in the Fight Against Terrorism. Ed. Giuseppe Nesi, 3–23. Burlington, VT: Ashgate.

Glover, Jonathan. 1991. "State Terrorism." In *Violence, Terrorism, and Justice.* Eds. R. G. Frey and Christopher W. Morris, 256–75. New York: Cambridge University Press.

———. 2001. *Humanity: A Moral History of the Twentieth Century.* New Haven, CT: Yale University Press.

Goldstone, Richard. 2009. Statement by Richard Goldstone on behalf of the Members of the United Nations Fact Finding Mission on the Gaza Conflict before the Human Rights Council. Available from http://www.ohchr.org/EN/HRBodies/HRC/SpecialSessions/Session9/Pages/FactFindingMission.aspx.

———. 2011. "Reconsidering the Goldstone Report on Israel and War Crimes." *Washington Post,* April 1, 2011. Available from http://www.washingtonpost.com/opinions/reconsidering-the-goldstone-report-on-israel-and-war-crimes/2011/04/01/AFg111JC_story.html.

Gordon, Michael R. and General Bernard E. Trainor. 1995. *The Generals' War: The Inside Story of the Conflict in the Gulf.* New York: Little, Brown & Co.

Govern, Kevin H. 2012. "Operation Neptune Spear: Was Killing Bin Laden a Legitimate Military Objective?" In *Target Killings: Law Morality in an Asymmetrical World.* Ed. Claire Finkelstein and Jens David Ohlin, 347–73. New York: Oxford University Press.

Grayling, A. C. 2006. *Among the Dead Cities: The History and Moral Legacy of WWII Bombing of Civilians in Germany and Japan.* New York: Walker & Company.

Greenawalt, Kent. 1984. "The Perplexing Borders of Justification and Excuse." *Columbia Law Review* 84: 1897–926.

———. 1987. *Conflicts of Law and Morality.* New York: Oxford University Press.

Greenberg, Karen J. and Joshua L. Dratel (eds.). 2005. *The Torture Papers: The Road to Abu Ghraib.* New York: Cambridge University Press.

Grotius, Hugo. 2005. *The Rights of War and Peace.* Ed. Richard Tuck. Indianapolis, IN: Liberty Fund.

Guevara, Che. 1998. *Guerrilla Warfare.* Lincoln: University of Nebraska Press.

———. 1998. "Message to the Tricontinental." In *Guerrilla Warfare,* 161–75.

Guillén, Abraham. 2004. "Urban Guerrilla Strategy." In *Voices of Terror: Manifestos, Writings and Manuals of Al Qaeda, Hamas, and Other Terrorists from Around the World and Throughout the Ages.* Ed. Walter Laqueur, 377–83. New York: Reed Press.

Haleem, Muhammad Abdel. 2011. *Understanding the Qur'an: Themes and Style.* New York: I. B. Turis.

Hamas Charter. 1988. Selected Documents Regarding Palestine. Available from http://www.thejerusalemfund.org/www.thejerusalemfund.org/carryover/documents/charter.html?chocaid=397.

Harman, Gilbert. 1982. "Moral Relativism Defended." In *Relativism: Cognitive and Moral.* Eds. Michael Kraus and Jack W. Meiland, 189–204. Indiana: University of Notre Dame Press.

Hartigan, Richard Shelly. 1966. "Saint Augustine on War and Killing: The Problem of the Innocent." *Journal of the History of Ideas* 27: 195–204.

Hasegawa, Tsuyoshi. 2009. "Were the Atomic Bombs of Hiroshima and Nagasaki Justified?" In *Bombing Civilians: A Twentieth-Century History*. Eds. Yuki Tanaka and Marilyn B. Young, 97–134. New York: The New Press.

Held, Virginia. 2004. "Terrorism and War." *Journal of Ethics* 8: 59–75.

———. 2005. "Legitimate Authority in Non-State Groups Using Violence." *Journal of Social Philosophy* 36: 175–93.

———. 2008. *How Terrorism Is Wrong*. New York: Oxford University Press.

Hitler, Adolf. 1995. "The Mission of the Nazi Movement." In *Fascism*. Ed. Roger Griffin, 116–17. New York: Oxford University Press.

Hobbes, Thomas. 1991. *Leviathan*. Ed. Richard Tuck. New York: Cambridge University Press.

Hoffman, Bruce. 2006. *Inside Terrorism*. Revised and expanded edition. New York: Columbia University Press.

———. 2015. "The Awful Truth Is That Terrorism Works." *The Daily Beast*. Available from http://www.thedailybeast.com/articles/2015/03/14/the-awful-truth-is-that-terrorism-works.html.

Holmes, Robert L. 1989. *On War and Morality*. Princeton, NJ: Princeton University Press.

Honderich, Ted. 2002. *After the Terror*. Great Britain: Edinburgh University Press.

Hooker, Brad and Elinor Mason (eds.). 2000. *Morality, Rules, and Consequences: A Critical Reader*. Lanham, MD: Rowman & Littlefield.

Human Rights Watch. 2014. "Saudi Arabia: New Terrorism Regulations Assault Rights." Available from http://www.hrw.org/news/2014/03/20/saudi-arabia-new-terrorism-regulations-assault-rights.

———. 2015. "China: Draft Counterterrorism Law a Recipe for Abuses." Available from http://www.hrw.org/news/2015/01/20/china-draft-counterterrorism-law-recipe-abuses.

Hume, David. 1964. "Of the Original Contract." In *Hume's Moral and Political Philosophy*. Ed. Henry D. Aiken, 356–72. New York: Hafner.

ICC-02/05-01/09. 2009. Available from http://www.icc-cpi.int/iccdocs/doc/doc639078.pdf.

ICJ. 2009. *Assessing Damage, Urging Action: Report of the Eminent Jurists Panel on Terrorism, Counter-Terrorism and Human Rights*. Available from http://www.un.org/en/sc/ctc/specialmeetings/2011/docs/icj/icj-2009-ejp-execsumm.pdf.

ICRC. 1988. Convention on the Non-Applicability of Statutory Limitations to War Crimes and Crimes Against Humanity, 26 November 1968. Available from http://www.icrc.org/applic/ihl/ihl.nsf/Treaty.xsp?documentId=735456606A8F58FDC12563CD002D6C51&action=openDocument.

ICRC. 2004. "How 'grave breaches' are defined in the Geneva Conventions and Additional Protocols." Available from https://www.icrc.org/eng/resources/documents/misc/5zmgf9.htm.

ICRC. 2004. "What is international humanitarian law?" Available from http://www.icrc.org/eng/resources/documents/legal-fact-sheet/humanitarian-law-factsheet.htm.

Ignatieff, Michael. 2004. *The Lesser Evil: Political Ethics in an Age of Terror*. Princeton, NJ: Princeton University Press.

International Human Rights and Conflict Resolution at Stanford Law School and Global Justice Clinic at NYU School of Law. 2012. *Living under Drones: Death, Injury and Trauma to Civilians from US Drones Practices in Pakistan (2012).* Available from http://www.livingunderdrones.org/wp-content/uploads/2013/10/ Stanford-NYU-Living-Under-Drones.pdf.

Ipsen, Knut. 2004. "Combatants and Non-Combatants." In *The Handbook of Humanitarian Law in Armed Conflict.* Ed. Dieter Fleck, 65–101. New York: Oxford University Press.

Iraq Body Count Project. 2004. Available from http://www.iraqbodycount.org/.

Jaggar, Alison. 2005. "What Is Terrorism, Why Is It Wrong, and Could It Ever Be Morally Permissible?"*Journal of Social Philosophy* 36: 202–17.

Jenkins, Brian M. 2003. "International Terrorism: The Other World War." In *The New Global Terrorism: Characteristics, Causes, Controls.* Ed. Charles W. Kegley Jr., 15–26. Upper Saddle River, NJ: Prentice Hall.

Jervis, Robert. 1976. *Perception and Misperception in International Politics.* Princeton, NJ: Princeton University Press.

———. 1988. "War and Misperception." *Journal of Interdisciplinary History* 18: 675–700.

Johnson, James Turner. 1975. *Ideology, Reason, and the Limitation of War.* Princeton, NJ: Princeton University Press.

———. 1999. *Morality and Contemporary Warfare.* New Haven, CT: Yale University Press.

Johnston, Douglas and Cynthia Sampson (eds.). 1994. *Religion: The Missing Dimension of Statecraft.* New York: Oxford University Press.

Johnston, Douglas (ed.). 2003. *Faith-Based Diplomacy: Trumping Realpolitik.* New York: Oxford University Press.

Jones, Sam and Owen Bowcott. 2011. "Osama bin Laden's death—killed in a raid or assassinated?" *Guardian* (UK). http://www.guardian.co.uk/world/2011/may/06/ osama-bin-laden-death-assassination.

Jones, Seth G. 2014. *A Persistent Threat: The Evolution of Al Qa'ida and Other Salafi Jihadists.* Santa Monica: CA: RAND Corporation. http://www.rand.org/content/ dam/rand/pubs/research_reports/RR600/RR637/RAND_RR637.pdf.

Judt, Tony. 1992. *Past Imperfect: French Intellectuals, 1944-1956.* Berkeley: University of California Press.

Kamm, F. M. 2007. "Toward the Essence of Nonconsequentilialist Constraints on Harming: Modality, Productive Purity, and the Greater Good Working Itself Out." In Francis Kamm, *Intricate Ethics: Rights, Responsibilities, and Permissible Harm,* 130–89. New York: Oxford University Press.

———. 2008. "Terrorism and Intending Evil." *Philosophy and Public Affairs* 36: 157–86.

———. 2012. *The Moral Target: Aiming at Right Conduct in War and Other Conflicts.* New York: Oxford University Press.

Kant, Immanuel. 1964. *Groundwork of the Metaphysic of Morals.* Trans. H. J. Paton. New York: Harper and Row.

———. 1991. *The Metaphysics of Morals.* Introduction, translation, and notes by Mary Gregor. New York: Cambridge University Press.

———. 1999. "Perpetual Peace: A Philosophical Sketch." In *Kant: Political Writings*. Ed. Hans Reiss, 93–130. New York: Cambridge University Press.

Kapitan, Tomis. 2002. "Terrorism in the Arab-Israeli Conflict." In *Terrorism: The Philosophical Issues*. Ed. Igor Primoratz, 175–91. New York: Palgrave MacMillan.

Kennedy, Ellen. 2004. *Constitutional Failure: Carl Schmitt Weimar*. Durham, NC: Duke University Press.

Kershner, Isabel. 2014. "Israel Braces for War Crimes Inquiries on Gaza." *New York Times*, August 14, 2014. Available from http://www.nytimes.com/2014/08/15/world/middleeast/israel-braces-for-war-crimes-inquiries-on-gaza.html?_r=0.

Khadduri, Majid. 2010. *War and Peace in the Law of Islam*. Baltimore, MD: Johns Hopkins University Press, 1955; reprint, Clark, NJ: The Lawbook Exchange.

Khatchadourian, Haig. 1988. "Terrorism and Morality." *Journal of Applied Philosophy* 5: 131–45.

Kiernan, Ben. 2007. *Blood and Soil: A World History of Genocide and Extermination from Sparta to Darfur*. New Haven, CT: Yale University Press.

Kolb, Robert. 1997. "Origin of the Twin Terms Jus ad Bellum/Jus in Bello." *International Review of the Red Cross* 320: 553–62. Available from http://www.icrc.org/eng/resources/documents/misc/57jnuu.htm.

Kwakwa, Edward K. 1992. *The International Law of Armed Conflict: Personal and Material Fields of Application*. Boston: Kluwer Academic Publishers.

La Caze, Marguerite. 2007. "Sartre Integrating Ethics and Politics: The Case of Terrorism." *Parrhesia* 3: 43–54.

Lal, Rollie. 2005. "Terrorists and organized crime join forces." *New York Times*. Available from http://www.nytimes.com/2005/05/23/opinion/23iht-edlal.html?_r=0.

Laqueur, Walter. 2002. *A History of Terrorism*, with a new introduction. New Brunswick, NJ: Transaction Publishers.

Laqueur, Walter (ed.). 2004. *Voices of Terror: Manifestos, Writings and Manuals of Al Qaeda, Hamas, and Other Terrorists from Around the World and Throughout the Ages*. New York: Reed Press.

Law, Randall D. 2010. *Terrorism: A History*. Malden, MA: Polity Press.

League of Nations Convention for the Prevention and Punishment of Terrorism (1937). 2012. In *Terrorism*. Ed. Ben Saul, 1. Portland, OR: Hart Publishing.

Lemos, Ramon M. 1986. *Rights, Goods, and Democracy*. Cranbury, NJ: Associated University Presses.

Levi, Primo. 1986. *The Drowned and the Saved*. New York: Summit Books.

Lewis, Aidan. 2011. "Osama Bin Laden: Legality of killing questioned." *BBC News*. Available from http://www.bbc.co.uk/news/world-south-asia-13318372.

Lewis, H. D. 1991. "Collective Responsibility." In *Collective Responsibility: Five Decades of Debate in Theoretical and Applied Ethics*. Eds. Larry May and Stacey Hoffman, 17–34. Lanham, MD: Rowman & Littlefield.

Lewis, Lloyd. 1958. *Sherman: Fighting Prophet*. New York: Harcourt, Brace and Company.

Lewis, Paul. 2014. "Obama admits CIA 'tortured some folks' but stands by Brennan over spying." *Guardian*. Available from http://www.theguardian.com/world/2014/aug/01/obama-cia-torture-some-folks-brennan-spying.

Locke, John. 1980. *Two Treatises of Government*. 2nd ed. New York: Cambridge University Press.

Mackie, J. L. 1980. *Hume's Moral Theory*. Boston, MA: Routledge & Kegan Paul.

———. 1990. *Ethics: Inventing Right and Wrong*. New York: Penguin Books.

Mangan, Joseph T. 1949. "A Historical Analysis of the Principle of Double Effect." *Theological Studies* 10: 41–61.

Mardini, Ramzy. 2014. "The Islamic State threat is overstated." *Washington Post*. Available from http://www.washingtonpost.com/opinions/the-islamic-state-threat-is-overstated/2014/09/12/acbbebb2-33ad-11e4-8f02-03c644b2d7d0_story.html.

Marighella, Carlos. From the "Minimanual." In *Voices of Terror: Manifestos, Writings and Manuals of Al Qaeda, Hamas, and Other Terrorists from Around the World and Throughout the Ages*. Ed. Walter Laqueur, 370–76. New York: Reed Press.

Martin, Gus. 2014. "Terrorism and Transnational Organized Crime." In *Transnational Organized Crime: An Overview from Six Continents*. Eds. Jay L. Albanese and Philip L. Reichel, 165–92. Thousand Oaks, CA: SAGE.

Martin, Patrick. 2014. "Elie Wiesel accuses Hamas of child sacrifice in news ad." *The Globe and Mail*. Available from http://www.theglobeandmail.com/news/world/elie-wiesel-accuses-hamas-of-child-sacrifice-in-news-ad/article19944809/.

May, Larry. 2005. *Crimes Against Humanity: A Normative Account*. New York: Cambridge University Press.

McDowall, Angus. 2014. "Saudi Arabia's top clerics speak out against militancy." *Reuters*, September 17, 2014. Available from http://www.reuters.com/article/2014/09/17/us-saudi-islam-security-idUSKBN0HC0XD20140917.

McMahan, Jeff. 2009. *Killing in War*. New York: Oxford University Press.

Medina, Vicente. 2002. "Locke's Militant Liberalism: A Reply to Carl Schmitt's State of Exception." *History of Philosophy Quarterly* 19: 345–65.

———. 2010. "Militant Intolerant People: A Challenge to John Rawls' Political Liberalism." *Political Studies* 58: 556–71.

———. 2013. "The Innocent in the Just War Thinking of Vitoria and Suárez: A Challenge Even for Secular Just War Theorists and International Law." *Ratio Juris* 26: 47–64.

Meir, Golda. 1973. *A Land of Our Own: An Oral Autobiography*. Ed. Marie Syrkin, 242. New York: G. P. Putnam's Sons.

Meisels, Tamar. 2007. *The Trouble with Terror: Liberty, Security, and the Response to Terrorism*. New York: Cambridge University Press.

Mei Sze, Jennifer Ang. 2010. *Sartre and the Moral Limits of War and Terrorism*. New York: Routledge.

Melzer, Nils. 2008. *Targeted Killing in International Law*. New York: Oxford University Press.

Merleau-Ponty, Maurice. 1969. *Humanism and Terror: An Essay on the Communist Problem*. Trans. John O'Neill. Boston: Beacon Press.

Meron, Theodor. 1995. "International Criminalization of Internal Atrocities." *American Journal of International Law* 89: 554–77.

Mill, John Stuart. 1971. *Utilitarianism*. In *Utilitarianism with Critical Essays*. Ed. Samuel Gorovitz. New York: The Bobbs-Merrill Company.

Mitchell, Andrew D. 2001. "Does One Illegality Merit Another? The Law of Belligerent Reprisals in International Law." *Military Law Review* 170. Available from http://www.pegc.us/_LAW_/Volume170Mitchell.pdf.

Moeller, Robert G. 2009. "The Bombing War in Germany, 2005-1940: Back to the Future." In *Bombing Civilians: A Twentieth-Century History*. Eds. Yuki Tanaka and Marilyn B. Young, 46–76. New York: The New Press.

Morgenthau, Hans J. 1985. *Politics among Nations: The Struggle for Power and Peace*. 6th ed. Revised by Kenneth W. Thomson. New York: Alfred A. Knopf, Inc.

Mueller, John and Mark G. Stewart. 2011. *Terror, Security, and Money*. New York: Oxford University Press, 2011.

Murphy, Jeffrie. 1973. "The Killing of the Innocent." *Monist* 57: 531–32.

Musharbash, Yassin. 2009. "Al-Qaida Kills Eight Times More Muslims Than Non-Muslims." *Spiegelonline*. Available from http://www.spiegel.de/international/world/surprising-study-on-terrorism-al-qaida-kills-eight-times-more-muslims-than-non-muslims-a-660619.html.

Nagel, Thomas. 1986. *The View from Nowhere*. New York: Oxford University Press.

———. 1991. "Moral Luck." In Thomas Nagel, *Mortal Questions*, 24–38. New York: Cambridge University Press.

———. 1997. *The Last Word*. New York: Oxford University Press.

Nathanson, Stephen. 2006. "Terrorism, Supreme Emergency, and Noncombatant Immunity: A Critique of Michael Walzer's Ethics of War." *Iyyun: The Jerusalem Philosophical Quarterly* 55: 3–25.

———. 2007. "Terrorism and the Ethics of War." In *Intervention, Terrorism, and Torture: Contemporary Challenges to Just War Theory*. Ed. Steven P. Lee, 171–86. Dordrecht: Springer.

———. 2010. *Terrorism and the Ethics of War*. New York: Cambridge University Press.

Nebehey, Stephanie and Ahmed Rasheed. 2014. "U.N. accuses Islamic State of mass killings." *Reuters*. Available from http://www.reuters.com/article/2014/08/25/us-iraq-security-idUSKBN0GP0L020140825.

New American Bible. 1970. Saint Joseph Edition. New York: Catholic Book Publishing Co.

Newport, Frank. 2003. "Seventy-Two Percent of Americans Support War Against Iraq." *Gallup*. Available from http://www.gallup.com/poll/8038/seventytwo-percent-americans-support-war-against-iraq.aspx.

Niebuhr, Reinhold. 1986. "Augustine's Political Realism." In *The Essential Reinhold Niebuhr*. Ed. Robert M. Brown , 123–41. New Haven: Yale University Press.

Nietzsche, Frederick. 1954. *Thus Spake Zarathustra*. In *The Philosophy of Nietzsche*. New York: The Modern Library.

———. 1967. *The Will to Power*. Trans. Walter Kaufmann and R. J. Hollingdale. New York: Random House, 1967.

Norman, Richard. 1995. *Ethics, Killing and War*. New York: Cambridge University Press.

OAU Convention on the Prevention and Combating of Terrorism. 1999. Available from http://treaties.un.org/doc/db/Terrorism/OAU-english.pdf.

Obama, Barack. 2009. "Remarks by the President at the Acceptance of the Nobel Peace Prize." Available from http://www.whitehouse.gov/the-press-office/remarks-president-acceptance-nobel-peace-prize.

Öberg, Marko Divac. 2009. "The Absorption of Grave Breaches into War Crimes Law." *International Review of the Red Cross*: 163–83. Available from http://www.icrc.org/eng/assets/files/other/irrc-873-divac-oberg.pdf.

O'Donovan, Oliver. 2003. *The Just War Revisited*. New York: Cambridge University Press.

OIC Convention to Combat Terrorism. 1999. Available from http://www.oicun.org/7/38/.

O'Sullivan, Christopher D. 2010. *Colin Powell: A Political Biography*. Lanham, MD: Rowman & Littlefield.

Orend, Brian. 2005. "Is There a Supreme Emergency Exemption?" In *Just War Theory: A Reappraisal*. Ed. Mark Evans, 134–53. New York: Palgrave.

Origen. 2006. *Against Celsus*. In *The Ethics of War and Peace: Classic and Contemporary Readings*. Eds. Gregory M. Reicheberg, et al., 64–65. Malden, MA: Blackwell.

Overy, Richard. 2004. *The Dictators: Hitler's Germany and Stalin's Russia*. Old Saybrook, CT: Konecky & Konecky.

Owen, Richard. 2006. "Catholic Muslim forum condemns religious terrorism." *TimesOnline*. Available from http://www.timesonline.co.uk/tol/comment/faith/article5100320.ece?.

Pallitto, Robert M. (ed.). 2011. *Torture and State Violence in the United States*. Baltimore, MD: Johns Hopkins University Press.

Pangle, Thomas L. and Peter J. Ahrensdorf. 1999. *Justice among Nations: On the Moral Basis of Power and Peace*. Lawrence: University Press of Kansas.

Pape, Robert A. 2005. *Dying to Win: The Strategic Logic of Suicide Terrorism*. New York: Random House.

Parfitt, Derek. 2011. *On What Matters*. Vol. 1. New York: Oxford University Press.

Paul. 1970. "The Epistle of Paul to the Romans." In *The New American Bible*. Saint Joseph edition. New York: Catholic Book Publishing Co.

Pennington, Kenneth. 2005. "Innocent Until Proven Guilty: The Origins of a Legal Maxim." In *The Penal Process and the Protection of Rights in Canon Law*. Ed. Patricia M. Dugan, 45–66. Montreal, CA: Wilson & Lafleur.

Perera, Amrith Rohan. 2011. "Response to Global Terrorism: UN Initiatives to Enhance International Cooperation in Combating Terrorism." *International Institute for Middle East and Balkan Studies*. Available from http://www.ifimes.org/en/researches/response-to-global-terrorism-un-initiatives-to-enhance-international-cooperation-in-combating-terrorism/.

Plato. 1978. *Crito*. In *The Collected Dialogues of Plato*. Eds. Edith Hamilton and Huntington Cairns. Princeton, NJ: Princeton University Press.

———. 1978. *The Republic*. In *The Collected Dialogues of Plato*. Eds. Edith Hamilton and Huntington Cairns. Princeton, NJ: Princeton University Press.

———. 1978. *Gorgias*. In *The Collected Dialogues of Plato*. Eds. Edith Hamilton and Huntington Cairns. Princeton, NJ: Princeton University Press.

Posner, Richard A. 2003. *Law, Pragmatism, and Democracy.* Cambridge: Harvard University Press.

————. 2006. *Not a Suicide Pact: The Constitution in a Time of National Emergency.* New York: Oxford University Press.

Powell, Colin. 2003. "Remarks to the United Nations Security Council." U.S. Department of State Archive. Available at http://2001-2009.state.gov/secretary/former/powell/remarks/2003/17300.htm.

Power, Samantha. 2001. "Bystanders to Genocide." *Atlantic.* Available from http://www.theatlantic.com/doc/200109/power-genocide.

Primoratz, Igor. 2004. "State Terrorism and Counter-Terrorism." In *Terrorism: The Philosophical Issues.* Ed. Igor Primoratz, 113–27. New York: Palgrave MacMillan.

————. 2005. "Civilian Immunity," *Philosophical Forum,* 36: 41–58.

————. 2006. "Terrorism in the Israeli-Palestinian Conflict: A Case Study in Applied Ethics." *Iyyun/The Jerusalem Philosophical Quarterly* 55: 27–48.

————. 2007. "Civilian Immunity in War: Its Grounds, Scope, and Weight." In *Civilian Immunity in War.* Ed. Igor Primoratz, 21–41. New York: Oxford University Press.

Quinn, Warren S. 2010. "Actions, Intentions, and Consequences: The Doctrine of Double Effect." In *The Doctrine of Double Effect: Philosophers Debate a Controversial Moral Principle.* Ed. P. A. Woodward, 23–40. Indiana: University of Notre Dame Press.

Ramsey, Paul. 1961. *War and the Christian Conscience.* Durham, NC: Duke University Press.

Rapoport, David C. 2003. "The Four Waves of Rebel Terror and September 11." Ed. Charles W. Kegley Jr., 36–52. *The New Global Terrorism: Characteristics, Causes, Controls.* Upper Saddle River, NJ: Prentice Hall.

Ratner, Steven R. and Jason S. Abrams (eds.). 2001. *Accountability for Human Rights Atrocities in International Law: Beyond the Nuremberg Legacy.* New York: Oxford University Press.

Rawls, John. 1999. "Two Concepts of Rules." In *John Rawls: Collected Papers.* Ed. Samuel Freeman, 20–46. Cambridge, MA: Harvard University Press.

————. 1999. *A Theory of Justice.* Revised edition. Cambridge, MA: Harvard University Press.

————. 1999. *The Laws of People.* Cambridge, MA: Harvard University Press.

————. 2001. *Justice as Fairness: A Restatement.* Ed. Erin Kelly. Cambridge, MA: Harvard University Press.

Reisman, Michael and Chris T. Antoniou. 1994. *The Laws of War: A Comprehensive Collection of Primary Documents on International Laws Governing Armed Conflict.* New York: Vintage Books.

Reuters. 2011. "China passes law to help fight 'acts of terror.'" Available from http://in.reuters.com/article/2011/10/29/idINIndia-60189920111029.

Rice, Condoleezza. 2011. *No Higher Honor: A Memoir of My Years in Washington.* New York: Crown Publishers.

Richardson, Louise. 2007. *What Terrorists Want: Understanding the Enemy, Containing the Threat.* New York: Random House.

Roberts, Adam and Richard Guelff (eds.). 2004. *Documents of the Laws of War.* 3rd ed. New York: Oxford University Press.

Robespierre, Maximilien. 2007. "On the Principles of Political Morality that Should Guide the National Convention in the Domestic Administration of the Republic." In *Virtue and Terror: Maximilien Robespierre.* Ed. Slavoj Žižek,108–25. New York: Verso.

Rodin, David. 2003. *War and Self-Defense.* New York: Oxford University Press.

Rollins, John and Liana Sun Wyler. 2013. "Terrorism and Transnational Crime: Foreign Policy Issues for Congress." *Congressional Research Service.* Available from http://fas.org/sgp/crs/terror/R41004.pdf.

Rome Statute of the International Criminal Court. 2011. ICRC. Available from http://www.icc-cpi.int/NR/rdonlyres/ADD16852-AEE9-4757-ABE7-9CDC7CF02886/283503/RomeStatutEng1.pdf.

Rorty, Richard. 1989. *Contingency, Irony, and Solidarity.* New York: Cambridge University Press.

———. 1999. *Philosophy and Social Hope.* New York: Penguin Putnam.

Rummel, R. J. 1997. *Death by Government.* New Brunswick, NJ: Transaction Publishers.

Russell, Frederick H. 1977. *The Just War in the Middle Ages.* New York: Cambridge University Press.

Ryan, Alan. 1991. "State and Private; Red and White." In *Violence, Terrorism, and Justice.* Eds. R. G. Frey and Christopher W. Morris, 230–55. New York: Cambridge University Press.

Salisbury, John of. 2006. *Policraticus.* In *The Ethics of War and Peace: Classic and Contemporary Readings.* Eds. Gregory M. Reicheberg, Henrik Syse, and Endre Begsy, 128–30. Malden, MA: Blackwell.

Samora, Mwaura. 2011. "Carlos de Jackal: Terrorist and revolutionary to some." *Daily Monitor.* Available from http://www.monitor.co.ug/News/Insight/-/688338/1275892/-/rq2o30/-/index.html.

Sardar, Ziauddin. 2011. *Reading the Qur'an: The Contemporary Relevance of the Sacred Text of Islam.* New York: Oxford University Press.

Sartre, Jean-Paul. 2004. Preface to Frantz Fanon, *The Wretched of the Earth.* In Frantz Fanon, *The Wretched of the Earth.* New York: Grove Press.

Savage, Charlie. 2014. "Decaying Guantánamo Defies Closing Plans." *New York Times.* Available from http://www.nytimes.com/2014/09/01/us/politics/decaying-guantanamo-defies-closing-plans.html?emc=edit_th_20140901&nl=todaysheadlines&nlid=13987239&_r=0.

Schmid, Alex P. and Albert J. Jongman. 2005. *Political Terrorism.* New Brunswick, NJ: Transaction Publishers.

Schmidle, Nicholas. 2001. "Getting Bin Laden: What Happened That Night in Abbottabad." *New Yorker.* Available from http://www.newyorker.com/reporting/2011/08/08/110808fa_fact_schmidle?currentPage=all.

Schmitt, Carl. 1988. *Political Theology: Four Chapters on the Concept of Sovereignty.* Trans. George Schwab. Cambridge, MA: The MIT Press.

———. 1996. *The Concept of the Political.* Trans. George Schwab with a new foreword by Tracy Strong. Chicago: The University of Chicago Press.

————. 2006. *The Nomos of the Earth in the International Law of the Jus Publicum Europeum*. Trans. G. L. Ulmen. New York: Telos Press Publishing.

————. 2007. *Theory of the Partisan*. Trans. by G. L. Ulmen. New York: Telos Press.

Schabas, William. 1999. "The Genocide Convention at Fifty." *United States Institute of Peace*, Special Report 41. Available from http://www.usip.org/sites/default/files/sr990107.pdf.

Schabas, William A. 2004. *An Introduction to the International Criminal Court*. 2nd ed. New York: Cambridge University Press.

Schwenkenbecher, Anne. 2012. *Terrorism: A Philosophical Inquiry*. New York: Palgrave Macmillan.

Selden, Mark. 2009. "A Forgotten Holocaust: U.S. Bombing Strategy, The Destruction of Japanese Cities, and the American Way of War from the Pacific War to Iraq." In *Bombing Civilians: A Twentieth-Century History*. Eds. Yuki Tanaka and Marilyn B. Young, 77–96. New York: The New Press.

Serle, Jack. 2014. "Drone Warfare: More than 2,400 dead as Obama's drone campaign marks five years." *The Bureau of Investigative Journalism*. Available from http://www.thebureauinvestigates.com/2014/01/23/more-than-2400-dead-as-obamas-drone-campaign-marks-five-years/.

Shalev, Sharon. 2008. *A Sourcebook on Solitary Confinement*. London: Mannheim Center for Criminology. Available from http://solitaryconfinement.org/uploads/sourcebook_web.pdf.

Singer, Peter. 2004. *The President of Good and Evil: Questioning the Ethics of George W. Bush*. New York: Plume.

————. 2006. "Famine, Affluence, and Morality." In *Ethics: History, Theory, and Contemporary Issues*. Eds. Steven M. Cahn and Peter Markie, 789–96. New York: Oxford University Press.

————. 2009. "A life to save: Direct action on poverty." Available from http://www.opendemocracy.net/article/a-life-to-save-direct-action-on-poverty.

Skinner, Quentin. 2002. "Meaning and understanding in the history of ideas." In Quentin Skinner, *Visions of Politics, Vol. I: Regarding Method*, 57–89. New York: Cambridge University Press.

Slim, Hugo. 2003. "Why Protect Civilians? Innocence, Immunity and Enmity in War." *International Affairs* 79: 481–501.

Smart, J. J. C. 1990. "Act-Utilitarianism and Rule-Utilitarianism." In *Utilitarianism and Its Critics*. Ed. Jonathan Glover, 199–201. New York: Macmillan Publishing Company.

Statman, Daniel. 2006. "Supreme Emergencies Revisited." *Ethics* 117: 58–79.

Sterba, James P. 1992. "Reconciling Pacifists and Just War Theorists." *Social Theory and Practice* 18: 21–38.

————. 2003. "Terrorism and International Justice." In *Terrorism and International Justice*. Ed. James P. Sterba, 206–28. New York: Oxford University Press.

Stern, Jessica. 2003. *Terror in the Name of God*. New York: HarperCollins.

Stirner, Max. 1918. *The Ego and His Own*. Trans. Steven T. Byington. New York: Modern Library.

Stone, Geoffrey R. 2005. *Perilous Times: Free Speech in Wartime.* New York: W. W. Norton & Company.

Stumer, Andrew. 2010. *The Presumption of Innocence: Evidential and Human Rights Perspectives.* Portland, OR: Hart Publishing.

Suárez, Francisco. 1995. "On War." In Francisco Suárez, *Selections from Three Works of Francisco Suárez.* Trans. Gwladys L Williams. Buffalo: William S. Hein & Co.

———. 2006. Disputation XIII: On War *(De bello).* In *The Ethics of War and Peace: Classic and Contemporary Readings.* Eds. Gregory M. Reicheberg et al., 13. Malden, MA: Blackwell.

———. 1995. "On Charity." In Francisco Suárez, *Selections from Three Works of Francisco Suárez.* Trans. Gwladys L. Williams. Buffalo: William S. Hein & Co.

Tanaka, Yuki. 1996. *Hidden Horrors: Japanese War Crimes in World War II.* Boulder, CO: Westview Press.

———. 2009. "Introduction." In *Bombing Civilians: A Twentieth-Century History.* Eds. Yuki Tanaka and Marilyn B. Young. New York: The New Press.

Tenet, George. 2007. *At the Center of the Storm: My Years at the CIA.* New York: HarperCollins.

Tertullian. 2006. *On Idolatry.* In *The Ethics of War and Peace: Classic and Contemporary Readings.* Eds. Gregory M. Reicheberg et al., 63. Malden, MA: Blackwell.

Thomas, Jakana. 2014. "Actually, sometimes terrorism does work." *Washington Post.* Available from http://www.washingtonpost.com/blogs/monkey-cage/wp/2014/04/22/actually-sometimes-terrorism-does-work/.

Thomson, Judith Jarvis. 1971. "A Defense of Abortion." *Philosophy and Public Affairs* 1: 47–66.

———. 1976. "Killing, Letting Die, and the Trolley Problem." *Monist* 59: 204–17.

———. 1990. *The Realm of Rights.* Cambridge, MA: Harvard University Press.

Thucydides. 1998. *The Peloponnesian Wars.* Trans. Steven Lattimore. Indianapolis, IN: Hackett.

Toye, Richard. 2010. *Churchill's Empire: The World That Made Him and the World He Made.* New York: St. Martin's Press.

Trotsky, Leon. 1995. *Marxism and Terrorism.* New York: Pathfinder Press.

———. 2007. *Terrorism and Communism: A Reply to Karl Kautsky.* New York: Verso.

Tzu, Sun. 2003. *The Art of War.* Ed. Dallas Galvin. New York: Barnes & Noble.

UK Terrorism Act 2000. 2000. Available from http://www.opsi.gov.uk/acts/acts2000/ukpga_20000011_en_2#pt1-l1g1.

UN. 1948. Universal Declarations of Human Rights. Available from http://www.un.org/en/documents/udhr/.

UN. 1976. International Covenant on Civil and Political Rights. Available from http://www.ohchr.org/en/professionalinterest/pages/ccpr.aspx.

UNCLOS. 1982. United Nations Convention on the Law of the Sea. Available from http://www.un.org/Depts/los/convention_agreements/texts/unclos/closindx.htm.

UN Human Rights. 1987. Convention against Torture and Other Cruel, Inhuman or DegradingTreatment or Punishment. Available from http://www.ohchr.org/EN/ProfessionalInterest/Pages/CAT.aspx.

UN. 1994. A/Res/49/60. Available from http://www.un.org/documents/ga/res/49/a49r060.htm.

UN. 1995. E/CN.4/1995/52. Report on the situation of human rights in Cuba, prepared by the Special Rapporteur, Mr. Carl-Johan Groth, in accordance with Commission resolution 1994/71. Available from http://www1.umn.edu/humanrts/commission/country51/52.htm.

UN. 2001. S/Res/1373. Available from http://www.un.org/Docs/journal/asp/ws.asp?m=s/res/1373(2001).

UN. 2004. S/Res/1535. Available from http://www.un.org/Docs/journal/asp/ws.asp?m=s/res/1535(2004).

"UN Interfaith conference rejects religious terrorism." 2008. *yaLibnan*. Available from http://yalibnan.com/site/archives/2008/11/un_interfaith_c.php.

UN Action to Counter Terrorism. Available from http://www.un.org/en/terrorism/instruments.shtml.

UN Fact Finding Mission on the Gaza Conflict, Press Release. 2009. Available from http://www.ohchr.org/EN/HRBodies/HRC/SpecialSessions/Session9/Pages/FactFindingMission.aspx.

UN Human Rights. 2014. *Report of the detailed finding of the commission of inquiry of human rights in the Democratic People's Republic of North Korea*. Available from http://www.ohchr.org/EN/HRBodies/HRC/CoIDPRK/Pages/CommissionInquiryonHRinDPRK.aspx.

UNTC. US Declarations and Reservations upon ratification of Convention against Torture and Other Cruel, Inhuman or Degrading Treatment or Punishment. 1994. Available from https://treaties.un.org/Pages/ViewDetails.aspx?mtdsg_no=IV- 9&chapter=4&lang=en#EndDec.

U.S.C. Title 22 2656f(d). 2010. Foreign Relations and Intercourse. Available from http://www.gpo.gov/fdsys/pkg/USCODE-2010-title22/html/USCODE-2010-title22.htm.

U.S.C. Title 18 2332B. 2011. Acts of Terrorism Transcending National Boundaries. Available from http://www.gpo.gov/fdsys/granule/USCODE-2011-title18/USCODE-2011-title18-partI-chap113B-sec2332b.

U.S.C. Title 18 2340. 2011. Torture. Available from http://www.gpo.gov/fdsys/pkg/USCODE-2011-title18/pdf/USCODE-2011-title18-partI-chap113C-sec2340.pdf.

USCCB. 1983. *The Challenge of Peace: God's Promise and Our Response, A Pastoral Letter on War and Peace*. Washington, DC: United States Catholic Conference.

US Department of State. 2013. Country Report on Terrorism. Available from http://www.state.gov/r/pa/prs/ps/2013/05/210103.htm.

US Department of State. 2014. Country Report on Terrorism. Available from http://www.state.gov/j/ct/rls/crt/2013/224831.htm.

US Senate Select Committee on Intelligence. 2015. *The Official Senate Report on Torture: Committee Study of the Central Intelligence Agency's Detention and Interrogation Program*. New York: Skyhorse Publishing.

Valls, Andrew. 2000. "Can Terrorism Be Justified?" In *Ethics and International Affairs*. Ed. Andrew Valls, 65–79. Lanham, MD: Rowman & Littlefield.

Vasquez, John A. 1993. *The War Puzzle*. New York: Cambridge University Press.

VCLT. 1969. The Vienna Convention on the Law of Treatises. Available from https://treaties.un.org/doc/Publication/UNTS/Volume%201155/volume-1155-I-18232-English.pdf.

Vitoria, Francisco de. 1991. "On the Law of War." In *Francisco de Vitoria, Political Writings*. Eds. Anthony Pagden and Jeremy Lawrance. New York: Cambridge University Press.

———. 1991. "On Civil Power." In *Francisco de Vitoria, Political Writings*. Eds. Anthony Pagden and Jeremy Lawrance. New York: Cambridge University Press.

Volpi, Frédéric. 2010. *Political Islam*. New York: Columbia University Press.

Vonnegut, Kurt. 2008. "Wailing Shall Be in All Streets." In Kurt Vonnegut, *Armageddon in Retrospect and Other New and Unpublished Writings on War and Peace*, 33–45. New York: The Penguin Group.

Walzer, Michael. 1977. *Just and Unjust Wars: A Moral Argument with Historical Illustrations*. 2nd ed. New York: Basic Books.

———. 1988. "Terrorism: A Critique of Excuses." In *Problems of International Justice*. Ed. Steven Luper-Foy, 237–47. Boulder, CO: Westview Press.

———. 2004. *Arguing about War*. New Haven, CT: Yale University Press.

Weber, Max. 1958. "Politics as a Vocation." Eds. H. H. Gerth and C. Wright Mills, 77–128. *From Max Weber: Essays in Sociology*. New York: Oxford University Press.

Wehberg, Hans. 1959. "Pacta Sunt Servanda. " *American Journal of International Law* 53: 775–86.

Wellman, Carl. 1979. "On Terrorism Itself." *Journal of Value Inquiry* 13: 250–58.

Wilgoren, Jodi. 2001. "Swept Up in a Dragnet, Hundreds Sit in Custody, and Ask 'Why?'" *New York Times*. Available at http://www.nytimes.com/2001/11/25/national/25DETA.html.

Wilkinson, Paul. 2006. *Terrorism Versus Democracy: The Liberal State Response*. 2nd ed. New York: Routledge.

Williams, Bernard. 1972. *Morality: An Introduction to Ethics*. New York: Harper & Row.

Wood, Paul. 2009. "Breaking silence on Gaza abuses." *BBC News*. Available from http://news.bbc.co.uk/2/hi/middle_east/8151336.stm.

Woodward, P. A. 2010. *The Doctrine of Double Effect: Philosophers Debate a Controversial Moral Principle*. Indiana: University of Notre Dame Press.

Yetiv, Steve A. 2013. *National Security through a Cockeyed Lens: How Cognitive Bias Impacts U.S. Foreign Policy*. Baltimore, MD: Johns Hopkins University Press.

Yoo, John C. 2005. "Letter to Alberto R. Gonzales, Counsel to the President," August 1, 2002. In *The Torture Papers: The Road to Abu Grahib*. Eds. Karen J. Greenberg and Joshua L. Dratel, 218–22. New York: Cambridge University Press.

Young, Robert. 2004. "Political Terrorism as a Weapon of the Politically Powerless." Ed. Igor Primoratz, 55–64. *Terrorism: The Philosophical Issues*. New York: Palgrave MacMillan.

Zanetti, Véronique. 2007. "Women, War, and International Law." In *Civilian Immunity in War*. Ed. Igor Primoratz, 217–38. New York: Oxford University Press.

Ziauddin, Sardar. 2011. *Reading the Qur'an: The Contemporary Relevance of the Sacred Text of Islam*. New York: Oxford University Press.

Žižek, Slavoj. 2008. *Violence: Six Sideways Reflections*. New York: Picador.

Index